# COMMON KNOWLEDGE?

# COMMON KNOWLEDGE?

## ▮ AN ETHNOGRAPHY OF WIKIPEDIA ▮

## DARIUSZ JEMIELNIAK

STANFORD UNIVERSITY PRESS ▮ STANFORD, CALIFORNIA

Stanford University Press
Stanford, California

Printed in the United States of America on acid-free, archival-quality paper

Library of Congress Cataloging-in-Publication Data

Jemielniak, Dariusz, author.
    Common knowledge? : an ethnography of Wikipedia / Dariusz Jemielniak.
        pages cm
    Includes bibliographical references and index.
    ISBN 978-0-8047-8944-8 (cloth : alk. paper)
    ISBN 978-0-8047-9723-8 (pbk. : alk. paper)
        1. Wikipedia.    2. Organizational sociology.    3. Electronic encyclopedias—Social aspects.
I. Title.
    AE100.J46 2014
    030—dc23

                                                                                        2013047786

ISBN 978-0-8047-9120-5 (electronic)

Typeset by Newgen in 10/14 Minion

# CONTENTS

# PROLOGUE

I woke up, drank my coffee, and scanned e-mails. I nibbled at a sandwich. As I did every day, still in my pajamas, I launched my browser and started casually perusing the news. I also opened Wikipedia to check recent changes in the articles I followed. Bam! There it was. I could not log in. It took me a minute or so to realize that it was not a mistake of the server and that I was really, genuinely blocked. I was shocked and furious. "How dare they!" I thought. "I should do something about this!" I then recalled the events that led to my being blocked.

In September 2008 a request to become an administrator (request for adminship; RfA) was made on behalf of Lorry, a Wikipedia user, or editor, with the support of another administrator, or admin. Lorry was a promising editor (she later became a highly trusted member of the Polish Wikipedia's Arbitration Committee and the author of twenty-five featured articles) with a decent and diverse edit count, so her candidacy was no surprise to anyone in the community.

Yet the RfA took an unexpected turn. One of the first votes came from Prot, an experienced editor (now with a five-digit edit count), notorious for his right-wing beliefs and for polarizing the community (which led to him being blocked quite a number of times), and respected for his intelligence and excellent understanding of Wikipedia rules. He wrote,

> How many users would vote for a candidate, who, just one day before the RfA, on their own userpage would declare "This user loves Adolf Hitler"? And this candidate had a declaration that she "loved Lev Trotsky." Anybody who dazzles readers with admiration to one of the biggest murderers and criminals in the world history is not, in my view, a good candidate for an admin. She also had other userboxes, expressing her political engagement, and this shows that the candidate has a strong need to show political declarations, and thus I doubt that she would be able to be neutral in related dispute resolutions.[1]

This comment led to a 3,300-word discussion on Trotsky and the rationale for disqualifying a candidate just because of such a declaration. Even though several administrators (including me) defended Lorry's right to make her political views explicit, and one of the administrators declared that she also was a Trotsky admirer, several others expressed doubts, and the general opinion and votes turned against the candidate. In the end, 76 percent of the collected votes were in support, but because 85 percent is required, she was not made an administrator at the time. The whole discussion was relatively civilized.

Fast-forward to February 2009: Lorry was again nominated for adminship (this time by a bureaucrat and steward). And again Prot was the first to oppose her:

> [I have] distrust for her role as an admin. You can't separate political and world view radicalism from your doings, as hard as you believe you might. Especially admins are often engaged in more complex and more difficult situations. Moreover, the candidate declares that she needs the flag to watch over the subjects in which she is most active—which means politics. With all apologies, but communists watching over politics did happen in the past. They were not particularly good as neutrality guardians. (February 12, 2009)

This time, he was met with much fiercer opposition. An ardent 2,200-word discussion followed.

A couple of users expressed their frustration with Prot's stance, pointing out that Lorry was able to keep a neutral point of view and was extremely balanced in her discussions with people, even if they were clearly declaring views far from her own (including a civil discourse with a user who stated that gay people should not have equal rights).

Several other disputants tried to persuade him that even extreme declarations of views, as long as they did not lead to extreme behavior on Wikipedia, should be acceptable. The only result was that Prot deleted a sentence from his vote ("I value her as an editor, remember interesting and important articles on Russia"), explaining that since some voters gave their support because respected Wikipedians did, he had crossed out the positive statement because he did not respect some of the supporters.

At this, I could not take it anymore and wrote,

> I suggest that this discussion be discontinued. Horribly, lamentably low level of some of Wikipedians here should not serve as an excuse to match down. I'd

only like to add that I find voting against a candidate, only because of support from people we dislike, shocking and totally in disconcert with the Wikipedia spirit. (February 13, 2009)

Prot reiterated his argument:

I've already explained in short below: declaring your support for Trotsky, Pol Pot, Stalin have the same weight as being a supporter of Hitler or Himmler. All of these people committed manslaughter and created murderous theories. (February 13, 2009).

And he mocked mine: "Is consistency an enemy of dialectics?" He added,

Naturally, I realize that criticizing Hitlerism or Trotskyism, or communism in general, is "insulting to many people in the world," but my only regret is not towards their feelings, since they apparently don't care about the feelings of the victims of Holocaust or Holodomor or lagers, but that there are really many of them, which can be observed recently in Germany. (February 13, 2009)

Then I retorted,

Please, don't continue this despicably low series of comments. Trotskyism is a school of thought; just like Rosa Luxemburg or Marx are cited up to this day by sociologists, since they had something specific and academically interesting to say, regardless of what they did. Just as Cioran or Eliade cannot be judged only by their actions. There is always some dissonance between action and literature, some people are known for one, some for the other, and some for both (Karadžić or John Paul II would probably not make history because of their writings, but Marx surely would). Before you start creating risky analogies, be so kind as to learn a bit more sociology and philosophy. (February 13, 2009)

I was angry that a good admin candidate might lose again because of what I saw as an ideological vendetta. I lost my head and commented on Prot's discussion page:

In case you sometimes wanted to read something, instead on going on autopilot, be so kind as to read a little: [six links to books on Trotskyism]. Besides exposing your own ignorance or viewpoint bias, don't transfer them onto a completely innocent candidate. (February 13, 2009)

Prot's reply was quick; he erased my message and replaced it with a comment: "Here was a comment of an admin and a bureaucrat. Because it contained personal attacks and was of lamentably low level, it has been deleted." This action was soon reverted by Seer, another admin, who warned Prot that blanking other people's comments and leaving such judgments would be considered trolling the next time. Prot also wrote on my talk page:

> Spare me your rude and provoking comments. If you can't behave with some minimum of culture, keep quiet, or preferably resign from adminship, so that you can embarrass only yourself, and not the wiki. I'm not going to discuss with you how great manslaughter systems were, I know that there are websites accepting discussions with people of your views, go there if you must. (February 13, 2009)

I never replied—I did not have to. Seer apparently was watching Prot's edits closely, and it took him just five minutes to block Prot for twenty-four hours "for vulgar behavior and a personal attack." Seer also wrote to me that I should refrain from saying that other users expose their ignorance. I was so convinced that I was right that I replied on Seer's talk page:

> Warm cheers and thanks for your comment. Let me explain what I wrote. A claim that Prot "exposes his ignorance" means two things: first, that in his activity so far he seemed to be competent and accurate (so ignorance has to be exposed—if he was a dilettante, it would be already obvious); second that he is clearly displaying ignorance in the area of Trotskyism. I quoted abundant academic literature to support this claim and for further discussion. I also allowed another possibility: that Prot has the knowledge, but is driven by a viewpoint bias against the candidate. I don't know if it indeed is so, but his comments in the RfA would indicate it and such an interpretation should not be surprising (a reminder: ". . . You can't separate political and the world view radicalism from your doings . . . ," ". . . communists watching over politics did happen in the past . . ."). Therefore a suggestion that perhaps he is not driven by ignorance, but rather a bias, seems to be grounded, even though I regret that he took offence. (February 13, 2009)

For three days I thought the case was over. After all, the entire situation was being discussed on the admin e-mail discussion list. I, as a member of the list, pledged not to quote it outside the group, but I can write here that the vast majority of admins were disturbed by Prot's behavior and considered it unproductive and damaging to the Wikipedia community. Means of responding to him were discussed, and even though most of us found it difficult to link a particular edit he made with a serious rule violation (except for occasional slips in civility), it was clear that he was crossing the line.

My complacency did not last long. On February 16, 2009, Prot filed a case against me with the Arbitration Committee, arguing that what I did was a series of personal attacks and that he was afraid he would not be able to continue his planned work on the articles on Nazis and communism. This last argument was important in the sense that all blocks on Wikipedia have to be preventive, not punitive. He requested removal of my administrator rights because of what he claimed to be personal attacks and persistent trolling.

This surprised me, and I decided that perhaps I should mitigate my stance. I wrote a five-hundred-word explanation on Prot's discussion page, explaining why I believed that judging people by their philosophical or sociological interests and beliefs, and not by their actions, was unfair as long as these interests and beliefs are acceptable in academic discourse. I also wrote,

> I regret that what I wrote upset you and you assumed that I wanted to insult or persecute you. In retrospect, I think that I could have phrased my view differently. I also admit that what I wrote on Seer's discussion page was illogical. Writing about your incompetence in (economic) sociology was not really meant to emphasize my admiration for your other edits. In fact, I literally wanted to criticize your categorical judgments without proper grounding in literature. I'm not going to retract this opinion now, although I realize it may be totally wrong. I also would like to apologize to you for everything in my comment, as well as in other postings, which you could interpret as insulting. (February 17, 2009)

I was pretty smug; I was certain that the Arbitration Committee would see that I had expressed my regrets and assume that there was no personal conflict to be resolved. At the same time, I knew that most of the arbiters were on the administrators' mailing list and must have known about the massive critique of Prot's behavior. But mostly I believed that I was protected by a procedural catch. The Arbitration Committee acts as "the final binding decision-maker primarily for serious conduct disputes the community has been unable to resolve" [[WP:Dispute_resolution_requests/ArbCom]].[2] In practice, this means that parties to the dispute should at least try to resolve their conflict by other means (e.g., reasoning with the disputant, requesting formal or informal mediation).

My sense of being right increased even more when on February 20, 2009, Prot was blocked by another administrator, Lud, for two weeks. The duration of the block was meant to last until the decision of the Arbitration Committee. The length of the block was approved by several other admins and also corresponded with the end of the committee's term. The assumption was, therefore, that this would be one of the last cases these arbiters would address. With the support of several other admins, I was confident that I was in the right but still expected that the case would not even be started.

To my dismay, the Arbitration Committee agreed to take the case (even though members expressed some reservations as to whether prior attempts at resolution were necessary). I still was not worried. From the discussions with other admins and from the fact that the committee took the case at all, I concluded that there had been pressure from the admin community to use this opportunity to temper Prot's behavior.

I wish I had known what was coming! The time pressure did not work in my favor. Even though the committee requested that both parties explain their points of view, the time limit on the block and, more importantly, the end of the committee's term caused pressure to speed things up.

In the meantime, Prot counterattacked. He prepared another arbitration case, against Lud. In his 1,170-word motion he described her alleged wrongdoings and the wider conspiracy against him, the lone wolf, defending Wikipedia's accuracy and value in spite of administrative cabal. He presented himself as a victim, a move that is universal among Wikipedia dissenters. Yet unlike most of the dissenters, he was capable of writing a coherent narrative. Prot was also a scholar, an assistant professor in his school's sciences department, with several publications in top journals of his discipline, and adept at producing a good argument.

The committee proceeded under additional tension as well: there was a clear expectation from the admin community that it "do something about Prot," who was perceived as generally disruptive to Wikipedia and, although not necessarily violating rules, was irritating many. Prot's recent activity on social network portals, criticizing the Wikipedia community (and accusing it of deliberately allowing copyright violations and promoting a point of view by brute force, through blocking editors), was clearly libelous, but it still could not have been a reason for any action on the part of Wikipedia: first, because there was no official confirmation linking his persona on Wikipedia with the persona on the social networks and, second, because almost all activities outside Wikimedia projects are not taken into account in Wikipedia proceedings.

On March 8, 2009, the committee finally announced its verdict. It recognized my good faith but gave me a symbolic twenty-four-hour block. I could only speculate that the committee wanted to seem impartial, especially in the face of Prot's accusations of favoritism, but I felt betrayed and misjudged by people whom I considered friends.

This incident made me realize how people who get blocked on Wikipedia may feel: mistreated and wronged, often with no recourse. It's no wonder that many of them subscribe to conspiracy theories. If I, with wide acceptance in the community, clear support from many admins, and only a minor, symbolic slap on the wrist, felt aggrieved, how much worse must it be for those who are used to editing Wikipedia but are not as welcome in the community and get longer blocks? I was so enraged that I wrote a lengthy letter to the admin community pinpointing procedural flaws and omissions in the committee's work (e.g., ignoring the omission of prearbitration dispute resolution, hastily and carelessly collecting facts, ignoring my reconciliation efforts, and treating a block as a punishment rather than a preventive measure). And yet, looking back, I know that the result was right, even if for the wrong reasons.

I should not have been rude to Prot, irrational and disruptive as his behavior was. In fact, my responses only fueled his rant. Had I explained everything peacefully, it would have had a much better impact. I probably was right about the Arbitration Committee's going a little outside its jurisdiction and the framework set by the procedures. Probably. But yet, even if it had somewhat bent the rules, it was essentially right. I should have been blocked or warned by some other admin even before the case was started, but my position in the community, as well as Prot's history, made it highly unlikely. The committee somehow corrected it.

This is how many of Wikipedia's formal and informal bodies work: rarely populated by professional lawyers and often filled with people with limited procedural experience but a lot of common sense, they try to do what is right rather than literally interpret the rules. Or rather, their interpretation of the rules often depends on the context of the rules' application, since open contestation of policies is also frowned on. Situations in which Wikipedia bodies or functionaries decide not to pick up cases because of their context are much more frequent.

This book shows how the Wikipedia community works—not in theory but in everyday social interactions.

# ACKNOWLEDGMENTS

This book would not have been possible without kind support from the Labor and Worklife Program at Harvard University (especially the support of Elaine Bernard, Richard B. Freeman, and John Trumpbour), a sabbatical from Kozminski University, and a research grant from the Polish National Science Center (no. UMO-2012/05/E/HS4/01498).

I am also grateful for comments, ideas, and feedback I received from the participants of the open-collaboration seminar at Berkman Center for Internet and Society, especially Shun-Ling Chen, B. Mako Hill, Brian Keegan, and Joseph J. Reagle, whose comments on the manuscript or its parts were very helpful. Discussions of the project with Yochai Benkler and Andreea D. Gorbatai were also enlightening.

Other scholars also kindly gave me constructive feedback. I am greatly indebted to Małgorzata Ciesielska, Davydd J. Greenwood, Piotr Konieczny, Tomasz Raburski, and Sebastian Skolik. Also, the reviewers, Jan English-Lueck and Gerald C. Kane, gave me many useful suggestions.

I am additionally indebted to my colleagues from the Center for Research on Organizations and Workplaces (CROW)—Małgorzata Adamczyk, Paweł Krzyworzeka, Dominika Latusek-Jurczak, Karolina Mikołajewska, and Marta Strumińska—who provided me with useful advice on the first draft of the book.

Fellow Wikimedians were extremely helpful as well, and in particular, Michał Buczyński, Natalia Szafran-Kozakowska, Daniel Malecki, Michał Rosa, and Wojciech Pędzich took time to help me improve the manuscript. Invaluable comments from Sue Gardner helped me improve the whole argument, even if we did not always have the same perspective on some topics.

The friendly home atmosphere provided by Bruce Petschek made writing this book during the sabbatical a true pleasure. Bruce should also be credited for coming up with the title of the book (and winning a bottle of wine for doing so). The stable support and encouragement from Joanna Jemielniak was invaluable during the many years this project was conducted.

The constructive help and guidance from Margo Beth Fleming, my editor at Stanford University Press, set the bar for professionalism in author-editor relations very high.

# COMMON KNOWLEDGE?

# INTRODUCTION

According to Michael Gorman, former president of the American Library Association, "A professor who encourages the use of Wikipedia is the intellectual equivalent of a dietician who recommends a steady diet of Big Macs with everything" (quoted in Reagle, 2010b, p. 138). I am such a professor. I not only approve of the use of Wikipedia but also strongly encourage my students to edit it and help it grow.

I am also an active member of the Wikipedia community.[1] Over the last six years, there was hardly a day when I did not log in to Wikipedia and make edits or check that the articles I follow had not been vandalized. I have participated in several reforms of the organization, witnessed it change, and discussed its growth. I have blocked vandals, quarreled with trolls, created and deleted articles, as well as debated their notability, and made a good share of friends and enemies.

While becoming a native Wikipedian, I was doing ethnographic research.[2] I observed, conducted interviews, and took field notes. This book is a result of my long-term anthropological study of the Wikipedia community. It is the first book on nonexpert open-collaboration communities that is based on longitudinal, participative ethnographic research.

## Why Study Open-Collaboration Communities?

Hardly any sphere of life has not been affected by the Internet revolution. The business strategies of many companies have had to be rewritten, because the value chains of most industries have been radically redesigned (Grant, 2010). The Internet has redefined modes of communication (Cairncross, 2001), changed society forever (Castells, 1996), and given birth to new tribalism (Adams & Smith, 2008), even though it remains to be seen whether the change has on the whole increased or decreased the scope of our freedoms (Lessig, 2004; Morozov, 2012). Arguably, the Internet has caused an even more radical change in the workplace and its related cooperation models.

As a result of novel Internet publication modes, the growth of a remix culture that relies on a collage of quotes and borrowings of other authors (Lessig, 2008; Hill & Monroy-Hernández, 2013), and consumer coproduction (Potts et al., 2008), paid professionals have to give way to unpaid ones: Photographers and reporters lose not only to the vast commercial stock picture archives but also to amateurs (often as skilled as the professionals) making their photos available under licenses that allow further sharing (Simmonds, 2010). Journalists compete with bloggers and community portals (Boehlert, 2009). Many projects developed in the free/libre and open-source-software (F/LOSS) movement, such as Linux, are more successful in the open market than their commercial counterparts (S. Weber, 2004; Benkler, 2011). The "copyleft" philosophy, developed from within the hacker and F/LOSS subcultures, redefines the boundaries of copyrights, intellectual work, royalties, proper attribution, and cultural production in general (Lessig, 2001; Coleman & Hill, 2004; Berry, 2008; Zittrain, 2008). Yet many, if not most, of these revolutionary projects are possible only thanks to the emerging peer-production and open-collaboration-organization movement rather than just technology (Kelty, 2010). This model of organization, emerging from open-collaboration projects, is fundamentally different from the one used in traditional commercial organizations and relies heavily on participative management, democratic decision making, and ad hoc structures (Castells, 1996, p. 164).

One example of such highly successful models is Wikipedia. It is an encyclopedia that "anyone can edit," which nevertheless has highly credible content (Chesney, 2006). In fact, it is much more popular (and, according to some, more factually correct) than the vast resources of *Encyclopaedia Britannica*; in as early as 2005 it was considered to "go head to head" with *Britannica* in an independent study published by *Nature* (Giles, 2005), even though at that time it had one-fifth the entries that it has now. (According to current estimates, Wikipedia has more than 2.5 billion words, which is more than sixty times as many as *Britannica*; see [[WP:Size_comparisons]].) According to some studies, it also maintains high overall linguistic readability (Yasseri & Kertész, 2013), although others disagree (Lucassen, Dijkstra, & Schraagen, 2012). Recent research, relying on expert evaluation of selected topics from fourteen websites with information on mental health (including those of *Britannica* and a psychiatry textbook), revealed that Wikipedia was the most highly rated in all tested criteria except readability (Reavley et al., 2012). Also, quite ironically, Wikipedia is better referenced than *Britannica* (Rivington, 2007), fulfilling the Mertonian criterion of scientific method and "organized scepticism" in its requirement of citing reliable sources for published claims (Merton, 1938), although it is prone to quality-perception bias (Flanagin & Metzger, 2011).

Wikipedia is a unique phenomenon among open-source collaboration projects in many respects. For instance, research shows that one of the main reasons why individuals help strangers online, even if they cannot get anything back, is to enhance their professional reputations (Von Hippel & Von Krogh, 2003; Wasko & Faraj, 2005). Such knowledge sharing makes sense, even in the traditional self-interest-driven economics discourse (Nahapiet, Gratton, & Rocha, 2005). There is no immediate gain, but a professional can build up a portfolio or gain higher respect among peers and expect long-term benefits in terms of career development. Reputation building is widely considered to be one of the main motivators for participation in F/LOSS endeavors (S. Weber, 2004).[3]

However, this is not the case on Wikipedia. In this respect Wikipedia differs from F/LOSS projects and is more similar to online games (such as World of Warcraft or Tibia), individual content aggregators, and social networks (such as Pinterest or Facebook), because recognition is built and career developed mainly within and for the community and not for the outside world. Writing many excellent articles on Wikipedia hardly ever gets a place on a résumé. Also, perhaps even more importantly, Wikipedia articles are predominantly created by nonexperts, and many professionals who contribute to it write about topics far outside their work fields. Their motivations are clearly different from those of F/LOSS contributors (Ciffolilli, 2003; Yang & Lai, 2010; Sun, Fang, & Lim, 2011). Interestingly, though, while expert open-collaboration communities such as F/LOSS have been studied by many researchers (e.g., Hippel, 1988; Lakhani & Von Hippel, 2003; Dahlander, Frederiksen, & Rullani, 2008; Ciesielska, 2010) using both qualitative and quantitative methods, qualitative studies of nonexpert open-collaboration communities, particularly studies using long-term, participative ethnographic research, have been few until recently. Since modes of collaboration developed in open-collaboration communities percolate into the traditional corporate world and serve as alternative designs for the formation of virtual teams (Bell & Kozlowski, 2002; Gibson & Cohen, 2003; Wakefield, Leidner, & Garrison, 2008), studying these communities is significant for practical reasons.

The collaboration exhibited by Wikipedia is particularly interesting in the context of the coming age of meritocracy. According to the predictions of some theorists, in the postindustrial turn (Mallet, 1975; Drucker, 1993; Castells, 1996), the organizations of the future will rely on a new occupational structure, independent of bureaucratic hierarchies, and be based instead on meritocratic relations (Argyris, 1973; Toffler, 1980; Ostroff, 1999). The social organization of Wikipedia, which is antihierarchical (Ayers, Matthews, & Yates, 2008; Bruns, 2008) and in which a person's standing in the community highly depends on evaluation of his or her input, strongly resembles these theoretical predictions.

With over nineteen million accounts (and three hundred thousand users, or Wikipedians, active every month), on the English Wikipedia alone (see [[WP:Wikipedians]]), Wikimedia projects[4] are arguably the largest collaborative initiative in the history of humankind. The people of all nationalities behind it form a significant, global, and iconic collective. They are developing some of the most popular websites in the world, and they perceive themselves as a distinct community. Even though the word "community" is often overused nonreflexively (Bauman, 2001), it is particularly fitting for Wikipedians: they form a unique culture, have a sense of identity, and often refer to people who edit Wikimedia projects as "the community" (Pentzold, 2011). This community[5] has a direct influence on what people all over the world know, believe, and think. It is thus important to research it, especially when such research includes comparisons between Wikipedias in different languages (so as to distinguish the elements of design specific to national and language cultures from those that are characteristic of the online open-collaboration environment in general).

The need for a solid study conducted from within the community is particularly great because of the many misconceptions and misunderstandings about the social mechanics of Wikipedia. While virtually everybody is familiar with Wikipedia and its content, very few people from outside the

Wikipedia community understand the social mechanisms driving the creation of articles, their development, and their quality control. Partly because of such misconceptions, Wikipedia is occasionally called fascist and undemocratic (Correa, Correa, & Askanas, 2006). It also often is accused of having a particular bias (right-wing, left-wing, Catholic, atheist, etc.). There are websites dedicated to criticizing Wikipedia (such as Wikipediocracy.com, Wikipedia-watch.org, and WikipediaReview.com). In some cases, the dissent is so strong that the opponents have set up their own wikis—often using the same engine as Wikipedia: Conservapedia (convinced that Wikipedia has a strong left-wing bias), Liberapedia (convinced that Wikipedia has a right-wing bias), and Homopedia (convinced that the Polish Wikipedia has a strong bias against lesbian, gay, bisexual, and transgender people).[6] Many of these accusations stem from a simple misconception of how Wikipedia works.

For example, the chances that an article on a sensitive or controversial topic will be unbalanced at some point in time are very high. Even though in most cases inaccuracies are removed soon after they are introduced, they stay longer if nobody notices them, which often is the case for less popular entries.[7] Some topics, on the other hand, are just prone to vandalism.[8] More importantly, though, articles on Wikipedia at different stages of development can be variously biased by diametrically different views at the same time. There are waves of slight biases on smaller Wikipedias, depending on the composition of editors at any given moment, but the larger a project gets, the less likely it is that biases prevail. In general, any purposeful, long-term universal bias on Wikipedia, detouring from the dominant beliefs of the general academic and para-academic community, does not prevail. (To understand how the system works in practice, it is enough to peruse Wikipedia articles on homeopathy or psychics.)

This does not mean that Wikipedia as a community is a heavenly Utopia. It has many problems and weaknesses, which can be analyzed only after careful examination from within. As an organizational ethnographer, I am both fascinated by the Wikipedia design, culture, and modus operandi, so alien to traditional organizational models, and acutely aware of its many shortcomings and the dangers looming over the community. Throughout years spent in the Wikipedia communities, I have gathered knowledge of its rites and social organization that are typically inaccessible to people from the outside. I believe I understand many of its weaknesses but also grasp why it still works and produces hard knowledge that is universally accessible and free.

## Structure of the Book

In this book, I present Wikipedia as a nonexpert open-collaboration-community organization studied from within. On a general level, I try to solve the puzzle of why Wikipedia's novel organizational design works; it should not, but it does. We still know very little about power and management in nonexpert open-collaboration communities, and this book is an attempt to begin filling this gap.

I focus on the issues that are typically inaccessible to people from the outside and are part of a consistent narrative of organizational culture:

- Status, power, and hierarchy enactment in a community so officially antihierarchical
- The Wikimedia business model and difficult relations between the Wikipedia community and the Wikimedia Foundation
- The role of conflicts and dissent as driving forces behind article development
- The "edit wars" and dispute resolution models on Wikipedia
- The scope of peer and bureaucratic control, which, contrary to the popular belief that Wikipedia is a totally free and anarchist community, is strongly exerted
- The abandonment of interpersonal trust and credential checks in favor of trust in procedures
- The organizational design, which balances chaotic, anarchist adhocracy with a formal bureaucracy in an environment run entirely by contingent volunteers
- The evolution of leadership in the Wikipedia community

An analysis of these issues leads to conclusions on how Wikipedia's chaotic logic makes it both effective and attractive for participants, as well as relatively structured and ordered. I also discuss the larger pattern of Wikipedia's shortcomings and weaknesses that emerge as responses to its increased scale and complexity, and I explore its unique and effective solutions to some of the problems of managing complex organizations. I emphasize the implications these problem-solving methods have for how Wikipedia legitimizes itself to its community and the rest of the world.

I also comment on the possibility of commercial endeavors copying the Wikipedia model and on why other, seemingly similar projects (such as Citizendium, created by one of Wikipedia's cofounders and aimed at avoiding some of Wikipedia's pitfalls) fail.

I begin the book with a brief history of Wikipedia, as well as a short description of the community life, core norms, and status and representation of self among participants. This information might be obvious to readers familiar with the Wikipedia community, but I include it because it lays the groundwork for later chapters and further interpretations.

In Chapter 2, I address the issues of career and hierarchy on Wikipedia. I analyze its community roles and reasons for the rapid decline in successful applications for administrative rights on the English Wikipedia. I discuss the obsession with edit count in a large part of the community and show the consequences of this phenomenon in deterring high-quality editors and promoting semiautomated minor edits in a perverse parody of a quasi-Taylorist system, a factory management system to speed up production. I describe the power tensions related to community elections and the perception by some members of the community that there is inequality and that a cabal exists—characteristics of the egalitarian system of power. In other words, I try to find out *why a community so egalitarian in its rhetoric and organized on a voluntary basis without monetary incentives experiences major power and hierarchy tensions.*

In Chapter 3, I describe means of conflict resolution on Wikipedia. I show how malicious edits are easily weeded out. I describe Wikipedia's official focus on consensus, which is commonplace for some participative organizations, and contrast it with the practice of an actual conflict: arguably, the worst "edit war" in Wikipedia history (whether the name of a Polish city should be written as "Gdańsk" or as "Danzig"). Through an analysis of this dispute, I show that under certain conditions, Wikipedia's dispute resolution methods fail, and settlement can be achieved only by abandoning the principle of consensus. I also present trajectories, or the progression, of certain conflicts. I conclude that a major part of Wikipedia development relies on conflict rather than understood collaboration and suggest that many online collaborative efforts are driven by dissent, which makes them more effective. I am interested in *how conflicts are handled and utilized in a community so seemingly oriented toward collaboration.*

In Chapter 4, I show that the Wikipedia community relies on peer control. All behavior on Wikipedia is monitored, registered, and tracked. User participation is also controlled through procedures, and the amount of regulation is much higher than in many even explicitly bureaucratic organizations. I show that the growing body of rules tends to increase the power of old-timers over newcomers and deters newcomers from participating in Wikipedia. I try to understand *why a community so opposed to structures and to formal regulation and so dedicated to ad hoc, semianarchist decision making insists on direct control of all behavior.*

In Chapter 5, I contrast this tight bureaucratic control with the extremely open approach of the Wikipedia community to credential verification. I describe the low interpersonal trust environment on Wikipedia, where the protection of online identity and privacy is sacrosanct. I show, through a case analysis of a major crisis of trust on Wikipedia, that credential control would undermine one of the attractors of Wikipedia (the ability to create a knowledgeable persona). I explain that, as a result, trust in procedures takes over the role of credentials, as well as interpersonal trust. The question here is *why does a community so focused on producing high-quality knowledge disregard real-life credentials and identities?*

The exploration of the issue of trust sets the foundation for Chapter 6, on governance. This discussion focuses on the entire movement rather than single communities. I describe the main stakeholders—the Wikimedia Foundation and its board of trustees, local Wikimedia chapters and the Wikimedia Chapters Association, and the community itself—and the relations among them, including past and present tensions. By analyzing the power struggle and the rivalry for resources, I consider the possibility of successful splits from the community (called "forking") but find them unlikely given the flexible conduct of the foundation and its hold over strategic resources. I conclude with general observations on Wikimedia governance and lessons for further studies of virtual communities. I explore *how this voluntary movement is dealing with advancing professionalization and competition for resources and what governance processes ensure its relative stability.*

In Chapter 7, I write on authority and leadership in the Wikimedia movement. I analyze the changing role of the founder of Wikipedia, Jimmy "Jimbo" Wales. I demonstrate how authority figures are not treated preferentially by the community on Wikipedia. I also describe the decline of Wales's operational leadership, in his conscious withdrawal from leadership and in two cases of leadership failure. I show that Wales's declared mode of leadership was incompatible with his actions. I also show how Wales's influence and power actually increased as a result of his withdrawal from micromanagement. By examining a minor community rebellion against him and his subsequent reformulation of his leadership, I draw wider conclusions for open-collaboration leadership. Ultimately, I am interested in *what types of leadership are used and under what circumstances they are used in open-collaboration communities.*

The final remarks in Chapter 8 bring together the observations from the previous chapters and open a discussion on the directions for Wikimedia's development and the impact of Wikipedia and its sister projects on the world. I show that Wikipedia is just one example of a broader revolution in knowledge production. I also describe how the enactment of conflict, trust, and leadership in open-collaboration communities can influence our understanding of organization of human work. I then draw conclusions for participative management theory by revealing the pros and cons of a fully collaborative design and the challenges to growth for an organization presenting itself as radically different (yet facing problems similar to those of others in matters such as scaling, management, and bootstrapping).

Appendix A describes the methods and other methodological considerations of this research. For people who are unfamiliar with ethnographic studies and the issues and concerns typical in qualitative research, this appendix may be a useful description of methodological choices a researcher has to make when conducting a longitudinal, qualitative study, especially one using virtual ethnography. For many other readers, these considerations may seem overly theoretical, and that is why they do not appear at the beginning of the book, in the typical academic manner.

Appendix B is an abridged glossary of Wikipedia slang and common lingo.

In conclusion, I express one caveat: As the nineteenth-century poet John Godfrey Saxe said in a quote often incorrectly attributed to Otto von Bismarck, "Laws, like sausages, cease to inspire respect in proportion as we know how they are made" (Shapiro, 2008). In this book I describe how Wikipedia works, not in theory, but in practice, and if you do not know the Wikipedia community, reading this book may change the way you perceive it.

**1**

# WIKIPEDIA IN SHORT

## Numbers, Rules, and Editors

### Wikipedia: Basic Facts

To analyze Wikipedia as a phenomenon and a community, it may be useful to understand its origins, history, and growth. Wikipedia, contrary to popular belief, was not the first wiki. A "wiki" (derived from the Hawaiian word for "quick" and named after the Wiki Wiki shuttle at Honolulu International Airport) is a website technology that tracks users' changes, which can be made in a simplified markup language (allowing easy additions of, for example, bold, italics, or tables without the need to learn HTML syntax). The first wiki was created and released in 1995 by Ward Cunningham as WikiWikiWeb. WikiWikiWeb was an attractive choice to enterprises and was (and sometimes still is) used for communication, collaborative idea development, documentation, intranets, and knowledge management. It grew steadily in popularity.

In 2000 Jimmy "Jimbo" Wales, then the CEO of Bomis, started up his encyclopedic project, Nupedia, which was meant to be an online encyclopedia, with free content written by experts. In an attempt to meet the standards set by professional encyclopedias, the creators of Nupedia based it on a peer-review process. The website relied on an assumption that scholars would generate content for free. But Nupedia developed slowly, and its editor in chief, Larry Sanger, hired by Wales to oversee its development, adopted a suggestion by Ben Kovitz[1] to use wiki software and philosophy for the creation of encyclopedic content. This idea resonated with Wales's vision of making a publicly editable and accessible encyclopedia, and in January 2001 Wikipedia.com (later Wikipedia.org) was launched, originally as a content feeder for Nupedia.

It was an instant success. The first year produced about twenty thousand articles, and the second year brought a nearly fivefold increase. Meanwhile, either Nupedia was not reaching the academic community with its message or the academic community was not interested in its mission. In September 2003 it was closed down, with only 24 articles finished and 74 in development. By then, the English Wikipedia already had more than 150,000 articles. (See Figure 1.1.) In the meantime, many editions of Wikipedia in other languages had started to spin off. The first was German (originally a subdomain of Wikipedia.com launched on March 16, 2001). The largest Wikipedias as of January 2013 are listed in Table 1.1.

The total number of articles in all Wikipedias (in more than 270 languages) exceeds twenty million. The English Wikipedia is by far the leader. However, positions from number 2 to number 10 are relatively close. There

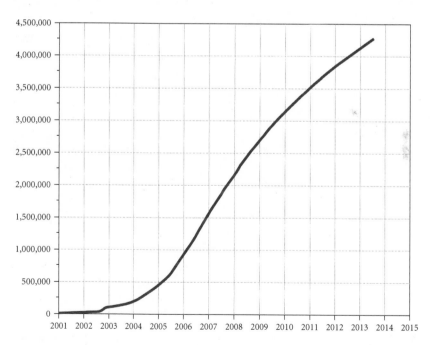

FIGURE 1.1. Number of articles on the English Wikipedia. Source: Illustration by HenkvD, [[File:EnwikipediaArt.PNG]].

TABLE 1.1   The ten largest Wikipedias in the world as of January 21, 2013

| Rank | Language | Number of articles | Number of articles per capita (per thousand native speakers) |
|---|---|---|---|
| 1 | English | 4.1 million | 10.9 |
| 2 | German | 1.5 million | 15.2 |
| 3 | French | 1.3 million | 11.3 |
| 4 | Dutch | 1.1 million | 47.7 |
| 5 | Italian | 983,000 | 16.0 |
| 6 | Spanish | 938,000 | 2.3 |
| 7 | Polish | 934,000 | 23.4 |
| 8 | Russian | 933,000 | 6.5 |
| 9 | Japanese | 834,000 | 6.9 |
| 10 | Portuguese | 760,000 | 3.2 |

SOURCE: "List of Largest Wikis," 2013.

is a larger gap between number 10 and number 11, the Swedish Wikipedia, which has 564,000 articles. When the number of articles per capita of native speakers is considered, among the ten largest Wikipedias, the Dutch one takes the lead by far, and the Polish one also significantly stands out. The English Wikipedia is near the middle in this ranking (at number 5, almost equal to the French one), which is surprising given that English is the most popular second language in the world—practically a lingua franca, unlike Dutch and Polish. Approximately twenty-nine thousand English Wikipedia users declare themselves native speakers,[2] and twenty-seven thousand who contribute to it are self-declared nonnatives. On the basis of these rough estimates, there are about as many nonnative editors as native ones, probably because the English Wikipedia had a head start on the other Wikipedias (especially in media coverage). In addition, the relative number of articles on the English Wikipedia is surprisingly low compared to those of other major languages. Furthermore, the page and editor growth rate on the English Wikipedia has slowed, while organizational costs of coordination have increased (Suh, Convertino, Chi, & Pirolli, 2009).

However, number of articles alone is not a good indicator of an encyclopedia's quality: many articles on the English Wikipedia are much better written and richer in sources and data than articles on the same subjects on other Wikipedias. Perhaps editors on the English Wikipedia more often decide to deepen and expand the existing articles rather than seed stubs (or start short new articles). Moreover, since the number of articles is the simplest and the most visible measure of encyclopedic size, some Wikipedias employ bots (software scripts) to automatically create articles, such as on villages in China (each receiving a separate entry) by using geographic lists and maps. This expansion strategy has been used by most Wikipedias since October 2002, when a bot added thirty thousand stubs on American cities and towns to the English Wikipedia in little over a week. Clearly, nonhuman contributors have a significant influence on the development of Wikipedia (Niederer & van Dijck, 2010; Geiger, 2011; Halfaker & Riedl, 2012). Thus, all the metrics should be taken with a grain of salt.[3] Note, however, that Wikipedia's growth is slowing (Suh et al., 2009), and some studies indicate that its growth follows an S curve (Lam & Riedl, 2011), which is not surprising.

Also interesting is that the criteria for topic notability vary significantly among Wikipedias. In a study of twenty-five Wikipedias, only 1 percent of their article topics were covered in all of them, and as many as 74 percent of the article topics were present in one language only (Hecht & Gergle, 2010). Yet the various Wikipedias have a similar rational and meritocratic development path, because the differences between average and featured (exemplary) articles within each Wikipedia are significantly greater than the differences between the Wikipedias (Hammwöhner, 2007). Different-language Wikipedias, after they reach a certain level of maturity, develop along similar patterns (Zlatić, Božičević, Štefančić, & Domazet, 2006).

In spite of its tremendous overall growth and undisputed maturity, the development of the English Wikipedia in some ways does not seem to be slowing down. For instance, one intriguing measure of Wikipedia stability is the time it takes to achieve ten million edits (a measure independent of the number of contributors). It took 211 weeks for the number of edits to increase from ten million to twenty million and then 17 weeks to increase to thirty million. The pace soon stabilized at about 7 weeks and has stayed there ever since. In 2007 it sped up to a little below 6 weeks, and since 2011 it has been 8 weeks; nevertheless, it is amazingly consistent. See Figure 1.2. It is quite possible that editing Wikipedia has become part of a work-life routine for many editors. Also, the proportion of administrative and other coordinative edits to the overall number of edits may be increasing (Kittur & Kraut, 2008). In August 2013 the total number of edits on the English Wikipedia reached 632 million.[4] Yet when the variations in the number of new editors, the number of those quitting, and general activity are taken into account, the stability in this data is surprising.

Other Wikimedia projects, and Wikipedias in particular, flourish as well. "As of October 2013, Wikipedia includes over 29.8 million freely usable articles in 287 languages that have been written by over 42 million registered

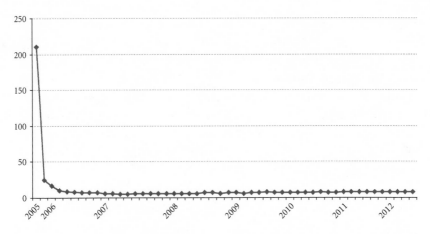

FIGURE 1.2. Number of weeks between every ten million edits on the English Wikipedia. Source: [[User:Katalaveno/TBE]] (retrieved September 2, 2012).

users and numerous anonymous contributors worldwide. According to Alexa Internet, Wikipedia is the world's seventh-most-popular website" (see [[History_of_Wikipedia]]). The total number of edits on all Wikimedia projects as of August 2013 exceeded 1.9 billion,[5] and the number of pageviews has been growing steadily (see Figure 1.3, which covers 2008 to 2012). Similarly, the number of unique visitors rose from 242 million in January 2008 to 469 million in June 2012.[6]

The Wikimedia community[7] has evolved, and some changes are not as positive as the pageview statistics would imply. For instance, according to the report "Editor Trends Study," on the five largest Wikipedias, by the Wikimedia Foundation, until 2005 nearly 40 percent of editors were still active a year after they started editing. However, after 2007, no more than 15 percent of editors remained active after a year (Wikimedia Foundation, 2011b). Clearly, integration with the Wikimedia community has become more difficult. This may be related to increased decentralized and informal gatekeeping—that is, small-scale actions of experienced community members aimed at discouraging newcomers (Shaw, 2012), possibly to assert status and flaunt seniority. The community has undertaken many efforts to reverse this decline (see, e.g., [[WP:Teahouse]]).

According to *Wikipedia Editors Study*, published in April 2011, 91 percent of all Wikipedia editors are male (Wikimedia Foundation, 2011a, p. 2). This figure may not be accurate, since it is based on a voluntary online survey

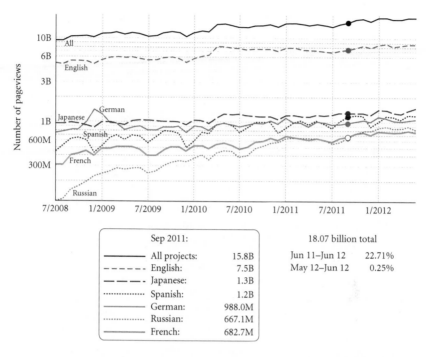

FIGURE 1.3. Pageviews for all Wikimedia projects, July 2008–June 2012. *Note:* The box shows the data for September 2011, the point selected on the graph. Source: http://reportcard.wmflabs.org (retrieved August 28, 2012).

advertised to 31,699 registered users and resulting in 5,073 complete and valid responses (p. 42). It is possible that male editors are more likely to respond than female editors. Similarly, a study of self-declarations of gender showing only 16 percent are female editors (Lam et al., 2011) may be distorted, since more females may choose not to reveal their gender in a community perceived as male dominated. Even taking into account that opt-in surveys of Wikipedia participation must be biased (Hill & Shaw, 2013), studies consistently show that the number of female editors is dismayingly small, especially when the gender gap is much smaller among nonediting readers (Glott, Schmidt, & Ghosh, 2010; Bywater, 2011). This extreme disparity is difficult to explain just by Wikipedia's geeky past or a reproduction of social and economic inequalities (Morell, 2010).[8] Some studies suggest that it may be a result of a high level of conflict on Wikipedia or a generally critical and uncooperative environment (Collier & Bear, 2012). Clearly, gendered perception of editor roles and careers could be at play, too (Bourne & Özbilgin, 2008). The phenomenon is far from being sufficiently explored and requires more Wikipedia-focused studies from a variety of angles, as well as studies of collaboration technologies and gender (Zhang & Kramarae, 2008). In general, the free-cultural-works and free/libre-and-open-source-software (F/LOSS) movements have a significant gender gap (Reagle, 2013).

As a possible side effect, Wikipedia may be missing more biographies of women than of men compared to *Britannica*, even though in general Wikipedia provides better coverage and more comprehensive articles (Reagle & Rhue, 2011). Also, articles about gender inequality and topics of interest for women may be more likely to be deleted (Carstensen, 2009). However, there is a huge variation in recognizing people across different-language Wikipedias (Callahan & Herring, 2011). Even clear sexism occasionally occurs: the *New York Times* writer Amanda Filipacchi observed that Wikipedians categorized American women novelists separately from men, who remained in the general American novelists category (Filipacchi, 2013). After publication of Filipacchi's article women authors were reincorporated into the general category.

Another finding from the *Wikipedia Editors Study* (Wikimedia Foundation, 2011a) is that as many as 61 percent of Wikipedia editors have finished college (8 percent attaining a doctorate, 18 percent a master's, and 35 percent a bachelor's degree), so the stereotypical image of a Wikipedian as a nerdy kid or, most commonly, a high school student (Greenwood, 2012) is clearly false. Only 36 percent of Wikipedia editors are able to write computer programs by themselves, so the geeky stereotype is also partly false. Moreover, Wikipedia editors are not so young; the average age is thirty-two, and 27 percent are twenty-one or younger. In another major study, however, 50 percent of respondents report being younger than twenty-two (Glott et al., 2010). In general, most quantitative studies of Wikipedia make some assumptions and are vulnerable to one methodological bias or another, since bias-free recruitment of subjects is a challenge.

Reasons for participation in surveys among Wikipedians vary greatly, and survey interpretation depends on the paradigm and discipline of the researcher. Some studies indicate that a dominant motivator for participating in surveys is the possibility of gaining recognition in the community (Forte & Bruckman, 2005), which is particularly attractive when paired with a relatively low transactional cost of entry and participation (Ciffolilli, 2003). Other motivators are gaining self-fulfillment, having fun, and acquiring and sharing knowledge (even if just to boost one's ego; Rafaeli & Ariel, 2008), maintaining a positive self-image, contributing to the common good (Ciffolilli, 2003; Bay-tiyeh & Pfaffman, 2010; Yang & Lai, 2010), and enjoying a sense of accomplish-ment (Kuznetsov, 2006). Such reasons are not uncommon for other online knowledge-sharing activities (Lee & Jang, 2010). As research on other virtual communities shows, many users participate to elevate their communal social status (Lampel & Bhalla, 2007) or simply feel that they belong (Lampe, Wash, Velasquez, & Ozkaya, 2010). Other motivations may be ideological (e.g., a strong belief that information should be free) and driven by principle (Nov, 2007; E. G. Coleman, 2013). Incidentally, even as beginners, those who become die-hard Wikipedians differ in how they participate in the community and edit (Panciera, Halfaker, & Terveen, 2009). This could indicate a significant selection bias in the Wikipedia community. Long-standing Wikipedians are sometimes perceived as a different kind of person by newcomers, and this perception adversely affects retention of new editors (Antin, 2011). They also take the role of gatekeepers in the eyes of the newcomers, especially in the case of breaking news articles (Keegan & Gergle, 2010).

At the same time, high user retention in the Wikipedia community does not have exclusively positive effects, contrary to popular belief. In fact, mod-erate levels of membership turnover on Wikipedia improve the production of collaborative articles (Ransbotham & Kane, 2011).

## Basic Rules and Norms

The English Wikipedia, and to a lesser extent the Polish Wikipedia, has hun-dreds of rules, norms, policies, and guidelines. Whereas many other virtual communities rely on governance by a few leaders (Lessig, 1999; Butler, Sproull, Kiesler, & Kraut, 2007), the Wikipedia community establishes these strictures. A proliferation of rules, statutes, deliberations, and meetings is typical of truly community-driven cooperatives (Whyte & Whyte, 1991; Cheney, 2002). Rule formalization and emergence of coercive institutional structures are discussed later. Here I summarize the chief policies pertaining to editing on most Wiki-media projects.

Wikipedia is distinguished from other contemporary Internet fora by one hard-and-fast rule: no personal attacks (NPA),[9] which possibly evolved from Usenet traditions. Editors are not allowed to attack each other, not even in retaliation for a personal attack; the attacked editor must try to reason with the attacker. Retaliation most likely leads to both parties being blocked. If an intervention is necessary, an administrator can be asked for help (or take the initiative to do so, upon spotting aggressive behavior). Editors are expected to comment only on content. A similarly strong and related norm is civility (CIV). It requires editors to treat each other with respect and consideration and to refrain from personal comments. Wikipedians are advised to forgive and forget (FORG) when insulted or wronged.

Enforcement of the civility and no-personal-attacks rules depends on the project, the people involved, and the situation. Sometimes a single snide comment may be a reason for blocking a user, at other times a major offense will go without a reaction. In one case, a Wikimedia Foundation employee who was also an administrator on the English Wikipedia called his disputant "a troll." Although the disputant had a long history of criticizing Wikipedia, in this instance he was actually making a point in a discussion and in my judgment not trolling. I suggested the employee retract the name-calling comment, but he refused.[10] Nobody else reacted. Clearly, the norm was bent because of the status of the people involved, one high, one low, but the outcome was not typical. I have blocked other admins (administrators) for not mincing their words when they should have and have witnessed others doing so often enough to believe that status and position in the community are no protection from policy enforcement. In general, all users, regardless of their experience and standing in the community, are expected to follow the rules of etiquette (EQ). The rules of civilized discourse reflect those used in academia: discussion is based solely on the strength of the argument rather than eristic tricks or participant status. In any case, blocking users is meant to be preventive rather than punitive and to ensure that, in the future, norms are respected.

A word enormously respected on Wikipedia is "consensus" (CON). The norm of consensus requires all editors to seek a solution acceptable to the community. It does not necessarily mean unanimity, but it emphasizes striving for hypothetical unity. In practice, dedication to consensus may coerce an agreement and dilute minority views, although it helps in achieving better understanding and increases the perception of participatory decision making. Because participation and the exchange of views are important, polling and voting are generally discouraged. In fact, voting is considered anticonsensual, as it does not allow the full expression of all views in a discussion. One of the norms explicitly says that "Wikipedia is not a democracy" (DEM); another states that "polling is not a substitute for a discussion" (POLL), and the page "Wikipedia:Straw polls" explains,

Having the option of settling a dispute by taking a poll, instead of the careful consideration, dissection and eventual synthesis of each side's arguments, actually undermines the progress in dispute resolution that Wiki has allowed. This is a strength, not a failing, and is one of the most important things that make Wiki special, and while taking a poll is very often a lot easier than helping each other find a mutually agreeable position, it's almost never better.

Polling encourages the community to remain divided by avoiding that discourse; participants don't interact with the other voters, but merely choose camps. Establishing consensus requires expressing that opinion in terms other than a choice between discrete options, and expanding the reasoning behind it, addressing the points that others have left, until all come to a mutually agreeable solution. No one can address objections that aren't stated, points that aren't made.

Yes, establishing consensus is a lot harder than taking a poll. So are most things worth doing. ([[WP:Straw_polls]])

The practical applications of rules referring to consensus seeking and conflict resolution are discussed in more detail in Chapter 3.

Other norms of conduct pertain to article content and to editor behavior and code of conduct. One of the most important behavioral rules is assuming good faith (ASG): all editors are required not to assume ill intentions and to respond as if others had acted in good faith, despite appearances to the contrary and even to users with a troubled history. This rule is quite flexible for obvious reasons, and its occasional minor breaches are rarely penalized. This rule is connected to the rule requiring that editors do not bite newcomers (DNB). New editors often make silly mistakes and cannot write articles following standards that they do not know about. They also often unintentionally break other rules. The DNB rule emphasizes that hostility toward newcomers is particularly damaging to the project.

Newcomers are especially prone to violating the rule against conflict of interest (COI). In general, editors are advised to not work on articles about which they may not be neutral. They are particularly discouraged from writing their own biographies. Similarly, writing about something one has interest in is not recommended, and editors are advised to disclose any possible conflict of interest. Administrators are forbidden to use their administrative privileges when they are also involved as regular editors (for example, an admin cannot block a user with whom he or she has a dispute, unless this dispute stems from the administrator trying to reason with a troublemaking user). Two other rules emphasize that all regulations are intended to make developing Wikipedia easier. Users are forbidden to disrupt Wikipedia to illustrate a point (POINT), which essentially means that editors may not hunt for inconsistencies in application of the rules looking for loopholes or enforce them in an arbitrary or absurd way. There is also a rule against gaming the system (GAME), or deliberately using Wikipedia rules in bad faith, seeking gotchas and loopholes, engaging in pettifoggery, or filibustering the consensus by reprimanding other editors for minor errors instead of simply correcting them.

Many other norms are content related and quite detailed but unrelated to the social organization of work and cooperation. All editors are expected to write from a neutral point of view (NPOV). That means that in principle an article must be objective, be accurate, and present information from reliable sources and in proportion to the sources' weight. Although the practical application of this policy is not always ideal (Oboler, Steinberg, & Stern, 2010), it is among the strongest norms of editing and one of three core content policies of Wikipedia. The other two, closely related, are verifiability (V) and no original research (NOR). The verifiability requirement means that all information that may be challenged should be attributed to a reliable published source. If it is not, editors are asked to look for a source themselves. Alternatively, they can add a citation-needed tag to signal to other readers and editors that a certain claim requires a source. The rule of no original research forbids publishing meaningful information without sourcing it to a publication, as Wikipedia is not a primary source of facts. This rule comes to bear especially when news stories are breaking. Then, sources are scarce and information changes quickly, and inexperienced editors often try to include information that has not yet been properly sourced (Keegan, Gergle, & Contractor, 2011). Keeping such an article accurate requires intense coordination (Keegan, Gergle, & Contractor, 2012).

Of course, the scope of these three core content policies varies and depends on the appropriateness to the claim; scientific topics have to rely on academic publications, and pop-culture news can refer to media news or occasionally even tabloids. The rule is interpreted on a project-by-project basis. Sometimes a simple calculation from well-sourced data, such as dividing a gross domestic product (GDP) by a country's population to arrive at GDP per capita may be considered original research, since the calculation is not in the source. Sometimes much more wide-ranging conjectures from sources are allowed. However, one requirement is unequivocal: all claims must use reliable sources (RS), and those notorious for unreliability are forbidden. Self-published and questionable sources can be used only as sources of information about themselves and only when they are not exceptional (i.e., deviating from the prevailing view; REDFLAG) or unduly self-serving. In other words, exceptional claims require multiple credible sources.

Wikipedia policies about original research and verifiability are quite strict. The extent to which this rule is applied depends on the topic and the editors, as well as the current trend in the community. A good exercise in understanding how it works is reading Wikipedia articles on topics such as homeopathy or ufology (on UFOs), in which sources are of varying verifiability and reliability and contradict each other, but the articles meet Wikipedia's requirements.

Over the years, both the Polish and the English Wikipedias have increased their requirements for sources. In some cases the results are absurd. For example, in September 2012 the American writer Philip Roth issued an open letter to Wikipedia in the *New Yorker* (Roth, 2012). He politely explained that he had tried to correct a misunderstanding about the origins of the story in one of his books, *The Human Stain*, on Wikipedia. One of the English Wikipedia administrators refused to permit the changes, because authors cannot make claims about their own work without confirmation from published secondary sources. Immediately after publication of Roth's letter the Wikipedia entry in question was amended, as it now met the requirement of a published source, and the entire incident was accurately reflected in the entry, but the incident shows that the sources and verifiability policies are taken extremely seriously on Wikipedia, to absurd results.

I had a similar problem with proper sourcing on the Polish Wikipedia. I found that in the infoboxes[11] of politicians, all female members of parliament were described with the male form of their function. I wanted to correct it, but one of the administrators insisted that the Polish parliamentary acts, in which only male nouns were used, should be considered authoritative. I argued that such acts are always written with just one form for ease of reading. However, my argument was moot without valid published sources using female forms of the positions, and I was not able to find any. Thus, I decided to create a source: through my publisher I contacted a well-known professor of linguistics and asked him to write an opinion in an online language advisory portal he ran, under the publisher's auspices. He agreed, and the opinion, recommending the use of female forms for female MPs, was published; no one could now object to changing the infoboxes, and they were immediately amended.

Many other detailed rules about reliability, required minimal notability, valid sources, and style depend on the topic of an article. One that applies to all is Wikipedia's rule preventing copyright violations (CV). Any excerpt spotted on Wikipedia that has been plagiarized from other sources is immediately removed. In addition, the use of materials without proper rights (in general, only some suitable free licenses are accepted)[12] is prohibited. Ironically, Wikipedia, often blamed for the epidemic of plagiarism, is a paragon of responsible copyright policies. Even more ironic is that mainstream professional media often use materials such as photos and article fragments from Wikipedia without the attribution required by the license, assuming that if it is free, crediting the source is not required. If Wikipedia used a rule of reciprocity against such violators, it would be much richer in content, but the community of amateur volunteers treats copyright more seriously than do many corporate journalists and professional authors. This surprising phenomenon does not apply only to Wikipedia: open-collaboration and F/LOSS communities are generally well versed in law because of their common ideological engagement in the free-speech and free-information movements (E. G. Coleman, 2009). A direct translation of F/LOSS ideas, related to code, into the world of other creative works is not possible, in spite of attempts advocated by Creative Commons (Hill, 2005; E. G. Coleman, 2013).

## Community Life, Status, and Representation of Self

A significant number of the most active Wikipedians on all projects are elected to community roles, but even more active users do not participate in the elections. Naturally, since egalitarianism and participative management do not suppress informal structures (Gruber & Trickett, 1987) and status play, users, whether participating in an election or not, resort to different strategies to present themselves and vie for standing among their peers. Their local identity building relies on adjusting to the organizational discourse and creating a fitting narrative (Łuczewski, 2012). Typically, for an open-collaboration environment, users rely on status building and social signaling meaningful mainly for other members of the community (Bianchi, Kang, & Stewart, 2010). In fact, status seeking is a powerful force behind virtual-community building (Lampel & Bhalla, 2007). Wikipedians, like hackers and contrary to the stereotype of computer nerds, are very social (E. G. Coleman, 2010b).

Wikipedians organize themselves into formal and informal groups. In addition to groups related to the real world, political views, or hobbies, there are groups related only to Wikipedia itself. The deepest philosophical divide among Wikipedians is between the inclusionists (editors believing that Wikipedia, as a digital resource, should not be limited by traditional encyclopedic constraints and should cover as wide an array of topics as possible) and the exclusionists (editors believing that Wikipedia should apply criteria about the notability of described phenomena as strictly as any other encyclopedia and that the virtue of sensible exclusion increases the project's quality). Both factions are pretty much equal in size, and only declaring an extreme stance in any of these camps can dampen one's chances in elections. I lean slightly toward inclusionism.

Some Wikipedia-centric groups are formed around typical tasks. For instance, some Wikipedians are vandal fighters or recent-changes patrollers and specialize in perusing others' edits, often focusing on anonymous edits or those from new editors. Many pranksters are shocked to find their vandalizing edits removed within minutes or even seconds. With the significant help of software tools, the vandal fighters play an important social role (Geiger & Ribes, 2010) by consolidating the Wikipedia community, since dense networks provide social rewards for those punishing norm violators (Piskorski & Gorbatai, 2011), and promoting Wikipedia as agile in correcting its mistakes.

Some take pride in taking care of new editors, welcoming them and providing guidance in basic Wikipedia policies. Some are interested in specific areas of knowledge (e.g., soccer, sociology, role-playing games, or railways) and form WikiProjects and WikiPortals, gathering other like-minded editors. WikiProjects ([[WP:WikiProject]]) often coordinate their efforts in their areas of specialization, create lists of articles within their scope of interest, and discuss notability of certain topics. There are more than two thousand WikiProjects on the English Wikipedia. They are important in the socialization of some specialized users and help them structure and coordinate their efforts (Forte et al., 2012). Specialization can include focusing on technical aspects of Wikipedia, such as preparing infoboxes, creating bots for specific tasks, or just helping with categorization.

Other, less formal forms of specialization naturally emerge. For instance, some Wikipedians frequently take part in policy discussions at the Village Pump, which is a platform with several topical forums for discussion on the development of Wikipedia. Others take part in debates on the notability of individual articles. Although there are notability guidelines for many topics, there are always borderline cases that require more consideration and weighing of the arguments for keeping, deleting, merging, or improving the article. Deciding which articles should be featured on the main page, which is updated daily, relies on some of the community, many members regularly participating. Featured-article designation is a rare honor, and the English Wikipedia has fewer than three thousand articles with this status (less than one article in a thousand).[13] Similarly, bestowing good-article status is a matter of communal debate, and some users specialize in it. Fewer than sixteen thousand articles on the English Wikipedia have been designated as good (not including featured articles). An article can attain good or featured status and then lose it. For instance, nearly one thousand articles lost their featured status because of failing to meet changed criteria.

The diversity of activities and areas where Wikipedians can interact is very high. This diversity dilutes the gradations of organizational authority. Some Wikipedians focus only on editing, but in general, credibility is built in interactions and participation in the common discourse (Forte & Bruckman, 2005), and to occupy a community position one has not only to edit but also interact. After all, collaborative editing of Wikipedia articles is a process of negotiating and constructing shared perspectives (Kane, Majchrzak, Johnson, & Chenisern, 2009), including the admissibility of sources, as well as balancing what constitutes neutral information and what does not. Even seemingly individual tasks have collaborative aspects.

Wikipedians like to socialize. Even though Wikipedia is not a social network and most interactions on Wikipedia are related to the encyclopedia, a plethora of cultural production is meant only for other Wikipedians. The community also shares many humorous essays and insider jokes [[Category:Wikipedia_humor]].

Most Wikipedians, after gaining some initial experience, create user pages, or personal pages, on Wikipedia. A user page has an important practical consequence: since links to nonexistent pages are marked in red on Wikipedia and since article editors are listed and linked in an article's history and on the list of recent changes, edits of registered but less socialized editors immediately stand out and receive more scrutiny. Not having a user page is an immediate sign of being either a novice or a rarity. Thus, one of the early lessons in Wikipedia culture is to create a user page and set up a talk page (a personal message board where other users can leave a message).

There are not many norms and rules about the organization of a user page. Most editors tell a little bit about themselves and their interests, sometimes also mentioning their occupation. They often include userboxes, or graphic representations of user statements. Userboxes can relate to Wikipedia roles and statuses, language skills, interests, or political and religious views. Some are humorous.[14] The number of userboxes displayed on a user page varies; some users do not have any, and some insert over a hundred (including declarations of one's "patronuses" [fictional guardians from the Harry Potter universe], favorite TV series, and eating habits). If there is a pattern, it is that users with declared radical views or sympathies are less likely to receive communal support in elections. In some cases, political or religious declarations have crushed a candidate's hopes for adminship, as voters assume that even if the candidate is able to put these views aside in everyday work, other users may think they have been mistreated because of a viewpoint bias. Similarly, excessive use of userboxes is rare among seasoned Wikipedians.

There is no one standard set of userboxes, but many Wikipedians use a box showing the rights they hold on a given project or their position (such as admin or bureaucrat). Some declare that they are not admins, although this sometimes indicates that they have gripes with the community. One of the most common userboxes is the Babel tower, with which editors declare their language skills on a scale from 0 (no ability to speak a given language) to 5 (professional-level fluency) or list a language with no number, indicating a native speaker. Babel-tower userboxes, like declarations of functions or rights held on a project, typically are used for most Wikimedia projects. Similarly, a declaration of gender is possible through a userbox (although most users do not display it) or, more recently, by a setting on the website that determines the way a person is addressed in some languages in automated messages.

Other userboxes are created spontaneously on each project, when a need arises and when there is an editor capable of creating one. Creation is not difficult but requires more than an elementary understanding of Wikipedia code and general project design, since even the simplest variants rely on using a properly sized image and linking the box with a matching user category (because adding a userbox also lists the user in a category with all other

Wikipedians sharing the same interest, ability, or view). On the Polish Wikipedia I created several userboxes, and when I joined the English one I noticed that there were no userboxes for Wikipedians practicing karate and tae kwon do, so I created them.

Most users develop their user page by observing those of more experienced editors. Copying bits of code and learning little technical tricks by imitation is usual and is just as important in enculturation as in article editing. Many advanced Wikipedians use a more complicated user page, incorporating floating elements and animations, embedding fragments from other subpages, and automating archiving of talk pages. Such displays of skill present a Wikipedian as experienced and enhances reputation. I have been asked a couple of times about a simple trick I use on my user page, showing a timer that counts seconds since I was born and is updated automatically with each page reload. The code is difficult to copy because it is specific to my age.

The user page is also a place to display honors and achievements related to Wikipedia work. Besides the highly prestigious accomplishment of being a major contributor to featured and good articles, there are many other accomplishments to sport. They are chaotically organized and differ across projects. Users of the English Wikipedia frequently use one of the twenty "service awards" ([[WP:Service_awards]]), displayed by those who satisfy edit count and participation levels. The highest service award, the Vanguard Editor is meant for future Wikipedians with at least 132,000 edits and a minimum of sixteen years on Wikipedia.

The levels have whimsical names (e.g., Yeoman Editor, or Grognard Extraordinaire; Master Editor, or Illustrious Looshpah; and Grandmaster Editor, or Lord High Togneme Vicarus), and possibly because of the slight tackiness of the awards, as well as socially expected humility, many editors who qualify for them do not display them.

Barnstars are found on most major Wikimedia projects (see [[WP: Barnstars]]). They are given for specific achievements, usually long-standing excellence in work on Wikipedia. There are no firm rules for creating types of barnstar awards, and any user who thinks that a barnstar is missing can create one. For instance, the Working Wikipedian's Barnstar "may be awarded to those who work tirelessly and endlessly on the more laborious or repetitive of Wikipedia tasks," and the Wine Barnstar is conferred on outstanding contributors to wine-related articles. Barnstars can be given by one editor to another without restriction; obviously they cannot be given to oneself. Even this is not explicitly forbidden, though.

Other types of awards on the English Wikipedia are personal user awards (see [[WP:Personal_user_awards]]), which can be given on any occasion specified by the creator of the award (examples include the Christmas award; the Mouldy Sandwich award for tireless work on bettering Wikipedia; the PSI award to polite, courteous, and helpful users; and the disco ball of knowledge award, which certifies that the recipient is among the finest contributors to Wikipedia). One-time awards are also available, such as the Zen Garden Award for Infinite Patience, given to "an editor who has shown extraordinary patience in the face of toil or turmoil" ([[WP:Other_awards]]).

The *Wikipedia Editors Study* (Wikimedia Foundation, 2011a) shows that peer recognition matters most for many Wikipedians: "Barnstars and rewards from fellow editors are very important to the community. Receiving compliments is another motivator. Editors value the appreciation of their peers much more than other perceived achievements, such as having their articles selected as featured articles, or making it to the front page" (p. 28). Experimental studies also show that receiving a barnstar, given randomly, results in further productivity increase (Restivo & van de Rijt, 2012; Hill, Shaw, & Benkler, 2013).

While reciprocity in giving awards is not a norm, as it may be in other open-collaboration communities (Stewart, 2005), it is not unusual. As with any award, some users are much more eager to receive them than others, and some occasionally even engage in an informal barnstars club, exchanging honors and enhancing their self-image. This process, while not so rare, is not typical either, and although some with a clear religious or political agenda make awards to pump up each other's image to increase their validity in the eyes of other community members, it is generally positive.

Giving barnstars is an important ritual, as the givers are also recognized (Mauss, 1954/2001). This may be why as of March 2013 Jimbo Wales has over ninety barnstars and other awards (see [[User:Jimbo_Wales/Barnstars]]. Since giving a barnstar is indisputably positive and does not have limits or costs, it is a socially acceptable way of appreciating another Wikipedian. It is also significant in identity work (Westenholz, 2006; Ashton, 2011). Also, in a community as large as any of the major Wikipedia projects, it is impossible for any member to know everybody else. Thus, social signaling and image building through user pages establishes a social position in an open-collaboration community (Stewart, 2005), and so does giving barnstars as much as receiving them. This is also perhaps why receiving a barnstar increases the likelihood of getting another one (Restivo & van de Rijt, 2012), as it reduces the risk of endorsing somebody who turns out to be unworthy. Barnstars and other awards have a strong positive social effect; other open-collaboration communities may not exploit rewards to the extent Wikipedians do (Kriplean, Beschastnikh, & McDonald, 2008). All in all, reputation is important on Wikipedia, as it is in the communities of collaborative consumption (Botsman & Rogers, 2010).

In addition to informal status building and seeking, as well as identity work, Wikipedia has a system of formal roles, organized in a para- and anti-hierarchical system, discussed in the next chapter.

# 2

## FORMAL ROLES AND HIERARCHY

### A Cabal That Rules the World

Wikipedia is full of paradoxes. On the one hand, it has a strong official ethos of avoiding power structures and of being democratically developed. On the other, or perhaps partly as a result of the ethos, the Wikipedia community, at least for some, feels unequal and alienated. Theoretically, access to roles of responsibility is open to anyone and anyone who is trustworthy can become an administrator. In practice, expected qualifications of administrator candidates rise every year. Large meritocratic contributions to Wikipedia develop it most, but many Wikipedians evaluate other users by their number of edits, which favors minor and automatic corrections. I believe that these contradictions are related to the increasing bureaucratization of Wikipedia. I also think that they stem from the fact that, in the absence of formal hierarchies, the Wikipedia community substitutes local power-knowledge differentials. Wikipedia's system of parahierarchy and its sources of social status are behind this.

Andrew Keen, when criticizing the nonexpert character of Wikipedia, insists that the Wikipedia cult of the amateur leads to "less culture, less reliable news and a chaos of useless information" (2007, p. 16). While this statement is unverifiable, one thing is certain: the nonexpert or at least nonprofessional (in the sense of formally certified knowledge) character of Wikipedia is indeed its distinctive feature. The chance to build one's meritocratic status and organizational standing in a knowledge-producing community through nonexpert contributions is the essence of the Wikipedia model and possibly the main source of its appeal, as in other virtual communities (Kelty, 2001;

Lampel & Bhalla, 2007). In addition, how powerful organizational roles are assigned on Wikipedia differs from traditional organizations' ways, including organizations with participative management (Greenwood, González Santos, & Cantón, 1991; Kim, 2002).

Open-collaboration communities often have flat, horizontal structures and dispersed coordination (Benkler, 2002), similar to hunter-gatherer communities (Barnard, 1983). They are usually much less hierarchical than traditional organizations and less reliant on formal authority (Powell, 1991; Barley & Kunda, 2001). It can be argued that they even generate new organizational phenomena and forms that are based on the model of a chaotic and ever-changing bazaar (Raymond, 1999; Demil & Lecocq, 2006) and without a clearly defined coordination center. Yet successful collaborative online endeavors have to rely on not only technology but also specific hidden and overt cultural rules and roles (Orlikowski, 2002; Hemetsberger & Reinhardt, 2009).

Although some open-source projects benefit from a clear hierarchy (Crowston & Howison, 2006), Wikipedia displays a spontaneous and ad hoc "division of labor, because people gravitate to work they enjoy, but little hierarchy" (Ayers, Matthews, & Yates, 2008, p. 217), and is generally described as ahierarchical (Bruns, 2008). However, unlike ventures in free/libre and open-source software (F/LOSS), which allow their contributors to build their professional recognition and expert standing (Lakhani & Wolf, 2003; Von Hippel & Von Krogh, 2003), no activities and roles on Wikipedia offer occupational benefits to most contributors and cannot be used for career-building purposes. While people programming in open-source environments often enjoy some recognition from their colleagues or can put their experience on a résumé, this is almost never the case for Wikipedia editors or functionaries. On Wikipedia, unlike in open-source-software projects but similar to online games such as World of Warcraft or Tibia, recognition and career advancement are gained mainly within and for the community and not for the outside world.

However, there are still many similarities with open-source ventures (Shirky, 2005). For instance, Wikipedia has developed under the influence of hacker culture, enforcing antielitism, having status based on peer recognition, and receiving mainly symbolic remuneration (O'Neil, 2011a). Following its ethos, it

> consciously distrusts and despises egotism and ego-based motivations; self-promotion tends to be mercilessly criticized, even when the community

might appear to have something to gain from it. So much so, in fact, that the culture's "big men" and tribal elders are required to talk softly and humorously deprecate themselves at every turn in order to maintain their status. . . . There's a very strict meritocracy (the best craftsmanship wins) and there's a strong ethos that quality should (indeed must) be left to speak for itself. The best brag is code that "just works", and that any competent programmer can see is good stuff. . . . The taboo against ego-driven posturing therefore increases productivity. (Raymond, 1999/2004, pp. 88–89; emphasis in original)

This passage refers to open-source programmers and hackers, but it is equally true of Wikipedia: the most prominent editors are socially obliged to show humility and not explicitly desire community recognition. Accepting any role in the community is strongly linked with an ethos of service, not of leadership, at least in the official discourse. Egos are constantly downplayed, and though substantial contributions to articles are valued, editors are reminded that "no one, no matter how skilled, and regardless of their standing in the community, has the right to act as if they are the owner of a particular article" ([[WP:Ownership_of_articles]]).

In such an environment, in which both the organizational culture and the formal design are strongly antihierarchical, none of the motivators are economic, and all interactions are virtual, the distribution of community-trust roles and power may be different from that of traditional organizations. This topic has been largely neglected by organizational scholars, especially in terms of rich, qualitative studies. Some authors theorize that "the fundamental egalitarianism within the community even goes beyond the roles and authority of the members of the community" (de Vugt, 2010, p. 71) of Wikipedia, but in my view such judgments are related to these authors' lack of actual Wikipedia editing experience. The Wikipedia community has many egalitarian features, but it also has established stratification and very real power play. After all, "to strive for a 'structureless' group is as useful and as deceptive, as to aim at an 'objective' news story, 'value-free' social science or a 'free' economy" (Freeman, 1972, p. 152), since structures and hierarchies naturally emerge in all communities, irrespective of their formal governance. According to some authors, organizations even have an "essential hierarchic nature" (Kerr, 2004, p. 83), and organizational actors are often unwilling to partake in a democratic system, even if they can. Clearly, there is a lot of skepticism about organizational democracy, despite its proven efficiency (Viggiani, 2011).

However, research shows that a cooperative organization often does not develop into a full democratic setting but rather into a mix of democracy and oligarchy (Hernandez, 2006). This does not necessarily mean that egalitarian ideals are doomed to disappointment. Rather, the democratic setting does not prevent hierarchies from emerging (Viggiani, 1991). Paradoxically, these hierarchies are perceived as more unjust than in traditional organizations, because of the egalitarian discourse, and may advance the "us versus them" alienation (Viggiani, 1997).

Virtual communities can expect formal and informal roles, including jesters, vandals, and flamers, to develop (Orton-Johnson, 2007), and Wikipedia is no different.[1] Open-collaboration projects also entrench many inequalities, in spite of their official egalitarian lingo (Ortega, Izquierdo-Cortazar, Gonzalez-Barahona, & Robles, 2009). As Sheizaf Rafaeli and Yaron Ariel observe,

> Perhaps the single most important insight about contributors to Wikipedia is that, in spite of their popular image and in possible conflict with some of the "democratic" rhetoric, they are neither equal nor uniform. . . . Even IP-only [or unregistered] users are stratified according to whether they visit Wikipedia from the same (repeated) IP [address] or are completely sporadic and unknown. Among those who decide to register, there are fine gradations of status, role, and hierarchy. (2008, p. 246)

In Chapter 1, I cover the informal status display symbols used by Wikipedians (the barnstar system, the Babel tower, and other displays of technical skill). In this chapter I describe the quasi-hierarchical system of roles used on Wikipedia, its pros and cons, and its current problems. I show that the expectations for elected functionaries on Wikipedia increase with time and that as chance for success in an election decreases so do the number of candidates. I link this observation with the number of edits each Wikipedian makes being commonly used as the single indicator of his or her contribution to the community and with the increased bureaucratization of Wikipedia. I also show that the community increasingly sees hierarchical inequality, which is reflected in both elections and recurring conspiracy theories. By emphasizing the growing us-them perception, I show that the egalitarian ideology of Wikipedia, when contrasted with even minimal procedural hierarchy, causes problems and deepens communal divisions. I conclude by linking these problems of a deeper conflict in organizational values that contradict the rhetorical equality with the everyday nonequal practice.

Describing the parahierarchical system of functions on Wikipedia and presenting the community's complaints with its performance, I discuss selected aspects of inequality and hierarchy perception on Wikipedia and lay the groundwork for further analysis of bureaucratic control, trust, leadership, and governance.

## Community Roles

The most common formal roles that contributors can assume in Wikipedia and across all Wikimedia projects, in descending order, are:[2]

- Steward
- Checkuser
- Oversighter
- Bureaucrat (or crat)
- Administrator/sysop (or admin)
- Rollbacker
- Registered user
- Newly registered user
- Unregistered user
- Blocked user

The last three roles have restricted rights compared to a registered user. A rollbacker has the ability to use a tool that simplifies reverting vandalisms; any administrator can grant this privilege to any user. This tool is vital for the stability of Wikipedia, since open-collaboration projects rely to huge extent on the low costs of elimination of in-error or bad-faith contributions (Benkler & Nissenbaum, 2006), and vandalisms and trolling are widespread (George, 2007; Schachaf & Hara, 2010).

The steward role was introduced in 2004. Jimbo Wales, the only steward who was appointed rather than elected, held his position between 2006 and 2010. Currently, there are slightly more than forty stewards (including me) for all Wikimedia projects. Many nations, languages, and projects do not have a representative among the stewards. Every year new stewards are elected by active editors of all Wikimedia projects from all over the world.

Stewards have the highest (unlimited) access to all projects: they can edit and perform any task that any other user group can (they are limited only by general and project-specific policies). They can remove rights from other users' accounts, to fulfill the community's consensus or at their own discretion in emergencies. Since they serve all Wikimedia projects, and since they are not supposed to use the rights that come with stewardship on their home projects (ones they are most associated with), they are independent parties. For example, when an administrator or a bureaucrat loses the community's trust the community can request that a steward remove that person's status. Stewards can also take the role of administrators and bureaucrats on smaller projects.

All candidates for stewardship have to be administrators on at least one Wikimedia project, and most also have significant experience with other roles of trust. Entering a steward election without having been previously recognized in the wider community is quite risky. Even of those who meet the criteria and expectations (such as having a high edit count, having experience with antivandalism, and holding other positions), many do not receive the required minimum of 80 percent support from the voters.[3] If voters notice early on that there is a groundswell against a candidate, he or she may experience a precipitous decline in support, because many voters decide how to vote on candidates they do not know well on the basis of how others are voting. Since elections are community-wide, candidates who speak only one language fluently are at a disadvantage. English speakers are at a natural advantage, since that is the language of most of the discussions. Approximately one-third of stewards are native English speakers, and a vast majority of the rest speak English fluently. As of 2013, only one steward speaks only one language (English), and even though he had significant experience on several Wikimedia projects at the time of his candidacy, that he was conversant in no other language cost him votes.

Becoming a steward is a sign of high (even sometimes blind) trust from the community, since stewards often use their own judgment in interpreting the rules. Stewards can perform the functions of both checkusers and oversighters. Checkusers are allowed to check IP addresses of users, usually to confirm or disprove that one person is editing from several accounts. Although formally one does not have to be an administrator to become a checkuser, in practice only some administrators receive these rights. Oversighters are allowed to hide revisions, user names, and other entries in an article's record of revisions (its log) so that only other oversighters and stewards can see them (called "suppression"). Large Wikimedia projects usually have several checkusers and oversighters whose responsibilities require a great deal of discretion and limited access to sensitive data. Given the sensitive nature of the roles of a steward, checkuser, or oversighter, those who are elected to them have to provide proof of their identity to the Wikimedia Foundation and must be age eighteen or older. Verification of identity and credentials on Wikipedia is an interesting issue and is discussed in Chapter 5. In general, the other roles do not have this requirement and users are allowed to fully hide behind their virtual personas even to the foundation.

Bureaucrats (typically not more than a dozen on a project, although exceptions occur; for example, on Spanish Wikipedia most administrators are also bureaucrats) grant administrative privileges to registered users. Their responsibilities are technical in the sense that bureaucrats cannot use their discretion in making nominations but must follow community consensus. Bureaucrats can change names on user accounts and perform usurpations (take over the name of a dormant or inactive account without taking over its editing history). Even on major projects, bureaucratic work is performed by just a couple of active people. The English Wikipedia is an exception, having as many as thirty-five as of November 2013. In my experience, most bureaucratic tasks are simple and involve mostly granting requests for renaming or taking over accounts.

The major problem that bureaucrat candidates face is the difficulty of making the case that a new bureaucrat is needed, because there are a sufficient number. As a result, the number of candidates has been gradually decreasing. On the English Wikipedia in 2005–2008, the number of candidates ranged from fourteen to twenty-three per year, but as few as 20 percent were elected to a bureaucrat position. In 2009 eleven entered the elections, and four were approved. In 2010 only six candidates entered the elections, and three were approved. In 2011 two administrators entered, and both were elected. In 2012, two out of five candidates were successful. Clearly, the unfavorable odds influenced potential candidates, and the number of bureaucrats has stabilized at a level that does not justify adding more people.

On the Polish Wikipedia only one or two people have been entering elections each year, with the exception of 2008, when seven people were approved (including me; the spike was related to an expected increase in work because of the introduction of the so-called global log in). Most candidates entered the 2008 elections with ample support, and only one candidate was unsuccessful.

The last and largest group of users with additional technical privileges is administrators. They are experienced users whose most important prerogatives are the authority to block and unblock other users and to delete articles (and see and restore deleted content). They also have the ability to protect or partially protect articles from editing. An administrator role, even though much less demanding than other roles, still confers considerable responsibility, and successful candidates for administrative positions must receive about 80 percent of the vote (there are minor differences across Wikimedia projects regarding the required support, eligibility, the freedom of bureaucrats to discard some votes, etc.). There are many informal requirements for candidates. Following policies and guidelines, being friendly to newcomers, being a recipient of barnstars, never having been blocked, having written or coedited a couple of good articles, and having a certain percentage of articles that he or she marked for deletion all play an important role. Participation in policy creation and community life is also valued (Burke & Kraut, 2008). Typically, the required minimum number of total edits varies from project to project, but it is used mainly as a justification to vote against a candidate whose edit count is regarded as too low. Candidates are also expected to participate in community discussions, assist newcomers, monitor recent changes, and report vandalism. As of November 2013, there are 148 administrators on the Polish Wikipedia and a little over 1,400 on the English Wikipedia.[4] Unlike bureaucrats, the number of administrators is not limited by little work, because administrators deal also with many simple tasks every day, such as page deletions and protections. See Figure 2.1 for an illustration of the typical paths among these most common roles.

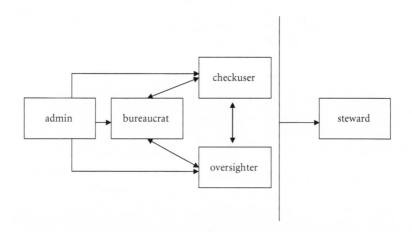

FIGURE 2.1. Typical involvement paths for functionaries

## Requests for Adminship

On the Polish Wikipedia, an average of 62 percent of requests for adminship (RfAs) in 2005–2011 were granted; in 2011, 59 percent were granted. Many of the successful candidates had slightly more than two thousand edits. On the English Wikipedia, the average edit count of successful RfA candidates has been hovering above ten thousand edits since 2008. While in the first years of Wikipedia the success rate of candidates was reasonably high (79 percent in 2004 and 65 percent in 2005), in the following years it plummeted to an average of about 36 percent, or nearly two-thirds of all Wikipedians who wished to be elected were not. The number of RfAs on the English Wikipedia has dropped steadily since 2007 (see Figure 2.2).

These figures for the English Wikipedia are disturbing. In 2008 the number of RfAs was just 64 percent of what it had been in 2007. These numbers have fallen consistently in all subsequent years (in 2009, 2010, and 2011 the number of candidates was approximately 60 percent of what it had been each preceding year). Even popular magazines, such as the *Atlantic*, noticed administrators on the English Wikipedia were declining (Meyer, 2012). This rapid change is not directly related to the number of new or active users, although recruiting new members has become a bigger challenge (Lam & Riedl, 2011), and retaining new editors has been a growing problem (Halfaker, Geiger, Morgan, & Riedl, 2013).

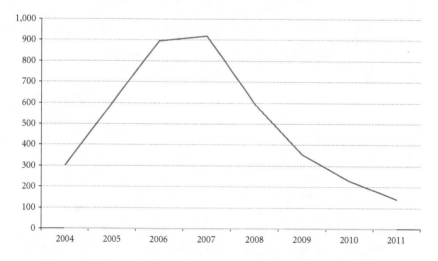

FIGURE 2.2. Number of requests for adminship on the English Wikipedia per year

There are many possible explanations for this phenomenon in addition to the one that an online collective project differs in participant engagement and dedication according to project stage, and Wikipedia is not an exception (Crowston, Jullien, & Ortega, in press). One of the most striking changes on the English Wikipedia since 2005 is the rapid increase in the expected edit count for administrator candidates (Ortega & Gonzalez-Barahona, 2007; Burke & Kraut, 2008). In 2005 the successful candidates had an average of five thousand edits. In 2006 this number had grown to six thousand, and since 2008 successful candidates have at least ten thousand edits. But what is an edit?

If each edit were a new article, the creation of ten thousand full articles from scratch would be comparable to writing between fifty and sixty books; this is a rare achievement even in a lifetime of paid work and not the usual in volunteer work. Therefore, editors who prefer to compose lengthy original articles or make significant improvements and expansions of existing ones cannot achieve the number of required edits. However, this is also the group that Wikipedia needs most for consistent and undisturbed development. Wikipedia has more or less reached its saturation point—that is, it now has articles on nearly all major subjects—and further development has to increasingly rely on either adding more specialized and niche articles. Established and aspiring subject experts are, obviously, those who can make such significant contributions. Yet on the English Wikipedia (and other projects) they seem to be discouraged from being active in the community: what they do seems to have little or no value in the eyes of other Wikipedians, at least in terms of an administrator candidate.

The unrealistically high expectations on edit count also implicitly force all candidates who want to win to make thousands of semiautomatic corrections and reversions, or reverts. Most have to familiarize themselves with special JavaScript tools and programs allowing faster edits. Even though they are quite easy to use, for less technically sophisticated editors they may create an entry threshold of disproportionate significance, since it limits access to community trust positions. Also, for users committed mainly to knowledge-intensive input, they may be just too boring. For instance, patrolling for recent changes in search of vandalism and hoaxes in Wikipedia articles, a task helpful in building edit count and reputation in the community, is boring. One must continually refresh the recent changes list (or use specialized tools for live tracking, such as LiveRC) and wait for a vandalism to show up. After spotting one, the patroller has to quickly click a couple of buttons (to revert the vandalism and issue a semiautomatic warning to the vandal or block the vandal from making edits for a defined time), hoping to be faster than other patrollers. Depending on the day, hour, and speed of one's Internet connection, it is possible to make anything from one to more than a dozen edits in ten minutes. This work requires no thought and only basic skills in Wikipedia policies. It resembles work at a McDonald's cash register—hitting the correct buttons, in the correct order, as quickly as possible, in a perverse new version of Taylorism. Although knowledge-work deskilling and Taylorism in knowledge-creating organizations is not unusual (Greenwood & Levin, 2001), it is remarkable that the Wikipedia community, one focused on generating and preserving knowledge, by its own design promotes manual over knowledge-intensive labor. This paradox may be related to power relations in the community and its organizational structure and egalitarian design, discussed earlier. While minor edits are important, using the edit counter as a major measure for evaluating candidates promotes a single editing style and, most importantly, deters valuable candidates from requesting adminship.

## Editcountitis

As of October 2012, the English Wikipedia has 187 users (43 percent of them administrators) who have made more than one hundred thousand edits. The top 10,000 editors have made more than five thousand edits each. Their input totals about 36 percent of all edits on the English Wikipedia (see [[WP:List_of_Wikipedians_by_number_of_edits]]).[5] That a minority makes the largest number of contributions is by no means unusual for F/LOSS projects (Mockus, Fielding, & Herbsleb, 2000; Lerner & Tirole, 2002).

Since over one-third of Wikipedia contributions come from heavy editors, who are also usually the most active in the community, they naturally dominate the elections. Still, most users realize that the number of edits alone is not a good measure of value (as I detailed earlier, heavy editors may account for many, many insignificant minor edits, while major, knowledge-intensive contributions may add up to a total of one or two edits). On Wikipedia "one's edit count is a sort of coin of the realm" (Reagle, 2010b, p. 157), and using it as a measure then serves a particular group of editors, just as the focus on quality and accountability in academic governance serves university administrators (Shore & Wright, 1999).

The problem is that it is difficult to create any quantitative measure of editor quality. There are some other measures and possible ideas, but all of them are flawed. For example, for simple spelling or punctuation corrections to not count in the same way as creating a full article, the amount of text added by a user could instead be measured. But that measure still does not reflect the value of the text added. In fact, quite often the most valuable editor is the one who is able to cut, rather than expand, an article. In software, a sign of an application's quality is that it cannot be shortened without harm (Raymond, 1999/2004). Thus, perhaps the most sensible idea would be to measure both the amount and the prevalence of one's input. Unfortunately, implementing this method in real time requires resources to overcome inherent complexities.

As a result, one of the few quantified measures of user-contribution value is the number of edits he or she has made. Everybody on Wikipedia knows that this measure is flawed (in Wikipedia jargon, obsession with edit count is called "editcountitis"; see [[WP:Editcountitis]]), but in the absence of other quantified indicators, it is used nevertheless. Many editors routinely check the volume of edits of other editors (O'Neil, 2010).

The situation resembles the amount of time spent at work as a measure of effectiveness of programmers and other knowledge workers: even though everybody agrees that it does not signify anything, many managers of software companies use it anyway since there is no better alternative (D. Jemielniak, 2009). Similarly, it creates pathologies, as organizational actors understand how the system works and act accordingly (for example, by working late to create a better impression).

Moreover, even though Wikipedia is a voluntary community and geared to collaboration rather than playing a zero-sum game, the problem with editcountitis is exacerbated by friendly competition. Even users whose organizational status cannot change as a result of their edit count (for example, because they are well established or are already administrators) still often compete with another on doing something quicker. For instance, administrators often compete in deleting articles marked for speedy deletion, bureaucrats may compete to promote a successful candidate to adminship in as short a time after an election as possible. Even stewards compete in applying global locks (blocking editors from logging in to any Wikimedia projects) or desysoping (removing administrator rights of) users. Different roles influence different behavioral patterns and strategies of legitimization.

Inactive bureaucrats are subject to demotion, and stewards must prove that they have been useful, thus slight competition is common, although it is playful and definitely friendly. Yet the competition for edits, administrative actions, or other tasks adds to their value. The number of bureaucrats on the Polish and English Wikipedias and stewards on Wikimedia is higher than strictly necessary, although a slight surplus is probably desirable and organizationally understandable, since volunteers can leave at any time and there are seasonal highs and lows of active users.

For a significant portion of the Wikipedia community the number of edits is an important measure of value, often more important than whether a user is an admin. Edit count, even more than participation in community discussion, is perceived as legitimization for participation by many: often users taking part in general debates are reminded that their recent contributions to Wikipedia articles are scanty and thus they should focus more on improving their standing in the community by editing than on discussing.

## Running the Gauntlet

The bigger picture is even more alarming. The editcountitis that is infecting RfAs on the English Wikipedia and on other projects is only part of the problem. Administrator elections are increasingly perceived as a gruesome and unpleasant process, and many editors do not want to take part, because they know what they can expect. The process, both on the Polish and the English Wikipedias, is described as "running the gauntlet" or "the bloodbath" and indeed sometimes takes the form of both an examination of a candidate's skills (often through difficult questions) and a list of gripes and derogatory comments from others. In the words of Sue Rangell in a recent election, "I wouldn't wish the RfA process on anyone. It is an inhuman nitpicking that is often unfair, and in many cases confrontational. I know that good editors have left Wikipedia over RfA scrutiny" ([[WP:Requests_for_adminship/Darkwind]], December 29, 2012).

Many candidates fail after one voter points to some relatively minor flaw or mistake of the candidate, and then others join in an attack. According to an experienced administrator,

> The results of RfA are sometimes a lottery: apart from a handful of regulars who generally (but not always) know what they are doing, the !voting is in the

hands of a flux of one-time commentators, fans, detractors, and newcomers. In some cases a lot of canvassing clearly goes on behind the scenes, some base their comments ostensibly on how others have commented, and some !voters clearly do not fully understand the process. Other participants will go to extraordinary lengths to support their !votes, often retrieving old and no longer relevant diffs from the archives. ([[User:Kudpung/RfA_criteria]])

Another administrator put it even more bitterly:

Users who grossly exaggerate even tiniest deficiency cause incessant drama-mongering can cause a deserving user's RfA to spiral into the depths of failure. It really is too bad that bureaucrats often [overlook] . . . what's actually being said in an RfA and pass or fail it based on margins of support. ([[User:Animum/RFA]])

Indeed, the reasons given for votes in opposition have even been parodied in Wikipedia folklore (see, e.g., [[WP:WikiSpeak/Decoding_RfA]]). Also, since reasons do not necessarily have to be well founded ("lack of trust" is often justifiable enough), RfA ballots often draw those with a gripe against Wikipedia, who perhaps do not have much against a candidate but are eager to express their dislike of the social organization of Wikipedia community by voting against the candidate.

Admin Kudpung analyzed 20 percent of the questions asked in RfAs in 2010. According to Kudpung's analysis, as many as 43 percent could be classified as "irrelevant, or prying into private personal opinion," 14 percent as "plain silly," and 12 percent as "time wasting/fishing for advice" Other less common but recurring categories include asking questions meant to "trick" the candidates or that were "deliberately misleading" ([[User:Kudpung/RfA_criteria]]). Scholars have shown that supporting or opposing a candidate strongly depends on the similarity of the characteristics of the candidate and the voter (Leskovec, Huttenlocher, & Kleinberg, 2010).

Many RfA candidates on Wikipedia are disappointed by the unfavorable climate, and there are numerous cautionary tales, such as the following one from the user Dayewalker, who described his experience with an RfA immediately after it failed on November 17, 2011:

No matter what people say, no matter how unfounded their accusations are, you must remain silent. Even if you are criticized by someone who is obviously insane, you shouldn't reply. You dare not appear touchy, even in rebutting pure lies. You must suffer the slings and arrows of outrageous fortune, even when they are slung by someone who doesn't even grasp the language. Of the first 175 edits to my RfA, forty of them were from one editor who opposed. Forty! And no one raised an eyebrow, or asked him to even slow down. It's like some kind of frat pledge where you let idiots spank you, just to prove you're a big enough idiot to be in the club.

My first ten "Oppose" votes were from editors with a combined 26 blocks. Who would know better what qualities an admin should embody than a freshly blocked, still-bitter problem editor? It's like letting felons sit on the jury because they know what a criminal looks like.

One of them said I was impolite and not level-headed. Another oft-blocked and still-restricted editor said I stalked him and filed specious reports. Other editors asked for diffs [evidence of the differences between versions of edits, used to point to specific edits of a given user]. Evidence? Nope, never another comment or diff, just drive-by douchebaggery. People went so far as to fill the talk pages of people who didn't even support my nomination to run me down. One went rogue and basically started campaigning for his own RfA during mine. Truly insane things happen on those pages, and they're all permitted. It's Thunderdome.

I had an editor (who had been blocked six times himself) oppose and accuse me of being part of some vague conspiracy, since I apparently picked up the lingo too fast and had too sharp of a "learning curve" when I started editing here in May of 2008. ([[User:Dayewalker]])

Such reflections by disappointed candidates are in no way unusual on Wikipedia.


## Is the System Broken?

On March 18, 2011, Jimbo Wales, consoling My76Strat, an unsuccessful administrator candidate, wrote on his talk page that "RfA is a horrible and broken process" ("User talk:John Cline," 2011). On August 23, 2011, Wales observed on his own talk page, in a discussion on how to improve the RfA, that "the mere existence of that process deters quite a large number of good candidates" and that he was "concerned about good candidates who don't bother standing for the current process because it is a nightmare and not worth the effort" ("User talk:Jimbo Wales: Difference," 2011). Other users often describe the process similarly, referring to it as a "very stressful and oft humiliating experience" ([[User:Kudpung/RfA_criteria]], April 13, 2011).

Many discussions have been started and proposals made for ways to repair the RfA process. The topic is quite popular among some Wikipedians. Discussions and viewpoints on the possible directions for the brave new RfA proceedings on the English Wikipedia exceed one hundred thousand words by my count, and it is likely I missed some of the less popular and older discussions and essays. Similar discussions, of corresponding length, have also occurred on the Polish Wikipedia and, I believe, on many other projects. Popular ideas have included appointing rather than electing administrators, training volunteers and allowing them to learn the responsibilities through a formal, academy-like process, apprenticeship and tuition systems, and breaking down the responsibilities of an administrator into smaller roles, which could be taken on incrementally. More radical proposals have also been discussed. For instance, automatic rights granting to users satisfying certain criteria has been proposed. Sophisticated algorithms and formulas, assigning points for achieving specific tasks, and automatically "unlocking" the administrator status (making admin tools available to anyone who satisfies given criteria) have been considered. Refining the requirements for candidates has been suggested. Similarly, introducing tighter requirements for voters has been discussed. Changing the format of the debate (reducing the number of allowed questions) has been another recurring idea. Even secret ballots by eligible voters has been discussed every year, as have been many other, more or less exotic, ideas. Keeping the current RfA procedure and introducing a concurrent alternative one has been also considered. As of November 2013, no consensus has been reached as to how and what kind of change would be introduced; in all likelihood the discussion will continue.

Some users do not perceive the RfA process as broken at all. For instance, user Errant commented on Wales's talk page,

> RFA was a highly positive experience for me, with a little useful feedback in the couple of opposes. I too did um and ah over submitting my RFA (especially as a self-nom), but I think in some respects that is an *important part of feeling ready*. Perhaps RFA is too scary (in fact, it probably is) but I think removing all the fear is not good. Similarly we have double standards which annoy me— admins regularly get away with behaviour that would have insta-failed any RFA (or acted as a major roadblock). I see nothing wrong with picking apart

contributions and making criticism of candidates; except we do it too harshly, and we don't continue to do it after RFA. —Errant 14:37, 24 August 2011 (UTC) ([[User_talk:Jimbo_Wales/Archive_82]]; emphasis in original)

User Vejvančický went even further:

Wow. Yes. I keep seeing the same phrases over and over: Unimaginable nightmare. Hell week. Ritual humiliation. <<<an insulting part of my comment redacted>>> Honestly, if you can't face criticism, ignore the irrelevant stuff and address the valid points of the criticism in a calm and civil way, you should grow up. That's how it works in real life and that's how it should work also here. People's opinions are not always packed in a rose gift box, and if you can't stay on top of things, the RfA is not for you. Just my opinion. —Vejvančický 10:31, 1 September 2011 (UTC) ("Wikipedia talk," 2011)

Apparently, the trauma some users associate with elections is sometimes perceived as useful by others, since it tests the emotional maturity of candidates who, as administrators, must be able to respond to irrational and angry users in a civil manner.

Nonetheless, most Wikipedians see something wrong with the RfA process. They analyze its consequences and see the unwelcome outcome of how the system works:

The problem is that the casual and quiet type of editors are those most likely to completely quit or leave one of the all too common wiki fights because they're here just to have fun. Whereas those who are in cabals or pushing their view will stick it out because they have an agenda—this type of editor has way too much influence on wiki and is a major reason why wiki is broken. I recently saw a comment about an RFC [request for comment; an informal procedure in which editors discuss solutions] on the RFA process, but that RFC misses the point. It's not just RFA that's broken, the whole system is broken and needs a major overhaul. PumpkinSky 10:04, 29 September 2011 (UTC) ([[Wikipedia_talk:RfA_reform_(continued)/Radical_alternatives]])

Ignoring the reference to cabals for the moment in this otherwise astute analysis of the system, the main point remains salient: some good and mature editors do not like the confrontational style of RfAs and may decide not to apply for adminship just because of the voting process or even leave Wikipedia because of distaste for the fights there and in some other discussions. Clearly, in the view of this editor, as well as many others expressing similar opinions, the current RfA is broken in the sense of not only not serving the purpose of electing the best candidates but also deterring participation in Wikipedia in general.

What is fascinating is that the election of administrators has been perceived as flawed at least since 2006 (see [[User:Aaron_Schulz/New_RfA_method]]). Interestingly, the RfA process is considered broken and nightmarish also on the Polish Wikipedia, which has not experienced such a dramatic decline in either the number of candidates or the percentage of successful candidates in RfA elections. On both the Polish and the English Wikipedias, RfA is used as a channel to express anger against the community itself. This could indicate that regardless of any changes to the mechanics of the election, users will express their opinions and the result may not change much. This is something also indicated by some editors. For example, on April 19, 2011, the user Fetchcomms observed, "The problem with RfA is NOT the process. It is the participants," and argued that no voting system can change voter attitude ([[Wikipedia_talk:RfA_reform_(continued)]]). Clearly, the RfA process is important for many Wikipedians, and the rampant dislike for it most likely is not just the result of how it elects administrators but rather a product of deeper discontent within the community.

Indeed, many elections occupy a lot of the community's time and escalate into fierce debates, sometimes going beyond the discussed candidate. The problems manifested on RfAs indicate that the elections are treated very seriously and as related to important and rare privileges by many users. This is particularly striking when contrasted with the official Wikipedia rhetoric emphasizing that functions and roles should be treated as unimportant.

## Is Adminship a Big Deal?

As noted previously, Wikipedia organizational culture promotes the service aspect of every role of responsibility. Most community roles, though described formally, are learned through informal socialization (Welser et al., 2011) and through their performance, and Wikipedia functionaries are often reminded that they are servants to other users. The welcome message given to new stewards on the IRC (Internet Relay Chat) channel is often the one I heard when new: "Welcome, new slaves!" On both the Polish and the English Wikipedias, administrators are often called "janitors," and being assigned administrator status is described as "being given the mop." Administrators are frequently reminded that they are not higher in the hierarchy than regular editors are, that their voices count just the same, and that they cannot use the technical abilities they are granted (especially when protecting articles from editing, deleting them, or blocking other users) in disputes in which they are personally involved. Wikipedia policy on the administrator role clearly states that "administrators were not intended to develop into a special subgroup. Rather, administrators should be a part of the community like other editors. Most maintenance and administration aspects of Wikipedia can be conducted by anyone, without the specific technical functions granted to administrators" ([[WP:Administrators]]). Many administrators honestly share this egalitarian view.

One of the most commonly repeated adages about being an administrator is that it "is not a big deal." This line comes from a statement made by Jimbo Wales in 2003, in Wikipedia's early days, but the statement has achieved a status similar to policies and describes the philosophy held by many Wikipedians:

> I just wanted to say that becoming a sysop [admin] is *not a big deal*.
>
> I think perhaps I'll go through semi-willy-nilly and make a bunch of people who have been around for awhile sysops. I want to dispel the aura of "authority" around the position. It's merely a technical matter that the powers given to sysops are not given out to everyone.
>
> I don't like that there's the apparent feeling here that being granted sysop status is a really special thing. (Jimbo Wales, February 11, 2003, WikiEN-l distribution list, quoted at [[WP:Administrators]])

This fragment is often cited in discussions on the role of administrators. The "Wikipedia:Administrators" page puts this idea this way:

> In the very early days of Wikipedia, all users functioned as administrators to perform various administrative functions, using a single password that was handed out fairly freely. The current form of administratorship is the result of a code modification which changed from password access to role-based access control. Under this system, individual accounts could be flagged per the roles they could perform, which in turn determined the functions and tools they could access. . . . [W]hile the correct use of the tools and appropriate conduct should be considered important, merely "being an administrator" should not be. ([[WP:Administrators]])

Despite this egalitarian discourse, adminship is a very big deal for many users. Moreover, there is a strong resentment of administrators and their true or imagined abuses of power, and adminship is perceived more than ever as a proof of editors' inequality. This is happening independently on both the Polish and the English Wikipedias and on some other projects, which indicates that the phenomenon may be characteristic for the organizational design they use, rather than contingent and dependent on the local situation and particular actors. Even the users actively seeking solutions to the RfA deadlock and trying to improve the situation often perceive administrators as part of the problem. For example, the user Dank wrote, "We need to disengage ourselves from the community's anger over admin abuse, and we need to find a way not to get in a candidate's face when they show up for RFA" ([[WP:RfA_reform_(continued)]]).

Apparently, a deeper and more universal problem is at the core of the flaws in the RfA process: a large part of the community believes in the us-them division and considers administrators to be a highly privileged elite, regularly abusing their rights.

Also, many of those who do not have administrator status, and as such are unable to see the limited technical scope of the extra powers it gives, additionally mythologize the already symbolic role.

## Administrator Recall

A significant part of the problem with the RfA process is that administrator status, once granted, is difficult to remove.[6] When users become admins, as long as they do not break rules to the extent that they would be blocked or judged by the Arbitration Committee, they keep their admin status, despite possible loss of confidence from the community and despite possibly falling below the standards set for administrator candidates (for example, admins may withdraw from active editing or behave uncivilly, which would be held against them if they were RfA candidates but is not a serious enough offense to make them accountable to the Arbitration Committee (ArbCom) or even to another administrator).

The view of many editors is expressed in a comment made on Jimbo Wales's talk page:

> Much of the problem lies in the fact that adminship is a lifetime appointment, so people are wary of the tiniest hint that someone could turn out to be

unsuitable. Term limits are the obvious answer, since this would assure people that admins who were nasty and overreaching though not quite to the point of full-blown Arbcom action would eventually age out. But the admin corps is implacably opposed to any such proposal; the prevailing attitude is "I'll give up my adminship when you take it from my cold, dead hands." Short Brigade Harvester Boris 16:21, 22 March 2011 (UTC) ([[User_talk:Jimbo_Wales/Archive_73]])

Whether to limit administrator terms or make administrators open for recall has been the subject of many heated debates on Wikipedia. There is consensus that it would be a good idea to force administrators who have lost the community's trust to resign, but there is disagreement over how to organize the details. The biggest problem is deciding who should be able to initiate the recall procedure (it should be easy but also exclude vandals, trolls, and single users unhappy because of correct actions of a particular administrator). Administrators agree that it is difficult to be a good one without making enemies. After all, most blocked users bear a grudge and consider their treatment unfair or at least disproportionate to their deeds. In fact, the more involved an administrator is in what he or she is supposed to do, the more likely it is that he or she will accrue a larger opposition from those in the community who were justly prevented from disrupting Wikipedia (but not banned permanently). Thus, a recall procedure ideally should apply only to administrators who do not perform their role well and who abuse their power.

Since the community has not been able to establish clear rules in this respect, an ad hoc, semiformal solution has been developed: some admins voluntarily agree to a recall, depending on liberally described rules. Conditions vary under which an admin is subjected to a democratic recall vote. There are minor differences between the Polish and the English Wikipedias and between other projects, because the procedure is voluntary and an administrator can declare his or her own requirements.

On the Polish Wikipedia one of the most popular minimum requirements of administrators open to recall is support of the recall motion by three editors, each with at least five hundred edits. Forty of 156 administrators are open to recall as of May 2012 (on the English Wikipedia 199 of 1,484 administrators are open to recall under similar but more diverse conditions depending on their individual choice). Note, however, that approximately 50 percent of all administrators on the Polish Wikipedia made fewer than thirty edits in two months, and among more active ones the idea of voluntary recall is much more popular.

I am one of the administrators who agree to be recalled. I made history on the Polish Wikipedia in October 2011 when I became the first (and as of November 2013 the only) administrator to be recalled. The experience was far from pleasant, and after having been reconfirmed in my role, with 95 percent support, I limited future recalls by excluding users with a history of being blocked for longer than seven days or in arbitrated conflict with me as an administrator. My case made several other administrators decide to not make themselves open for recall. Adminship may not be a big deal, but only as long as an administrator is not going to lose it.

Through this experience I understood even more clearly that adminship was a big deal to me. Had I not received at least 80 percent of votes in my reconfirmation, I think I would have shifted my presence to the English Wikipedia and limited my participation in the Polish one. After all, just as electing an administrator is a signal of trust, a recall is a clear message of distrust from the community.

As with reforming the RfA process, establishing and enforcing a uniform administrator-recall process presents difficulties because of a deeply rooted perception by users, mostly among the nonadministrator Wikipedians, of the inequality of power. The consensus-reaching procedures, described in Chapter 3, also are a barrier.

## Cabal

Some users view Wikipedia as hierarchical and oligarchic and also believe that it is home to different cabals and powerful "inner circles" (Metz, 2008b). In fact, cabal is a concept that has been discussed on Wikipedias since their beginning (and commonly addressed in wiki folklore as well (see [[WP:Cabals]]), regularly recurring over the years as a heritage of Usenet and hacker culture (Pfaffenberger, 1996; Grossman, 2001). Usenet experienced emergence of a caste of "baron" administrators who autocratically managed their servers and recognized themselves as a separate class of users (Pfaffenberger, 1996). Although administrators on Wikipedia have much less power than on Usenet and in practice just share the function name, the fear of a group of users usurping power over the rest is very much alive on Wikipedia. In the words of one of the most radical critics of Wikipedia, "contrary to the mistaken impression that everyone is on an equal footing, Wikipedia has an elaborate hierarchical structure which is infested with cliques and factional conflicts" (Finkelstein, 2008). In an egalitarian environment, any hint of power inequality and possible abuse naturally raises red flags, irrespective of validity (Konieczny, 2009a). Parker Peters elaborates on this idea:

> If a wikipedia administrator's conduct is questioned? "You don't get anywhere by attacking an admin." Not even if they were in the wrong. The dirty secret of Wikipedia adminship is that it's a cult, a good old boy's network, a masonic society of sorts.
>
> Administrators will stand up for administrators, no matter what, because they want the others to stand up for them when they decide to protect their "owned" article(s) from some newcomer trying to improve or change them. (2007)

The core of this idea of a cabal, or sometimes "admin mafia," is that some groups of users (particularly those in positions of power) try to rule the community invisibly, coerce it to agree to the cabal's ideas, have their own ends, and also occasionally gang up on the innocent rebels fighting for true liberty. Of course, in many cases a perception of a cabal is no more than a typical conspiracy theory, emerging because of users' refusal to admit they may be wrong. This is the official view, shared by many administrators: there is no cabal whatsoever. This statement is used so often in discussions that it is often abbreviated as TINC (see [[WP:TINC]]). Those indulging in the idea of a secretive, coordinated power group are regarded as conspiracy theorists. This paranoia is a frequent topic of jokes among Wikipedians and a subject of many parodies (see, e.g., [[WP:List_of_cabals]] or [[WP:Rouge_admin]]).

I too view the notion of a cabal on Wikipedia as absurd and laugh, with other admins, when it comes back. We are such a diverse group, often not able to agree on the most obvious and simple decisions. Whoever believes we could form a working, operational collective clearly overestimates administrators' abilities. At the same time, I cannot help seeing a glimmer of truth in the idea. As a researcher, I know that organizational power is often used by the dominant players to legitimize their demands and to delegitimize and ridicule those of others.

It is possible that even if changes made by an anonymous or less known user are reasonable and justified, they may be perceived as part of an edit war and not scrutinized by the first intervening administrator, who reverts them. Others, seeing that an administrator reverted edits by a nonadministrator Wikipedian, may assume that the administrator is simply one of many ideological POV, or point of view, pushers who do not carefully consider edits. Especially when editing a highly sensitive topic, the first revert may determine subsequent ones.

Scenarios like this are what often creates the perception of a cabal. Administrators tend to rely on the judgment of other administrators or of established editors. It saves time to assume that another administrator or a trusted user was right, especially on high-traffic projects such as Wikipedia. We revert a change and quickly score another edit to our count. Yes, we should always check the content and if deciding that we are not competent to judge whether an edit should be reverted, refrain from action or ask somebody else for help. But we do not always do this, and that is enough to create a strong sense of injustice and create the impression of administrators' solidarity against others.

To be fair, though, from my own experience as an administrator, we do gang up on some users sometimes, at least sort of. Not all of us, obviously, even though some Wikipedia projects have e-mail lists accessible only to administrators, and these lists sometimes host discussions on the proper course of action toward a user who is thought to be trouble. Many of us prefer to ask a colleague to intervene in a situation in which we risk entering a "wheel war" (when two or more editors revert each others' edits over and over) or when we believe we need a consultation with a fresh eye. There is nothing wrong with that, of course, since by referring to someone else's judgment we are allowing our own actions to be evaluated, too. However, we naturally tend to ask for help from those whom we know well and can expect to share our point of view and often do so outside Wikipedia, and so the user, unaware of this background, obviously feels singled out and surrounded. Such a user may not verbalize it, but she or he is right to feel a subject of power play, even if just because she or he did not have the same means to defend her or his ground, contacts on Wikipedia, or an established position. Clearly, hierarchy-attenuating organizations are also prone to social dominance strategies (Haley & Sidanius, 2005), and what administrators may perceive as an elegant way of addressing a problematic user, such as trading off among themselves in addressing him or her, from the viewpoint of the user may be considered to be more similar to a group assault, where the administrators have better grounds, tools, and procedures to process the conflict even by themselves. Also, quite likely, administrators minimize the importance of colleagues' behavior that is not in line with official policies (Glasford, Dovidio, & Pratto, 2009).

Possibly because of this inequality in terms of social capital, the fact that Wikipedia administrators communicate with each other on a "secret" e-mail list enrages some users. As one website that is highly critical of Wikipedia (and offers an alternative encyclopedia development website) put it,

> Sophisticated control systems are in place to make sure that the content on Wikipedia remains aligned with Jimbo Wales' vision. Superficially, Wikipedia appears to be very transparent, with visitors being able to see contribution histories and talk pages of every user. There are large areas of Wikipedia devoted to mock judicial proceedings and various processes, policies, discussions.
>
> However, behind the scenes, Jimbo and a small group of administrators control the site through the use of mailing lists. The Arbitration Committee has a private mailing list, and there are the Wikimedia "internal-l" and "private-l" mailing lists. ("Wikipedia," 2012)

That administrators communicate with each other without the community's control was a topic of several intense debates on both the English and the Polish Wikipedias and was strongly criticized on several occasions, usually in the wake of some administrative failure. The "secret" e-mail list was even described in the information technology media:

> Controversy has erupted among the encyclopedia's core contributors, after a rogue editor revealed that the site's top administrators are using a secret insider mailing list to crackdown on perceived threats to their power.
>
> Many suspected that such a list was in use, as the Wikipedia "ruling clique" grew increasingly concerned with banning editors for the most petty of reasons. But now that the list's existence is confirmed, the rank and file are on the verge of revolt. (Metz, 2007)

Clearly, the nonpublic means of communication give rise to most fantastic theories. The idea that all administrators actively target "perceived threats to their power" does not hold water: if true, the brave heroes of justice would also be persecuted in their RfAs (discussion of which, interestingly, most often turns to failures by votes of nonadministrators), and the Wikipedians proposing reforms of the system (including administrator recall) would soon be blocked, which is not the case. In addition, as noted earlier, administrators do not make up a uniform group: they are highly diverse, differing in opinions, views, and beliefs. This discourse confirms something obvious: limiting access to anything (especially in a community valuing equality) immediately becomes a status symbol for the haves and is hated by the have-nots.

This problem cannot be easily solved. Asking for a second opinion from other administrators is, generally, a good idea. Enforcing that all such consultations go through open, public channels does not make any sense, since it would lead to information overflow if it were to be managed by the administrators' notice board ([[WP:Administrators'_noticeboard]]). Naturally, some form of social control could be exerted through keeping public archives of the e-mail lists. But administrators wanting to socialize and befriend each other off the record is both positive and inevitable. Making e-mail lists public would likely move the informal discussions to different channels rather than eliminate them. Wikipedia organizational routines in this particular case result in a wide discrepancy between the egalitarian story that everybody is equal on Wikipedia and the practice of having well-established, privileged users.

In practical terms, secret channels of communication can become a safety valve for open communication, and this is of special importance when the overwhelming scope of bureaucratic organizational control exerted on Wikipedia (covered in Chapter 4) is considered. All users are under public communal social control basically all the time. The e-mail list is the only exception, and it allows expressing honest and unfiltered opinions of other administrators' actions and establishing consensus for reverting them, if needed.

And yet, as Michel Foucault has put it, "people know what they do; they frequently know why they do what they do; but what they don't know is what what they do does" (quoted in Dreyfus & Rabinow, 1983, p. 187). Well-intended administrative behavior and communication patterns may sometimes create an image of a cabal even in the eyes of good-faith Wikipedians, to say nothing of people outside the community. Especially in a voluntary organization that makes equality of all editors such a strong principle, even the slightest signal indicating that it sometimes is otherwise can cause frustration and anger. If the official discourse emphasizes ahierarchical principles, but there are symbolic manifestations of hierarchy (including secret communication channels), the ones who are not privileged perceive it as a blatant contrast and a proof of its falsity. They also may want to get back at the ones putting on airs.

Thus, one reason why RfA is becoming such a gruesome experience on different projects may be because it is in many respects the only power the community has over administrators. Naturally, administrators who repeatedly break the rules lose their privileges. But most of them, as long as they follow the guidelines, are untouchable; even when it is clear that the community would not reelect them, they do not lose their position, unless they satisfy the criteria for being demoted. RfA is the only process in which users can protest the perceived power differential. Interestingly, neither the Polish nor the English Wikipedia has clear policies for administrator recall by the community, which again confirms that administrators constitute a privileged caste.

## Egalitarian System of Power

Participation in social interactions and in organizations is related, according to the social exchange theory, to the opportunity for gaining approval, respect, or status (Blau, 1964). Indeed, building one's reputation and recognition in the community is an important motivator in virtual communities (Donath, 1999), just as in the traditional workplace (Herzberg, Mausner, & Bloch-Snyderman, 1959). On Wikipedia, the status-building rituals and the forms of presentations of self in the community, described in Chapter 1, and the winning of the community's support through taking up a formal role of an administrator (or higher), discussed in this chapter, are motivating and clearly important in the enactment of power and hierarchy. Yet, possibly because of the participative and egalitarian design, the very presence of privileged roles causes disproportionate stir, similar to the uneasy relations of the Wikipedia community and the Wikimedia Foundation, described in Chapter 3.

Since its inception, Wikipedia has used accumulated reputation as an alternative to organizational hierarchy and as a source of informal authority (Ciffolilli, 2003). Building status within the community is also a lock-in mechanism, keeping the core group of dedicated contributors motivated (George, 2007). As shown in this chapter, Wikipedia culture (in both the English and the Polish communities) has drifted into ostensible appreciation of visible sacrifices (such as spending time on inflating one's edit count) more than the actual gains for the encyclopedia. The number of edits is appreciated more than their quality, and a thousand minor corrections help raise organizational standing more than creating a perfect one-thousand-word article does. This process is similar to what Leslie Perlow describes as "individual heroism" (1998): organizational appreciation of one's theatrical gestures and symbolic yields over quiet, systematic solid work. While this process is not surprising in knowledge-creating communities (D. Jemielniak, 2012), that the number of edits becomes the single most important value indicator independent from holding democratically elected seats is likely detrimental to Wikipedia in the long term, since it deters people who would prefer to specialize in a few high-quality, major contributions. However, such a process is one of the typical symptoms of organizational bureaucratization (Blau & Scott, 1962), which I address in Chapter 4.

The obsession with number of edits may be related with yet another phenomenon. For Alf Rehn (2004) warez (software pirate) communities depend on the gift-economy principle. Uploading pirated software is a symbolic gesture emphasizing participation in the community and influencing the giver's status. Other researchers point out that open-source communities in general rely on the principle of gift giving to organize the social relations within the community (Raymond, 1999/2004; Bergquist & Ljungberg, 2001; Kelty, 2006). They are a specific "marriage of altruism and self-interest" (Rheingold, 1994, p. 58) and form a gift economy, a postcapitalist form of society (Barbrook, 1998).[7]

Similarly, on Wikipedia the number of contributions has a strong symbolic value used in determining an editor's position in the group. This could be because of lack of other measures or because of the preference for measuring one's sacrifice rather than the value of the contribution. The reason could even be a side effect of general egalitarian philosophy, indirectly enforcing an environment in which people whose intellectual abilities are higher do not dominate the community. In any case, the number of contributions clearly corresponds with the author's status in the community (Ciffolilli, 2003; Rafaeli & Ariel, 2008).

In the classical Weberian understanding, power is "the probability that one actor within a social relationship will be in a position to carry out his own will despite resistance" (M. Weber, 1947, p. 152). In this sense, Wikipedia organization is extremely disempowered, and single individuals, regardless of their role, cannot impose their will on the others.

Nonetheless, this lack of individual power does not prevent Wikipedians from seeing Wikipedia as hierarchical. This occurs because, in the eyes of many nonadministrators, administrators form a separate and privileged caste. Even though the difference in real influence on encyclopedic articles and on organizational decision making between administrators and nonadministrators is minimal (especially when considering that there are many nonadministrator users of high communal status), and even though Wikipedia culture states that holding organizational functions does not confer higher status or greater authority, part of the community perceives inequality. The perception is exacerbated when administrators occasionally support each other in resolving disputes with other users and when they communicate with each other beyond public control. Although they do not perceive their collaboration and network as oppressive, and even though, because of the strong norms of civility, they quite likely use more polite language than newcomers (unlike in regular organizations; cf. Morand, 1996), inevitably they cocreate the system of dominance, even if just by exercising their system of connections and leveraging a good understanding of local norms and available technology (Foucault, 1977; Heller, 1996; Ball & Wilson, 2000; Bjørn & Ngwenyama, 2010). Those who are underprivileged in this system perceive it as unjust, in particular because of the stark contrast with the discourse of equality Wikipedia promotes.

Unsurprisingly, especially among online tribes, the rhetoric of absence of authority may rather indicate that the authorities do not welcome scrutiny or critique (O'Neil, 2009). If the official discourse insists that there are no hierarchies, but in practice participants feel unequal, the egalitarian narrative may, inadvertently, have a silencing effect on the dissidents. Although I do not believe voices are silenced, Wikipedia's highlighting of democracy and equality fuels the Wikipedia community's obsession with hierarchy and authoritarianism as a consequence of generating fears about them.

However, in "democratic hierarchies," the issues of accountability, ownership, authority, and power are addressed more often and more openly than in conventional organizations (Viggiani, 1997), which may seem to be, especially to a newcomer and a nonparticipant observer, a much bigger problem than it actually is. The open expressions of disagreement, which would normally indicate that the situation is dire and critical, in egalitarian organizations signify also that the participants can air their concerns freely and vent their dissent without fear.

Since the scope of organizational control on Wikipedia is extremely wide (as is discussed in Chapter 4), this exclusion is striking for some members of the community. And because Wikipedia rhetoric is extremely egalitarian, even the smallest potential inconsistency with this image disturbs. While discrepancy, even a little, between the official organizational discourse and what is perceived to be the reality is often a source of organizational stir (Rosen, 1985/1991; Fleming & Spicer, 2007), in the case of Wikipedia it relates to its fundamental values and, unsurprisingly, makes some users disappointed with the system itself. These users also find the fact that administrators are difficult to be recalled another sign of power inequality. Both processes act in favor of making the RfA elections more and more difficult, since on one hand, these elections are one of the rare occasions in which Wikipedians may influence decisions (one negative vote weighs four times as much as a positive one) and on the other, increasing expectations toward RfA candidates are natural, when the appointments, for all intents and purposes, are for life.

The years-long inability of the Wikipedia community to deal with the broken RfA ballots on many Wikipedias is symptomatic of deeper problems permeating it. I discuss these further through a study of the Wikimedia Foundation's relations with the community and through an analysis of conflict trajectories, bureaucratic control, trust enactment, declining leadership, and governance tensions on Wikipedia in the following chapters.

# 3

# CONFLICT RESOLUTION ON WIKIPEDIA

## Why Die for Danzig?

## Online Conflict Resolution

Conflict is possibly the most common form of interaction that people take part in or observe on Wikipedia. While egregious errors are easily dealt with, when more fundamental and nuanced details are under consideration, conflicts on Wikipedia abound. I believe this is because conflicts play a crucial role in motivating people to participate (by increasing their involvement and fueling engagement). In fact, in spite of the vast majority of literature saying otherwise, Wikipedia cannot be described as solely collaboration driven; it is also dissent driven. And still, the Wikipedian ethos is very much consensus and agreement oriented. "Consensus" is a Wikipedia buzzword, and the assumption of good faith on the part of others is one of the most fundamental rules editors are obliged to follow.

To examine this intriguing paradox, I delve into one of the biggest edit wars in Wikipedia history (that of Gdańsk versus Danzig)[1] to show how the traditional dispute resolution methods on Wikipedia often prove to be ineffective, with consensus impossible to reach. While presenting possible alternatives (by seeking analogies with other participative organizations), I show that major reduction in the scope of these conflicts is unlikely, as conflicts are basically the fuel of Wikipedia growth.

M. Wasko and S. Faraj (2000) observe that when knowledge is considered a public good, rather than a precious resource to be guarded from looters, people are eager to exchange it and are driven by community interest and their moral obligation to others, rather than by self-interest. This concept accords with how the Wikipedia community operates: beyond any doubt and all other motivations aside, all established Wikipedians enjoy creating a common good. In fact, displays of ownership of knowledge are frowned on: editors cannot claim articles as theirs, should not take offence if somebody edits their sentences, and should participate collectively, although their authorship is attributed (in the page history, which records all the revisions of an article). Practice differs from this official point of view, and there is strong evidence that some editors display strong ownership behaviors (Halfaker, Kittur, Kraut, & Riedl, 2009; Thom-Santelli, Cosley, & Gay, 2009), violating communal norms.

One of the major advantages of Wikipedia is expressed in its credo: it is an encyclopedia that anyone can edit. As Clay Shirky observes,

> In a system where anyone is free to get something started, however badly, a short, uninformative article can be the anchor for the good article that will eventually appear. Its very inadequacy motivates people to improve it; many more people are willing to make a bad article better than are willing to start a good article from scratch. (2009, pp. 121–122)

This process is true of Wikipedia as well as other virtual communities, many online behaviors being driven by the observation that "someone is wrong on the Internet."[2]

The same process makes editing Wikipedia more oriented to disagreement than to collaborative efforts (Gorbatai & Jemielniak, 2012). In fact, calling Wikipedia a collaborative project may be misleading: actual conscious cooperation of editors, coordinating their joint efforts, is rare. In most cases, single users make their edits and then leave the page, turning to another task or leaving Wikipedia; most users are focused on what they themselves do and interact with other editors only when they disagree with them or need help.

Conflicts take place on Wikipedia every day. Many of them are resolved by the rules. For instance, Internet trolling is stopped much more effectively than elsewhere (Kendall, 2011; Brunton, 2012) by Wikipedia's norms regulating constructive behavior (see, for example, the guideline at [[WP:Do_not_disrupt_Wikipedia_to_illustrate_a_point]]).

Similarly, bad-will edits are easily eliminated. Many people and corporations try to influence Wikipedia articles about themselves. Examples from the past include edits attributable to the CIA, PepsiCo, Wal-Mart, or Exxon (Hafner, 2007) or done by public relations companies, such as Bell Pottinger, on behalf of their clients (Pegg & Wright, 2011). PR edits are usually quite blatant, even if they involve just papering over some inconvenient information, and are quickly removed. Disputing the reversion of PR edits is pointless, since there are detailed guidelines on encyclopedic content, neutral wording, weasel words, and general notability.[3]

Outsiders coming to Wikipedia with their own agendas are usually easy to identify. However, if users are determined to slant content, well versed in Wikipedia's policies and rules, and persistent, they prevail for a time. Users who persist in planting misinformation or massaging content are blocked. In the most extreme cases, entire organizations may be banned from editing Wikipedia. This happened with the Church of Scientology, which kept editing about four hundred articles related to it, trying to neutralize its critics and, by using multiple accounts, attempting to favorably slant the content. After regular methods failed and after the longest-running arbitration decision on the English Wikipedia (six months), on May 28, 2009, IP addresses from the Church of Scientology were banned from editing (Singel, 2009), and many of the users were banned individually (see [[WP:Requests_for_arbitration/Scientology]]).

Wikipedia has well-developed procedures for dispute resolution (see [[WP:Dispute_resolution]]). Most conflicts can be resolved through the normal protocol: parties focus on the content, remain calm, and try to reason with each other. Small-scale arguments on the English Wikipedia can also be resolved through an informal request for comment (RFC), in which fellow editors express their opinion and help find a satisfactory solution. RFCs date back to the 1970s, when they were used by network architects to resolve issues (Kelty, 2008; Brunton, 2012). They are not much used on the Polish Wikipedia, since they entice trolls and libelous editors. Disputes on the English Wikipedia are announced on the dispute resolution notice board ([[WP:DRN]]).

Formal mediation is meant to be the last resort of content disputes, while arbitration is used mainly for disputes over conduct, not content. Additional institutions are used to cool tempers and enforce respect for norms (and set examples) for personal conflicts. Arbitration and mediation as a standard method of dispute resolution has only recently been attracting interest in legal corporate practice (Jemielniak & Mikłaszewicz, 2010; J. Jemielniak, 2011), but on Wikipedia it is well developed and long practiced.

Content disputes are at the core of most conflicts and are more difficult to resolve than personal battles. Content disputes usually result in edit wars, in which editors representing conflicting viewpoints repeatedly change a contested article. Small edit wars are by no means rare. Many of them do not even draw the notice of other Wikipedians and administrators. Only when more editors get involved and administrators are asked to intervene do they become visible, but many of them are resolved locally, by several editors.

This tendency to local resolution is largely because Wikipedia rules suggest that editors seek agreement. These rules are interesting from the point of view of organization studies, as they are unique and oriented to consensus building. Consensus building as a mode of decision making has been growing in popularity in management circles over the past fifteen years (Drucker, 1993; Pursuer & Cabana, 1998). As Joseph Reagle (2010b) observes, many of Wikipedia's rules for reaching an acceptable solution are similar to those used by Quakers. Sue Gardner, executive director of the Wikimedia Foundation, concurs and has taken a keen interest in Quaker methods of reaching consensus.[4] Indeed, as Michael Sheeran, a Jesuit and one of the pioneers of consensus building, notes, Quakers strive for a consensus, not just a majority vote; they take breaks when consensus is difficult to reach, are receptive to other people's ideas, avoid direct leadership in conducting the discussions, are inclusive and egalitarian in inviting everybody with an idea to participate in a discussion, and set emotions aside (Sheeran, 1983). The informal part of the Society of Friends is cultivated, and it is possible to participate for years without formally asking to join (Louis, 1994).

These principles are reminiscent of many of the rules of Wikipedia. For instance, according to Wikipedia policies, all disputes about content should be resolved through seeking consensus. The policies and the official Wikipedia rhetoric are quite clear:

> When agreement cannot be reached through editing alone, the consensus-forming process becomes more explicit: editors open a section on the talk page and try to work out the dispute through discussion. Here editors try to *persuade others*, using *reasons* based in policy, sources, and common sense; they can also suggest alternative solutions or compromises that may satisfy all concerns. The result might be an agreement that does not satisfy anyone completely, but that all recognize as a reasonable solution. Consensus is an ongoing process on Wikipedia; it is often better to accept a less-than-perfect

compromise—with the understanding that the page is gradually improving—than to try to fight to implement a particular "perfect" version immediately. The quality of articles with combative editors is, as a rule, far lower than that of articles where editors take a longer view. ([[WP:Consensus]]; emphasis in original)

There are detailed advisories on how to seek consensus in a civilized manner. Voting is again considered to be generally bad. One Wikipedia adage is that Voting Is Evil (VIE), and a guideline essay stating the reasons for such an extreme stance has long existed on the English Wikipedia (and from 2007, on Meta-Wiki, a separate wiki set up to coordinate all Wikimedia projects). Similarly, a behavioral guideline on the English Wikipedia states,

> Wikipedia works by building consensus. When conflicts arise, they are resolved through discussion, debate and collaboration. While not forbidden, polls should be used with care. When polls are used, they should ordinarily be considered a *means* to help in determining consensus, not an end in itself. ([[WP:Polling_is_not_a_substitute_for_discussion]]; emphasis in original)

A Wikipedia policy adds,

> Wikipedia is not an experiment in democracy or any other political system. Its primary (though not exclusive) means of decision making and conflict resolution is editing and discussion leading to consensus—not voting. (Voting is used for certain matters such as electing the Arbitration Committee.) Straw polls are sometimes used to test for consensus, but polls or surveys can impede rather than foster discussion so should be used with caution. ([[WP:What_Wikipedia_is_not]])

This philosophy is shared across the major Wikimedia projects. Consensus in general discussions is usually considered to be reached if at least 80 percent of the good-faith disputants agree, but numeric, mechanistic rules are discouraged.

While the similarities to Quaker communities are striking, there are parallels to other communities and rules: for example, the rules of Wikipedia resemble the practices of the Search Conference, a method with a long history and tradition (T. A. Williams, 1979; Trist, 1983), often used by action researchers (Crombie, 1985; Oels, 2002; D. Jemielniak, 2006) and aimed at participative organizational autoreflection. "The whole [Search Conference] process emphasizes non-hierarchical structure and 'democratic dialogue' in which everyone's voice is respected, speaking time is shared, and open modes of communication among groups are developed and encouraged" (Schafft and Greenwood, 2003, p. 23).

The Search Conference and other variations of participative strategic vision building, such as Future Search (see Bryson & Anderson, 2000), similar to Wikipedia rules, aim at reaching consensus, although the accent is more on trying to build ways forward on a few items while holding other disagreements aside. They also focus on eliminating nonconstructive conflicts, neutralizing power play, and achieving communal agreement. Such processes are also not uncommon in different varieties of industrial democracy designs (Bass & Shackleton, 1979; Greenwood, González Santos, & Cantón, 1991) and are occasionally used in information technology project management (Koch, 2004; Marks & Lockyer, 2004).

As similar as Wikipedia rules are to processes of the Society of Friends, the Search Conference, and some other social systems, these rules often do not work the same way on Wikipedia. In particular, many conflicts are resolved not through consensus-building mechanisms but through persistence and wearing the other side down. This is characteristic of the larger conflicts and has not been more closely studied, although a study would shed light on dispute resolution trajectories in online communities. Studying extremes, observing what happens when conflicts grow and expand beyond their local context, is instructive. Extremes often make organizational processes more visible (Eisenhardt, 1989). Seeking "extreme situations, critical incidents and social dramas" has been encouraged by many case study researchers (Pettigrew, 1990, p. 275).

For this reason, in this chapter I analyze "the largest and longest-running article content dispute on Wikipedia" ([[WP:Wikipedia_Signpost/2005-03-07/ Gdansk_or_Danzig]]). The conflict was one of the biggest crises on Wikipedia (Ayers, Matthews, & Yates, 2008; Lih, 2009; J. J. Anderson, 2011).[5] It took place on the English Wikipedia and drew in some Polish editors. It erupted in 2001, peaked in 2003–2004, and lasted until 2005. The bone of contention was, essentially, whether the Polish city of Gdańsk should be listed and described on the English Wikipedia under its German name, Danzig, especially in the historical contexts. The debate over this relatively trivial issue exceeded four hundred thousand words.

Through an analysis of this epic battle I show that Wikipedia's practical conflict resolution system occasionally fails when both sides are confrontational and committed. I describe how such time-consuming conflicts can be resolved only by departing from the policy of consensus (and by resorting to mechanistic straw polls, once the participants are exhausted enough). This analysis leads to a typology of conflicts on Wikipedia and pinpoints important differences between Wikipedia policies and the rules used by the Society of Friends and the Search Conference.

## Feel like Danzig: The Beginning

The article on Gdańsk was written in the beginnings of Wikipedia, and the earliest edits of the article have not been preserved on Wikipedia servers. The Internet Archive Wayback Machine stores a copy of the article from November 9, 2001 (see "Gdansk," 2001a). An old backup of Wikipedia discovered in 2010 by Tim Starling shows that the article on Gdansk was written in early May 2001, as one of the first ten thousand articles, and consisted of just two sentences: "Gdansk is a city in Poland, on the Baltic Sea. Its old German name is Danzig" (see Starling, 2010).

The earliest edit stored on Wikipedia is from November 19, 2001, by the user JHK, and it shows a solid, 534-word entry. There is nothing controversial in its first paragraph: "Gdansk is a city in Poland, on the coast of Baltic Sea. Its German name is Danzig, which it was called until the region was conquered by the Soviet Union and transferred to Poland at the end of World War II" (see "Gdańsk," 2001b). Similarly, the earliest entry on Danzig on Wikipedia is from October 17, 2001, when the user Paul Drye put in one simple sentence: "The former name of Gdansk, which see for a complete history of the city" (see "Danzig," 2001).

The name of the city quickly became a controversial topic. On December 19, 2001, the user H. Jonat added the Latin name of the city and changed almost all instances of Gdansk to Danzig. At that time she was active in editing articles from this region and engaged in heated historical discussions on apportioning blame for massacres, the origins of the Polish nation, and Nazi and communist propaganda (Godwin's Law of Nazi Analogies[6] was known to the disputants at the time but, considering the topic, was not entirely applicable). Her adversaries fueled the fire. One of them was Polish, the user Szopen (the Polish transcription of "Chopin"). The tone of the discussion on the talk page of the article was not essentially different. Users exchanged lengthy references to history books, websites, and whatever sources they could find. Some tried to cool the hotheads. For instance, an unregistered user commented on December 22, 2001,

> To an English speaker, the city wasn't Gdansk up till 1939. When we read English language history books dealing with that particular city up till 1945, they most often call the city Danzig. It doesn't mean anything as to who the city belonged to—Most English speakers don't know or care (in the sense that they don't say to themselves "Danzig—must be German"). Could you just quit for a while and maybe listen to people who know what they're talking about (i.e., native speakers with an education). This is not about Prussia/Poland—it's about what title works best in an English language encyclopedia. ([[Talk:Gdansk/archive1]])

Many others edited the article and proposed what they believed to be an acceptable compromise (e.g., referring to it as "the city" rather than by a name). They also tried to incorporate the controversy into the article itself. On June 28, 2002, the user Greg Lindahl added, "The name of the city is still a sore subject even today; as an example, the official city history website . . . does not even mention the word 'Danzig'" (see "Gdańsk: Difference between revisions," 2002a).

A day later an unregistered user edited this as follows:

> The insistence on using of Polish names of this and other cities in English language publications is questionable, especially, since the current official Polish city history website . . . in it's German language version (black/red/gold button) uses "Danzig." ("Gdańsk: Difference between revisions," 2002b)

This edit did not last even an hour. Many similar edits and reversions (called "reverts") took place. Conflict over the name recurred throughout 2002–2003, both in edits and on talk pages. Comparisons to the Ku Klux Klan, skinheads, and totalitarian propaganda flew, alongside more serious arguments and sources supporting the views of both sides.

Wikipedia edit wars sometimes follow a pattern: as long as the most fanatical sides stay in the discussion, those with moderate comments have difficulty following because escalation is rapid (Staw, 1981). Opponents increase their stake in the dispute by investing time (cf. Shubik, 1971) and making quick replies, often even frequently checking whether their disputant has posted something so as to react quickly. The barrier to discussion entry or reentry increases dramatically for those not closely following the discussion, as they must read the lengthening chain of interactions, and participation becomes limited to a small group of the most engaged contributors (Gómez, Kappen, & Kaltenbrunner, 2011). Experienced editors sometimes use the tactic to their advantage: they build a series of lengthy arguments, which deter all who are not genuinely interested in the topic from entering the debate, although on Wikipedia long argumentations are much less likely to be dismissed as "tl;dr" (too long; didn't read) than they are on typical Internet fora (Narayan & Cheshire, 2010; Karatzogianni & Kuntsman, 2012).

In fact, Wikipedia consensus policies encourage discussion participants to voice concerns; "consensus is assumed when there's no evidence of disagreement" ([[WP:Silence_and_consensus]]), which naturally encourages disputing. As a result, quite often, when the rules and sources do not give one side the advantage, winning an argument is simply about staying in the discussion long enough.

However, in the case of the article on Gdańsk, at least four groups of editors stayed active:

- German and Prussian nationalists, insisting that Danzig had belonged to Germany/Prussia for millennia and thus on the use of the German name
- Polish nationalists, convinced that Gdańsk had been Polish for just as long, with brief periods of occupation
- Editors with no stake in the dispute who believed that whatever name was more frequently used in the sources should be applied (and who made several attempts to end the dispute)
- Editors with no stake in the dispute but who understood that it was a sensitive issue and that a sustainable solution had to address all stakeholders (and who tried to build a compromise and mitigated both sides of the argument by occasionally reverting disputants' edits)

## The Forever War

In 2003 the debate reached another stage when four new disputants began to edit frequently: Nico, a strong supporter of the Danzig option; Wik, a strong supporter of the Gdańsk option but not eager to join the discussion on the talk page; Space Cadet, a declared Pole and a supporter of the Gdańsk option; and John K., an American administrator with a declared doctorate in history and initially a proponent of using "Danzig" in all instances when the city before 1945 was described and possibly allowing "Gdańsk" for all later references. When the debates reached the general mailing discussion list the issue at times drew the interest of the general community, including Wikipedia luminaries like Jimbo Wales, and many suggested commonsense solutions without delving into the issue.[7]

Between January 2003 and February 2005 nearly 1,400 edits were made to the Gdańsk article, more than one-quarter of which were by one of these four editors, even though the article was periodically protected from editing because of persistent quarrels and alterations. One hundred and twenty-seven edits were marked as reversions, or reverts, in this period, and in many cases the changes, even though not marked as reverts, had the same result. Other recurring users also participated (including one whose name revealed his or her bias: Gdansk).

The war sporadically spread to other Wikipedias, since the participants, attempting to support their point of view, edited other language versions and tried to manipulate the interwikis (links to the article's counterparts in different languages) so that the English Wikipedia would list only the links to foreign counterparts showing references to Gdańsk or Danzig, depending on the faction.

The disputants also argued about what reference point to use, what the objective source should be. Some proposed Google searches, some insisted on common usage in the language (immediately refuted as unverifiable), some made queries to academic journal databases to determine names used to refer to historical periods, and some queried popular magazines and newspapers, which was more difficult then than now. The results were not immediately unambiguous. Predictably, the same arguments kept being made, and the disputants became weary of their repetition. But the repetition slowly started to bring results: the two sides each recognized that the other was behaving in a civilized manner and grounding arguments in valid sources.

In January 2004 the first attempt at a community-wide compromise was made, but the proposal suggesting that the city should be referred to as Danzig in the 1793–1945 period and as Gdansk otherwise, although accepted by John K., Nico, and Szopen, among others, was met with fierce opposition from several users. Some of the contingent visitors, unaware of the tedious discussions that had taken place previously, tried to make the international audience aware of the background of the issue for the Polish community and appeal to their sensitivity. The following is a comment from February 21, 2004, from an unregistered user:

> Only after the Kulturkamf (enforced Germanisation) in the 1870s the German name was enforced and Polish name forbidden. The German post-office delivered mail to German and Polish addresses and it started to refuse Polish placenames in the 1910s. Free City of Gdansk/Danzig (1919–1939) had a German majority 90%, but also special ties to Poland (cumstoms union, foreign policy, post office etc.) so both names (Gdansk/Danzig) were in use.
>
> The big problem arised during World War II, when people were murdered or sent to concenteration camps (Stutthof) just because they wanted to call the city with its Polish name. This is why the German names of Polish cities are very insulting to Polish people. I don't know why you call it a compromise. ([[Talk:Gdansk/archive3]])

While such arguments had no immediate effect and were not considered relevant, they helped some of the non-Polish editors understand the sensitivity of this issue.

The article was repeatedly protected from editing because of the edit wars (some related to the city's name, some to its history). Interestingly, most of the editors who participated in the discussion on the talk page for a longer time were trying to avoid the most controversial edits. They even made major conciliatory efforts. On February 10, 2004, an administrator (and bureaucrat, at some point), Ed Poor, tried to intervene by unprotecting the article and, in an attempt to, as he described it, "find a way to settle the 'name controversy' once and for all," changing the article's lead-in to the following:

> **Gdańsk** (or **Danzig**) is a famous European city with a long and colorful history. It is known in English by two slightly different names: in alphabetical order, *Danzig* (German) and *Gdansk* (Polish). ("Gdańsk: Difference between revisions," 2004)

He was immediately criticized on the article's talk page by John K., who had been a proponent of using "Danzig," at least in historical contexts:

> Sigh, Ed, I must say that I do not like your version. In the first place, *everyone* agrees that the city's current name is "Gdansk." Of course, earlier in its history

it was frequently known as "Danzig." The question is the best way to indicate this. I, of course, think that my way, which actually explains the situation (that it was usually called Danzig before 1945) is the best, but I think an article which tries to claim that both names are equally valid today is simply wrong. As to the edit war, that had nothing to do with the disputes going on on the talk page, which I think were basically simmering down. What happened was that a [name for user trying to cause trouble deleted], user:Gdansk, decided to start messing with the article in order to minimize the importance of the name Danzig by flooding the article with other, hardly used, names. I won't edit the introduction just yet, but I think the current version is quite poor john 18:56, 10 Feb 2004 (UTC) ([[Talk:Gdańsk/archive3]])

The editors who cared enough to participate in the debate were running out of ammunition. Also, since Wikipedia ethos enforces conduct similar to that in academia with respect to sources, the editors who stayed in the discussion were more eager to at least acknowledge the other side's arguments. Since objectivity is one of the greatest Wikipedia virtues, making an open concession to adversaries can bring respect. For instance, in another reply to Ed Poor's intervention, the user Delirium wrote,

> I made some hopefully acceptable edits to Ed's version. My edits were to move slightly in favor of the Polish argument, which hopefully is okay since I've mostly been taking the German side. I clarified that Gdansk is currently the predominantly used name, while Danzig is a previous name, and one that was once the predominant English name. —Delirium 09:41, Feb 11, 2004 (UTC) ([[Talk:Gdańsk/archive3]])

While a similar edit from a Gdansk proponent would be perceived as continuing the war, and could even incur being blocked, the same changes done by a person known to come from the other side of the fence were acceptable. They also helped instill a positive image of the user, as willing to go beyond his or her own point of view and to remain impartial.

Even more importantly, this situation showed that the users engaged in the edit war and participating in the discussion on the talk page, while disagreeing ardently on many points were trying for consensus. Even if these agreed points were not explicitly stated, violations of this consensus by good-faith incomers were unwelcome. An equilibrium between opposing sides emerged in the sense that both sides acknowledged some issues as unresolved and some as not worth further discussion and were clear on the basis of their disagreement. As with the Christmas Truce of 1916, when German and British soldiers spontaneously declared a cease-fire and even exchanged gifts, participants in the Gdańsk/Danzig edit war joined forces when third parties, unaware of what had already been agreed on, jumped in. It seems that process rules both facilitating and taming discord keep the Wikipedia development structure possible and sustainable.

Despite their debate being listed on March 8, 2004, as one of the "lamest edit wars ever" (see [[WP:Lamest_edit_wars]]), the debate raged on, with attempts at weighing the arguments but each side convinced it was right. On March 16, 2004, editor Gdansk proposed a compromise solution, which essentially was his point of view: only the Polish name should be used for Gdańsk on the English Wikipedia, and other names should be mentioned only once, in the headline. It received support from the Gdańsk faction and the expected veto from opponents. The war was more visible than ever in the community, and an administrator (now an elected member of the board of trustees) took part in the discussion, criticizing the compromise.

Several attempts to find a universal solution to general naming conventions have been undertaken, without much success.[8] On March 16, 2004, the user Mestwin of Gdansk, one of the pro-Gdańsk editors, requested a mediation between a faction promoting German names of Polish and other Central European cities on the English Wikipedia and the ones who objected to it. The user llywrch, an administrator, bitterly commented, "To be honest, I don't see where mediation will be of help in this matter. Both sides appear to me as being fairly hardened & upcompromising in their positions" ([[WP:Requests _for_mediation/Archive_04]]). Since the mediation request was more like a list of demands and since other parties were not interested in participating, this move served only as yet another forum for discussions.

John K. repeated the suggestion to "stick to standard English usage. Perhaps the determination of what this is should be left to us native speakers of English" ([[Talk:Gdansk/archive8]], April 2, 2004), which would completely defang his adversaries but was ignored. Clearly, legitimate solutions were being negotiated, but reducing the complex historical and sociological problem to just language and limiting its consideration to only natives could not work. He also made a significant effort in analyzing historical books and made queries to the JSTOR academic journal database to determine how historians referred to the city. This study of sources was important in the debate, but disagreements had progressed past resolution, and perhaps also the point of reason. Even what should have been the least problematic decisions, such as phrasing of the header, produced hours of disputes and nuanced consider-ations, and deciding among the four options turned out to be very difficult:

- Gdańsk (formerly Danzig)
- Gdańsk (German: Danzig)
- Gdańsk (formerly also Danzig)
- Gdańsk (in English formerly known as Danzig)

Apparently, writing that "Gdańsk" was formerly "Danzig" indicated that the Polish name had not previously existed, which was objectionable to the Polish faction; referring to "Danzig" as only a German name did not satisfy their adversaries, who insisted that it was also in widespread use in English at some point, when it was almost exclusively used as the city's name (which was also a reason for rejecting the "formerly also Danzig" proposal). Similarly, the last option was questionable because it sounded as if "Danzig" was actually an English name that had fallen into disuse. Differences between these choices seemed irrelevant to the general community but had become a headache for those involved, indicating again the escalation of commitment to extremes.

This mundane issue was just the tip of an iceberg. A separate lengthy thread was dedicated to the desirability of allowing diacritical spelling of for-eign words on the English Wikipedia.

Meanwhile, the user Wik, who had been active in the Danzig/Gdańsk quarrel, landed in trouble. Wik had made more than twenty-two thousand edits on the English Wikipedia (none on the Polish one) and was regarded as an experienced editor, but he was reluctant to discuss his changes and reverts. He also kept reverting entire edits that contained minor errors but a lot of good material instead of just correcting the minor errors. Eventually, because of his persistence in the article on Gdansk and his repeated offenses, the Arbi-tration Committee forbade him to make more than three reverts on any given page (see [[Wikipedia_talk:Requests_for_arbitration/Wik]]). He briefly tried to game the system by challenging the nuances of the wording of the rule and by requesting his supporters to act as proxies in daily reverting of articles (he listed twelve, including Gdańsk). Shortly thereafter, another arbitration case involving him was opened, which resulted in his being banned from Wikipedia in May 2004. He tried giving Jimbo Wales an ultimatum and, when it was rejected, attacked Wikipedia with a vandalizing bot; tried to edit from different accounts, which were also banned (see [[WP:Requests_for_arbitration/Gzornenplatz]]); and eventually left.

The prolonged edit wars and the success of the three-revert rule (3RR) in tempering Wik resulted in promulgation of 3RR as a strict policy for all editors on the English Wikipedia in November 2004 (but not introduced as a policy on the Polish Wikipedia and many other Wikipedias as of 2013). With few exceptions, following 3RR means that within any twenty-four-hour period one editor is allowed to perform only three reversions in an article, and editors violating this rule are blocked (see [[WP:Edit_warring]]. Wales personally endorsed this solution (see [[WP:Three_revert_rule_enforcement]]).

In the Gdańsk/Danzig discussion, strife continued. Occasional page protections (such as the one instituted in June 2004 by the administrator and bureaucrat Raul654) only enraged some users: editor Gdansk went on an editing spree of articles on German cities, adding their Polish names in a "retaliation action for blocking Gdansk and Szczecin" ("Kiel," n.d.), and was eventually temporarily blocked. Meanwhile, a subpage for voting on a naming convention was set up ([[Talk:Gdańsk/Naming_convention]]) by the user Halibutt. Instead of bringing a solution, it prolonged the argument. For example, already-familiar nuances of implications were debated, such as whether indicating that "Danzig" was a German name implied that it was not in use in other languages. Other encyclopedias (*Encarta*, *Britannica*, and *Columbia* and its online version infoplease.com) were consulted for their usage, leading John K. to comment with disappointment that there was "no apparent consensus over the web and other encyclopedias on how the city is called now," and the disputants seemed to slowly sink into a state close to paranoia—nothing was certain anymore. Even the use of "Gdansk" by the English-language media was questioned, since the omission of the acute accent mark over the letter *n* might have been deliberate (and might have indicated the correct English name) but might also have been a result of typographic negligence (and thus "Gdańsk" should be considered the correct English name). This voting was quite useful, however, in summarizing the pros and cons of different naming proposals, since all editors were able to add their comments and suggest advantages and disadvantages of the proposed solutions.

## Peace Without Consensus

The discussion continued intermittently on the voting subpage, simultaneous to that on the Gdańsk talk page, until October 2004. Occasional edit wars started and ended on related topics. The stalemate finally led the community to open the case for a wider discussion. On February 18, 2005, an administrator, Chris 73, acting with John K. and with help from Szopen, prepared a detailed voting page, allowing participants to express their opinions on names for the city in six historical periods, specific uses of the name in biographies, whether to always cross-reference one name to the other, and how to enforce an established consensus in the future. Proposals were made to accommodate the needs of readers from different countries and for different sensitivities: one of the Polish-faction editors suggested that for biographies of persons of clearly German origin, regardless of the time period, the German name should be used (and, respectively, Polish), since the readers coming to these biographies would be predominantly of the same nationality and be more familiar with the name in their own language.

The vote was advertised to the community and described in the *Wikipedia Signpost*.[9] The poll gathered a little more than eighty votes on the most popular question and fewer in the others. This is not a trifling number, but for such a seemingly important issue it is surprisingly small. Disputes on the vote's discussion page ([[Talk:Gdansk/Vote/discussion]]), barely exceeded five thousand words and were largely technical (how the voting should be conducted). The arguments on the vote page itself were longer, up to twenty-one thousand words, including the votes themselves. Still, all sides wanted to avoid repetition of arguments, occasionally suspecting newcomers of being their former adversaries and editing from new accounts or without logging in:

> Eeech are you Helga by chance? Cause I saw all these "arguments" before and I thought we were finished with them. I'm sure the answers and discussion is somewhere in history. Szopen 08:24, 1 Mar 2005 (UTC)

Many of the votes were cast soon after the poll opened, and only a few were cast on the last day of the poll (March 4, 2005), indicating that the most interested parties followed the issue closely. There might have been some cheating: in the vote for the 1466–1793 period, forty-seven votes were for Danzig and forty-eight for Gdańsk, but the latter included twelve votes by users with very low edit counts (indicating they were accounts set up on the English Wikipedia just to participate in this poll), which would be unusual. One of these votes was from an account that one year later was revealed to be a sock-puppet[10] of one of the strong supporters of the Polish option. However, it might have been that Polish Wikipedians learned of the vote and registered on the English Wikipedia to express their opinion. Excluding these twelve votes was not beyond dispute but did not cause a stir. Similarly, that the issue was of primary interest to Polish and German editors and that Germany has roughly double the population of Poland and thus could have skewed the vote did not raise much discussion.

All in all, the participants seemed to believe that everything had been said, and the vote was conducted peacefully, with only occasional accusations of propaganda. After the vote there was no drama; the users seemed to accept the results.

Of course, the issue did not disappear for good, and the topic has occasionally reemerged, as new editors stumble on the topic. As recently as July 2011, there was a short debate over whether a painting from 1608 by the Dutch artist Izaak van den Blocke, "Allegory of Gdańsk Trade," should not be called "Allegory of Danzig Trade" (see [[Talk:Gdańsk/Archive_13]]). Similarly, in May 2012 one editor, claiming to hold several academic degrees and awards, tried to reopen the discussion about the city's name but was persuaded that the community had already settled the issue. On June 26, 2012, an anonymous user tried to add a sentence to the article: "The city's German name prevailed in English texts until the end of World War II," but the edit was reverted within forty-one minutes (see "Gdańsk: Difference between revisions," 2012). Clearly, a decision has been reached, and experienced editors and administrators have been defending it. Any attempts to reverse the 2005 decision have been contingent, not initiated by regular editors of the topic.

The articles on Gdańsk and Danzig are relatively stable now,[11] even though the latter has occasionally been a reason for minor edit wars because it is a redirect to the article on the city and is not, as some would prefer, a disambiguation page about the American heavy metal band Danzig. Although the rules of Wikipedia state that a consensus can change (CCC), "longtime contributors do not want to waste time having arguments about issues that they consider to be solved. Pointing to prior consensus, just like linking to policies, provides a method for dealing with trollish behavior" (Kriplean, Beschastnikh, McDonald, and Golder, 2007, p. 174). This is probably why late entrants to editing particular articles usually stand on the losing side in Wikipedia disputes (O'Neil, 2011).

## Conflict Trajectories

The results of this edit war have influenced Wikipedia policies and have become a part of Wikipedia folklore, being cited to this day as a legendary dispute about a relatively insignificant issue.

In retrospect, the solution to the Gdańsk/Danzig case seems to have been extremely local in its impact. While it helped in establishing a working status quo, it had minimal influence on many other similar cases. Similar epic discussions and wars continue on Wikipedia all the time: the river commonly referred to as Ganga among native English speakers in India is described under "Ganges," a name more familiar to Western speakers of English. To many Indians this wording is a colonial relic and as such has huge symbolic and emotional importance. Many discussions have been held about changing the name (a list of fourteen debates can be found on "Talk:Ganges"), and all have failed. Similar discussions and lengthy debates have taken place about Ivory Coast (or Côte d'Ivoire), Kiev (or Kyiv), and many other locations, both historically and recently, and the geographic disputes are just a small fraction of many major conflicts. Polish-Lithuanian tensions on the English Wikipedia have been frequent and have found their way into many articles (see [[WP:WikiProject_Lithuania/Conflict_resolution]]).

Even more bizarre topics have become sources of heated debates. For instance, between April and June 2012, a fierce discussion was held on the English Wikipedia about whether Mexico has an official language (see [[Talk:Mexico/Archive_9#RfC:Does_mexico_have_an_official_language]]). Users exchanged sources, links, quotes, and arguments (exceeding seventeen thousand words), but no consensus was established. Even voting did not bring a solution, possibly because only the editors engaged in the dispute voted, and unlike Gdańsk/Danzig, it did not attract outsiders' attention and any result could not have confirmed wider agreement. In a similar spirit, deciding whether the name of an article should be "yoghurt" or "yogurt" took ten large debates, as well as an uncountable number of edit wars between November 2003 and December 2011, before it was resolved (see [[Talk:Yogurt/Archive_6#Move_page_to_yogurt]]). Discussion on whether a picture of a tarantula should be used for an article on arachnophobia was four times as long as a discussion about the rest of the article (Forte, Larco, & Bruckman, 2009). Such lengthy and intense conflicts are endemic to all major projects (for example, see an analysis of a conflict on the French Wikipedia as to whether Pluto should be described as a planet; Fréard et al., 2010). Even though less than 0.5 percent of pages are subject to larger edit wars (Sumi, Yasseri, Rung, Kornai, & Kertész, 2011), few editors have never been engaged in a dispute. Conflict on Wikipedia is said to be "as addictive as cocaine" (Reagle, 2010a, p. 161).

This process in itself is not necessarily harmful to the community and the encyclopedia. However, it may lead to systemic biases, based on a majority of culture, language, or gender, and consequently deter people who are underrepresented in the community from expressing their opinion. The Ganga/Ganges discussion is a good example: the consensus and the approach to the problem, relying on the Western English custom and ignoring other cultures' sensitivities, is quite likely related to the history of Wikipedia, which developed at first more dynamically in the United States and Europe, but is one that potentially discourages editors from India, who have to fight an uphill battle. Issues of low symbolic importance to the dominant population of Wikimedians are significant to those who fall victim to the systemic bias. More generally, editors with more mainstream views tend to win arguments. Young, male, Western, well-educated, and relatively affluent editors have more time, technical skills, commitment, and confidence to participate in Wikipedia. The homogeneous composition of editors affects the articles[12] and, quite obviously, undermines diversity even more.

As I have described, many interactions on Wikipedia are driven by disagreement. They are also rhetorical and argumentative (Famiglietti, 2012). Debates on Wikipedia substitute for face-to-face discussions and are inherently textual (Ong, 2002). Thus, the argumentative positions, already diminishing empathy because of the semianonymity of interactions, their asynchronicity, and lack of body language and face-to-face contact, further detach the discourse from the author (Olson, 1990), which makes all discussions more prone to dispute. Online discussions often serve as fora for venting frustration and anger (Lee, 2005; da Cunha & Orlikowski, 2008).

As conflict escalates and increases participants' time commitment, people become more engaged in discussions and also in improving the articles, since it is the only way to win the argument. Since aggressive behaviors are prohibited by the rules and the written norms are designed to reach a consensus, the social system of Wikipedia often channels the energy of disputes into article development.

As shown in this chapter, these rules, although participative and aimed at communal agreement, do not always work as planned. The Danzig/Gdańsk dispute had to be resolved in a way that violated Wikipedia policies: through polling and not discussion. The discussion proved ineffective, and consensus was never reached. The process of reaching a consensus, done by the book, failed. Only the brute force of widely discouraged vote counting brought acceptable results, although they were quite far from consensual. Some decisions introduced and enforced as a result of the vote received about 60 percent support but were accepted by the community (ordinarily a larger percentage is required for resolution).

It is possible that the lengthy disputes allowed the expression of all opinions, and even though neither side admitted that they understood their adversaries, knowing their positions probably softened the negotiation positions. In addition, everyone was so worn out that they were willing to accept a rotten compromise.

Though the scale of the dispute on Danzig/Gdańsk was extreme even by Wikipedia standards, its pattern of dispute resolution is much more common than one would assume. Beyond any doubt, even though the rules of Wikipedia are aimed at discovering facts and establishing well-sourced information through confronting different views and at acknowledging and reflecting all true disagreements if they are covered in the sources, they also encourage disagreements. The escalation of commitment to disputes raises the threshold of participation for everybody who is not involved. Those involved, on the other hand, often differ in determination. Thus, disputes on Wikipedia often do not end because one side persuades the other and is able to reach the holy grail of a consensus, to live happily ever after, but because the other side is bored to death and finds continued participation in the discussion a waste of time. In Wikipedia discussions, it more important to be persistent than right.

Wikipedia's official rules, so admired for their resemblance to Quaker and Search Conference consensus-oriented standards, work well if the conflict can be resolved by establishing the facts from reliable sources. When the issue is more complicated, that becomes clear within weeks. Table 3.1 depicts a typology of the most common nonfactual conflict trajectories on Wikipedia. Conflicts in which both parties agree that their point of view may not prevail are nonconfrontational, while the ones in which at least one party does not

TABLE 3.1 Typology of conflict trajectories

|  | Unequal commitment to rules | Equal commitment to rules |
|---|---|---|
| Confrontational | **Elimination**<br>Both sides blocked | **Stalemate**<br>Participants entrench |
| Nonconfrontational | **Domination**<br>One side surrenders | **Collaboration**<br>Participants cooperate |

consider it as an option are confrontational since they antagonize and engage the other party in the confrontation. The trajectory and outcome of the conflict depends on parties' commitment to rules.

## Elimination

When the conflict is confrontational, meaning the parties are unwilling to seek agreement (whether because of one stubborn editor or something else), and participants' commitment to the dispute and the rules is not equal, usually at least one of the participants breaks the no-personal-attacks rule or does not maintain general civility and is excluded from the discourse. The rule breakers do not have to be the ones who are seeking confrontation; they just have to be less committed to rules. Following the rules of civility and valid sources requires more time and commitment than throwing off insults and witty remarks, so high commitment levels correlate more with following the rules than emotional attachment with the topic. Also, some experienced users skillfully incite and provoke the other party to break the rules.

If both sides resort to uncivil behavior, both may be blocked, since retaliation is not a reason to break the rules. Such conflicts are rarely constructive, since they do not lead to refinement of articles. Only after they end, by driving the destructive contributor out, can the article be developed.

## Domination

When the conflict is not confrontational and the parties differ in their commitment to the dispute and the rules, replies from the more committed to the less committed party are prompt and long, so following the discussion requires time. Statements are supported by sources, sometimes difficult to find or requiring skill to handle. Even though there is no direct confrontation and in theory each side respects the other's viewpoint and just awaits proper argumentation in the discussion, it is the less committed party that surrenders and leaves the dispute, unable to keep pace with the committed opponent. As in a marathon, stamina is valuable. As Oliver Kamm observes,

Wikipedia seeks not truth but consensus, and like an interminable political meeting the end result will be dominated by the loudest and most persistent voices. This is an inherent flaw. The problem is not that there are too few voices in the editorial process, who can skew the result, but the opposite. Participation is prized more than competence. (2007)

This scenario is far from optimal, since people lacking commitment are often beginners, who have little stake in participating in Wikipedia. When they leave a conflict feeling mistreated or misunderstood, they also often leave Wikipedia for good. Article quality may also suffer, fulfilling one of Larry Sanger's hypotheses: "Over the long term, the quality of a given Wikipedia article will do a random walk around the highest level of quality permitted by the most persistent and aggressive people who follow an article" (2009, p. 64).

Tiring out one's opponent is a common strategy among experienced Wikipedians. I have resorted to it many times. This is so because Wikipedia's rules of consensus seeking encourage argumentation, as long as it is meritocratic, and because the experienced editors on Wikipedia are by natural selection the ones who enjoy (or at least do not despise) such discussions. As a result, all major debates on Wikipedia are quite long.

### Collaboration

When the conflict is nonconfrontational and both parties have the same commitment, cooperation is possible, as envisioned by Wikipedia rules. When both parties to the conflict abide by the rules of civil behavior and dispassionately seek valid sources and proper phrasing of the facts, they come to an agreement. The possibility to actually shape the outcome has quite a satisfying and empowering effect on the parties. The consensus, once reached, is usually satisfactory to everyone involved. This scenario is not by any means unusual but also is not dominant.

### Stalemate

When the conflict is confrontational and both parties are at a similar commitment level, the scenario resembles the chicken-run scene from *Rebel without a Cause*. On Wikipedia, however, the race does not end, and both sides end up entrenched in a long war, as in the Danzig/Gdańsk case. This scenario is typical of Wikipedia and, obviously, wastes the time and effort of the editors. Such a conflict usually cannot be resolved through consensus, but once both participants' enthusiasm wanes, a simple vote may suffice.

The social aspects of content production are crucial for the way Wikipedia develops (Kane, 2009), and the conflict trajectories must influence articles. In fact, the number of contributors is closely related to article quality, although only to a certain point (Kane, 2012); the positive aspects of collaboration, as well as of collaboratively oriented conflicts, are most visible when there are not too many participants.

While quantitative trajectories of conflicts have been a topic of extensive studies (Török et al., 2013) across different language versions (Yasseri, Spoerri, Graham, & Kertész, in press), they have rarely been a topic of a qualitative study. As a result, many topics are worth a deeper analysis, including leader-follower behavioral patterns in conflicts (Yasseri & Kertész, 2013) and the influence of national culture on topics' controversy levels (Yasseri et al., in press). The most important question remains: Is Wikipedia a collaborative project or a conflict-driven one?

## Collaboration, Conflict, or Both?

Discussion archives are an important part of the quality control system (Stvilia, Twidale, Smith, & Gasser, 2008), as is debating. However, even though Wikipedia encourages a dispassionate approach to editing, most editors take their work personally. Still, discussing is better than acting in a way that advances the conflict. Reverting newcomers' work, especially without explanation, discourages them (Halfaker, Kittur, & Riedl, 2011), and some do not come back. This is by no means rare: according to the *Wikipedia Editors Study*, "More editors reported their edits were reverted with an explanation, at 59%, in comparison to 43% who said that their edits were reverted without any explanation" (multiple answers were possible; see Wikimedia Foundation, 2011a, p. 25). This is why Wikipedia has a clear policy to not bite newcomers (see [[WP:Please_do_not _bite_the_newcomers]]),[13] and civility is of the highest importance. This is so to the extent that on the Polish Wikipedia, for example, the most prolific editor in the project's history (and a former administrator), editing on different projects since 2004 and with an edit count close to six digits, was in 2009 banned for the way he treated other users for their alleged misdoings.

These conflict patterns show that Wikipedia discussions are entirely collaborative only when specific conditions are met. This may well be a side effect of the truly participative design of decision making on Wikipedia. As long as the participants act in a civilized way and as long as the dispute is not over facts (for example, when reliable sources differ, and this difference is not covered by other sources), parties can continue arguing. Inevitably, "conflicts and editorial wars, although restricted to a limited number of articles which can be efficiently located, consume considerable amounts of editorial resources" (Yasseri, Sumi, Rung, Kornai, & Kertész, 2012, p. 11). Most conflicts are resolved within a reasonable amount of time, but others extend into lengthy campaigns among the few most fanatical editors (Yasseri & Kertész, 2013), deterring everybody else from even looking into the issue because of the sheer accumulation of arguments.

Some popular topics are still surprisingly underdeveloped (Gorbatai, 2011b), in spite of powerful social mechanisms of aligning collective production with demand (Gorbatai, 2011a), and well-intentioned editors trying to develop an article find themselves trapped in conflict (Suh, Convertino, Chi, & Pirolli, 2009). The scale of and proportions between conflict-driven and intentionally collaborative efforts on Wikipedia are difficult to measure (Rad & Barbosa, 2012; Rad, Makazhanov, Rafiei, & Barbosa, 2012), but both are significantly present. However, quite perversely, some conflicts, especially those relying on purposeful and bad-will violation of rules and trolling for the fun of wreaking havoc or resulting from frustration (Schachaf & Hara, 2010), have an important community-building role (Franco et al., 1995; Lesser, Fontaine, & Slusher, 2012): they allow editors to unite against a common enemy. On Wikipedia, "the system functions not so much to resolve disputes and make peace between conflicting users, but to weed out problematic users while weeding potentially productive users back in to participate" (Hoffman and Mehra 2009, p. 151).

All this leads to an important differentiation of Wikipedia from Quaker and Search Conference model communities: facilitators. Quakers have a clerk, whose responsibility is to synthesize the outcome of each debate and summarize the sense of the meeting (Hare, 1973; Burson, 2001). While this role is not related to authority or decision making, it is of utter importance: a clerk facilitates the discussion, suggests questions for discussion, and chooses the moment for silence (Gentry, 1982).

Similarly, in action research and the Search Conference methodology, a facilitator aids consensus reaching and problem solving by encouraging the participants to voice their concerns, ensuring their understanding of the discussion, and providing theorizations when required (Avgitidou, 2009). A facilitator has to be an unengaged reflexive listener (Cunliffe, 2002; Rutter, 2003) who does not take the leadership position and mirrors the community's discussion.

The facilitator's role is crucial for group conflict resolution through consensus seeking (Isenhart & Spangle, 2000; Cao, Chuah, Chao, Kwong, & Law, 2012), since it directs the conflict trajectories toward collaboration. However, on Wikipedia, the rules for establishing a consensus do not include such a role. Even worse, although the inherently political nature of disputes is recognized (having friends helps in winning arguments), there are no institutions for representation in conflict.[14] This, combined with the lack of facilitators, is striking, since the struggle between editors eager to intensify discussions and the ones who try their best to neutralize conflicts and mediate is visible in the most vitriolic debates (Iba, Nemoto, Peters, & Gloor, 2010).

Some projects have formal or semiformal mediators who mitigate interpersonal conflicts and who make a huge difference in terms of dispute resolution (Billings & Watts, 2010), but their involvement is not routine and not helpful on some projects. Notably, on the Polish Wikipedia successful mediation is rare. On the English Wikipedia a group of mediators ([[WP:Mediation _Cabal]]) ceased to operate because it was unused and ineffective. Thus, Wikipedia consensus-building rules are different from those of organizations using similar methods and possibly more prone to stalemate, domination, or elimination scenarios. This indicates that in participative management organization, group conflict resolution in the absence of an impartial facilitator is difficult and introducing ad hoc facilitators is hardly possible. In addition, the discourse of collaboration and consensus seeking, extremely popular when talking about Wikipedia and other open-collaboration communities, does not reflect the reality of everyday editing. Yochai Benkler's definition of collaboration as cooperating "without relying on either market signals or managerial commands" (2006b, p. 60) is broad, covering almost any communal activity conducted outside traditional structures and hierarchies.

Wikipedia article development is, in this sense, collaborative, but in the same way that adding bricks to a wall by individual passersby is or any other task "chunked out into bite-size pieces that individuals can contribute in small increments and independently of other producers" (Tapscott & Williams, 2006, p. 70). However, a more common understanding of collaboration brings images of at least some general agreement, as well as of simultaneity and collective work. It "involves two or more contributors discussing, cooperating, and working together to create something or share information" (Preece & Shneiderman, 2009, p. 20). From this perspective it is clear that the Wikipedia community relies as much on cooperation as it does on conflict and on what Barry Wellman refers to as "networked individualism" (2002). In this light it is not surprising that a study by Yair Amichai-Hamburger, Naama Lamdan, Rinat Madiel, and Tsahi Hayat (2008) showed that Wikipedians are less agreeable, less open, and less conscientious than non-Wikipedians. As shown in this chapter, much of the participation in Wikipedia is disagreement driven, and many of the highly idealized procedures of consensus seeking result in flamed disputes, even though truly collaborative and coordinated efforts and friendly support do take place on Wikipedia, more often resulting in better articles (Turek, Wierzbicki, Nielek, Hupa, & Datta, 2010; Nemoto, Gloor, & Laubacher, 2011). Perhaps, as Lewis A. Coser postulated more than half a century ago (1957), social conflicts foster creativity and innovation.

In some ways, Wikipedia forms a "community of dissensus." It "does not pretend to have the power to name and determine itself; it insists that *the position of authority cannot be authoritatively occupied*" (Readings, 1996, p. 187; emphasis in original), as dissent is one of several powerful secrets to its success. The participants in many conflicts on Wikipedia seem to assume a positivist model of establishing and negotiating facts, rather than a pragmatist one, which John Dewey postulated to be more cooperative (Campbell, 1995).

Such a chaotic and uncoordinated way of seeking consensus and resolving disputes reflects a laissez-faire and hands-off approach to Wikipedia, which is unlikely to change if only because it draws people to this community. Yet that approach is somewhat surprising when the sheer number of rules and the level of social regulation in general organization of cooperation is considered. This is the topic of the next chapter.

# 4

## BUREAUCRACY AND CONTROL

### Big Brother Is Watching

Wikipedia relies on a community of volunteers, who cooperate in a democratically and participatively created environment. Everybody is allowed to focus on any form of improving the encyclopedia they want, and freedom of choice and the fully open character of collaboration are strongly emphasized. Still, the amount of peer control that all Wikipedians experience is extremely high. There is a Panopticon-like record of everyone's actions, and Wikipedia's control of participation through a high degree of regulation and procedures would be surprising even for a highly bureaucratic organization. This paradox may stem from the community's need to stratify users and create barriers to entry for newcomers and the natural tendency to introduce informal strategies of domination and differentiation of user status. To study this further, it may be useful to focus on how open-collaboration communities, and Wikipedia in particular, solve the problem of control and regulation.

Molly McLure Wasko, Robin Teigland, and Samer Faraj (2009) observe that in some electronic networks of practice, the community is sustained not necessarily through strong ties among the members but rather by the ties between members and the community. This is true of Wikipedia. One of the reasons for this phenomenon is the asynchrony of its interactions. So is not knowing if the person we are trying to communicate with is even going to read our message, since only some editors opt to be e-mailed when their talk page has been edited, and this choice is not revealed to the public. Wikipedians cannot know whether a favorite collaborator will be available and thus must rely on the community rather than on a personal network of contacts, although the most active Wikipedians often communicate with each other on IRC and through other channels when they need assistance. This is why most editor requests to administrators are posted on the administrators' notice board for any administrator to address. Beginners sometimes simultaneously ask one or a couple of administrators they know by posting their request on the administrators' talk pages, but this is counterproductive; once the issue has been resolved by one administrator, the others still have the request on their talk pages.

Wikipedia editors rarely form strong ties with each other, simply because of the sheer number of Wikipedians. Some editors do specialize in certain topics, and after some time they recognize other users with similar interests.[1] Yet the chaotic, voluntary, contingent, and irregular character of the majority of contributions precludes development of closer ties and relies on weak ties much more than the traditional social structure (Granovetter, 1973; Constant, Sproull, & Kiesler, 1996; Wasko & Faraj, 2005). This is especially true of the English Wikipedia, which has many more active editors than other projects, but the Polish Wikipedia also experiences this atomization.

However, there is another explanation for the reluctance of editors on Wikipedia to develop interpersonal relations. It is the specific way that peer control is exerted on Wikipedia, unlike in other traditional and virtual communities. This issue has not been a topic of much academic discussion. In fact, most studies of Wikipedia focus on the freedom of participation, the relative anarchy of the community, and the autonomy of its members (Konieczny, 2010; Reagle, 2010). While rules and the coordination of cooperation projects have been analyzed and the antiorganizational organization principles of Wikipedia (Shirky, 2009; Benkler, 2011) have been studied, rarely has the actual application of organizational control and the scope of procedural rules been the topic of inquiry. In fact, most publications acknowledge the participative character of rules and the equality and freedom of contributors (Ayers, Matthews, & Yates, 2008), and they stress the creative vibe of volunteer enthusiasts engaged in a decentralized, fluid, and generally unmanaged activity (Bruns, 2008).

This image is to some extent true but presents only part of the picture. Although Wikipedia is a free and egalitarian community, its members are closely controlled, in some aspects to an unprecedented extent. As I show, while the scope of paramanagerial control is limited, since administrators rarely exert their supervision and other privileges, organizational control in its normative (Kunda, 1992) and peer, or concertive (Barker, 1993), aspects is much wider than elsewhere. Wikipedians are subjected to extreme forms of liquid surveillance (Bauman & Lyon, 2012). Discussing it is essential for better understanding of the problems of social control by administrators indicated in the previous chapters and the issues of organizational trust and credential enactment, which are covered in Chapter 5.

Even though the Wikimedia Foundation does exist, organizing on each of the Wikimedia projects is done without organization and with minimal structure (Shirky, 2009). But the absence of strict managerial supervision and hierarchies does not mean that organizational control is not exerted: in fact, it is pretty tight. In this chapter, I show the extremely wide scope of social control employed on Wikipedia through control over discourse and interactions and through procedures.

I show how all actions on Wikipedia are recorded and used to control community members and then describe how even the structure of discourse is shaped in such a way that makes peer control easier. I present the array of procedures and rules in this seemingly antibureaucratic community and argue that the absence of clear hierarchy and the low management environment have been replaced by advancing proceduralization and bureaucratization of Wikipedia.

## Control Through Revisions Tracking

The first powerful experience of control on Wikipedia is experienced by anonymous and newly registered editors without their even knowing it. Users who are unknown, have done little editing, and especially, edit without registering an account (known as IPs because their edits are marked with their Internet protocol address instead of a username) are under close scrutiny from the established members of the community.

Many Wikipedia editors pay special attention to the most recent edits made by anonymous or new users. This makes sense in terms of preventing vandalism, since the most common ones, such as page blanking, adding curse words, or inserting bizarre information (such as "John X. smells" into an article on a high school, or "He was a ninja" into a biographical article on a famous composer, or switching birth and death dates), are frequently committed by pranksters who do not log in or who have just created an account.

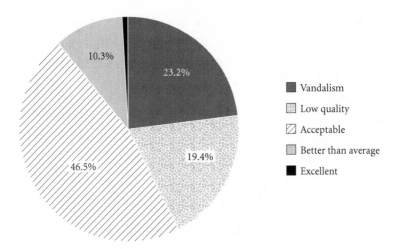

FIGURE 4.1.  Quality of 155 randomly selected edits of new account creators who have made at least one edit

Similarly, many edits that are clearly not neutral or not properly sourced (e.g., blatant self-promotion; advocating for one point of view; and propagating religious, political, and other biases) are often done by newly registered editors.

The quality of edits of new contributors (or, to be more precise, new account creators) is quite good on average.[2] According to a recent study by the Wikimedia Community Department (Walling, 2011), based on a sample of 155 new editors' first edits, only about 23 percent are clear vandalism, and 19 percent are of poor quality (see Figure 4.1). Anonymous Good Samaritans who are one-time contributors also show a high quality of contributions (Anthony, Smith, & Williamson, 2009).

Still, although most new editors make useful contributions to Wikipedia and react very well to constructive criticism as well as simple courtesy (Choi, Alexander, Kraut, & Levine, 2010), those who vandalize articles create a bad image of all new editors. Possibly as a result of this, many Wikipedians are suspicious of anonymous editors and do not treat them the same as other editors. This is so to the extent that in an advisory essay on proper Wikipedia behavior, editors are bizarrely reminded that "IPs are human too":

Many users believe that unregistered users' sole contributions to Wikipedia are to cause disruption to articles and that they have fewer rights as editors compared with registered users. . . . As current policy stands, unregistered users have exactly the same rights as registered users to participate in the writing of Wikipedia. . . . Remember this when dealing with unregistered users. They are not a lower category of users. They are not a special subset that we tolerate. They are not locust swarms intent on destroying your article. ([[WP:IPs_are _human_too]])

In a similar spirit, another essay explains that not every IP is a vandal (see [[WP:Not_every_IP_is_a_vandal]]). This mistrust seems to be growing. As Aaron Halfaker, a Wikimedia Foundation research analyst, observes,

> The quality of new editors has not substantially changed since 2006. Moreover, both in the early days of Wikipedia and now, the majority of new editors are not out to obviously harm the encyclopedia (~80 percent), and many of them are leaving valuable contributions to the project in their first editing session (~40 percent). However, the rate of rejection of all good-faith new editors' first contributions has been rising steadily, and, accordingly, retention rates have fallen. What this means is that while just as many productive contributors enter the project today as in 2006, they are entering an environment that is increasingly challenging, critical, and/or hostile to their work. (2012)

There may be several explanations for this phenomenon, but one is the growing alienation of the Wikipedia community from the rest of the world and the community's feeling that it is "us versus them." With the mess in community elections (indicating power play and resentment of the espoused equality; see Chapter 2) and the dissonance of egalitarian rhetoric with the hierarchy of experience, more users than ever engage in power play. Since editors covet administrator positions and see their attainment as increasingly limited, they may take out their frustrations on those lower in Wikipedia ranks: newcomers and anonymous editors.

The Wikipedia community operates on an informal and delicate parahierarchy, relying on the perception of one's experience and usefulness to the community. Some users with more experience believe newcomers are inferior and disruptive. This is by no means an isolated phenomenon; according to the *Wikipedia Editors Study* (Wikimedia Foundation, 2011a), as many as 28 percent of surveyed editors reported that more experienced editors looked down on them. Even more interesting, though, is that the concertive control (Barker, 1993) exerted by the community does not stop at controlling unregistered and new editors. In fact, all Wikipedians are subject to close peer monitoring, which has serious consequences for organizational life. This is most striking for requests for adminship (RfAs), which often reflect and magnify the troubles and trends in community lives. RfAs, as it turns out, are often tales of acute community control. In the words of the user Dayewalker, describing the voting in his lost RfA bid soon after it, on November 17, 2011,

> As I expected, everyone I'd ever crossed paths with in any sort of negative light returned to take their shots, stalking my edits from #1 to #13990, looking for something I'd done wrong. Editors who I'd generously describe as "troubled" took their time to track down any misunderstandings and paint me in a negative light. Almost fourteen thousand edits in three years and no blocks, not even a serious warning that I can remember. All of that time, I tried to calm things down in this ticking time bomb of a website. My reward? A trip before the firing squad, where editors who broke policy and were rightfully blocked in the past took their opportunity to take revenge without fear of reprisal. ([[User:Dayewalker]])

He added later, in an even more blistering tone,

> Anything in your past is fair game. Any detail of your life you've admitted, or that can be inferred from your editing patterns, can and will be used against you. What you've done by volunteering your time here isn't nearly as important as what other editors think you should have done. Protect your information. ([[User:Dayewalker]])

This is by no means an isolated experience. In fact, most RfA candidates can expect anything they ever wrote on Wikipedia, including arguments with vandals, to be dug up and pointed to, including edits deleted by the candidate and comments removed from the current record. Even one questionable comment, deleted seconds after posting, may be disqualifying. Since wiki technology allows tracking all changes ever made, any time the editor presses the save button he or she leaves a permanent and visible track.

Similarly, any edits the candidate ever made to his or her own user page and talk page are carefully reviewed by some voters. If they find that the candidate removed declarations (even honest disclosure of religion, political views, or stance in a social or economic rights debate), they will suspect the objectivity of the candidate. If a candidate has taken sides in major social questions, even if such statements have been removed by the candidate before the RfA, those positions will likely add fuel to the fire.

Even editors without community career ambitions can expect some occasional routine control. First, many editors casually read through other discussions on talk pages they edit. Second, there is a whole group of recent-changes patrollers, who avidly check the latest changes made to Wikipedia. Even though they focus on articles and not on discussions, some make random checks of talk pages. Third, in the case of conflicts or disagreements, and especially when an editor seems about to become disruptive, it is not unusual to examine a large sample of his or her edits and what was written in debates and to other editors. Finally, in formal dispute resolution (conducted by the Arbitration Committee), actions of the analyzed editor are carefully reviewed. In all cases, since Wikipedia technology allows retaining all edits (including those changed by the same person or other editors later), every single edit stays on Wikipedia until the end of days. It is only a matter of access priority as to who can see the historical version of the page: in most cases the history is available to everybody, including anonymous surfers; in some cases (when content is deleted) only administrators can see it; and in the rarest cases (such as heavy policy violations), access to deleted and historical content may be limited to oversighters and stewards.

This means that, since written or edited interactions are the only form of behavior available on Wikipedia and take the place of both communication and actions, all behavior on Wikipedia is controlled and recorded. This may be equivalent to being constantly watched on cameras and having everything we say filmed and accessible for all other organizational actors at any time. In this sense Wikipedia resembles a Panopticon (Foucault, 1977) or an open-space office: everybody is watched by everybody else, and all actions remain on the record, forever.

Even though this system balances the freedom to edit with protection from disruptive behaviors, it affects behavior on Wikipedia, even if the issue of control is not verbalized and the official discourse emphasizes freedom and egalitarianism. All conversations on Wikipedia are conducted as if they were semiofficial, in the sense that they are kept for the public and stored for the purpose of social control. Asking for going off the record (for example, by continuing the conversation through other communication channels) is not practiced, with some exceptions listed later, and perceived as potentially aimed at bending the rules. Similarly, even personal conversations on users' talk pages are supposed to be conducted in the main language of the Wikipedia. This leads, for example, to two native Polish speakers communicating in intermediate-level English because they interact on Commons (a central media repository for all Wikimedia projects) and want to make the content of their communication transparent. Transparency of communication deprives personal interactions of their private character.

From the point of view of social control, there are almost no regular and unanimously accepted private channels of interaction for Wikipedians who do not know each other. The exceptions are a semiformal IRC network, which is used by only some members of the community; e-mail messages to users who agreed to be contacted this way; and the e-mail lists of administrators and stewards (and several others) used on some Wikipedias that are private, in contrast to other e-mail lists.[3] All discussions not adhering to the purpose of such restricted-access lists (namely, discussing proper administrative actions and not discussing anything else—in particular, policies or changes in rules, since these require a general community consensus) are quashed.

## Control Through Structured Discourse

One striking difference between the Polish and the English Wikipedias is the way the discourse on talk pages is conducted, and this difference relates to social control on Wikipedia. Wiki software notifies a user whenever his or her talk page is edited by somebody else. It has the obvious useful functionality of alerting the owner of the talk page that another editor requires his or her attention. On the Polish Wikipedia talk pages are used as probably intended: a message system that makes messages publicly accessible but retains only messages left for the talk page owner, not his or her replies. Whenever I want to leave somebody a message, I go to his or her talk page, and I expect his or her reply on mine; the same applies to longer conversations.

Oddly enough, even though the technology is the same, the system is not used this way on the English Wikipedia. Instead, both sides of a discussion are conducted on the talk page where it started. This way, the outcome resembles more a threaded forum rather than a publicly accessible messaging system. The rationale is explained on a page suggesting how to be elected as an administrator. Since January 2010, the following piece of advice has been given in a list of ten ways to prepare for an RfA:

> If you are one of those types that responds to comments on the other person's
> talk page, STOP. These pages are extremely hard to assess as a reviewer, and

they can actually kill your chances. If somebody comes to your page with a criticism/warning, you want others to be able to see your response/side of the story. You don't want them to have to dig for the truth. ([[WP:How_to_pass _an_RfA]])

This approach has one obvious disadvantage, especially for the most active users: they are not automatically notified about replies to messages they wrote to others. Instead, they are supposed to add the talk pages of the editors they are corresponding with to their list of watched pages (often already containing tens of thousands of pages) and spot the reply when it appears. For editors who participate in many discussions, it is difficult to track all the threads. Also, when in discussions with people who have many messages from others, editors will have to search through all discussions their correspondent is in. Some editors on the English Wikipedia have dealt with this problem by notifying the recipient when they have replied in a discussion, but this is not common practice.

This difference has been the deepest culture shock I have experienced since I began editing the English Wikipedia in March 2007. I have found it annoying and unreasonable that the majority of Wikipedians on the English Wikipedia choose not to make our digital life easier by using the convenience of the new-message notification system. I gave it some consideration, and now I understand why it is used this way. The reasons are given in the essay for prospective administrator candidates: keeping discussions in one place may be at the cost of your convenience but is for the convenience of other editors who may exert social control over the discussions. Using wiki software as intended forces the community to work to find messages, since it is more difficult for uninvolved Wikipedians to follow the discussion. On the English Wikipedia, therefore, the control of flow of discourse by the community is more important than the ease of conversation between two or more editors.[4]

Using wiki software this way is symptomatic of editor relations on Wikipedia: peer control permeates all interactions, and everything we say may be used against us if we go out of line. The reason why this control is not so tight on the Polish Wikipedia is probably the result of the size of the community. The more atomized it gets and the less it relies on a semipersonal network of users whose nicknames we recognize, the more control is needed. Still, all edits are closely monitored, and many users on the Polish Wikipedia are accustomed to reading through the talk pages of all disputants to keep track of their debates.

In a similar spirit of watching the users, the Wikipedia community opposes deletion of any part of a discussion without good reason (which is a matter of debate). The Wikipedia policy against personal attacks puts it this way:

> There is no official policy regarding when or whether most personal attacks should be removed, although it has been a topic of substantial debate. Removing unquestionable personal attacks from your own user talk page is rarely a matter of concern. On other talk pages, especially where such text *is directed against you*, removal should typically be limited to clear-cut cases where it is obvious the text is a true personal attack. ([[WP:No_personal_attacks]]; emphasis in original)

In general, no alterations to other editors' comments are allowed: "Editing another editor's signed talk page comments is generally frowned upon, even if the edit merely corrects spelling or grammar" ([[WP:Etiquette]]).

The article "Avoiding Common Mistakes" lists one of the typical errors made by newcomers:

> Deleting or removing text from any Talk page without archiving it, except in your user space. Talk pages or any discussion pages are part of the historical record in Wikipedia. Every time the pages are cleaned up, don't forget to store the removed text in its corresponding archive ([[/Archive]]) page. ([[WP:Avoiding_common_mistakes]])

Similarly, the "Talk Page Guidelines" state firmly,

> *Never* edit or move someone's comment to change its meaning, *even on your own talk page*. Striking text constitutes a change in meaning, and should only be done by the user who wrote it or someone acting at their explicit request.
>
> Editing—or even removing—others' comments is sometimes allowed. But you should exercise caution in doing so, and normally stop if there is any objection. ([[WP:Talk_page_guidelines]]; emphasis in original)

The exceptions to this rule (e.g., severe personal attacks, disclosure of sensitive data, trolling, or vandalism) do not include mere incivility or occasional invectives. In 2010 on the Polish Wikipedia, within minutes of its publication I deleted a derogatory comment aimed at another editor that stated, "You should not worry about this 'Wikipedian.' Her hobby is patronizing others

and being miffed." I was hoping that the insulted Wikipedian would not
see this comment. Other administrators later criticized my action. Thirteen
months later, when my administrator recall procedure was under way, this
deletion was dug out with a demand for an explanation.

The policies on editing one's own posts are even stricter:

> It is best to avoid changing your own comments. Other users may have already
> quoted you with a diff . . . or have otherwise responded to your statement.
> Therefore, use "Show preview" and think about how your amended statement
> may look to others before you save it.
>
> Removing or substantially altering a comment after it has been replied to
> may deprive the reply of its original context. It can also be confusing. Before
> you change your own comment, consider taking one of the following steps:
> - Contact the person(s) who replied (through their talk page) and ask if it is
>   okay to delete or change your text.
> - Use deletion and insertion markup or a place-holder to show the comment
>   has been altered.
>   - Deletion, which in most browsers is rendered as struck-through text, is
>     coded <del>like this</del> and ends up ~~like this~~.
>   - An insertion, which in most browsers is rendered as underlined text, is
>     coded <ins>like that</ins> and ends up <u>like that</u>.
>   - A placeholder is a phrase such as "[Thoughtless and stupid comment
>     removed by the author.]". This will ensure that your fellow editors' ir-
>     ritated responses still make sense. In turn, they may then wish to replace
>     their reply with something like, "[Irritated response to deleted comment
>     removed. Apology accepted.]"
>   - *Please* do not apply any such changes to other editors' comments with-
>     out permission.
> - When modifying a comment, you can add a parenthetical note pointing out
>   the change. You can also add an additional timestamp by typing ~~~~~
>   (five tildes). ([[WP:Talk_page_guidelines]]; emphasis in original)

Alterations (with the possible exception of obvious spelling and punctuation mistakes) to whatever has already been posted are regarded with suspicion. This is most striking given that on many Internet fora, as well as on
Facebook, deleting one's posts is socially acceptable and so is post-factum editing, even though the editing mechanisms do not allow as perfect a version

tracking as does Wikipedia (Facebook has introduced history tracking for edited posts). Apparently, Wikipedia does not allow much leniency in retracting one's actions, or rather, it allows only later expression of discontent with what we have said by crossing our own words out but still leaving them in public, possibly to allow all readers to react to our original words in context (some editing is allowed; see [[WP:Refactoring_talk_pages]]).

## Control Through Procedures

Wikipedia culture is influenced by a hacker ethos in terms of its antielitism and dislike for hierarchies but also in its apparent disregard for formalities and organizational bureaucracy (Raymond, 1999/2004).

Common sense outweighs procedures, and users are expected to do what they believe is good for Wikipedia, using their best judgment, rather than following the letter of law:

> Instead of following every rule, it is acceptable to use common sense as you go about editing. Being too wrapped up in rules can cause loss of perspective, so there are times when it is better to ignore a rule. Even if a contribution "violates" the precise wording of a rule, it might still be a good contribution. Similarly, just because something is not forbidden in a written document, or is even explicitly permitted, doesn't mean it's a good idea in the given situation. . . . The *principle* of the rules . . . is more important than the letter. ([[WP:Common]])

A Wikipedia policy states, "If a rule prevents you from improving or maintaining Wikipedia, ignore it" ([[WP:Ignore_all_rules]]), and one of five pillars of Wikipedia insists,

> Wikipedia has policies and guidelines, but they are not carved in stone; their content and interpretation can evolve over time. Their principles and spirit matter more than their literal wording, and sometimes improving Wikipedia requires making an exception. Be bold, but not reckless, in updating articles and do not agonize about making mistakes. Every past version of a page is saved, so any mistakes can be easily corrected. ([[WP:Five_pillars]])

There is even a "rule" that instruction creep should be avoided ([[WP:Creep]]), and one of the policies, describing what Wikipedia is not, insists that Wikipedia is not a bureaucracy:

While Wikipedia has many elements of a bureaucracy, it is not governed by statute: it is not a moot court, and rules are not the purpose of the community. Written rules do not themselves set accepted practice. Rather, they document already existing community consensus regarding what should be accepted and what should be rejected.

While Wikipedia's written policies and guidelines should be taken seriously, they can be misused. Do not follow an overly strict interpretation of the *letter* of policy without consideration for the *principles* of policies. If the rules truly prevent you from improving the encyclopedia, ignore them. Disagreements are resolved through consensus-based discussion, not by tightly sticking to rules and procedures. Furthermore, policies and guidelines themselves may be changed to reflect evolving consensus.

A procedural error made in a proposal or request is not grounds for rejecting that proposal or request. ([[WP:What_Wikipedia_is_not]]; emphasis in original)

Indeed, procedural slips are not grounds for discrediting most proposals (even though such slips do matter, for example, in elections in which the validity of votes cast before the candidate's formal confirmation of agreement to participate is questioned).

Trying to use the rules in bad faith, or gaming the system, is strictly forbidden. It is assumed that

an editor gaming the system is seeking to use policies in bad faith, by finding within their wording apparent justification for disruptive actions and stances that policy is clearly not at all intended to support. In doing this, the gamester separates policies and guidelines from their rightful place as a means of documenting community consensus, and attempts to use them selectively for a personal agenda. An editor is disruptive if they are using a few words of policy to claim support for a viewpoint which clearly contradicts those policies, to attack a genuinely policy-based stance by willfully misapplying Wikipedia policies, or to detail Wikipedia processes. ([[WP:Gaming_the_system]])

Being overly clever about procedures may be considered suspicious. Behaving "like a lawyer" is unacceptable, and there is even an essay explaining why being a "wikilawyer" is bad:

A "wikilawyer" is an image drawn from a lawyer, and the term may also be used in other cases, e.g., when a person superficially judges other editors and

their actions by jumping to conclusions and slapping labels while brandish-
ing Wikipedia policies as a tool for defeating other Wikipedians rather than
resolving a conflict or finding a mutually agreeable solution.

Wikipedia policies and procedures should be interpreted with common
sense to achieve the *purpose* of the policy, or help dispute resolution. Typically,
wikilawyering raises procedural or evidentiary points in a manner analogous
to that used in formal legal proceedings, often using ill-founded legal reasoning. Occasionally wikilawyering may raise legitimate questions, including fairness, but often it serves to evade an issue or obstruct the crafting of a
workable solution. ([[WP:Wikilawyering]]; emphasis in original)

Apart from this odd aversion to lawyers, this essay emphasizes something
in which the Wikipedia community strongly believes: procedures may be im-
perfect, but editors are supposed to seek the spirit of the rules and understand and respect the reasons for policies rather than try to find loopholes.[5]
Similarly to Basque cooperatives, more importance is put on solidarity than
on equality per se (Greenwood, González Santos, & Cantón, 1991). Obviously,
this would not work in a wider society, but on Wikipedia, where both the
possible losses and gains and the scope of "punishments" are limited to the
virtual world, the primitive antilegal culture is useful, as it forces users to seek
consensus and use arguments rather than using procedural leverage.

The real problem, though, that Wikipedia is experiencing is that the everyday Wikipedia practice has long deviated from the policy of disregarding
proceduralization and formalities. As early as 2008 users complained that the
number of rules was growing from year to year (Butler, Joyce, & Pike, 2008),
and the problem has become only more acute, on both the Polish and the
English Wikipedias.

Procedures on Wikipedia are covered in principles (see "Five pillars" and
"Principles," which are to large extent shared across Wikimedia projects),
policies, guidelines, and essays. Principles are similar in most Wikimedia
projects, but policies differ more, and guidelines and essays vary quite a lot.
Most Wikimedia projects decide their own policies, but they usually use the
English Wikipedia policy set as a starting point (for instance, on the Polish
Wikipedia, most of the original policies are translated, but some have only the
status of essays, since they have not been approved by consensus).

To make matters even more confusing, although the Wikipedia community introduces some distinctions between policies, guidelines, and essays,
that difference is often blurred to a reader. For example, on the English Wiki-

pedia, the page "Wikipedia Content Policies" contains subcategories with numerous guidelines and essays related to the policies and their interpretation (see [[Category:Wikipedia_content_policies]]). The distinction is fuzzy also on the practical level. Violating some policies and guidelines in many circumstances will not bring any consequences (for instance, the verifiability policy is most likely violated many times every day), while breaking other rules in what are formally labeled as essays (such as the ones at [[WP:Tendentious _editing]]), may cause the user to be blocked.

Currently, the English Wikipedia has over fifty official policies, and there are nearly forty on the Polish one. For a volunteer organization, this amount of regulation is huge. Policies govern Wikipedia life, from how to discuss notability of books or living persons through the rules of civilized discourse, the kinds of nicknames allowed on Wikipedia, technical nuances of how access to openproxy servers (intermediary servers accessible to any Internet user) is treated, and how bots can be operated. To put this in perspective, on the English Wikipedia, as of November 2013 the word count for the official policies alone was close to 150,000 words, which is 50 percent more than that of this book.

These official policies are just the beginning. In spite of the disdain for wikilawyering, Wikipedians have a lively and growing culture of rule interpretations and renditions, in guidelines (often created through the community consensus) and essays (sometimes just one Wikipedian's reflections but other times elaborate and community-generated texts). The number of Wikipedia guidelines and essays on proper conduct on the English Wikipedia exceeds 450. Even just the 9 guidelines on working with others total 14,000 words, and the additional 20 guidelines on proper behavior on Wikipedia total 45,000 words. There are many other guidelines for notability of particular topics, rules, dispute resolution, mediation, requesting comments, blocking, or arbitration. The number of essays discussing policies and guidelines, giving advice, and analyzing the community exceeds 1,200. It is difficult to estimate the total word count for all guidelines and essays, but it must be in the millions.

Reading through all the guidelines, for a new user who wants to familiarize him- or herself with the key ones, is impossible.

## Reasons for the Bureaucracy

One reason for the growing body of rules and interpretations is obvious: as the encyclopedia develops and as it improves in quality, more rules are needed to coordinate the workflow and control the outcome of work (Stvilia, Twidale, Smith, & Gasser, 2008). Moreover, in any organization, when the number of members increases and the entrepreneurial enthusiasts are joined by people more accustomed to rules and styles of mainstream organizations, there is a tendency to bureaucratize (Greiner, 1972). It is extremely difficult to suppress, even in organizations consciously struggling to overcome proceduralization and keep their innovative spirit afloat, such as Microsoft (Arthur, 2012). Even the companies used as examples of antibureaucratic philosophy tend to slide into paperwork hell (Girard, 2009). Wikipedia's increasing bureaucracy is, in this sense, a sign of its maturity and growth, even if this normalization deprives it of its originality. However, there are other reasons for Wikipedia's need for control.

In a typical organizational setting, the purpose of bureaucratic control is to establish a hierarchy and set the grounds for managerial supervision (Braverman, 1974), which have some benefits (Du Gay, 2005; D. Jemielniak, 2010). In the contemporary world, especially in knowledge-intensive environments, this kind of control gives way to fluid organizational designs (Lewin & Stephens, 1994), and its structural aspect disappears, even though the control itself stays put (Cobb, Stephens, & Watson, 2001). This is so on Wikipedia: because of its antihierarchical, declaratively egalitarian, and somewhat antiorganizational design, as well as the contingent and chaotic nature of virtual interactions and roles, the community decided to rely more on organizational control (in the sense of reciprocal peer supervision, recording of all actions and words, and use of bureaucratic scripts and rules). In a way, the Wikipedia community returns to the premodern communal form of symmetric control by peers (Bauman, 1987/1998). Instead of appealing to authority, Wikipedians appeal to rules. This is discussed in Chapter 5. Yet one thing is clear: the lack of policy on Wikipedia is a fiction (Butler, et al., 2008). According to Sabine Niederer and José van Dijck, Wikipedia is a "gradually evolving sociotechnical system that carefully orchestrates all kinds of human and nonhuman contributors by implementing managerial hierarchies, protocols and automated editing systems" (2010, p. 1373). These procedures, like the actions of human and nonhuman (bots) contributors, determine its development at least as much as meritocratic editors and create powerful defense mechanisms, which simultaneously inhibit the retention of new editors (Geiger, Halfaker, Pinchuk, & Walling, 2012).

This bureaucracy's use of technology depends on controlling behaviors and spotting infractions. For instance, the use of semiautomated countervandalism tools often results in good-will edits being discarded simply because it is easier for an experienced editor to delete them than correct them and explain the need for doing so. As a result, new editors are squeezed between high regulation and being treated as vandals, even when making innocent mistakes. One solution, as current research suggests, is that the available technology and algorithms be employed with equal care to recognize good new editors, to reverse the unfavorable trend in editor retention (Halfaker, Geiger, Morgan, & Riedl, 2013). This solution would also undermine the layers of internal order and status enactment and reduce the number of easy edits, such as one-click reversions of edits not fully adhering to the standards.

This phenomenon is taking place also because beyond any doubt, the bureaucratization of the Wikipedia community raises, even if not in a planned way, entry barriers for new users by making status and community standing easier to recognize. In the absence of traditional hierarchy, and with the importance of quasi-hierarchical official community roles kept to a minimum, the number of rules allows Wikipedians to be easily stratified. Most organizations develop oligarchies, which eventually take control, according to the iron law of oligarchy, and Wikipedia is no exception (Konieczny, 2009a). While displays of technical skills and of understanding wiki code and getting symbolic rewards such as barnstars are an important part of community status enactment, so is showing an understanding of Wikipedia rules and referring to them in regular conversations. "The discussion pages also work to discursively discipline new or dissenting contributors. It is in these spaces that undesirables are 'sorted out'" (Tkacz, 2010, p. 50). After all, bureaucratic control helps in justifying the dehumanization of certain categories of people, through creating pseudorational, linear scripts of behavior (Bauman, 1989/2000; Burrell, 1997).

E. Gabriella Coleman's description of hackers can be equally applied to Wikipedians:

> Much in the same way that a guild artisan learned and followed the techniques cultivated by their guild, a hacker enters a world of standardized conventions and preferences and unique social organization when volunteering on a free software project. (2001, p. 29)

Newcomers need to prove their usefulness to a Wikipedia but also, through an apprenticeship of a sort, show that they have acquired the knowledge of customs, rituals, and rules. Unregistered, anonymous editors contribute as much as one-quarter of the content, but they create only one-twentieth of the regulations, which sometimes is a political exercise in itself (Aaltonen & Lanzara, 2010). Because the majority of rules were established before 2007 (also the year the decline in editor retention and RfAs began on the English Wikipedia), for all incomers they form a given, large, and inert set. The creation and modification of behavior-related guidelines has significantly slowed down since (Forte, Larco, & Bruckman, 2009). The status quo violates E. Ostrom's third principle of stable common-pool resource management, which requires "collective-choice arrangements that allow most resource appropriators to participate in the decision-making process" (1990, p. 90).[6] This situation is especially damaging to newcomers, who are more vulnerable to regulation, treat it as more stable than the veterans, and are incapable of changing it in any significant way (Halfaker et al., 2013) and who also perceive the bureaucratic nature of regulation of Wikipedia work as a problem, "thwarting anarchic ideas" of the community (Muller-Seitz & Reger, 2010, p. 469). As Andrew Lih observes,

> With the slow morphing of policy to be more restrictive, and the challenge of editing more complex pages and simply scaling up from hundreds to millions of users, the Wikipedia community might be like the frog slowly boiling to death—unaware of the building crisis, because it is not aware how much its environment has slowly changed. (2009, p. 222)

Experienced editors often use cryptic abbreviations in discussions, along with Wikipedia slang. Phrases such as "fails to meet WP:GNG," "out per snowball," "fails WP:N," or "SD—copyvio" are immediately clear to experienced Wikipedians but intimidate newcomers and enforce a pecking order of informal parahierarchy, based on the understanding of Wikipedia rules. As Mathieu O'Neil points out, "Means of domination are not limited to the crude use of blocking tools. In fact, such measures are less effective than more subtle means relying on superior project knowledge" (2011, p. 318). Even though Wikipedia lingo is picked up by editors who persevere (Beschastnikh, Kriplean, & McDonald, 2008), this may indicate just that they recognize the social norm and importance of using the lingo and not give insight into how much proceduralization deterred those who left Wikipedia after trying to edit it. As a result, to some extent,

> Wikipedia has changed from the encyclopedia that anyone can edit to the encyclopedia that anyone who understands the norms, socializes him or

herself, dodges the impersonal wall of semi-automated rejection and still wants to voluntarily contribute his or her time and energy can edit. (Halfaker et al., 2013, p. 683)

Additionally, the redundancy of the rules and their excess allows for a more flexible mediation of desired actions. Since there are many policies and guidelines, the ability to navigate them adds a layer of expertise for all Wikipedia veterans. At the same time this variety supports consensus seeking, since (much as in Talmudic interpretations) in meanders of rules, the process of debating their application becomes more important than their letter. As Travis Kriplean and colleagues observe:

> Contributors may interpret a situation differently and draw on different policies to substantiate their views. A precise rule may not even exist. In this ambiguity, we find many examples of complex power plays that contributors make to control content and coerce others during the consensus process. At the same time, the ambiguity of the consensus process and its shared language, the policy environment, draws the community together. (2007, p. 167)

The accumulation of policies and rules increases the practical organizational standing of the administrators, since they effectively become their interpreters, judges, and executioners at the same time (O'Neil, 2009). In this light it may not be surprising that rules are rarely invoked in article content disputes (Goldspink, 2010): their purpose is not functionally normative but symbolic, as it stratifies Wikipedians on the basis of their command of norms and by its very existence increases the imbalance of power between the veterans and newbies.

The Wikipedia community is characterized by what Ostrom refers to as *radical autonomy* (1990), as it operates with few external rules and rigorous internal control of member behavior. It operates in what Jonah Bossewitch and Aram Sinnreich call an "information flux" (2013, p. 224), a perpetual Foucauldian Panopticon of observing each other combined with "the end of forgetting," an era of recording and storing everything, quite typical for many online communities (Albrechtslund, 2008). All interactions are conducted under the assumption that they may be controlled by the peer public and clearly differ from regular conversations (Laniado, Tasso, Volkovich, & Kaltenbrunner, 2011). The Wikipedia interface also encourages surveillance of others' contributions (Bryant, Forte, & Bruckman, 2005). In the words of a Wikipedia critic, "It's important to keep in mind that while it's hyped as a quasi-mystical collective endeavour which spins straw into gold, in reality it's a poorly-run bureaucracy with the group dynamics of a cult" (Finkelstein, 2008).

Thus, that ahierarchical: Wikipedia, in spite of its egalitarian, freedom-oriented, and ahierarchical approach, uses extraordinarily tight bureaucratic control (by tracking everything anyone ever writes or edits and through insane and constantly growing amounts of rules) should not be surprising. The collectivist organization may be perceived as an alternative to bureaucratization (Rothschild-Whitt, 1979), which open-collaboration communities often take pride in avoiding (Fuggetta, 2003), and is understood as an interesting alternative to growing power asymmetry and vertical control that is typical for modern organizations (Bauman, 1987/1998). In practice Wikipedia relies on some forms of collectivist organization (De Laat, 2007; Holck & Jørgensen, 2007).

However, in one area Wikipedia control is surprisingly slack: identity checks and real-world credentials. This phenomenon is related to the enactment of trust and the way the Wikipedia community replaces interpersonal and organizational trust and credential control with trust in bureaucratic procedures. This is the topic of the next chapter.

# 5

## TRUST IN PEOPLE AND TRUST
## IN PROCEDURES

### The Truth Is Out There

The previous chapter describes the sweeping sense of organizational control that Wikipedia editors experience and the Panopticon of peer supervision felt at every stage of work on Wikipedia. The study of organizational control leads us to yet another atypical phenomenon of this open-collaboration community: its construction of interpersonal trust and credentials. This is particularly important, since even though Wikipedia is a community controlling every possible behavior very tightly, it rejects the idea of credential checking, as this chapter shows. How can a community that is so strict in terms of procedures and rules be so lax in terms of identity verification? This seemingly contradictory approach is rooted in the community's notions of trust in general and the relations between the editors' created online personae and their real identities in particular. The Wikipedia community does not care much about true identities or credentials for a reason: the possibility of building one's credibility only within the community, irrespective of real-world status, encourages nonexperts to participate. However, this process naturally results in lower interpersonal trust, which the community addresses by substituting trust in people with trust in procedures. Over the course of this chapter, we see these tradeoffs in action through the case study of a major scandal, a well-known Wikipedian claiming to be a professor and turning out to be an impostor.

Trust has been a common topic of organization studies on both the interorganizational level (Newell & Swan, 2000; Hoffmann, Neumann, & Speckbacher, 2010) and the intraorganizational level (Gambetta, 1988; Thau,

Crossley, Bennett, & Sczesny, 2007; McEvily, 2011). The profound influence of new technologies on trust relations has also been a topic for considerable academic speculation and investigation (English-Lueck, Darrah, & Saveri, 2002; Latusek & Jemielniak, 2007; Latusek & Gerbasi, 2010) in the open-source environment (Ciesielska & Iskoujina, 2012) and in nonvirtual distributed work (O'Leary, Orlikowski, & Yates, 2002).

The issue of trust is particularly important in the new knowledge society and its virtual environments, which present challenges for both trust and control (Knights, Noble, Vurdubakis, & Willmott, 2001). For obvious technological reasons and in lack of regular face-to-face interactions, identity enactment, trust creation, and manner of credential checks differ significantly from traditional organizational environments (Oxley, Morgan, Zachry, & Hutchinson, 2010; Green & Carpenter, 2011).

Identity, trust, and credentials are of particular concern in open-source community environments, where participation is voluntary, incentives or punishments are limited, membership dispersed, and identities only virtual (as discussed in earlier chapters). Trust enactment on Wikipedia, in particular in the context of credential checks, has not been a subject of a major academic analysis. In this chapter I address trust enactment, since it is vitally important for understanding how previously discussed issues of power relations, hierarchy, control, and management work in this online community. The analysis of trust is also a starting point in the later discussion on Wikipedia leadership and governance.

## Trust and Open-Source Communities

The development and social production of knowledge requires cooperative relationships within organizations. However, these relationships are hampered by the dominant assumption that people are mainly motivated by self-interest (Nahapiet, Gratton, & Rocha, 2005) and may not necessarily engage in activities that bring them no material gain or reward over the long term. The collaboration typical for open-source communities proves this assumption to be false, however, as many people are willing to cooperate and contribute without material benefits and able to successfully develop products and ideas that compete with their commercial counterparts on equal grounds (Benkler, 2006b). Examples of such successful endeavors have been discussed in previous chapters. As pointed out, Wikipedia differs significantly from other large open-collaboration communities in the sense that it is composed mostly of nonprofessional authors (as opposed to free/libre-and-open-source-software, or F/LOSS, projects created by professional software engineers). While contributors can, and often do, leverage their participation in the F/LOSS movement to advance their careers, on Wikipedia it is practically impossible: writing encyclopedic articles is not a profession one could specialize or prove skills in. Thus, even though Wikipedians represent all kinds of professions, virtually none of them have professional experience in encyclopedia development, and their motivations to contribute are not job related. Open-collaboration organizations seem to rely on a hope of a collective good, a hope that is used as a method, rather than just faith (Miyazaki, 2006).

While there have been many studies on the trustworthiness of Wikipedia articles (Dondio, Barrett, Weber, & Seigneur, 2006; Kwan & Ramachandran, 2009; Sundin, 2011), the mechanism of trust and credential creation within the Wikipedia editor community has rarely been a subject of serious academic inquiry (Krupa, Vercouter, Hübner, & Herzig, 2009). Other studies indicate, however, that online communities with no offline interaction among their members (which, in most cases, applies to Wikipedians) enact trust differently from groups with face-to-face contacts (Matzat, 2010). When this lack of traditional credential verification is taken into account, Wikipedia becomes a particularly interesting topic for the study of trust enactment. Also, as we have already established, Wikipedia is a model example of an organization that relies on empowerment, a flat structure, and decentralized authority; in such an environment, trust unavoidably plays a crucial role (Jones & George, 1998; De Jong & Elfring, 2010). Previous chapters addressed power and status enactment within the community and organizational control; understanding how sustaining it is possible in an organization so dispersed and virtual requires a more detailed look at how credentials and trust are addressed on Wikipedia.

Deborah G. Johnson (1997) argues that in our contemporary society credentials have become more important in the enactment of trust than have personal identity and relationship status. She sees the lack of confirmed credentials in the online environment as a major obstacle to regular and effective social activities. Similarly, according to other authors, the lack of transparency in terms of revealing Wikipedia contributor identity also calls into question the validity of the outcome—that is, article content (Waters, 2007). Adele Santana and Donna J. Wood, when criticizing Wikipedia, even make the melodramatic point that "the anonymous production and use of information prevents human users from achieving the deepest possible meanings in life, and violates as well the ethical principle of integrity of information. In addition, anonymous providers need not exercise moral responsibility for there is no accountability" (2009, p. 143). I believe this statement is not only flawed (considering both the popularity and proven quality of Wikipedia) but also testifies to the authors' ignorance of the Wikipedia community and human relations involved in its communication of knowledge. Yet the authors do have a point—namely, that quasi-anonymous online communities do need to address the problem of accountability in their own way. Thus, it is vital for organization studies to examine and understand and perhaps define the mechanisms of trust and credential control in the new world environment that is now often deprived of typical incentives, punishments, and hierarchies but allows much more fluid, even obscured, identities. Open-collaboration projects are growing in popularity and becoming a great part of mainstream organizational design (Neus & Scherf, 2005).

In Internet environments especially, strong assurance control systems are often portrayed as a solution to the nagging problem of trust (Cheshire, 2011). Identity and credential verification provide a threshold or gate check, as it were, so that interpersonal trust is not needed later. As I show in this chapter, this scenario is not the case for Wikipedia. The community has undergone some trust crises, but it decided against introducing a tighter system of credential verification. It has seemed however, to substitute for the typical trust-credentials control functions by adding bureaucratic scripts. In other words, the community discarded the idea of increasing control or credential checks and of trusting users in favor of trusting organizational routines and processes instead (in particular, in the case of Wikipedia, these include behavioral guidelines, essays, and policies and the technologies and norms of dispute resolution). A Wikipedia crisis of interpersonal trust was resolved by means of strong institutional trust and organizational paralegalistic remedies, which in traditional, nonvirtual organizations would often increase and deepen interpersonal distrust (Sitkin & Roth, 1993).

This chapter examines the community of Wikipedia and its approach to trust and credentials through a step-by-step analysis of one of the largest crises in both trust and virtual identity that the community experienced (the so-called Essjay controversy) and the internal debates within the community that followed it. The chapter analyzes relevant discussion, talk, and comment pages (a total of roughly five hundred thousand words of field material).

The 2007 scandal shook Wikipedia's community and was widely commented on in the media (entering "Essjay controversy" in the Google search engine still brings over 34,500 hits). The scandal resulted in several lengthy internal discussions and debates on editor trust and credibility. While the event is now long passed and the scandal quite gone, it is worthwhile to interpret the reaction and decisions of the community related to it, since they reveal several social mechanisms and basic assumptions regarding Wikipedia. This case has also been mentioned in several academic publications (Bruns, 2008; Lih, 2009) but has not been a subject of detailed analysis, in particular from an organizational point of view, which might shed light on the enactment of trust and credentials in the online community context.

## The Essjay Controversy

Someone calling himself Essjay started to edit Wikipedia in 2005. From the beginning, he claimed on his user page that he was a tenured professor of religion, with doctorates in theology and canon law and other degrees in his field, and that he taught theology to undergraduate and graduate students at a private university in the United States. He was indeed quite active in the articles on religion, and in just five months he earned enough respect from the community to became an administrator (with tremendous support, over 98 percent of voters). He then increased his engagement in Wikipedia and was active in the community, mediating conflicts, fighting vandals, and doing well what any administrator does. This success led to his being elected a bureaucrat and a checkuser (a member of the Wikipedian elite who is trusted to check sensitive information about other users' IP addresses) and becoming the chair of the Mediation Committee.

He was such a dedicated and efficient editor, a paragon of Wikipedia's collaboration with the academic world, that he was invited in July 2006 to participate in an interview for the *New Yorker* (Schiff, 2006), via a recommendation from the Wikimedia Foundation. His experience on Wikipedia was wide enough to help him get hired by Wikia (a commercial company offering wiki-based hosting solutions, also created by Jimmy Wales, the cofounder of Wikipedia) in January 2007. Soon after, the scandal broke: Daniel Brandt, a social activist dedicated to exposing misconduct on Wikipedia (and harshly criticizing Wikipedia, in ways that sometimes bordered on conspiracy theories), discovered that Essjay was not who he said he was. Brandt wrote to the *New Yorker* and posted his suspicions on his website.

As it turned out, upon achieving employment at Wikia, Essjay had published an online biographical note on the company's website in which he admitted to being a twenty-four-year-old former paralegal clerk and an account manager for a Fortune Twenty company (a statement that many also doubted later). When some of the Wikipedia editors saw the discrepancy between this note and the one posted on Wikipedia, they expressed doubts about his identity. In early February, he admitted creating a false persona but said he did it for security reasons:

> One of the things that tends to happen as you become, let us say, "popular" on Wikipedia is that you attract the attention of an unsavory element. There are a number of trolls, stalkers, and psychopaths who wander around Wikipedia and the other Wikimedia projects looking for people to harass, stalk, and otherwise ruin the lives of (several have been arrested over their activities here). . . . Many people have tried many things to keep their identities secret: They worry over every little detail they may have released, or refuse to answer anything about themselves, making it very difficult to form any personal ties. Quite unfortunately, it simply isn't possible to keep your details quiet: You will eventually say something that will lead back to you, and the stalkers will find it. My approach was different: I decided to be myself, to never hide my personality, to always be who I am, but to utilize disinformation with regard to what I consider unimportant details: age, location, occupation, etc. . . . I was actually under the impression that the stalkers and psychopaths were the only people who actually believed the story; a quick examination of the time I've spent here should lead to the conclusion that there's no way I could be who the statistics said I was. . . . Essjay 06:07, 2 February 2007 (UTC).[1]

This explanation was sufficient for many editors. That Daniel Brandt had a record of attacking Wikipedia and stalking and exposing the real identity of some administrators worked in Essjay's favor; he seemed to be the target of malicious attacks, and it seemed reasonable to protect his identity. Later, Essjay confessed that he was subjected to weekly death threats, torture monologues, and legal threats, which won him additional sympathy. In my roles on Wikipedia, I also was threatened a couple of times (I do not believe the number of death threats that Essjay reported). In my view, many other Wikipedia activists related to and sympathized with the situation that Essjay described.

Possibly to show solidarity with this singled-out Wikipedian, on February 23, 2007, Wales nominated Essjay to the Arbitration Committee, a highly prestigious body that is responsible for resolving conflicts and disputes in the community and has high decision powers. A couple of days later, the *New Yorker* published an update to its earlier article, clarifying that Essjay had misled the interviewer about his credentials. The update also quoted Wales, who said he did not regard the situation as problematic and insisted on Essjay's right to use a pseudonym. This rendering immediately led to a discussion on Wales's talk page, simultaneous to the one appearing on Essjay's. Various editors now were accusing Essjay of serious misconduct and lying.

However, Essjay still had his defenders. An example of a supportive comment on his talk page reads, "Just wanted to express my 100% support for everything you do around here. I think you were totally entitled to protect your identity. Don't let all the fuss get you down! WjBscribe 16:49, 1 March 2007 (UTC)."[2] The point of view of the defenders is summed up by a comment from a different administrator (also a checkuser) on Wales's talk page:

> Since qualifications don't matter here, who cares? WP:V and WP:RS are required both from PhDs and junior high kids if they're editing articles. As far as personal integrity is concerned, in cyberspace, nobody knows you're a dog; people make up personae right and left around here. —jpgordon 21:36, 28 February 2007 (UTC). ([[User_talk:Jimbo_Wales/Archive_19]])

"WP:V and WP:RS" refer to Wikipedia's policies on verifiable and reliable sources, both fundamental principles that apply to all Wikipedia articles. They determine precisely what kinds of statements and references are allowed and are meant to eliminate editors' original research and opinions. The user basically made the point that, since all information has to be verifiable and based on trustworthy materials, it does not matter what credentials editors claim. He also pointed out that online identities are not particularly trustworthy anyway ("nobody knows you're a dog") and that creating virtual identities is a common practice on Wikipedia.

But the tide started to change. Wales was reported as accepting Essjay's apology and considering the whole matter settled (Cohen, 2007), but he was not able to fully participate in the debate because he was traveling in Asia and had limited Internet access (which likely limited his ability to delve into the issue in detail). One of the other administrators and bureaucrats succinctly declared on Wales's talk page what many others had expressed:

> We enjoy our fantasy of an exclusively merit-based system, but it really is nothing more than a fantasy. If someone says he has a Ph.D., no amount of protesting the egalitarianism of the project will change the effect this claim has on other editors' opinions of him (or, in this case, the opinions of the New Yorker's readership, who are doubtless accustomed to put much stock by advanced degrees). He could easily have chosen a set of fake characteristics which did not carry such strong preconceptions if he wished to be anonymous. He has introduced a biasing factor—I cannot say whether it was deliberate, but we cannot pretend it has no effect. —Dan 21:45, 28 February 2007 (UTC). ([[User_talk:Jimbo_Wales/Archive_19]])

In the wake of a scandal now gone public, many editors started to look more closely into Essjay's editing history and did not like what they found. For example, in one of his early edits, he insisted on using *Catholicism for Dummies* as a source, writing, "This is a text I often require for my students, and I would hang my own Ph.D. on its credibility" (see [[Essjay_controversy]]). In another discussion, he referred to his personal experience as a monk to validate a point he was making about Psalms. He claimed he had been the head of his department and that he wrote a letter to a few other professors in which he explicitly represented himself as "a tenured professor of theology" (see [[Essjay_controversy]]). On the basis of these credentials, he was referred to as "one of Wikipedia's foremost experts on Catholicism," a comment that he was happy to quote himself when offering his advice in disputes (see [[User:Essjay/RFC]]). On several occasions he used his faked credentials to add weight to specific disputes on Wikipedia.

Many Wikipedians expressed disappointment with Essjay's conduct. The "Request for Comment" page dedicated to the case contained nearly forty thousand words of different opinions, statements, and views. While some supported Essjay's right to create a fake identity, the vast majority were critical and occasionally even hostile (a fact also pointed out by Wikipedians appealing for more civility).

Among the many disappointed editors, Erik Möller, a member of the Wikimedia Foundation board of trustees, urged Essjay (on Essjay's talk page) to step down:

Creating a pseudonym is one thing. Creating an elaborate fake persona with fake credentials, and using it in arguments, letters, and interviews is another. I am deeply troubled by this behavior, consider it highly unethical, and would like to ask you to seriously consider stepping down from your official Wikimedia roles. At the very least, I believe you owe the community an apology for this behavior. You have damaged both the reputation of the project, and your own. I am deeply saddened and disappointed. —Eloquence 22:13, 1 March 2007 (UTC).[3]

Finally, Wales posted a statement (after archiving his talk page, so that the statement would be immediately visible at the top), and he explained,

I only learned this morning that EssJay used his false credentials in content disputes. I understood this to be primarily the matter of a pseudonymous identity (something very mild and completely understandable given the personal dangers possible on the Internet) and not a matter of violation of people's trust. I want to make it perfectly clear that my past support of EssJay in this matter was fully based on a lack of knowledge about what has been going on. . . . —Jimbo Wales 06:42, 3 March 2007 (UTC). ([[User_talk:Jimbo_Wales/Archive_20]])

He also asked Essjay to resign his positions on Wikipedia. On the very same day, Essjay decided to do just that, deleted his talk page, and left.

## What Did Essjay Do Wrong?

While for the rest of the world, Essjay's wrongdoing was one of creating fake credentials, it seems that for a huge majority of Wikipedians, such wrongdoing was not a problem at all. This view may be related to the fact that many people come to edit on Wikipedia to gain the status and authority they lack in regular life (Jemielniak & Gorbatai, 2012). Since creating an alter ego is a widely accepted behavior in online communities (Bailenson & Beall, 2006; Boellstorff, 2008) and since the Wikipedia user page is considered to be one's private turf and is less regulated, even though creating a totally fictional profile is not widely condoned, it is not frowned on either.

Also, privacy is a serious concern. As mentioned before, many administrators are subject to different kinds of threats. Even editors sometimes fall victim to stalkers or occasionally are targeted by deranged people because of their work on Wikipedia (Shankbone, 2007). According to the *Wikipedia*

*Editors Study* (Wikimedia Foundation, 2011a) 24 percent of surveyed editors believed other editors harassed them on Wikipedia, and 5 percent were harassed outside Wikipedia (including via phone calls, social networks, and e-mails). I was cyberstalked and bullied by a person who did not like the content of his biographical article on Wikipedia, to the extent that he (a martial arts instructor, with a history of violent behavior and a legendary persistence in suing everybody he considered his enemy, including Internet disputants) tried to find where I lived and also tried to contact my employer with his delusional accusations. After this incident, I removed all identifying data from my Wikipedia pages, but I know of several similar incidents involving other administrators. Unsurprisingly, Internet trolls and frustrated everyday freaks with aspirations to garnering encyclopedic fame often end up interacting with the administrators. Some people are less able to deal with it than others.

In light of this, Essjay's first reply resonated with the community with respect to identity protection, which is perceived as a fundamental right. Essjay's initial explanation was perfectly legitimate. After all, he changed several facts about his occupation, age, and so on, only to make it more difficult for stalkers to find him. When his masquerade was revealed by somebody considered hostile toward Wikipedia in general and selected administrators in particular, it is not surprising that the community, including some influential figures, supported Essjay in the beginning.

For Wikipedians, the problem with what Essjay did was not that he created a false persona. What infuriated many members of the community was that he referred to his fake credentials in discussions, inflating his arguments and adding weight to his point of view in interactions, which by design were meant to be meritocratic and not based on formal authority. Wikipedia guidelines clearly state that edits have to stand (or fall) on their own merit. Thus, even using one's true credentials in a discussion may display bad manners (an editor is supposed to clearly present arguments as his or her own, rather than trump a disputant's comments with a reference to a diploma or degree).

With assuming good faith being one of the fundamental guidelines on Wikipedia and in recognition of Essjay's position of power, most of his disputants thought they indeed had to be mistaken when Essjay disagreed with them in articles in his fake specialization area. This use of a fake persona created a feeling of major trust violation. Indeed, Essjay's use of fake credentials quite likely persuaded other editors not to perform reference checks, since they simply trusted his professional judgment.

## The Post-Essjay Disputes

Wales, who initially declared himself anticredentialist (possibly because of the failure of Wikipedia's predecessor, Nupedia, which was intended to be developed by experts, but turned out to be a flop), announced to Associated Press in March 2007 that Wikipedia would start requiring contributors claiming higher credentials to identify themselves (Read, 2007). It seemed that this issue of credentialing and use of personae had been finally decided.

However, Wikipedia relies on a participatory design and draws heavily from shop-floor democracy roots (Rayton, 1972; Greenwood, González Santos, & Cantón, 1991), and a decision had to be made by the community itself and not by any of its representatives. Although appalled by Essjay's conduct, the community remained reluctant to accept Wales's proposal.

On March 7, 2007, Wales proposed simply that credential verification could rely on other Wikipedian testimonies and be completely voluntary (applying only to users who wanted their credentials checked). A fierce debate in the community lasted about two weeks and produced over 130,000 words. The vast majority of commentators considered credential verification a horrible idea. They were afraid it "[would] become a bragging rite" (JoeSmack), and that "it [would] make[] a class of privileged editors, which was totally against the spirit of Wikipedia. Issues should be solved using cited, verifiable facts, not credentials" (pschemp) (see [[User_talk:Jimbo_Wales/Credential _Verification/Archive_1]]). Many users pointed out that Wikipedia policies and guidelines (requiring, among other things, verifiability, reliable sources, and no original research) made the problem of credentials irrelevant. Also, they insisted that introducing official credential verification would allow users with formal qualifications to gain the upper hand in disputes, when in normal meritocratic circumstances they would not have such a high standing. In general, a visible majority believed that existing policies already regulated discussions and adequately allowed argumentative practices and that allowing the use of credentials and credential verification would disturb the system by both weakening meritocratic discussion and stratifying users.

There were other minor concerns, such as the possibility of faking the credentials and the indispensable right to remain anonymous. Some editors saw the proposal as an opportunity to attract more experts to Wikipedia (a long-standing concern), but they were criticized, occasionally even with slightly hostile comments: "There we go. 'stewardship.' Appeal to authority already, and this hasn't even been implemented yet" (Corvus cornix) (see [[User_talk:Jimbo_Wales/Credential_Verification/Archive_2]]).

On March 14, 2007, one of the disputants, Netesq, created an alternative proposal—namely, to ignore all credentials. As he explained,

> The idea of verifying credentials on Wikipedia is a bad one, and THERE SHOULD BE A POLICY in place stating that any information which people choose to set forth on their Wikipedia user pages is inherently unreliable and *NOT* subject to any sort of verification. ([[User_talk:Jimbo_Wales/ Credential_Verification/Archive_3]])

This proposal gained some interest and even support from Wales himself, who commented,

> I would support the elevation of that to a more fundamental position of re-spect within the community. I actually suspect that the problem of people inappropriately relying on credentials in an argument is much more likely in cases where people are faking the credentials. Actual PhDs are not normally pompous jerks; they are actually well trained intellectuals who have devoted themselves to a life of rational discussion and debate, and they know quite well that "I have PhD so STFU" is not a valid argument. It's the fake PhDs who are likely to try that nonsense. Jimbo Wales 07:19, 16 March 2007 ([[User _talk:Netesq#Ignore_all_credentials]])

However, this solution, too, was contested. Wikipedians made the point that Wikipedia already suffers from low expert retention and that emphasiz-ing that credentials would have no value on Wikipedia did not exactly help. In about eight thousand words the disputants continued to deliberate the pros and cons of the proposed solution. Around the same time, one of the admin-istrators (WikiLeon) created an essay explaining that "credentials are irrele-vant." A discussion on this essay took up seventeen thousand words, generally repeating the arguments for the other two proposals. It was clear a consensus would be difficult to reach. A couple of other proposals emerged in the mean-time, including a full credentials ban.

Finally, a poll was organized to make a decision, and the community flatly rejected the idea of credential verification. Wales's proposal received only five votes in favor and twenty-nine against. Other proposals to regulate (or ban) credentials were also refused. The vote indicated the community's desire to stay with the status quo, in which credentials could be listed but would not be officially confirmed and so should be always treated with caution and not taken into account in meritocratic discussions.

One of the few stable results that emerged from the Essjay case was the creation of an information page (with a poll showing fourteen in favor and thirteen against) on the communal consensus about the rules of conduct for an honest Wikipedian. That page states,

> *Honesty* is expected in all processes of Wikipedia, including content discussion, the dispute process and all other functions of the community. . . . An honest Wikipedian *does not* intentionally misrepresent their identity or credentials. The choice of anonymity and pseudonymity is part of Wikipedia, but it is not a license to fabricate real world credentials. It is strongly recommended that you decline to share details you wish to keep secret rather than to invent alternatives. Fabrication of credentials will lose an editor his or her credibility and damage the credibility of the project as a whole. ([[WP:Honesty]]; emphasis in original)

## Trust and Credentials Control

Trust has often been portrayed as reciprocal in nature; it is built (or destroyed) in a mutual relationship (Fox, 1974). However, more recent publications show that the process may be asymmetrical (Schoorman, Mayer, & Davis, 2007); trust in someone does not necessarily invoke trust from that someone. In the case of Wikipedia, trust in another editor is often asymmetrical and can be reduced to the expectation that the other editor argues with good faith and in the honest belief that his or her reasoning is valid.

The norm of reciprocity indeed is in and of itself a trust-building mechanism and may be perceived as seminal to both social group and group norm formation (Gouldner, 1960). One important difference shown by the regular social context on Wikipedia is that interpersonal trust is built from scratch through online interactions and article editing with no stigmas present (Goffman, 1963) that relate to dress code, appearance, social class, gender, or race (since editors have the liberty to represent themselves freely in this respect), although it is likely that they have other stigmas related to text (vocabulary, punctuation, grammar, etc.).

Personae in online communities are liquid, typical for the "age of uncertainty" (Bauman, 2005, 2007). Virtual identities can be created easily on

Wikipedia, and this ease makes Wikipedia, along with other online communities, particularly attractive for users who are seeking the chance to interact without the usual stigmas they have previously displayed. Additionally, any unblocked editor has the right to leave and come back under a different name or persona (see [[WP:Clean_start]]), which makes the creation of identities potentially transient and also temporary (but the more an editor edits, the more his or her identity becomes stable, since the edits build up trust and standing for a single particular identity, and this investment is of course nontransferable to a new identity).

Curiously though, creating a couple of different accounts and identities and using them simultaneously (called "sock-puppetry"), especially if done to create an illusion of independent support, is considered to be one of the most serious crimes a Wikipedian can commit and often results in a lifetime ban, at least for the alternative accounts. The act also disqualifies an editor from community service roles (Welham & Lakhan, 2009). Even if the edits are relatively innocent, editing from two or more different virtual identities is considered fraudulent, much more so than just inventing a single online persona. This view is so because within the community the virtual identity is the only one that should matter. One can create any identity representation one chooses but should not use more than one identity at a time. There is, of course, also a practical side to the issue; a person operating multiple avatars could create an illusion of support for his or her ideas and generate extra votes in a cause and thus falsely inflate a discursive argument.

In this online community, a world where everybody can easily create a fake persona and where everybody can (and is allowed to) choose or change the presentation of self, trust can be earned only through actual participation in Wikipedia and a history of edits and interactions. Such capital is definitely required for any elected functions. As Shun Ling Chen observes, "Although Wikipedia permits users to edit without a user name, editing with a consistent identity—either real name or pseudonym—is an important factor when one wishes to participate in the internal governance structure of the community" (2010, p. 272). Considering the sheer size of all Wikipedias (250,000 accounts created every month, three hundred thousand editors making changes every month, five thousand editors making more than one hundred edits every month, more than seven hundred active administrators, etc.), for most members of this community it is impossible to employ more sophisticated trust-evaluation strategies. Thus, interpersonal trust, in theory, should be replaced by credential checks.

In some online communities, a so-called swift trust serves as a useful surrogate. Debra Meyerson and Karl E. Weick (1996) introduced this notion to describe a phenomenon that is typical for virtual teams formed around a common project, clear tasks, and a defined project life span. Team members suspend their doubts about others while reasonably expecting beneficial outcomes for the project and stability within the team (most if not all people should remain part of the team). This process quite understandably cannot emerge on Wikipedia. It is useful, therefore, to consider why credentials are not considered useful in this community.

External credentials on Wikipedia are much less useful than in other online communities of practice oriented toward knowledge generation. In fact, in this respect Wikipedia resembles much more an online game system or a public forum: users are allowed to introduce themselves any way they want. While credential control systems are believed to be a common answer to the problem of low trust in most Internet interactions (as observed and critiqued by C. Cheshire, 2011), the case of Wikipedia clearly proves this speculation at least partially wrong. Even during its most extreme trust crisis, the community firmly rejected the idea of credential verification. I believe this view ruled because one of the fundamental assumptions of the Wikipedia community is that it provides a clean slate for all participants. This focus is an embodiment of the form of citizen participation (Arnstein, 1969) the community believes in; everybody is on equal grounds with everybody else. Status and trust have to be earned within the community, and attempts at shortcuts (such as leveraging one's high social standing outside the community) are generally discouraged. Thus, digital have-nots and pariahs (because of their true or alleged misbehaviors or social maladjustment) can get a new identity and start all over.

Control, in the sense of credential assurance, is thus nonexistent, and even such public relations disasters as the Essjay incident do not justify changing the status quo. Similarly, the forms of control that are speculated to emerge in ahierarchical organizational designs, such as technocratic control (Burris, 1989) and having expertise (and, partly, professional credentials), are significantly reduced or even become nonexistent on Wikipedia, because of the basic rejection of credential checks. This, however, is in clear contrast to the general approach to control on Wikipedia described in the previous chapter, which relies on many bureaucratic rules and recording of everything any user ever said or did. Overall, the scope of credential verification on Wikipedia seems narrow, just as it is in the case of trust, and credential verification is strikingly different from control requirements generally introduced on Wikipedia.

## Trust in Procedures

Active participation on Wikipedia helps build a local (intracommunity) identity, status, and reputation (Anthony, Smith, & Williamson, 2007). Relinquishing the means of control (such as assurance, credential checks, hierarchical control) and accepting the low-trust environment (anybody can present himself any way he wants; trust is developed locally and has a fluid nature), apart from its obvious disadvantages, produces significant organizational benefits.

Rejecting credential control allows full democratic participation by different people with different backgrounds. Paradoxically, since credentials are not checked, claiming expertise is an empty gesture, as all arguments still have to make valid points to be considered. However, making a point valid according to Wikipedia standards is not something everybody is born to do. The amount of formalized rules, described in the previous chapter, is astonishing and still growing. Apparently, trust or credential control is substituted with precise behavioral scripts and formalization of discussion rules.

While Essjay's case showed that the Wikipedia community is prone to crises of trust in the ranks of its contributors, it also proved that more formal rules of discussion, dispute resolution, and decision making can provide a necessary alternative to the introduction of tighter credentials checks. Thus, legalistic remedies, often perceived as ineffective substitutes for trust in organizations (Granovetter, 1985; Sitkin & Roth, 1993), worked in a democratic, participative online environment.

Clear article-editing rules do allow for nonexpert administrators to exercise judgment in meritocratic disputes. Wikipedia has successfully reduced the problem of truth to the problem of sources. In the same way, it has reduced the problem of credentials and low trust to the problem of following the rules of editor behavior and proper discussion (see Chapter 3 for how they work in everyday practice). Thanks to the creation of such precise and elaborate guidelines, requiring well-grounded points of view from all disputants, Wikipedia is probably one of the few communities in the world where a teenager can win a meritocratic debate with a person holding a PhD in the field (Kapiszewski, 2011). That knowing all the guidelines and rules is not mandatory also adds flexibility to discussions as long as beginners make a point that is valid in the eyes of others; not adhering to the letter of the rules is not a problem. Not following guidelines is a powerful formal argument, however, that experienced users may call on, situation allowing.

Also, since building one's reputation within the community is an important motivator for participation in it (as described in Chapter 2), introducing external credentials would destroy an important part of Wikipedia's attractiveness to newcomers: instead of a system in which they can create their standing and recognition on the basis of only their merit and actions in the community, Wikipedia would simply replicate real-world hierarchies. After all, it is an encyclopedia anyone can edit, and the accessibility, on equal footing, is important for many participants. This is, perhaps, why even though Wikipedia culture enforces enormous amounts of organizational control (as described in the previous chapter), it still is extremely flexible in terms of credentials.

Part of Wikipedia culture and heritage is disregard of externally imposed regulations and conventions. As Elinor Ostrom observes, "Norms seem to have a certain staying power in encouraging growth of the desire for cooperative behavior over time, while cooperation enforced by externally imposed rules can disappear very quickly" (2000, p. 147). But this reliance on internal normative regulation naturally exacerbates the tendency to reject all forms of external validations.

Shifting the weight from a trust–credential checks duo to formalization (or in other words, trust in the procedures and not the individuals and their credentials) is not a universal remedy and has other, somewhat undesirable, implications. For example, even though in theory the Wikipedia community does not want to turn into a bureaucracy, the bureaucratic creed is clear and affects the organizational culture, as mentioned in the previous chapter. The initially loosely coordinated egalitarian community systematizes its rules into procedures, and then some of the procedures are fossilized through embedding them in the technical environment, in a form of algorithmic governance (Müller-Birn, Dobusch, & Herbsleb, 2013).

Additionally, as also described in the previous chapter, rules are not listed or collected in a single consistent manner. These circumstances add to newcomer confusion and give a discursive advantage to experienced editors. Clearly, the number of regulations and guidelines and their chaotic and inconsistent presentation using hermetic slang, even if unintentional, increase difficulties for less experienced and new editors. When trust in people and credential verification are substituted by only trust in procedures (also known as institutional trust; see, e.g., Shapiro, 1987; Sitkin & Roth, 1993), apparent proficiency in those procedures can have a trust-building value. Anybody can claim to hold a doctorate, and with so many different academic fields the claim is difficult to verify. However, expertise in Wikipedia rules and language is immediately apparent to natives of this online culture. Editors displaying good understanding of Wikipedia policies are naturally considered more trustworthy, at least not to make the mistakes typical for those who do not have much Wikipedia article-editing experience. One criticism of this solution is that "since experts enjoy no special privileges in dispute resolution, and since there are many aggressive non-experts who care deeply about a wide variety of topics, Wikipedia's anti-expert tendencies unsurprisingly work against continual improvement" (Sanger, 2009, p. 64).

The scope of the adverse phenomenon is definitely disputable, and the results speak for themselves. Wikipedia, all in all, undergoes impressive continual improvement, and its quality is also clear: for many practical applications, it is simply good enough to use. The disregard for formal expertise may result in failing to hold to an article version theoretically more correct, at least in the eyes of an expert, as persistence in discussions is often more important than being right (see Chapter 3). But since credential checks could undermine the fundaments of Wikipedia's informal structure and collaboration philosophy, they are not likely to be accepted by the community.

In fact, institutionalized appreciation of experts may strongly deter and effectively prevent the masses from participating, damaging the Wikipedia model of widely distributed, low-cost participative crowd sourcing of knowledge creation. While open-source software projects are elitist (Mockus, Fielding, & Herbsleb, 2000) and "important contributors are few and ascend to the 'core group' status, the ultimate recognition by one's peers" (Lerner & Tirole, 2002, p. 206), Wikipedia relies almost entirely on the power of massive participation. Although, admittedly, a small group of users is responsible for the largest number of edits (Ortega, Gonzalez-Barahona, & Robles, 2008; Ortega, 2009) and serves as a community hub (Laniado & Tasso, 2011), most article development is done by a larger population (Swartz, 2006), and low-level users are increasingly taking over the workload (Kittur, Chi, Pendleton, Suh, & Mytkowicz, 2007). In a community in which legitimate peripheral participa-

tion—that is, initially participating in small ways (Lave & Wenger, 1991)—
is crucial, of much bigger importance is supporting retention of new users,
rather than pleasing the experts.

Larry Sanger's ideas of expert oversight have been tested in practice with
his Citizendium project, founded in 2007. This online encyclopedia community has been able to generate about 16,500 articles, of which fewer than 200
are expert approved (even though some featured articles from Wikipedia were
used as "seed capital"), over its six years of existence so far ("Welcome," 2013),
which does not give hope for creating anything even remotely close to what an
encyclopedia should be in the foreseeable future. Apparently, the costs of credentialing and identifying experts in open collaboration exceed the possible
benefits (O'Neil, 2010). The social software of Wikipedia makes vandalizing
an article more time-consuming than restoring its acceptable version (Lih,
2004), since it dramatically reduces costs of protection against graffiti attacks
(Ciffolilli, 2003).

Also, as shown in the previous chapter, understanding bureaucratic rules
and their cryptic abbreviations leads to status in a community. Therefore,
building one's status through external credibility and expert status could disturb this delicate social system. In this sense, controlling credentials would
make exerting organizational control, in the form Wikipedia uses, more difficult. Wikipedia, similar to other sociotechnical communities (STC), has
evolved "from an informal trust-based community with only a few formal
roles to a[n] STC where social mechanisms, and not the software architec-
ture, support knowledge management processes" (Jahnke, 2010, p. 544).

What is most striking in the Wikipedia Essjay crisis is seeing that this
online community prefers to trust rules of conduct that are precise and appropriate and developed in a participative manner rather than more interpersonal trust or precise credentialing and general control systems. Even though,
as some authors indicate (Sitkin & Roth, 1993), legalistic solutions may have
limited effectiveness in restoring trust, this is not the case for Wikipedia. The
fully democratic and participative character of its rules and procedures may
be decisive in their communal acceptance and preference over credential verification or local trust development. It may also have something to do with
the high reverence Wikipedians have for reliable sources (in creating articles),
and their own procedures, once established and institutionalized, become
externalized and receive a similar status. As it seems now, procedures and organizational routines do substitute for the need for trust and true identity

checks, even though this process is possibly limited to only virtual communities, which are able to develop their own rules and structures and also have naturally limited regular trust-building face-to-face interactions. Also, antielitism and disregard for real-world formal expertise is typical in hacker circles, which emphasize that people should be judged by their real abilities and "not bogus criteria such as degrees, age, race, or position" (Levy, 1984, p. 43). This approach heavily influenced the development of open-source communities. As a result, "[Wikipedia] stands for the most radical form of anti-credentialism: expertise is no longer embodied in a person but in a process, the 'wisdom of the crowd', that is to say interactions between individual authors and a massively distributed peer community" (O'Neil, 2011a).

Although some researchers suggest that distributed work and virtual communities require high levels of interpersonal trust (Jones & Bowie, 1998; O'Leary et al., 2002), as this chapter shows they can operate perfectly well in the absence of trust, and also credential checks, by employing bureaucratized procedures (Gallivan, 2008); credentials are unimportant, since expertise is transferred from persons to processes (O'Neil, 2009). As hypothesized by Dominika Latusek and Karen S. Cook (2012), on larger scales the social order is provided much more typically by institutions rather than general trust.

The conclusion that sometimes formalization of discursive practices may successfully substitute for credential checks in low-trust environments is unusual and certainly worth further research. Even if this phenomenon is limited to only online open-source communities, it is still significant, because it indicates that traditional identity-verification methods can serve as an ersatz solution to trust deficiency, but so can clear rules of conduct and behavior as long as those rules are created in an ahierarchical, self-managed community and created by the community itself.

The conclusions of the analysis of trust and credential enactment serve as an opening for a discussion of governance in Wikipedia community. This is the topic of the next chapter.

# 6

# BETWEEN ANARCHY AND BUREAUCRACY

## Wikimedia Governance

Anyone who has followed the wide community discussions must have been amazed by the amount of disagreement they contain. Conflicts about articles on Wikipedia, as described earlier, are one thing, but the level of frustration and anger vented in general debates is also surprising. Moreover, there are many occasional power struggles or tensions between the main internal stakeholders of the movement: the Wikimedia Foundation (WMF); the local chapters, which organize and support local Wikimedians and Wikimedia-related events and actions; and Wikimedia project communities. As the movement grows, the local chapters want to professionalize and take over some of the operations in the niche already occupied by the WMF. Even Wikimedians not affiliated with a chapter often criticize decisions and actions of WMF staff. Or any other activist in the movement. In fact, one thing is guaranteed: a decision will be criticized. Occasionally, discussions are initiated spontaneously: the WMF pays too much to its employees. Or too little. All work should be done by volunteers. All operations should be professionalized. These are just some of the common issues debated within the community.

To a bystander, Wikimedia projects may seem on the verge of splitting from their main project (known as "forking"). But the internal stakeholders miraculously survive, carry on, and cooperate as if nothing happened. A high number of disputes are actually typical for open-collaboration communities. There is no hierarchy to fear, and people can express doubts. Additionally, expressing concern is considered a sign of caring and, generally, good activism.

To understand conflict on Wikipedia better, I analyze the power dynamics between stakeholders, explain how funds are allocated, and discuss cultural and ideological backgrounds of existing tensions.

The Wikipedia community's need for leadership and clear governance is clearly visible (Collier, Burke, Kittur, & Kraut, 2010). Despite its anarchist features and being an arena of conflicting philosophies for managing the movement, the Wikipedia community puts great emphasis on coordinating and sustaining its internal order (Viégas, Wattenberg, Kriss, & van Ham, 2007). In this chapter I describe the governance of the Wikimedia movement, the composition of stakeholders, and the tensions among them. Analyzing governance in the context of open-source and open-collaboration projects may be approached from the perspectives of organizational control, roles, norms, and trust (Markus, 2007; O'Mahony & Ferraro, 2007). However, while there have been discussions of Wikipedia governance in terms of a single project (Forte, Larco, & Bruckman, 2009; Konieczny, 2009a), discussions of different projects and their coordination has been rare (Morell, 2011b). Governance and consensus on terms of authority and legitimization boundaries play crucial parts in the overall long-term stability of open-collaboration organizations (O'Mahony, 2007; Jensen & Scacchi, 2010; Kemp, 2010), just as in any other organization (Etzioni, 1959; J. S. Coleman, 1980; Huse, 2003), despite their uniqueness (O'Mahony, 2003; Von Hippel & Von Krogh, 2003).

Wikimedia meets many criteria for being a large social movement (Konieczny, 2009b), with a definite social agenda and a goal (making knowledge freely available to everyone and challenging its traditional distribution), and is also part of an intellectual movement (Frickel & Gross, 2005) advocating free information access and open licensing (Morell, 2011a). It is a hybrid (Ciesielska, 2010), or rather a boundary, organization (O'Mahony & Bechky, 2008), aligning to divergent interests of the academic, educational, social, and political worlds. Despite these characteristics it also exists in the environment and tradition typical for open-source projects: slightly anarchist, without a clear hierarchy, and highly dependent on participative organizational designs.

It uses its own organizational model, characteristic of free/libre-and-open-source-software (F/LOSS) projects, that resembles a chaotic bazaar with its independent agents rather than a cathedral with the coordinated effort to build it, according to the famous metaphor coined by Eric S. Raymond (1999), called a "chaordic organization" (Hock, 2005). Wikipedians are directly involved in the organizational governance and shape the community rules and structures. The successful organizational model of Wikipedia serves as inspiration to more traditional organizations, yet it remains to be seen if nondigital environments will be able to adopt it.

The policies of "What Wikipedia Is Not" state that Wikipedia is not a democracy, a bureaucracy, or an anarchy:

> Wikipedia is free and open, but restricts both freedom and openness where they interfere with creating an encyclopedia. Accordingly, Wikipedia is not a forum for unregulated free speech. The fact that Wikipedia is an open, self-governing project does not mean that any part of its purpose is to explore the viability of anarchistic communities. Our purpose is to build an encyclopedia, not to test the limits of anarchism. ([[WP:What_Wikipedia_is_not]])

The procedures, as well as firm democratic governance rules, show that Wikipedia is far from an anarchy. At the same time, Wikimedia communities are chaotic and rely on adhocratic principles (Mintzberg & McHugh, 1985). Adhocracy in this case is not incompatible with bureaucracy (Autier, 2001), as the community operates in a strictly regulated environment but remains agile and detours from rules on many occasions or even ignores them; rules are not hard and fast and can be challenged by anyone in the community, as long as he or she is successful in gathering support and reaching consensus for change.

Sometimes even well-established procedures and rules are not followed when a sufficient number of stakeholders decides that this is the right thing to do. In one case the English Wikipedia Arbitration Committee imposed the restriction on a user, a prominent expert in climatology, of only one revert per day. But the administrators refused to respect the restriction, as they considered it a bad decision. Eventually, ArbCom changed the ruling. This case shows how decentralization and anarchy are embedded into the governance design (Forte & Bruckman, 2008) and that the concept of *dura lex sed lex* is not considered natural or useful.

In some sense, Wikipedia indeed is not just a bureaucracy and is not merely an anarchistic adhocracy, but at the same time it draws liberally from both designs. Such an arrangement is not entirely unusual in knowledge-intensive organizations (Bailey & Neilsen, 1992; Robertson & Swan, 2004). Yet since Wikimedia is the largest movement of nonexperts in the history of humankind, since it relies on a highly diverse community (in terms of culture, race, class, and education and political, economic, and religious views), and since it is based almost entirely on virtual interactions, its governance is uncharted territory (Morell, 2009; Konieczny, 2010), especially since governance instruments of open-collaboration communities differ significantly from mainstream organizations (Lattemann & Stieglitz, 2005).

"Wikipedia . . . has developed a system of self-governance that has many indicia of the rule of law without heavy reliance on outside authority or boundary" (Zittrain, 2008, p. 143). Wikipedia (or rather, Wikipedias) and other Wikimedia projects exist within a movement that influences the shape of the communities in it. This delicate system relies on a balance among internal stakeholders who, although in most cases collaborate closely, are still not entirely unanimous and do experience some tensions. I describe them here and present the possible conflicts and contradictory directions that stakeholders may try to choose for the movement. I also show that the possibility of successful forking from Wikimedia is quite low but exists.

## Wikimedia Internal Stakeholders

The key Wikimedia internal stakeholders include the Wikimedia communities and projects run by them, the WMF, the board of trustees, and the local chapters (see Figure 6.1). While many others may have an impact on the movement (such as some of the arbitration committees, especially on the largest projects, the Ombudsmen Commission, and the Language Committee), these four groups of stakeholders have the largest effect on the relations within the movement. The communities do not require further explanation, as their social organization and customs have been the topic of analysis so far (however, putting them all in one box is misleading).[1] The other bodies, however, I describe briefly, before discussing the relations among them.

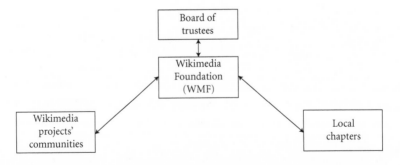

FIGURE 6.1. The main internal stakeholders of the Wikimedia movement

### The Board of Trustees

"The Wikimedia Foundation Board of Trustees oversees the foundation and its work, as its ultimate corporate authority" ("Board of Trustees," 2013). As the highest authority of the movement, the board strategically directs the WMF and is the only body that can issue resolutions that cannot be overturned by the communities (in practice, this applies mainly to situations in which the communities could put the WMF in legal trouble). Since 2008 it has consisted of ten members:

- Three seats elected directly by the Wikimedia community
- Two seats selected by the Wikimedia chapters
- One board-appointed "founder's seat" (reserved for Jimmy Wales)
- Four board-appointed "specific-expertise" seats

Because of this composition, as well as the scope of power it holds, the board is relatively neutral to organizational power shifts between other stakeholders. The board is tightly linked to the WMF and for practical purposes can be considered its managing board.

However, the other three stakeholders, although collaborating in many areas, often disagree on governance matters. The relations of these three have a huge impact on the development of the movement.

### Wikimedia Foundation

The WMF was established in June 2003 and for the first couple of years relied almost entirely on volunteers. Only after Sue Gardner became the executive director of WMF in 2007 did the organization grow significantly, both in number of employees and size of budget ([[Wikimedia_Foundation]]). The WMF employs over a hundred people.

The WMF's current organizational chart has a simple two-level structure (see "Staff and Contractors," 2013). The departments of the WMF include the following:

- Engineering and Product Development (102 people)
- Grantmaking and Program Development (23 people)
- Fund-raising (12 people)
- Legal and Community Advocacy (20 people)
- Finance and Administration (12 people)

- Human Resources (9 people)
- Office of the Executive Director (2 people)

Most of the work is technical (55 percent of staff numbers), and a significant part of it relates to global development, which means bringing Wikimedia projects to undeveloped or underdeveloped places, especially in the Southern Hemisphere (14 percent). Legal and community advocacy is quite important, too (10 percent), since Wikimedia projects require considerable licensing and copyright support. Fund-raising, obviously, is also crucial for the movement's sustenance (8 percent). Finance and administration, human resources, and the office of the executive director make up the remaining 13 percent of the total staff.

### Chapters

There are now thirty-nine chapters of Wikimedia ("Local Chapters," 2013). They are usually formed by Wikimedia activists from a country or a region, after being approved by the Affiliations Committee of the WMF, to support local Wikimedians. For example, the Polish chapter organizes get-togethers and conferences and takes responsibility for promoting Wikimedia values and ideas in the Polish media. Some chapters are large and well developed. For instance, the German chapter has over 6,500 members ("Wikimedia Deutschland," 2013) and is an established professional structure.

Relations between the editor communities and chapters are quite loose. In most cases, obviously, chapter members and functionaries come from the community. However, many community members do not feel the need to join the chapters and may believe them redundant. In fact, only about 5 percent of active editors join a chapter. Some editors even may be unaware of chapters' existence since the vast majority of community discussions have nothing to do with chapters, some may not have a local chapter, and some may be simply uninterested. The situation depends on the country, but chapter membership or function usually does not influence an editor's position and standing in the community. For instance on the Polish Wikipedia, one of the chapter members, holding an important position in it, requested adminship twice and both times was rejected, possibly because of a homophobic comment he once made (and apologized for later, but it was enough to raise suspicions about his objectivity).

Considering the proportion of chapter members in the general population of Wikimedians, the chapters have a relatively strong voice. This should not be surprising, however, since they are organized.

## WMF Relations with the Chapters

The main bones of contention between the WMF and the chapters are, naturally, resources and the power to allocate them.

The WMF relies on funds from corporate donors and from worldwide fund-raising campaigns directed to Wikimedia project readers. Chapters, in contrast, rely on support from the WMF and in many cases on local donations made directly to the chapter or a share in the money raised for Wikimedia through the chapter.

According to the WMF's annual plan for 2012–2013, the biggest budget allocations for 2011–2012 had been WMF Engineering ($11.9 million), other WMF programs ($5.6 million), chapters ($6.4 million), and WMF Legal, HR, Finance and Administration ($5.8 million) (Wikimedia Foundation, 2012, p. 56).

For 2012–2013, spending on WMF Engineering increased to $16.4 million, and WMF Legal, HR, Finance and Administration spending increased to $7.1 million, but the spending on other WMF programs decreased to $3.2 million, and spending on chapters fell to $4 million (Wikimedia Foundation, 2012, p. 56). The last cut is explained by the creation of a new body, called the Funds Dissemination Committee (FDC), to recommend how to allocate up to $11.5 million through grant competitions, open to chapters and also to WMF project proposals. The decision to create the FDC was explained in the plan document:

> In 2011–12, many discussions were held on movement roles and fundraising and funds dissemination, and some resolution was achieved, with the WMF Board approving new models for affiliation in the Wikimedia movement (thematic organizations, movement partners, and user groups), approving the creation of a Funds Dissemination Committee designed to empower a volunteer-driven and WMF-supported committee to disseminate money to chapters and movement partners, and putting in place a moratorium on local payment processing for all but four chapters. (2012, p. 26)

At the time of this writing, it is not yet clear what success the FDC will have or whether chapters will see it as a threat or support.[2] Apparently, it is a move to limit the influence of Wikimedia chapters, but also of the WMF, over funds allocation (whether it will also make the expenditures more effective is, of course, a different story). For the inception of the committee, members were appointed by the WMF board from the community, but in future they will be elected by the community.

In addition to gaining greater transparency, accountability, and effectiveness of fund allocation, setting up the FDC neutralizes some concerns expressed by the chapters. Chapters want to have a say in how to spend the money collected through fund-raising. The WMF has recognized the chapters as partners but insists that it is accountable to the community, not to member associations. As Sue Gardner explained to me in an interview,

> The issue is: Who does the money belong to? The money belongs to the global community of editors. The global community of editors needs an entity to hold the money in trust for it and to act as a proxy for it. We're the closest thing that exists to that, the Wikimedia Foundation. (July 13, 2012)

Making the FDC responsible for grant recommendations on a no-entitlement basis means that the WMF is going to be competing with the chapters for funds, but the WMF can prepare very professional applications by itself. Also, the board and the WMF decide which of the activities requesting funding are considered core (essential for running the projects) and which are noncore (not critical for functioning). The way they are defined is discussed by some activists.[3] In the past the validity of some expenses was disputed by a former employee of the WMF (Metz, 2008a), and now some members of the community feel that there is a need for radical transparency and frugality.

In short, relations between the chapters and the WMF are complicated. As a WMF employee (and also a former administrator) told me in an interview, "To be honest, I try and avoid the chapters—solely because I don't think their perspective is necessarily a useful one for me to bring into my daily work."[4] And another interviewee from WMF commented to me, "Chapters. Love them or hate 'em. You'd be mad not to hate 'em."

Some from the WMF see chapters as usurping the role of community representatives when the community can speak for itself. As for resources, the WMF and the board seem to believe that it is irrelevant whether chapters raise money and that funds redistribution is more effective when done through the WMF.[5]

Some chapters believe that they represent their community and that they should get a fair share in whatever resources are gathered through them and in their country or region. They also perceive the WMF as U.S.-centric and not accountable to the wider community to the extent they would like. U.S. centrism is indeed visible in the current board's composition, in which half are from the United States. It is impossible to win one of the community-reserved seats on the board without the support of American editors.

As one of the chapter representatives told me, chapters see the WMF as having a long reach and too much influence in the movement. This situation is not unusual for a cooperative organization; similar struggles and tensions took place in the Basque cooperative Mondragon when dealing with its co-operative bank (Whyte & Whyte, 1991). The chapters discuss their options on a separate, closed e-mail list that is hosted on independent servers in Austria and with no access by anybody in the WMF, so as to "scheme, plot, and dis-cuss strategy," as my informant sarcastically put it in an interview. One inter-viewed steward commented,

> Previously, all chapters could participate in fund-raising, and now only the chosen ones . . . , only they can get some peanuts. And the rest cannot re-ally collaborate hand in hand with the foundation; they can only apply for grants. . . . Somewhere in the way a trust has been lost—the conviction that all communities can take care of reasonable funds allocation. The arrangement is altered; previously it was based on partner relations, and now . . . some people mention aloud that if Wikipedia Deutschland wanted to fork, they could.

Although major forking is not yet seriously considered, in March 2012, twenty-five chapters declared their intent to create the Wikimedia Chapters Association, and seven others supported the move ("Wikimedia Chapters Association/Berlin Agreement," 2013). The association was founded at the Wikimania conference in July 2012, with twenty chapter members. It grew to twenty-six members, and its mission was "to further and represent the common interests of the Organizations within the Wikimedia movement" ("Wikimedia Chapters Association," 2013; "Wikimedia Chapters Association/ Charter," 2013), to have a stronger position in relation to the other stakehold-ers, and to be able to speak with one voice. The Wikimedia Chapters Associa-tion, as a new player, had the potential to complicate the dynamics between stakeholders. It was not clear to what extent it would counterbalance the in-fluence of the WMF, represent the chapters, or organize its turf. The WMF was already recognizing the need to narrow its focus and concentrate only on core activities while supporting and outsourcing the others.[6]

A few, mostly contingent, incidents might have influenced other stakeholders in their reception of the chapters. For instance, a situation that caused a bit of a stir and raised some eyebrows took place at Wikimania 2012, during the Wikimedia Chapters Association incorporation. As one of my interviewees who attended the inaugural meeting claimed, some supported making the chair of the association a paid position. The salary numbers discussed were high, comparable to WMF directorial levels. An initial idea was to set up an independent organization with full-time staff. The preliminary draft budget assumed a personnel annual budget of about $500,000 ("WCA Budget," 2012). For many Wikimedians, including chapter representatives, such an idea seemed to go too far, since most chapters do not have fully professional staff and the entire movement is based on volunteerism. In the end the idea was not accepted, but it indicated possible expectations from some of the participants. The strong tendency to apply corporate standards to activist work resurfaced in October 2012, when the Wikimedia Chapters Association passed a resolution to recruit a secretary-general by a committee that would have its expenses covered and use a paid consultant—before decisions had been made on the final place of incorporation and budget.[7] (For more examples of related tensions, see [[WP:Wikipedia_Signpost/2012-07-16/Special_report]] and C. Williams, 2012.) After discussions, the idea of the Wikimedia Chapters Association has been mostly abandoned (the chair and the deputy chair stepped down in August 2013 at Wikimania in Hong Kong; see [[WP:Wikipedia _Signpost/2013-08-07/News_and_notes]]), and the new models of cross-chapter collaboration are yet to emerge.

Such incidents cannot be considered to be representative of all chapters. Rather, the last example may simply indicate that some people who have been involved in the volunteer movement for many years eventually desire to act *pro publico bono*. In a way, it is part of the trend to professionalize activities that are already close to full time, although some chapters have had problems with professional hired staff who were not able to handle the workload and pressure.

Some members of the community fear that the activist and spontaneous character of Wikimedia grassroots associations is lost in some chapters when they favor nongovernmental-organization or even corporate-culture methods. Although professionalization of social movements is typical (Werker &

Ahmed, 2008; Elkington & Beloe, 2010), it distances the "discourse from ordinary individuals and thereby rob[s] the movement of its ability to capture the imagination of the public and to ensure accountability to important constituencies" (Land, 2009, p. 207), and it risks making a local organization's survival and administrative growth, rather than the movement's mission, a priority.

In addition, the professionalization trend is in stark contrast with the prevailing paradigm, which relies on one global professionalized foundation and a voluntary community, occasionally organized in voluntary chapters. Making Wikimedia activism a professional career path is hard to reconcile with the movement philosophy and would lead to an inevitable culture clash between the WMF and the chapters. It is difficult to conceive of two large professional organizations with large overheads operating simultaneously and serving the same purpose.

At the same time, the board and the WMF insist on semiprofessional standards being upheld by the chapters if they are to retain some of the money they raise and if they are to be eligible for WMF donations. The board issued a letter in August 2011[8] emphasizing chapters' need for tighter financial control, for higher accountability standards, and to offer tax deductibility of donations. Some chapter representatives criticized the requirements as being impossible to meet in some countries or contradictory.[9]

However, even such tensions as these are commonly addressed and attempted to be resolved in public in the Wikimedia community. After the board posted a letter withdrawing initial support to the Wikimedia Chapters Association in February 2013 (see "Talk:Wikimedia Chapters Association," 2013), the Wikimedia community discussed an association begun from a grassroots cross-chapter initiative, and association organizers agreed that developing structures first might not have been the way to go. Typically for the Wikimedia movement, harsh, open discussions and critiques quite often lead to some agreement.

## WMF Relations with the Communities

The Wikimedia project communities do not often need to communicate or deal with the WMF. When they do, it is usually because something has gone wrong, and that is often because of a programming error. If the error can be tied to the alleged U.S. centrism of the WMF, that magnifies the perceived mistake. This connection dates to the inception of Wikipedia, when development of the Polish Wikipedia was slowed by insufficient support for Polish diacritical characters (Enyedy & Tkacz, 2011), but it also has a more recent source: flagged revisions.

Flagged revisions are a function of MediaWiki software and allow unregistered or freshly registered users to introduce changes pending review by an editor. The idea, in Wikipedia's open philosophy of an encyclopedia that "anyone can edit," is controversial and was a topic of debate on many Wikipedias (de Laat, 2012). Yet this mechanism is now used by seventeen Wikipedias (see [[WP:Flagged_revisions]]) and had been implemented on ten of them when the English Wikipedia started testing it in 2010–2011. The developers kept making changes to the software, seeming to assume that if software worked for the English Wikipedia, it would work for all Wikipedias. But the changes caused immediate problems to Wikipedias already using flagged revisions. The IRC channel for MediaWiki software developers saw many reports of failures and disasters caused on other Wikipedias by the developers' tweaks. Ironically, after all the tests and turmoil and probationary periods, the English Wikipedia has not decided to use flagged revisions.

Smaller Wikipedia communities believe their feature requests are often ignored and that the limelight is on the English Wikipedia. This Wikipedia generates most of the traffic and hosts the largest Wikimedia community, so such a focus is somewhat understandable. But how feature requests are prioritized is not always well explained, and the bug report system (Bugzilla) does not allow the easy communication and discussion to which Wikipedians are so accustomed. In the words of a WMF employee I interviewed who often talks to software developers,

> The developers are interested in fixing old stuff because we have developers whose sole job is to fix old stuff. But communicating this to the community is difficult, as is getting developers to understand the impact of problems. Like if one of the parser functions is not working, that is, from a developer point of view, a very small problem because the site is still up and there aren't any glaring problems. From the community point of view, that is a hideous problem because all their internal templates and mechanisms have just broken and they don't understand why and can't fix it. But there is only one metric used to indicate the priority of a bug, which is how big a deal it seems from a purely technical standpoint.

The WMF's lack of understanding of the communities' decisions and careful consideration of their customs engenders ill will toward it in the communities. Also, the WMF pays little heed to them, even the English-speaking communities. For instance, Matt Bisanz, a student of law and also a steward, was frustrated enough to address the WMF on behalf of the stewards on one specific issue but followed that with more general observations:

> This specific concern does however tie into the larger issue we've recently noticed of developers not being aware of how their actions affect global policy and practice. See https://bugzilla.wikimedia.org/show_bug.cgi?id=26159 (giving local users the power to grant checkuser and oversight) and https://bugzilla.wikimedia.org/show_bug.cgi?id=32593 (disabling local steward powers).
>
> We appreciate that WMF creates the global policies and project mission, the developers code the software that permits the projects to function, and the stewards administer the global policies to ensure minimum basic standards on the projects, but are concerned with how things have changed as the foundation and projects have grown. We would appreciate it if the WMF could emphasize to the developers that while they have the technical power to alter certain things, they need to ensure their changes comport with global policy and practice by either consulting with the stewards when a change affects the stewards' practices or documenting to the stewards when the foundation has waived a global policy in a particular situation. We think this would help the projects run more smoothly and ensure better systemic compliance with the WMF's global policies. (Personal communication, March 19, 2012)

New functions that have been enabled without communicating and discussing them in advance are a source of frustration to experienced editors and functionaries. For instance, introduction of a system of edit monitoring using a new IP address standard caused panic among stewards in 2012, as none of them knew how to work with it, use "range blocks" (blocking a range of IP addresses, a technique important for dealing with dynamic addresses), or interpret the address syntax and no one knew whether bots created for monitoring IP edits (from unregistered users) would work in the new system. Such incidents are by no means isolated. However, the WMF is in the process of appointing community ambassadors who will pass important information to and from the communities.

Another example of miscommunication relates to a research project conducted by a team of scholars from the Berkman Center for Internet and Society at Harvard University and a French university led by Jérôme Hergueux (see "Research:Dynamics," 2012). The study had been prepared months ahead of time, had been discussed on the administrators' notice board since March 2011 (see [[WP:Administrators'_noticeboard/Archive222#Researchers _requesting_administrators'_advices_to_launch_a_study]]), had the support of the WMF and the Wikimedia Research Committee (see "Research Talk:Dynamics," 2012), and had even been discussed on the WMF's e-mail list in April 2011.[10] Despite the preparation, when a banner inviting participants to take part in a poll was placed on the English Wikipedia on December 8, 2011, it was immediately criticized in a community discussion (see [[WP:Administrators'_noticeboard/IncidentArchive731#Harvard.2F/ Science_Po_Adverts]]) and taken down within hours, well before it gathered enough respondents (see [[WP:Requests_for_comment/Central_Notices]]). The immediate reason for taking it down was the mistaken assumption by an administrator that the banner was displayed to all Wikipedians (it was not, as an algorithm showed the ad only to editors thought to match certain criteria; see "Research Talk:Dynamics," 2012), but the community strongly rejected using banner space, for the first time, for purposes other than fundraising (see [[WP:Wikipedia_Signpost/2011-12-12/News_and_notes]]). The general community was apparently unaware of all previous discussions on the research, and nobody from the WMF thought of posting a reminder a day or two before the study began and the banner was posted. The combination of lack of awareness, misconception of to whom the banner would be displayed, and a strong ideological opposition to advertising resulted in termination of this research campaign. As one of the editors commented,

> I write as a mildly-committed Wikipedia member, not at all related to WMF. But I have been observing these Wikipedia community–WMF communication difficulties with some concern (although I hate this sort of adversarial community vs WMF attitude some have, I view the two as interlinked and interdependent and ultimately interwoven) and I think one source of confusion (and I may be wrong here) is that there is a poor sense of where the WMF should make an announcement so that the community has the opportunity for sufficient say and sufficient notice. There seems to be a number of places, IRC, Mailing Lists, Village Pump, RFC's, Centralized Discussion template,

Signpost, etc. So I think there should be some discussion in this regard. It seems that WMF did announce this banner in some places, but not others, and so I think there should be some discussion to make clear what is the best place for the WMF announcements. I admit I'm not absolutely sure if this is a matter of confusion or not, but it seems that way for me, so just throwing it out there, discuss if you'd like. Jztinfinity 10:21, 25 December 2011 (UTC). ([[WP:Requests_for_comment/Central_Notices]])

The incident led to a wider-ranging discussion on what kinds of banners should be allowed on Wikipedia pages, and many editors insisted that only fund-raising campaigns should enjoy this privilege, with no exceptions. This is another good example of fuzzy ownership identity and competition for resources: the WMF saw the banner as using in its own space and assumed that displaying it for a clearly academic and carefully prepared project was something completely uncontroversial and within the WMF's decisional scope. The community, however, believed the banner's display required wide communal and open discussion about advertising principles and saw its actual display as going too far and making use of a resource reserved exclusively for Wikipedia's sustainability. Some also, on principle, protested any banner that took the user outside Wikipedia's domain space. The communal assumption was that banner space belongs to the community, even if it is customarily used by WMF for fund-raising purposes.

Some tensions arise from many WMF employees having accounts with high-level rights (e.g., administrator, oversighter) but not being well versed in project policies, which occasionally leads to a misuse of tools that frustrates the community.[11] Others are related to a lack of sufficient consultations about the decisions and actions of the WMF legal department, as is the case with issues of the Access to Nonpublic Information Policy (see "Talk:Access to nonpublic information policy," 2013) and community logo trademarking (see "Community_Logo," 2013), which as of November 2013 are hot and divisive topics.

The general perception of the WMF in the community ranges from neutral to quite negative. Tensions arise from the WMF having a role in everything, including content development, and from the inevitable clash of the radical ideological openness of the movement with the practice of running an organization (Morell, 2011b). What the WMF does is often taken for granted, and any mistake is long remembered as its fault. The WMF is run by people enthusiastic about the movement's ideology and usually qualified to obtain better-paid jobs elsewhere, but they are full-time employees, which in the eyes of some Wikimedians is a sin. In the past the WMF was also criticized for insufficient transparency (Martin, 2007; Bauwens, 2008). A WMF employee (a former administrator), asked in an interview whether his involvement in the community as an administrator helped, said,

> Overall I'd say my experience didn't necessarily help, though. What's helped
> is the status of being an administrator. Despite the constant refrain of "being
> an admin is no big deal," being an admin does count for something. And this
> can be very useful when trying to convince people that you are not in fact one
> of those assholes from the foundation [*laughs*], which seems to be a stereotype
> that I now work for the great Satan.

WMF is not generally perceived as negatively as the above statement might suggest, but a conviction prevails that the communities and the volunteers constitute the movement and the WMF is ancillary and subservient to their general will. The WMF to some extent shares this perspective.

Detachment and lack of communication are by no means only on the WMF side. Wikimedia communities are also surprisingly careless about communicating their actions, even those that have immediate and direct impact on the WMF. One recent example that shocked the WMF was the Italian Wikipedia blackout.

In 2011 the Italian Wikipedia community protested the DDL intercettazioni (Wiretapping Bill), especially its paragraph 29, which required all websites operating in Italy to publish, within forty-eight hours of the request and without a possibility to comment, a correction of any content that applicants deemed detrimental to their image, under a penalty of a fine of up to twelve thousand euros.[12] In protest, Italian Wikipedia was blacked out from October 4 to 6. This was the first time that any Wikimedia project had blanked all its content as a show of protest.

Discussions were held within the Italian Wikipedia community and spread to the international Wikimedia community only later.[13] The news was posted on the WMF e-mail list the day the protest started, and the WMF was apprised of the situation only hours before the blackout.[14] In the words of one of my interviewees from the WMF,

> There was definitely an environment of shock and, "Shit, what do we do now?
> This hasn't happened before." But again, the reason I found it most [frustrat-

ing] was the fact that we only found out twenty-four hours [before], and not just that: we hadn't noticed that they were reaching a decision but that the community didn't feel the need to notify the foundation until twenty-four hours before. Like, of all the Italian editors, not one of them went, "Gee, someone should probably tell the guy who runs the servers" and went across to do it. Either because, like, they're actually more independently minded as a community than the foundation. Whether this is the reason they don't talk to us much or because they don't talk to us much or even just [*inaudible*] entirely, I don't know. But it was fascinating to watch this vastly different attitude towards the relationship between the foundation and the community come to the fore.

The WMF's shock had nothing to do with the WMF or the board not approving of the community's decision. In fact, on the day the protest started, the WMF issued an official statement in support (J. Walsh, 2011), firmly standing behind the protest. The problem was that the WMF, bombarded with media requests for comment on this major political move, had to first figure out what was going on.

The Italian protest set a precedent though, and soon after, on January 18, 2012, the English Wikipedia was shut down for twenty-four hours to protest the Stop Online Piracy Act (SOPA) and Protect Intellectual Property Act (PIPA) bills under discussion by the U.S. Congress (see [[Protests_against _SOPA_and_PIPA#Wikimedia_community]]), and on July 10, 2012, the Russian Wikipedia shut down in protest against the Duma's proposed amendments to Russia's Information Act, which would have allowed blacklisting websites and prohibited their use (see [[Russian_Wikipedia#Blackout]]).[15]

The question of whether Wikimedia communities should engage in local political debates had not been asked before, and it is not clear whether allowing an online encyclopedia to go dark to make a statement is not a violation of its main mission. However, the WMF and the board recognized that local communities have a strong sense of ownership of their Wikipedias. In fact, this feeling is part of the organizational design. Wikipedia creators "wanted all the members of the community to feel a greater sense of power and ownership of Wikipedia—and thus to be motivated to contribute to its success" (Malone, Laubacher, & Dellarocas, 2010, p. 28). Also, all three shutdowns were related to Internet freedom and opposition to censorship of information, which are intrinsically related to F/LOSS movement roots (Brincker & Gundelach, 2010; E. G. Coleman, 2013) and at the heart of the Wikimedia movement (Gardner, 2011; Morell, 2011a). The Wikimedia community has started developing procedures for administrating project-wide protests (see "Project-wide Protests," 2013).

It is rare but not unheard of for a community's decision to be reached through a regular discussion when a project has been rejected by the WMF (see "Limits," 2013). For instance, in May 2011 the English Wikipedia community decided by a more than two-thirds majority from more than five hundred editors that creating articles should be limited to autoconfirmed editors (those who have made at least ten edits and whose accounts are at least four days old), meaning that neither anonymous nor new editors would be able to create articles (see [[WP:Village_pump_(proposals)/Proposal_to_require _autoconfirmed_status_in_order_to_create_articles]]). The proposal was intended to minimize the amount of vandalism and also to teach new editors how to participate.

The discussions were long and difficult, but eventually the disputants agreed that for the English Wikipedia, at its current stage, such a solution would work best. Yet, after the consensus had been reached, the trial period approved by the community, and the request submitted to software developers, the proposal was met with staunch opposition from the developers and the WMF. The initial reason developers gave for the rejection was that there had not been a clear consensus, but it was immediately pointed out that it is not for the developers to decide these matters, since the discussion had been closed according to custom and not protested. Moreover, the community was puzzled that the developers would dispute its decision. As the user Snotty-wong commented in the relevant Bugzilla ticket on August 4, 2011,

> Can someone explain to me how things work here when editors need to interface with the developers to make a change? We were hoping to just clearly explain what we need, point to the successful proposal which shows community consensus for a trial of the change, and get a dev to flip the user-rights switch for us.
>
> We were not aware that the entire concept was subject to another round of re-litigation by the developers at the 11th hour once the request is made on bugzilla. In particular, I'm concerned that these bugzilla discussions are not visible to any of the hundreds of editors who participated in the actual request for comments on enwiki.
>
> If there are technical issues with making this change, please let us know and we will work with you to resolve them. If you have editorial concerns

about the change, then my feeling is that those concerns should have been voiced at the proposal, which ran for nearly 2 months and was widely advertised all over the village pump and centralized discussion areas.

I don't want to come off as hostile and I don't want to dismiss anyone's legitimate concerns, but I feel like the comments being made here are essentially editorial comments by editors who missed the original proposal, and I find these comments to be out of place in this venue.

Please let me know if my concerns are unfounded, or if this is the status quo here. Many editors have been planning the details of this trial for close to 6 months and are itching to see it get underway. ("Bug 30208," 2013)

As the discussion continued in the bug ticket it involved WMF representatives, who argued that enacting this proposal would be in direct opposition to WMF strategic goals and that an abundance of research indicated that such a change could result in serious damage to, if not failure of, a collaborative project. Eventually the request was rejected, mostly because it contravened the main purpose of the movement and the strategic goal to be more inclusive, rather than raising entry barriers for new users.

Even though WMF representatives, including its deputy director, Erik Möller, tried to be conciliatory and promised that the request would be further discussed and possibly addressed, the points raised against the request came late and should have been disputed when the issue was first discussed on the English Wikipedia. The WMF's concerns were legitimate, but they should have raised them earlier, during the months the proposal was discussed and advertised in the English Wikipedia community. In the end, much of the communal effort and discussion was in vain. As Erik Möller explained in his final comment on the issue on September 19, 2011,

I empathize with expressions of anger and frustration, and I'm very sorry that we haven't been able to handle this issue in a way that minimizes both.

With that said—if your view of WMF is that the only legitimate engagement toward a request like this one is to execute it, then there's not much point in continuing a conversation. That's simply not our view, nor has it ever been our practice.

My own take is pretty straightforward: The community has certain blind spots and biases; WMF has certain blind spots and biases. Having spent years deeply immersed in both, I can safely say that the two are very different animals. ("Bug 30208," 2013)

The role of legitimate peripheral participation in open-collaboration communities is important, and even just readership can be treated as the first step to entering the community, not as free riding (Antin & Cheshire, 2010). In this sense, contributions from IP-signed, or unregistered, users can be seen as introductory Wikipedia editing, and the high volume of vandalism may be the inevitable cost of attracting new editors. But the fundamental reason is irrelevant; the WMF failed to give timely notice of its different interpretation. As a WMF employee admitted to me in an interview, "I think the right decision was reached, I think the right action for that decision would have been to step in and say, 'We're not going to do this' before they spent three months arguing over the implementation and reaching a decision and so on and so forth."

This incident also shows that who owns Wikipedia is a sensitive issue. The communities obviously believe that they run the Wikipedias and the WMF is responsible for administration and execution of the communities' resolutions, given the available resources. The WMF contends that the communities can decide their own organization and rules only within the limits of the strategic vision set by the board and that the WMF has the final say. As Edward Castronova (2005) observes in online gaming communities, when members lack the technical powers to perform acts of governance, the community-driven governance becomes questionable. However, reminding community members of their lack of expertise and throwing this technical disempowerment in their faces is risky, especially when social organization of production relies on both coordinating efforts of the most dedicated members of the community, who perform free labor (S. Levine, 2008), and empowering grassroots governance by design (Butler, Joyce, & Pike, 2008; Andrea Forte et al., 2009). After all, governance structure and its enforcement can have a huge impact on motivation and willingness to participate in open-collaboration projects (Shah, 2006). This is perhaps why such disagreements are extremely rare and why miscommunications and misunderstandings between the WMF and the Wikimedia communities, as well as local chapters, have not so far led to any major schism, or forking.

## Forking

"Forking" is the splitting of a community in an open-collaboration project.

> On a whim, because of a fundamental technical disagreement, or because of
> a personality conflict, anyone could take the Linux code base or the Apache

code base and create their own project around it, with different decision rules and structures. Open source code and the license schemes positively empower this option. (S. Weber, 2004, p. 93)

According to research on twenty-six F/LOSS projects that experienced forking, dissatisfaction with project governance was an important motivation to fork (38 percent), second only to technical considerations (Viseur, 2012), which obviously play a crucial part. Members take their version of the project elsewhere when it is not developing as they would like (Li, 2009; Nyman & Mikkonen, 2011). Open-collaboration projects often have strong reservations about forking (Stewart & Gosain, 2006), but dissatisfaction with the movement governance could lead to it.

Several small forks from some Wikimedia projects have already taken place. For example, in 2011 theopenglobe.org forked from WikiNews, only to go defunct in less than a year (see "Wikinews:Water Cooler," 2012). The Wikimedia community has occasionally disputed such schisms on a larger scale, usually for ideological reasons—for example, controversial-image filtering. The image-filtering case (discussed in Chapter 7) shows that different Wikimedia communities have different sensitivities but often share a strong commitment to defending their principles. Even though the majority of the Wikimedia community supported some form of controversial-content filtering in the largest referendum ever held on the subject in 2011[16] and the board passed a resolution encouraging development of technical means to allow users to opt in to having such content filtered,[17] resistance from a dedicated minority resulted in abandoning the idea on the global level. As Sue Gardner, the executive director of the Wikimedia Foundation, told me in an interview,

We could have said, "We're going to build it anyway because roughly two-thirds are in favor," but we wanted to recognize the one-third that was seriously very opposed to it, and we wanted to recognize from a practical perspective, too, if we were to go ahead and build it anyway, there would be a really heavy lift in terms of developing any kind of consensus around it, and we would risk potentially a German fork, a French fork, et cetera. So it was a divisive issue, and it had the potential to split the Wikimedia movement, to cause bad feelings and lots of hostility, and to cripple the Wikimedia Foundation's ability to do other work. And in a movement like ours, those are real repercussions, those are real implications; they're not nothing because our ability—the

Wikimedia Foundation's ability to do our job—is predicated in the expectation that we're going to be good partners working together. (July 13, 2012)

This decision was probably not made just because of the commitment to seeking consensus and unanimity. Image filtering had general support globally and not just from hardcore Wikimedians, who have the most influence on local projects. While the referendum reached Wikimedians of all editing frequencies, some communities held their own polls, engaging the most active editors and not the occasional ones, and it turned out that on several major Wikipedias image filtering was strongly opposed (79 percent opposed on the Spanish Wikipedia ["Wikipedia:Encuestas," 2011], 81 percent on the French Wikipedia ["Wikipedia:Sondage," 2013], and 85 percent on the German Wikipedia ["Wikipedia:Meinungsbilder," 2012]), sometimes for ideological reasons and sometimes because the move was perceived as undue interference with individual Wikipedias' prerogatives. The board and the WMF had to be careful about making resolutions that would potentially or actually challenge convictions of any of the major communities. Discussions about forking did actually start on the German Wikipedia (see "Wikipedia:Wikipedia-Fork," 2013). As the German Wikipedia has a strong administrative backbone, it could probably carry out forking both technically and financially.

Forking, often despised in open-collaboration communities as detrimental to common goals, is an option that ensures that the collaboration is truly free (Reagle, 2004; Cheliotis, 2009). The theoretical possibility of forking is itself a safety valve that all stakeholders are aware of and that empowers the minorities. It is the "invisible hand of sustainability" of projects, allowing them to develop (Nyman, Mikkonen, Lindman, & Fougère, 2011). Yet its practical possibility highly depends on the governance model used in the community (Kogut & Metiu, 2001). On Wikipedia, even though the theoretical possibility of forking has been discussed occasionally and a few attempts have been made (e.g., Citizendium, Wikinfo, the Spanish Enciclopedia Libre; for an analysis of Wikipedia forks, see Tkacz, 2011), a forking resulting in a success comparable to the original Wikimedia movement seems unlikely.

First, even though many websites, such as About.com, are openly and legally copying everything from Wikipedia and entirely relying on its content with only occasional creative additions, Wikipedia is extremely well positioned among and well treated by search engines. Also, it is massively linked to by other websites. Even if a majority of the Wikimedia community jumped ship today, chances are that Wikipedia would go on and cultivate a new generation of editors, while the new project would find it extremely difficult to find readers and new editor attention. Thus, unlike different Linux distributions, Wikipedia does have a privileged position in terms of user access.

Second, and as a corollary, although the value of Wikipedia initially came only from the content, currently much of it relies on the brand name as well. Since the content is not owned by the WMF, it cannot be taken away, because of the open-licensing model, and the value of the brand becomes the major added value of the project when compared to all other websites using Wikipedia content. An average reader neither knows nor cares about the community behind the content. Possibly slightly different from OpenBSD or Java or Unix (Kumar, 2010), much of Wikipedia's current standing and readership relies on external conditions (such as positioning) and on a stable and respected brand. While the product is obviously important, with thousands of mirrors of Wikipedia content, Wikipedia and Wikimedia logos differentiate the official projects from the rest, and it is the brand, not the product itself, that makes the difference and generates the traffic (Klein, 2000). Paradoxically, the high number of Wikipedia mirrors makes the original Wikipedia stand out more rather than less (Famiglietti, 2011). Many of the mirrors are set up as "link farms" to make modest revenue on traffic directed from the search engines, and Wikipedia has better quality control. It also benefits from the copyright requirement that those mirror websites link back to it.

Third, the likelihood of forking is highest when there is a total lack of coordination or when the control exerted over the community by the coordinating center is too tight (Kumar, 2010). The WMF has kept this in mind and not confronted local communities on issues that could result in a schism, trying not to interfere in local communities in the areas that they consider important while making an orchestrated coordinating effort for the movement. Even the incorporation of the WMF, which abandoned a business-start-up approach and implemented a radical opening of content, might have been influenced by the need to prevent forking and keep a volunteer community active (Chen, 2011; Enyedy & Tkacz, 2011).

Fourth, online collaboration systems require a certain critical mass to make the cooperation work and for the positive aspects of the system to prevail over its shortcomings (Bonaccorsi & Rossi, 2003; Prasarnphanich & Wagner, 2008). The failure of previous forks is a serious warning sign that outside the Wikimedia movement it may be impossible to maintain an organization.

This is possibly why Wikimedia's governance tensions concentrate on debating and reformulating roles and influence between the stakeholders, rather than on possible forking.

However, the potential for forking is an important factor to account for in Wikimedia movement management. For instance, the Spanish fork of Wikipedia, Enciclopedia Libre, even though not a successful independent encyclopedic project, quite possibly tilted the scales toward the decision that Wikipedia would not use ads to bring in revenue in 2002, when that was still considered a viable option (Tkacz, 2011).

Also, with the incorporation of the Wikimedia Chapters Association and with discussions of the movement's vision and future development taking place (for instance, the WMF proposes a narrowed focus to concentrate on its crucial objectives, while some members of the community believe a narrowed focus would undercut some key initiatives; see "User Talk:Sue Gardner," 2012), the potential for a divisive issue is growing, as observed by Victoria on the Wikimedia e-mail list on October 19, 2012:

> So WMF will collect the money and then will distribute it by the means unknown. As a former member of the Grant Committee I can say that the current process is not very efficient and there is no alternative proposed. And if WMF focus on distributing grants instead of helping directly, it will become incredibly difficult for people with no experience in a highly specific task of grant-writing (=community members) to get their initiatives off the ground, and the money will go to third parties. During the "restructuring time" WMF will stop supporting really working things such as Wikimania, leaving it to fend for itself, just like chapters.
>
> I wonder at what point European Chapters, lead by highly efficient German, will realise that they don't need WMF, buy servers and fork.[18]

Especially in the wake of the founder's leadership crisis (see Chapter 7), the view that governance is stable seems somewhat distorted.

## Incomplete by Design?

One thing is important to remember when interpreting tensions among stakeholders and conflicts on Wikipedia more generally: standards for reading the scale of dissent cannot be reliably adopted from the more typical hierarchical organization. For a bystander, used to disagreement, frustration, and anger being suppressed out of fear of more powerful others and being voiced only when they have escalated, the Wikimedia movement may seem incredibly querulous.

However, the Wikimedia community is accustomed to expressing dissent. In fact, as noted before, not expressing disagreement is often treated as agreement to what has been proposed. Also, as is typical for cooperatively managed organizations (Greenwood, González Santos, & Cantón, 1991; Whyte & Whyte, 1991), voicing different opinions and confronting drastically different views is a standard practice for almost any topic. Within the Wikimedia movement one thing is guaranteed: any decision is going to fuel a discussion. What is worth remembering is that the discussion signifies fundamental divisions or embedded inequalities and injustice to a much smaller extent than it would in a hierarchical organization. What would be an extreme conflict, likely leading to a schism in a hierarchical organization, in an online open-collaboration community governed cooperatively is business as usual. As Clay Shirky observes,

> Open systems are open. For people used to dealing with institutions that go
> out of their way to hide their flaws, this makes these systems look terrible at
> first. But anyone who has watched a piece of open source software improve,
> or remembers the Britannica people throwing tantrums about Wikipedia, has
> seen how blistering public criticism makes open systems better. (2012)

As described in this chapter, the larger picture of governance of the Wikimedia movement is that it does not rely on just the community. While individual Wikipedias are at liberty to decide most of their policies and rules, doing so through group discussion (Black, Welser, Cosley, & DeGroot, 2011), and "Wikipedia has been developed with almost no centralized control" (Malone et al., 2010, p. 21), there is a backbone of organizational governance provided by the incorporated WMF and more or less developed chapters (and the new chapter association). Interactions among these lead to occasional frictions on the boundaries of what is not clearly ascribed to one of the stakeholders' prerogatives. There is also a rivalry and indirect competition over governance philosophies and resources.

The emergence of community leaders and of governance tensions in the highly ahierarchical and egalitarian environment is by no means surprising:

> Collectively intelligent crowd-based organizations such as open source soft-
> ware projects and Wikipedia may be thought to be flat, egalitarian, and self-

organizing. However, research has examined a core group of leaders that emerge through formal election processes from the "crowd." Elected leaders in crowd-based organizations often provide centralized coordination of long-term objectives, mediate conflict within the organization, and develop formal organizational policy. (Collier & Kraut, 2012, p. 1)

While this process is highly regulated and mostly frictionless within each of the communities,[19] it seeks an equilibrium in their global coordination. Several different approaches are possible. At one extreme, the WMF is an annually renewed contractor that provides Wikimedia communities with computer servers, legal counsel, and professional fund-raising, but the communities are organized so well that they can terminate this relationship at any point or decide that some other organization may serve them better. At the other extreme, the WMF owns the movement and the communities may be easily replaced if they are not willing to follow. Fortunately for the movement, so far all stakeholders have not followed anything close to these extreme strategies and are aware that, regardless of which of these philosophies is better in theory, pushing for one of them would lead to a serious crisis. Even so, some power struggle, as described, is evident and possibly related to not following the design principle for self-organizing communities (Ostrom, 1990) that requires clearly defined community boundaries. This is the case of the global Wikimedia movement: while each of the communities has a pretty stable and known governance organization, the balance between the players on the global level is still in flux. Quite understandably, when the governance structure is not crystal clear, games and strategies must fill the void. The organizational power of the WMF, rooted in ownership of the Internet domains, fund-raising proficiency, and administrative backbone (with legal, technical, and coordinating centers), is mitigated by the growing expectations of professionalizing chapters (and their association), a strongly ideological community of volunteers, and the practice of discussing any concerns. Moreover, the many ideas for both stakeholders' roles and the desired direction for the movement further destabilize the system. Ultimately, the decisive issue will be communal legitimization. Paradoxically, the lack of immediate accountability to the community makes the WMF more vulnerable (Kearns, 1994; Guo & Musso, 2007), especially because it operates according to a logic of e-governance, promising decentralized empowerment and the immediate rule of the community (Mazzarella, 2006).

At the same time, Wikimedia movement governance, like that of many other genuinely participatory, self-managed organizations, is incomplete by design (Garud, Jain, & Tuertscher, 2008), as participant engagement in its constant creation is part of its attractiveness, and reflexive self-organization constitutes an important part (Jessop, 2010). The governance structure of the movement is in constant flux, and the untamed creativity of the participants, combined with a radical transparency, results in what seems on the surface to be fighting factions but is peaceful, continuous re-creation of organizational structure. The result resembles a network form of organization (Powell, 1991) in the sense that it detours from hierarchical and market patterns typical for traditional organizational forms, even though it is also radically antieconomic. Since it is built on adhocratic principles (Konieczny, 2009a, 2010), or rather as a heterarchy, it is an ad hoc meritocracy with dispersed power (Bruns, 2008; Kostakis, 2010). It is blending bureaucratic procedural control with agile organizational adjustments and spontaneity and requires flexible procedures and somewhat imprecise governance principles. This novel mixture may form what Mathieu O'Neil calls an "online tribal bureaucracy" (2009, p. 5), an equivalent of modern nonvirtual "soft bureaucracies" (Courpasson, 2000), balancing formalization with entrepreneurial ferment. It is self-reproducing, self-adjusting, and self-created. Unfortunately, self-organization tends to lead to perfecting the procedural rationality rather than focusing on the goal (Meyer & Rowan, 1977; Herman & Renz, 1997). In the Wikimedia movement perfecting the procedural rationality can be observed in the concentration of debates on egalitarianism, inclusivity, freedom of information, and respect for significant minorities (all related to how collaboration is conducted) and not reaching the goal of a moment when every human being can freely share in the sum of all knowledge (which is the movement's purpose, but the amount of time spent discussing how to reach it is significantly less).

Despite the shifts in influence among the stakeholders, both the WMF and the board are legally and organizationally potent and legitimized in policy and governance decisions. They also perceive their role to be much more than serving the community by silently supporting and executing its will: they intend to lead the movement and formulate its goals. Yet because of the strong ideology of participation followed by the community, its perception of ownership of the project, and the strong position and aspirations of the chapters, the

WMF's practical power, understood as the ability to shape the direction for the movement and its further development, is somewhat limited. In general, "the community has been able to keep the WMF in its designated role—as an institutional interface between the community and society and as an institutional buffer that enhances enrolment" (Chen, 2011, p. 364), adopting policies and resolutions almost exclusively by following the community's consensus (Chen, 2010).

On one hand, the Wikimedia community, characteristically for activist- and ideology-driven groups (which makes organizational change more likely; Dobosz-Bourne & Kostera, 2007), is highly sensitive to anything it perceives as out of step with the movement's philosophy (such as image filtering, thought by some a step toward censorship and limiting digital freedom, one of its ultimate values; cf. Kelty, 2008), since it perceives itself as ethos driven (Pentzold, 2011). On the other, Wikimedia chapter activists professionalize and build organizational structures alternative to those of the WMF. Both of these trends strictly limit the scope of WMF power, but the entire process relies much more on negotiation than conflict, despite appearances to the contrary. To understand governance in the Wikimedia movement it may be worthwhile to take a look at leadership models used in it.

# 7

## LEADERSHIP TRANSFORMED

### The Pros and Cons of Benevolent Dictatorship

As discussed in the previous chapter, the Wikimedia community seems to desire some form of leadership while ideologically opposing it on many occasions. Open-collaboration communities exercise different forms of leadership; some are, in fact, quite authoritative, and some are fully collaborative.

Quite understandably, Wikipedia's lack of formal leadership only makes it more difficult for natural leaders to legitimize their role. New leaders emerge as in any other organization, yet they cannot institutionalize their position. Only the role of Wikipedia's founder, Jimmy "Jimbo"[1] Wales, carried a classic form of authority at some point. Interestingly, his influence on the movement increased only when he stepped down from operational, daily activities and attempts at direct management and only after his authority took a direct hit, following a series of unfortunate incidents.

This chapter presents the evolution of Wikipedia's direct leadership, through Wales's position in the movement. Over the years, his role has changed from being the unquestioned leader of the English Wikipedia to being the spokesperson of a movement. This transition has not been entirely smooth, and analyzing its background and the reasons why the Wikimedia community stood up to its founder only to recognize his influence in hindsight is essential for understanding this quirky organization and developing a perspective on its novel leadership. As this chapter reveals, the change in Wales's involvement was the result of both a clear and communicated strategy and a contingent major transformation in leadership, which seemed to culminate in his symbolic demotion by the community but then led to a new role—as the spokesperson for the movement's values. I frame these events as part of a larger discussion on open-collaboration-project leadership and draw conclusions from them, showing that open-collaboration communities seem to accept both democratic and dictatorial leadership models, but leadership practices must be compatible with the chosen model.

## Founder's Exit?

Research in venture creation indicates that founders of successful organizations often depart after their creations have grown (Boeker & Karichalil, 2002). This may be related to organizational life cycle (L. E. Greiner, 1972), in which needs shift from an entrepreneurial, creative, and market-opportunity orientation to an operational, managerial, and coordinative orientation (Rubenson & Gupta, 1992), requiring different skills and expertise from the leaders. Development from a start-up to an established venture may depend on replacing at least some of the founders (Hambrick & Crozier, 1985), though some studies contradict this conventional wisdom (Willard, Krueger, & Feeser, 1992).

In commercial organizations, the entrepreneur's exit is a critical component in organizational development (DeTienne, 2010), signifying its professionalization (Gedajlovic, Lubatkin, & Schulze, 2004). "[The] founder's ongoing involvement in general management activities may be decreasingly valuable or even detrimental to the company's success as the firm grows" (Jayaraman, Khorana, Nelling, & Covin, 2000, p. 1216).

Similarly, in nonprofit organizations, founder exit is often considered a natural stage in organizational growth (Riggio & Orr, 2004), even though founders sometimes wield more power than in commercial organizations (Sharir & Lerner, 2006), possibly because of looser external control from stakeholders and smaller possibility of removal from the leadership position by the board or shareholders (Chu, Kolodny, Maital, & Perlmutter, 2004).

Wikipedia experienced some planned shifts in leadership, marked by several milestones. For example, Wales, who created, inspired, developed, and nurtured Wikipedia, gave up chairing the board of trustees of the Wikimedia Foundation in 2006 (but retained the "founder's seat"; see Chapter 6). Sue Gardner became the executive director of the Wikimedia Foundation in 2007. She has brought the foundation to financial stability; the number of donors increased tenfold from 2008 to 2011, and the total amount of donations in that time frame increased almost fivefold (J. Walsh, 2012).

The changes in Wales's direct role have been much more important for the culture of Wikipedia communities. From the beginning, he has been the visionary of Wikipedia, its sole authority figure, a "benevolent dictator" (Gillmor, 2004, p. 149), even though he more often performed the tasks of an editor and an administrator (O'Neil, 2011). After the first years he gradually began limiting his involvement in direct leadership of the movement, until in 2010 his authority in the community suffered a crippling blow, which led to a redefinition and a successful transformation of his leadership.

The evolution of his role and the small communal revolt against him sheds light on leadership in ahierarchical and participative managed communities.

## The Founding Fathers

The analysis of Wikipedia leadership should start with a description of the debate that rolled through the English Wikipedia on whether Wales was the sole founder of Wikipedia or whether he should share the credit with others. This discussion reflects the unusual approach of Wikipedians to notability and facts, and it shows that even Wikipedia big shots cannot count on leniency.

In the beginning, Wales was the only person with the right to ban other users. He was also the project's representative and promoter. However, Wikipedia was originally coordinated by Larry Sanger, then a graduate student in philosophy, who Wales hired full time to help develop it.

This has led to ardent disputes in the Wikipedia article on Larry Sanger, since Wales later questioned Sanger's role as cofounder. Wales, CEO of the company taking the entrepreneurial risk of starting both Nupedia and Wikipedia, author of the idea, and project leader for many years after Sanger's departure and before Wikipedia's worldwide success, understandably did not want to share the credit with his former employee. After all, it was Wales's own crazy concept to create a free-access online encyclopedia, and it was he who hired Sanger to coordinate Nupedia and start Wikipedia in 2001. Wales was both the originator and the investor in this venture, not the hired help.

Sanger's strong involvement in the beginning is, however, beyond question. He was the editor in chief of both Nupedia and Wikipedia and is also credited with the idea of using wiki software. But "it was Jimmy Wales who added the third critical ingredient to the mix. He directed Sanger to give essentially unrestricted editorial access to this new wiki to the 'non expert' public" (see [[Larry_Sanger]]). Sanger designed many of the basic policies, including those permitting ignoring all rules when the good of the encyclopedia needs it, requiring a neutral point of view, and requiring verifiability (Schiff, 2006). However, he was laid off because of lack of funds in 2002, after which he apparently lost faith in the project (in his farewell message he skeptically wrote that "Wikipedia still might succeed brilliantly"; Berstein, 2011). Since then he has been very critical of it. In 2007 he launched his own online encyclopedia website, Citizendium. Clearly, both being let go from Wikipedia and having his cofounder status questioned left Sanger resentful. Nonetheless, as late as December 2010, when criticizing WikiLeaks and addressing Julian Assange, he mentioned his former affiliation rather than his later projects: "Speaking as Wikipedia's co-founder, I consider you enemies of the U.S.—not just the government, but the people" (Crovitz, 2010). Identifying himself as Wikipedia's cofounder might have created the impression that he was speaking for the Wikipedia community or the Wikimedia Foundation, but his view was far from unanimously shared by Wikipedians.

His hostility toward Wikipedia might have made editors reluctant to accept that reliable sources label Sanger as Wikipedia's cofounder in the Wikipedia article about him. Many discussions have been held over several years (with the most heated discussions in 2007–2009). Wales rarely commented on the issue, but his disagreement with describing Sanger as a cofounder was clear, and he expressed it outside Wikipedia, too.

This case is possibly the ultimate proof of the efficiency of Wikipedia's content management system: with reliable sources even the information most unwanted by Wikipedians, and contested by their leader himself, still prevailed. Naturally, if Wales participated more actively in discussions and presented counterarguments, his voice would be treated with respect by the community and would add considerable weight to any point of view. Wales apparently decided against it—possibly out of respect to Wikipedia's rule on conflicts of interest ([[WP:Conflict_of_Interest]]), a rule many editors ignore. But even if he did insist on his perception, unless he provided the proper countersources, he would not be able to prevent Wikipedia from mentioning that according to some sources Sanger is its cofounder, because early press releases named both Wales and Sanger as such ([[WP:Press_releases/

January_2002]]). Thus, Sanger is credited with being a cofounder, based on the data and not on editors' biases or preferences.

Unlike many other policies and norms on Wikipedia, the rules regarding content are similar in both their ideological or rhetorical aspect and their practical application, and they indeed are quite antiauthoritarian and democratic. They expand direct power to the lower levels by stripping organizational leaders of the power to do anything beyond the script and not allowing status in the community to be an exception to the rule. This observation of content rules, possible also because no one in the Wikipedia community receives compensation, is worth emphasizing and showing on another case, since such disempowerment is truly exceptional.

Angela Beesley is a cofounder of Wikia and was a member of the board of trustees of the Wikimedia Foundation in 2004 and 2005. On April 1, 2005, a biographical article was created to describe her. Beesley protested the article and submitted it as an article for deletion (AfD) with the following comment: "Unfactual article about a non-notable person. Is this meant to be an April Fool's Day joke? Angela. 09:06, Apr 1, 2005 (UTC)" ([[WP:Articles_for_deletion/Angela_Beesley]]).

A weeklong discussion followed, in which some users expressed respect for her decision to have the article deleted, others suggested correction of factual mistakes in the article, and the majority maintained that, according to Wikipedia rules, she was a notable person and did not have standing to complain about the article's existence. The article was kept. This decision was sustained in another AfD discussion.

Beesley made one more attempt to have the article removed on July 12, 2006, when she again nominated the article for deletion. She appealed to fellow Wikipedians by pointing out her disagreements with the article and claiming that she no longer qualified as notable:

> I'm sick of this article being trolled. It's full of lies and nonsense. My justification for making a third nomination is that my circumstances have changed significantly since the last AfDs—I have resigned from the Board of Trustees of the Wikimedia Foundation. Given that this was previously kept on the grounds I was on that Board, there is no longer any reason for this page to be kept. This has already been deleted on the French and German Wikipedias. ([[WP:Articles_for_deletion/Angela_Beesley_(3rd_nomination)]])

An administrator (Kimchi.sg) initially deleted the article because policy allowed deletion of articles with little likelihood of survival ([[WP:SNOW]]), but another user requested a return to the debate.

And discuss Wikipedians did, in more than thirteen thousand words. Several of Wikipedia's widely respected and recognized users took stances. For instance, the deputy director of the Wikimedia Foundation, Erik Möller, commented,

> We need to be careful not to give Angela preferential treatment because she is a Wikimedian, and the "troll magnet" argument shouldn't weigh too strongly either. Whatever precedent we establish here needs to be applied consistently to other articles. As noted above, I vote for *delete and re-evaluate in one year* right now, with the rationale: "borderline case, subject requests it to be deleted." I might be convinced to change my vote to "keep," though. —Eloquence 14:52, 12 July 2006 (UTC). ([[WP:Articles_for_deletion/Angela _Beesley_(3rd_nomination)]]; emphasis in original)

A person from outside Wikipedia might expect Wikipedians to discuss whether they should do their long-term colleague a favor and agree to her request, maybe bending the rules. Most of the debate, however, stuck exactly to the point and related to deciding whether the described person should or should not have a biographical note on Wikipedia according to notability rules. This sentiment is best explained in the words of one of the disputants:

> This is almost starting to become some sort of inverse vanity page argument. And in my opinion, the conclusions are the same: the wishes of the subject of an article as to its existance or nonexistance do not over-rule the policy and notability criteria. If I want to have an article about myself, but I am not notable, no amount of me protesting will get it included. If I don't want to have an article about me, but am notable, the same thing applies. The trolling is regretable [sic], but until we develop the software to read the minds of editors and determine whether they are acting in good faith or not, it is a necessary evil for the continued existence of the Wikipedia project as a whole. Perhaps our most relevant rule here, however, is WP:OWN. Which is an official policy, I might add. You don't own articles which are *about* you any more than you do those you *wrote*. An opt-out system would violate this rule. Also, I think we have a slight conflict of interests here. —tjstrf 21:54, 16 July 2006 (UTC). ([[WP:Articles_for _deletion/Angela_Beesley_(3rd_nomination)]]; emphasis in original)

The policy on ownership of articles ([[WP:OWN]]) explains that nobody owns an article or a page on Wikipedia (and cannot forbid editing it, discussing its deletion, or keeping it).

In total, there were more than 130 votes, divided almost equally between those against and those in favor of deletion (the latter were also strict about rules but believed that a former presence on the Wikimedia Foundation board is not reason enough for a person to be included in an encyclopedia). With this lack of consensus there were no grounds for deleting the article.[2]

This example and the case of Larry Sanger show that on Wikipedia the procedures take precedence over the people. More importance is assigned to the participatively created set of rules than to formal roles, as would be more typical. The requirement of verifiable sources is taken seriously and works both ways: information without proper sources cannot be included, but well-sourced information cannot be removed.

Both cases expose the lack of direct power in the Wikipedia organization, even by the most prominent and privileged users (Zittrain, 2008), which contributes to both the attractiveness and the seaminess of the Wikipedia organizational design. On Wikipedia even the most respected people rarely receive special treatment. This is most important for understanding the changes in Wales's role.

## Wales's Changing Role

In Wikipedia's early days, Wales's position was unquestionable. Regardless of the cofounder title, he was the final authority. On September 26, 2001, he posted his statement of principles:

> I should point out that these are *my* principles, such that *I* am the final judge of them. This does not mean that I will not listen to you, but it does mean that at some ultimate fundamental level, this is how wikipedia will be run, period. (But have no fear, as you will see, below.) . . .
>
> Newcomers are always to be welcomed. There must be no cabal, there must be no elites, there must be no hierarchy or structure which gets in the way of this openness to newcomers. Any security measures to be implemented to protect the community against real vandals (and there *are* real vandals, who are already starting to affect us), should be implemented on the model of "strict scrutiny." ([[User:Jimbo_Wales/Statement_of_principles]])

In those times, when Wales said something, it was the law. He rarely used this privilege, preferring to defer to community consensus, but his decisions were final. He disliked elitism, hierarchies, and baroque structures, viewing them as discouraging to newcomers. He also disputed the existence of cabals.

In December 2003, an article on Wikimedia was created describing Wales as "the benevolent dictator of the English Wikipedia" ("Benevolent Dictator," 2013). Wales edited the article himself in September 2004, not deleting or revising it but only adding one line: "It should be noted that Jimbo disputes this term." His comment resulted in an inquiry on the article's talk page on why he opposes the name at all. Wales replied in a reflective description of his role in the community:

> I am more comfortable with the analogy to the British monarch, i.e. my power should be (and is) limited, and should fade over time. Wikipedia is not an anarchy, though it has anarchistic features. Wikipedia is not a democracy, though it has democratic features. Wikipedia is not an aristocracy, though it has aristocratic features. Wikipedia is not a monarchy, though it has monarchical features.
>
> The situation in nl.wikipedia.org is probably a good example of how I can play a productive role through the judicious exercise of power. My role there is mostly just as advisor to people in terms of just trying to help people think about the bigger picture and how we can find the best ways to interact and get along to get our incredibly important work done.
>
> But it is also a role of "constitutional" importance, in the sense that everyone who is party to the discussion can feel comfortable that whatever agreements are reached will be *binding*, that there is a higher enforcement mechanism. It's not up to me to *impose* a solution, nor is it up to me directly to *enforce* a solution chosen by the community, but I do play a role in guaranteeing with my personal promise that valid solutions decided by the community in a reasonable fashion will be enforced by someone.
>
> Notice that very little of *that* involves actual power. Rather, it involves respect for me and my role, and that respect last only so long as I act thoughtfully and with fairness and justice to everyone, and in accordance with the broad consensus of the community.
>
> And notice, too, that I believe such authority should be replaced as time goes along by institutions within the community, such as for example the ArbCom in en.wikipedia.org, or by community votes in de.wikipedia.org, etc.

We have very few problems, other than isolated things, with sysop abuse or cabals, even in smaller languages, and in part because everyone is quite aware that I would take whatever actions necessary to ensure due process in all parts of wikipedia, to the best of my ability.

None of this is like being a dictator, benevolent or otherwise. Jimbo Wales 01:07, 27 Oct 2004 (UTC). ("Talk:Benevolent dictator," 2011)

Wales recognized his need to release his power to the community, envisaged Wikipedia being taken over by community-created institutions such as the Arbitration Committee, and described his role as more advisory than having power. Rather than being a figure of authority, resolving disputes and making the final calls, he preferred to be the guarantor of consensus.

Also, quite likely, Wales did not think that the term, coined or at least popularized by Eric S. Raymond (1998) in his highly acclaimed essay on open-source software project management, is immediately recognizable as a quote. Raymond maintained that "benevolent dictatorship" is an effective model for organizing work, proved by the example of the Linux operating system:

Typically, a benevolent-dictator organization evolves from an owner-maintainer organization as the founder attracts contributors. . . . [A] benevolent dictator does not in fact own his entire project absolutely. Though he has the right to make binding decisions, he in effect trades away shares of the total reputation return in exchange for others' work. . . .

By custom, the 'dictator' or project leader in a project with codevelopers is expected to consult with those co-developers on key decisions. . . . A wise leader, recognizing the function of the project's internal property boundaries, will not lightly interfere with or reverse decisions made by subsystem owners.

Some very large projects discard the benevolent dictator model entirely. One way to do this is turn the co-developers into a voting committee (as with Apache [Software Foundation]). Another is rotating dictatorship, in which control is occasionally passed from one member to another within a circle of senior co-developers; the Perl developers organize themselves this way. (1999/2004, pp. 101–102)

Raymond possibly took the term from the "Benevolent Dictator for Life" nickname arguably given to Guido van Rossum, the creator of the Python programming language (Van Rossum, 2008). In Raymond's concept, benevolent dictatorship is quite close to what Wales would refer to as a constitutional monarchy. Yet Wales was probably right to say that the term "benevolent dictatorship" may be obscure outside the hacker and open-source community and even evoke association with the likes of Ho Chi Minh, Josif Broz Tito, or Fidel Castro (interestingly, the Wikipedia entry on "benevolent dictatorship" has been a field of an ongoing edit war on who should be given as an example of a benevolent dictator, and so far no clear consensus has been established). Still, as some Wikipedians pointed out, the "constitutional monarchy" term preferred by Wales is not much better because of its different meanings in the United States and in Europe, historical connotations, and the idea of succession.

Wales's description in the article as benevolent dictator was uncontested for several months. Founding principles of Wikipedia were formulated as late as May 2004. The user UninvitedCompany described them this way:

> Wikipedia as a community has certain foundation issues that are essentially beyond debate. Any challenge to these issues is usually ignored, and people who disagree with them usually end up leaving the project:
>     1.   The "wiki process" as the final authority on article content
>     2.   Ability of anyone to edit articles without registering
>     3.   NPOV [neutral point of view] as the guiding editorial principal
>     4.   GFDL [GNU Free Documentation License] licensing of content
>     5.   Jimbo Wales as ultimate authority on any matter
>     . . . The presence and unchangable nature of these foundation issues is one of the factors that has led to charges of cabalism. ("Founding_Principles," 2004)

Wales's status was explicitly established as superior to that of everyone else: according to the fifth point, whatever he said was law. But change was already apparent: Wales's authority was recorded as law. Even though seemingly confirming the status quo, following the governing metaphor its recording reflected a subtle shift from absolute to limited monarchy.

Wales evidently did not mind. In fact, he was keen on promoting the idea of the Arbitration Committee taking over some of his responsibilities and he helped that take shape in 2003.

In 2008 the following discussion took place, reflecting some of the communal concerns:

> I think it's been a long while since anyone actually considered Jimbo to have any real authority. Naerii 06:43, 28 June 2008 (UTC)

My question is, when did we ever decide he no longer had any authority? Tiptoety

> I have no idea. I just doubt that anyone takes seriously his hippie love-your-neighbour guff that he comes out with when he bothers commenting on community issues. Naerii 07:31, 28 June 2008 (UTC)

>> Experience and trust often give a Wikipedian informal authority. And while it might be hippie-love crap, it's still good advice, and I do try to take it to heart. —Ned Scott 07:38, 28 June 2008 (UTC)

>>> To respond to Tiptoety: From what I've heard in interviews and such, it's really been Jimbo himself that has tried to depreciate his formal authority, to help transition to a more community run system. —Ned Scott 07:40, 28 June 2008 (UTC). ([[Wiki pedia_talk:Role_of_Jimmy_Wales]])

Additionally, discussions about Wales being a steward kept arising. In February 2009, when the time for steward confirmations came, a confirmation for Wales was started as well (see "Stewards," 2009). Many users stated that since he was not really active as a steward, he should be removed from this group, possibly moved to the staff category. This did not seem right to others, who insisted that Wales was not really a member of the foundation staff. Some suggested that, since he was flagged as founder on the English Wikipedia, he could have a similar role across all projects. Wales decided to request creation of a project-wide founder flag, with the same privileges as those reserved for stewards. This solution seemed to satisfy everybody at the time and allowed Wales to keep his access and privileges and avoid further confirmations.

In July 2009 Wales blocked one of the administrators on the English Wikipedia because of her highly uncivil comments to an editor (who made wrongful but good-faith edits). The case was escalated to the Arbitration Committee, which pointed out that Wales had not followed blocking policy (see [[WP:Arbitration_Committee/Noticeboard/Archive_5#Arbitration_motion_regarding_Jimbo_Wales_and_Bishonen]]). As a result, Wales forfeited use of the blocking tools in the future. The event was not a big deal, but it is important, since it symbolically marks the moment when the Arbitration Committee started to exert its authority over Wales, rather than the other way around.

Also in July 2009, a proposal to form an advisory council on project development on the English Wikipedia, initiated by the Arbitration Committee and with endorsement from Wales ([[WP:Advisory_Council_on_Project
_Development]]), was poorly received by the community. Many Wikipedians
claimed that this move was an attempt to widen the ArbCom's scope of power
beyond the community's mandate. In particular, the nontransparent character of the new body was critiqued (invitations to join the council were sent
to undisclosed people handpicked by the initiators). Moreover, many were
infuriated that formation of the council was attempted without communal
discussion; this could be viewed as the feared cabalism.[3]

In September 2009 Wales declared that his appointments to the Arbitration Committee would henceforth be purely ceremonial. Shortly thereafter,
things went south.

## Breaching Experiments

In January 2010 the user Privatemusings created a page on Wikiversity about
ethical breaching experiments conducted at Wikipedia (e.g., creating bogus biographies to test users' and editors' reactions, adding plausible but fictional
references and citations). In February he added instructions on how to create
a sock-puppet for deceiving the Wikipedia administration. He was advised on
the same day that such content was unacceptable and that similar guides had
been removed from other Wikimedia projects before. He discussed the issue in
a quite civilized manner and started a community discussion on the topic in
March. One of the participants of this discussion asked Wales on the English
Wikipedia to look into the issue.

Wales responded not with love and understanding but instead by deleting
the whole page (and related subpages) and blocking Privatemusings. When
one of the administrators[4] started a community discussion about the situation, Wales issued a statement:

> I am currently discussing the closure of Wikiversity with the board. That is an
> unlikely outcome, but I mention it because I really want to press the point that
> the scope of Wikiversity has to be restricted to genuine OER [Open Educa-
> tional Resources]. I think that my actions here are strongly supportive of the
> genuine community who want to do that, making it clear to them that they

have very strong support for making it happen. Some may feel that Wikiversity should be a place for silly and juvenile experimentation. If people want to discuss such things, there is an entire Internet open to them—they should not hijack Wikiversity for these purposes. ([[WP:Wikipedia_Signpost/2010-03-15/News_and_notes]])

This comment was interpreted as a threat. Many editors commented also that while giving detailed instructions on how to cheat and experiment on Wikipedia should not be supported, documenting such occurrences and researching them should receive just as much coverage as computer security issues.

Meanwhile, a Wikiversity administrator and bureaucrat, SB Johnny, restored the pages deleted by Wales and unblocked Privatemusings. Wales immediately removed the pages, blocked Privatemusings again, and used his steward privileges to demote SB Johnny. He also declared that he would be happy to reinstate SB Johnny if he refrained from supporting Privatemusings. The user Thekohser, blocked on the English Wikipedia but active on Wikiversity, commented on the "Community Review" page that Wales's actions were "comically reminiscent of the schoolyard bully" and compared him to an Internet troll (see "Difference between revisions," 2010). Wales removed the comment and blocked the user.

These events raised a stir, mainly because many users believed that Wales had exceeded his authority. It was pointed out that he was not even an administrator on Wikiversity, he was not an elected Wikimedia steward, and his founder status, though including the technical abilities of a steward, should not be used at liberty and against the communal consensus. Six users addressed Wales on his talk page, requesting clarification. In Wales's terse replies he insisted that he acted with the full support of the foundation, which fueled further questions as to how and when this support was expressed.

Sue Gardner, executive director of the foundation, then posted her statement:

> There's a lot of talk on this page about whether Jimmy has the authority on Wikiversity to do what he did—the deleting and desysopping [or demoting]. With respect, I think that's a red herring. I support Jimmy because I think his main message is correct—and I am becoming a bit worried it may be starting to get lost in this authority conversation.

What Jimmy is saying is that he believes destructive trolling is happening on Wikiversity, and that the community here needs to figure out how to
better protect itself and its work. He says that it's important for a community
to be able to clearly define its mission, rather than to have a fully laissez-faire
attitude. I completely agree with that—if you can't define what you're doing in
a way that excludes destructive nonsense, you have a serious problem. . . . Sue
Gardner 05:38, 18 March 2010 (UTC). ("Wikiversity," 2010)

Meanwhile, the community was establishing policies to prohibit breaching experiments, at least with respect to giving detailed instructions. The following comment by Wales seemed reassuring:

My authority here does not derive from the community and isn't something
I'm interested in exercising in the future in any case. I recommend that this
portion of things simply be removed—in that it is an argument and discussion that we simply don't need to have, and which will make it much more difficult on all sides if a situation arises in the distant future. Don't make policy
which isn't needed. If you find me in your hair in 3 months time, then by all
means, do something about it at that time. . . . Jimbo Wales 16:03, 21 March
2010 (UTC). ("Wikiversity," 2011)

Wales agreed that Privatemusings seemed reasonable and unlikely to
restart the controversial pages and unblocked him on March 23, 2010 (see
"Wikiversity," 2011). But SB Johnny decided that he was no longer comfort-
able being an administrator and a bureaucrat of the project and resigned. One
other administrator followed suit.

The disputants had been aware that Privatemusings was an active member
of the Wikipedia Review, an Internet group extremely critical of Wikipedia
and often disparaging of Wikimedia projects. There he had discussed the
possibility of planting false information on Wikipedia as a breaching experiment and declared that he was going to try it.[5] Nevertheless, the discussion
was fierce and the community seemed most concerned about Wales's acting
outside allowed authority (neither in the capacity of an administrator or steward nor as an executor of an official decision by the foundation). His lack of
consultation with the community and the absence of reasonable explanations
were also pointed out. Most importantly, he used his steward powers to demote an administrator, bypassing approved procedures.

The debate, held at Wikiversity but also partly on Meta-Wiki[6] and on
the discussion lists, exceeded sixty thousand words and stimulated another

debate, started on Wikimedia on March 25, 2010, on whether Wales should have his founder flag removed because of his transgressions (see "Requests for Comment," 2013). Toward the end of March votes favored Wales: eighteen supporting removal, twenty-six against, three abstaining. Then another unfortunate event took place.

## Child Pornography?

In April 2010 Larry Sanger sent a letter to the FBI accusing Wikimedia Commons of hosting child pornography (Metz, 2010) and other hard pornographic images. The message, aimed at the media, was clear: Wikipedia, though positioning itself as an educational and knowledge-sharing website, contained explicit, potentially offensive, or even illegal images. The topic was eagerly picked up by FoxNews.com (Winter, 2010c). This could have been disastrous to the Wikimedia projects' image, and Wales decided a speedy reaction was necessary. He urged the community to set guidelines on sexually explicit pictures.

No clear consensus emerged. Wales initially argued that images defined as pornographic by the U.S. Child Protection and Obscenity Enforcement Act should be deleted. Later, however, he seemed to extend the argument to artworks and diagrams. Anticipating a PR disaster, he single-handedly deleted seventy-one files. These included illustrations made by Wikimedians themselves (and used in articles about sex), as well as historical drawings by renowned artists. Granted, some of them were indeed quite explicit and also deeply offensive to some groups of readers. For instance, a picture by the nineteenth-century Belgian painter Félicien Rops, *Saint Teresa*, depicted a nun, wearing only a coif and shoes, playing with a dildo with an ecstatic grimace on her face and blood spilling from her vagina.[7] Wales quite likely wanted to take the most controversial pictures offline, even if they were to be reinstated later, after giving full consideration to the matter.

The deletion of artistic images created an uproar. So did deleting educational drawings used as illustrations in articles about sex, such as the one depicting the act of fisting, which Wales insisted was "porn, pure and simple" ("User talk:Jimbo Wales/Archive/2010/5," 2010). Wikipedians are sensitive to any form of censorship and reluctant to impose limits on controversial but legal imagery.[8] Although several administrators followed Wales's lead, many users objected. Wales went on a deletion spree without discussion or presentation of an emergency plea for the speedy action. When confronted by several administrators on Commons, he entered an edit war (editors reverting each other's edits) with them and insisted that any discussion occur only after finishing the cleanup. In his haste, he did not ask people to help him but jumped into action himself, without responding to the questions from the community in the expected detail. To make matters worse, he ignored the serious technical consequences of deleting the images, which were in use by articles on different wikis,[9] and threatened to block people who undeleted some of the images.

Herbythyme, an administrator and a checkuser on the Commons, addressed Wales on Wales's talk page:

> I'm refraining (again) from being rude however the behaviour here is just not acceptable. If you are a dictator then fine. Those of us who care quite a bit about Commons—warts and all—will simply bugger off and leave the last one to turn out the lights if you keep up this style of "leadership" (yep that is sarcastic).
>
> There is work to be done and garbage to get rid of but there is also a community here who have been trying to improve this project for a fair time now and have "invested" in it quite a bit since you last showed up. Maybe go and reflect on this—this is not en wv [English Wikiversity]—this is a key wiki project that is of real value (particularly to those of us who are committed to it and care about it). —Herby 17:49, 7 May 2010 (UTC). ("User Talk:Jimbo Wales," 2010)

As one of the stewards then told me in an interview:

> There was a discussion among stewards: "Shit, what should we do? This guy [Wales] clearly lost his mind. Should we revoke his privileges or what?" Stewards who were in touch with the foundation employees also said that they were shocked; they didn't want to start anything as employees But there was finally an agreement from stewards that maybe he would have to be blocked and demoted, but then he calmed down.

In a huge, heated dispute that roiled not only Commons talk pages but also the foundation's discussion list, Wales was attacked, occasionally offended, and told that he was behaving as if Commons were a repository of pornographic materials (it contained only encyclopedic illustrations most of the time).[10] Wales defended himself on May 8, 2010:

> We were about to be smeared in all media as hosting hardcore pornography and doing nothing about it. Now, the correct storyline is that we are cleaning

up. I'm proud to have made sure that storyline broke the way it did, and I'm
sorry I had to step on some toes to make it happen.

He also received support from several of the board of trustees members
on the foundation e-mail list. Only about half the images deleted by Wales
were restored later; he was right about the others, according to community
standards and policies. Yet, clearly, the issue was much bigger than just being right or wrong about these deletions. As an experienced administrator
of Commons, Pieter De Praetere, observed in an impassioned response on
May 8, 2010,

> Nobody has the power to declare policy at commons but the community and
> the board. You are neither. You have behaved like a vandal, and every other
> user would have been blocked ad infinitum. This is not about porn, this about
> you abusing your status in the most evil way anyone could have imagined. If
> you had followed the correct procedure, instead of going on a deletion spree,
> everything would have been settled and most images would have been deleted
> anyway.
>
> This is unacceptible behaviour and is inexcusable. Delete first and discuss
> later is not the way commons works and it has never worked that way. You
> say you are proud? Well, you can be proud. You have destroyed all confidence
> people had in you, and frankly, you don't deserve any better.
>
> If you think stepping toes is the right way to do it, perhaps you should state
> [that] instead of "an encyclopaedia everyone can edit" [Wikipedia is] "a site
> that is run in accordance with the whims and fancies of the former owner."
>
> A disgruntled former Commons admin.

Some users, including experienced ones and a handful of administrators, announced that they would be leaving Commons and Wikimedia projects because of Wales's behavior.

Simultaneous with the discussion on the list, a petition was set up urging
Wales to respect the processes and policies established by the community and,
when he intervened, clearly state that immediate intervention was required,
with detailed explanations (see "Petition to Jimbo," 2013). The petition gathered support from over three hundred users in less than five days (and fewer
than forty votes in opposition).

Eventually, Wales apologized a couple of times for his actions and explained that he had had a feeling of urgency. It did not help much, though.
The uproar fueled a move to deprive Wales of his cross-project privileges

and resulted in the trend shifting on the voting page for removing Wales's founder flag.

The debate over Wales's status totaled twenty-eight thousand words and involved hundreds of Wikimedians. As of May 9, 2010, votes in support of depriving him of his powers totaled 329 (which increased by 76 in the next two months). Only 96 were against it (29 more in the following months). Only 9 people (including me) abstained (voted neutral). The high number of votes, the extreme polarization, and the emotional tone of the debate indicate that the community took the matter quite seriously.

Many voters expressed their anger in ridiculous ways (proposals to ban Wales from Wikimedia projects, repeated accusations of dictatorship, the time for god-kings long passed, etc.). More rational commentators pointed out that Wikimedia projects might be suffering from founder's syndrome and that it would be good for Wales to move on. More reasoned analyses often resembled what Dcoetzee, an experienced administrator on both the English Wikipedia and Commons, wrote in his vote in favor of removing the founder flag:

> Jimbo Wales is a great boon to Wikipedia as a figurehead and a spokesman. But he has a history of causing immense conflict whenever he tries to use his autocratic powers. . . . This will always be the consequence, no matter what individual carries these powers. His recent actions were particularly ham-fisted, demonstrating a fundamental disconnection from the processes and conventions of the Commons community. While I support the Board's priv-ileges to take unpopular action in emergencies, they should do so through an unnamed, impersonal account representing their combined will. I invite Jimbo to voluntarily step down and act as a normal admin subject to the same sanctions and requirements as the rest of us; or failing that, I ask the Board to review his special privileges, to minimise future conflict. Dcoetzee 21:50, 8 May 2010 (UTC). ("Requests for Comment," 2013)

On May 9, 2010, Wales acceded to the demands of his critics. In a letter sent to the foundation's e-mail list he stated,

> In the interest of encouraging this discussion to be about real philosophical/ content issues, rather than be about me and how quickly I acted, I've just now removed virtually all permissions to actually do things from the "Founder" flag. I even removed my ability to edit semi-protected pages! (I've kept permis-sions related to "viewing" things.)

I do not want to be a tyrant or dictator. I do not want us to fight about that kind of thing, as it's really a distraction from our work.

This seemed to bring the turmoil to an end. As it soon turned out, the debate on whether keeping the images was right or wrong notwithstanding, Wales's rapid deletions had been a well-timed preemptive tactical move. FoxNews not only continued to publish articles claiming that child pornography was being kept on Wikimedia projects but also requested comments from the Wikimedia Foundation's corporate donors (such as Microsoft, Google, Best Buy, Ford Foundation, Open Society Institute, USA Networks, and Yahoo!) about porn, quite likely trying to dissuade them from further support (Winter, 2010a). On May 14, 2010, FoxNews.com published "exclusive" material, again extremely critical of Wikipedia and revealing "chaos" in the community and "the eruption of a heated and chaotic debate over whether to delete the images, which legal analysts say may violate pornography and obscenity laws" (Winter, 2010b). Ironically, Wales's renouncing his active powers and limiting his founder-flag role was announced by some segments of the media in a way suggesting that Wales gave up his privileges to protest the majority's support for keeping pornography on Wikipedia (see, e.g., Barnett, 2010). However, some better-informed journalists commented that the whole issue proved that Wales should cut the cord and withdraw from involvement (Blankenhorn, 2010).

The view expressed in the Wikimedia Commons discussion on sexual content by an administrator on both the English Wikipedia and Commons prevailed:

It seems to me to have been a surprisingly inept action, but one undoubtedly taken in good faith. The main problems seem to have been (1) he panicked and went off half-cocked without building any consensus and (2) in the process of doing so, he invoked his authority as founder and as a Board member. The latter is what I think alienated the several admins and others who quit over this.
—Jmabel 04:47, 2 June 2010 (UTC). ("Commons Talk: Sexual Content," 2013)

In July 2010 the policies described in "Wikipedia:Child Protection" ([[WP:Child_protection]]) were made official by Wales on the English Wikipedia. This move did not create a stir. It was accepted that it was an invocation of the rule that decisions were not subject to consensus of editors ([[WP:CONEXCEPT]]), which states that "certain policies and decisions made by the Wikimedia Foundation ('WMF'), its officers, and the Arbitration Committee of Wikipedia are outside the purview of editor consensus." Apparently, the community, especially on the English Wikipedia, understood the need to eliminate harmful and illegal images. Its rabid side was visible only when procedures were perceived to be violated and informal authority exerted and abused.

In fact, while Wales has decreased his direct involvement in enforcing policies, editing, and in general with micromanagement of Wikipedia editors, his influence on the larger Wikimedia community has increased significantly. For instance, Wales's leadership has been pivotal in the English Wikipedia protests against the Stop Online Piracy Act (SOPA) and Protect Intellectual Property Act (PIPA) in the United States. In 2011 Wales initiated a discussion, started a poll, and organized the community's will so that the English Wikipedia, after much deliberation, went on strike.[11] On January 18, 2012, all pages on the English Wikipedia were blacked out, and thirty-seven other Wikimedia communities published some form of support.[12] The *New York Times* summed up the aftermath:

> The legislation, largely the product of media companies to protect movies, television shows, video games and music against online theft from rogue foreign Web sites, sparked a reaction that quickly shifted from an arcane policy debate to an online consumer rebellion.
>
> Wikipedia went black to protest SOPA and more than seven million people signed online petitions, many of which said the bills would "break the Internet." Congress, overwhelmed by the popular opposition, quickly backpedaled, leaving the legislation to die. (Chozick, 2012)

Although the protests were supported by other major websites (notably Google and Facebook), the blackout of Wikipedia, a direct result of an initiative started and led by Wales, made the difference. Such successful community mobilization would not have been possible without a good cause, appealing to a large part of the movement, but Wales's well-planned actions and direction setting for the initiative was what gave it legs. Arguably, this kind of leadership would have been difficult to assert before, when he was still attempting to be proactive on the projects. In a sense, the renunciation of active powers and withdrawal from hands-on directing marked Wales's transition from management to leadership.

Wales also has started to engage more in activism outside Wikimedia. For instance, he initiated a petition to stop the extradition of the British student Richard O'Dwyer to the United States. O'Dwyer had created a website with links to copyrighted content (posted by visitors, and removed upon request by copyright owners). His actions, although not clearly criminal, prompted American authorities to request his extradition. Wales gathered over 250,000 signatures and persuaded British authorities to stop the process (Wales, 2012). Wales also agreed to become an unpaid adviser to the British government (Hough, 2012).

Taken as a whole, his influence on the Wikimedia community, in terms of large-scale initiatives and leadership in selected, important issues, has grown since 2010. Fund-raising campaigns also prove that Wales has enormous impact on readers and editors. He is also unconditionally loved and respected by the Wikimedia community, and queues to shake his hand or exchange a couple of words at Wikimania conferences attest to this popularity. In fact, refraining from exercising direct power allowed Wales to introduce constitutional reforms on the English Wikipedia. On December 21, 2012, he wrote on his talk page, when formally approving ArbCom appointments,

> I'm planning in January to submit to the community for a full project-wide vote a new charter further transitioning my powers. Because the changes I hope to make are substantial, I will seek endorsement from the wider community. (There are powers which I theoretically hold, but can't practically use without causing a lot of drama, but it is increasingly clear to me that we need those powers to be usable, which means transitioning them into a community-based model of constitutional change. One good example of this is the ongoing admin-appointment situation . . . a problem which I think most people agree needs to be solved, but for which our usual processes have proven ineffective for change. Some have asked me to simply use my reserve powers to appoint a bunch of admins—but I've declined on the view that this would cause a useless fight. Much better will be for us to put my traditional powers on a community-based footing so that we, as a community, can get out of "corner solutions" that aren't working for us. ([[User_talk:Jimbo_Wales/Archive_122]])

At the time of this writing, discussion of the changes is still under way, yet it is quite clear that Wales recognized that his resignation from operational influence has further legitimized his strategic authority.

## Modes of Leadership in Open Collaboration

While the founder's exit has been shown to be a natural stage in organizational development, in this case the limitation of Wales's involvement was both consciously planned and a contingent process of management models and philosophies open-community leadership, both to some extent present in the free/libre and open-source-software (F/LOSS) environment.

E. G. Coleman (2011) points out that digital-generation communities may be governed by principles as diverse as those of WikiLeaks (with one charismatic leader making all decisions and monopolizing the limelight) to those of Anonymous (an antileader and anticelebrity group). Even though rarely falling on the extremes of that continuum, large open-collaboration projects tend to rely on two kinds of models: a democratic community-decision-making process (elections, representation) and "benevolent dictatorship" (Raymond, 1998, 1999/2004).

In the first case, the open-collaboration communities often start with the servant-leadership model (Taylor, Martin, Hutchinson, & Jinks, 2007), which requires the founder to take on a supportive, subservient, and noninterventionist role. In the case of such virtual self-managed teams, leadership is fluid and constantly emergent (Heckman, Crowston, & Misiolek, 2007). A study of the Debian (a free and open-source distribution of the Linux operating system) community, one of the often-researched examples from the F/LOSS movement, shows that in the beginning,

> charismatic authority mostly derives from earned respect often proven by leading a big, successful project. As a matter of fact, charismatic authority may be, in some circumstances, more "efficient" than authority deriving its legitimacy from well-established rules. (Garzarelli & Galoppini, 2003, p. 18)

Later, once the project matures, it may turn to more formal but still community-driven institutions, such as a constitution and elected temporary leaders in the Debian case (Sadowski, Sadowski-Rasters, & Duysters, 2008). The creation of more formal democratic procedures may be a result of the project's growth but also of the community's discontent with an authoritarian approach of ad hoc leaders. In fact, the creation of a constitution and formalized governance for the Debian project was a result of one attempt at authoritarian leadership (Mateos-Garcia & Steinmueller, 2006), which faced strong ideological opposition from a significant part of the community.

Antiauthoritarian resentments are strongly embedded in open-collaboration culture, harking back to the times of Usenet power struggles (Pfaffenberger, 1996). As a result of this process, the Debian community has neither one stable leader nor a clear decision-making cabal; it relies on "tribal distributed leadership" (O'Neil, 2009, p. 146). Similarly, Apache web server software relies on dispersed communities run by project leaders and supported (similar to Wikipedia) by a formal organization, the Apache Software Foundation (Conlon, 2007).

In contrast, the Linux community, started by Linus Torvalds, operates on a model that concentrates power in one person: Torvalds is the chief developer of Linux, which means that he is the final authority on what portions of code are admitted into the standard kernel. He is supported by lieutenants from his inner circle and sublieutenants who decide which contributor submissions to incorporate into their subsystems. This structure is informal and fluid but clearly hierarchical. While contributors work on whatever they find interesting and there is no clear coordination center that sets development directions, there is still firm hierarchical quality control. No organization supports the development of the project, however. What seems to be important for this model's sustainability is that Torvalds is one of the largest contributors to the project. In addition, his leadership, while clear and somewhat institutionalized, is not really authoritarian:

> One of the most noteworthy characteristics of Torvalds's leadership style is how he goes to great lengths to document, explain, and justify his decisions about controversial matters, as well as to admit when he believes he has made a mistake or has changed his mind. . . . In the end, Torvalds is a benevolent dictator, but a peculiar kind of dictator—one whose power is accepted voluntarily and on a continuing basis by the developers he leads. (S. Weber, 2004, p. 90)

Another F/LOSS community operating on a similar leadership model is the Emacs editors family, led by Richard Stallman (also the founder of GNU and the Free Software Foundation). According to some authors, the existence of a central authority figure is one of the essential ingredients in open-collaboration projects (Carr, 2007).

As history shows, though, both of these philosophies work just fine in the open-collaboration environment. And both, possibly, could have taken shape on Wikipedia. In fact, the history of the evolution of Wales's role in the community shows clear signs that it hovered between the two models. If events had turned out differently, Wikipedia could have taken the benevolent dictatorship route, as the community signaled its appreciation early on. Moreover, although Wikipedia communities are egalitarian, they still rely on informal leader-follower patterns (Yasseri & Kertész, 2013) and show a need for charismatic leadership.

However, the Linux model, to remain acceptable to the members, requires both the leader's heavy involvement in the project and his or her being open, explicit, and detailed in grounding any rationale for deviation from customary ways.

This is different from Wales's approach. While he has humility, mostly rejects authoritarian leadership, and is able to admit his mistakes, in both of the cases documented here he failed to communicate with the community and resorted to direct interventionism. Steven Weber makes the further point (2004, p. 168) that in open-source communities the main way a leader may fail his or her followers is by a lack of responsiveness. This is exactly what happened: Wales acted first and left the explanations for later. However, the benevolent dictatorship model, paradoxically, does not allow for such action if it is to be effective.

In fact, Wales's aversion to directing others backfired: in both situations, had he made an urgent appeal to the community to use his solution to the problem, rather than getting his own hands dirty and limiting interaction with the community to post-factum scanty replies, both scenarios would have developed differently. Even though the need for action was urgent, especially in the case of the porn scandal, posting an announcement about a force majeure situation and simply asking for a credit of trust before doing anything would have worked better.

"F/LOS communities only tolerate an individual's exercise of authority over her areas of expertise" (Mateos-Garcia & Steinmueller, 2008, p. 342). Following a model of epistemic communities, open-collaboration projects allow construction of authority that is based on knowledge differentials between participants, in particular, extensive knowledge of and contributions to the project. Alternatively, authority may come from coordination and increased communication with the community (Yoo & Alavi, 2004; Carte, Chidambaram, & Becker, 2006), as traditional management, if effective, may be also appreciated.

On the English Wikipedia Wales had authority to act, which came from his experience in the community. If either of the two described situations had happened there, in all likelihood his actions would have been accepted, though with minor disagreement.

But Wales acted outside his home project. On both Wikiversity and Commons he was respected as the founding father of the movement but lacked the local legitimization or the "idiosyncrasy credit" (Hollander, 1958). Joseph Reagle, when analyzing Wales's leadership before the incident, insightfully speculated that his authoritarian approach could be exerted only until it exceeded his accumulated merit or charisma (2010b). Wales was in shortage of both merit and charisma on Wikiversity and the Commons. He might have thought he had more influence because both of these projects operate in English, but they comprise distinct communities, each with its own standards, member hierarchies, and layers of interpersonal relations. Consequently, he was perceived as an intruder.

To make matters worse, he broke the rules. Both actual blocking and threatening to block are rigorously regulated in all major Wikimedia projects. Each project has specific rules of conduct. While rules differ in their details, only administrators can do routine blocks, and in special emergency cases sometimes stewards can. Although Wales had steward tools as the founder, he was not a steward and of course he had never been elected administrator. He also acted with nonchalant disregard for customs and policies. Even though this might have gone unnoticed if he had supreme standing and rock-solid authority in the local communities, he did not have this resource to spend. Also, Wikiversity and Commons communities are not the most peaceful within the Wikimedia universe; many vitriolic debates have taken place there and users are used to not mincing their words when they see a problem.[13] Additionally, Wales suggested he might leverage his position to exert control over the Wikiversity community if it did not obey. What was probably meant to be a gentle reminder of the common cause of all Wikimedia projects was interpreted as a threat. All this probably contributed to the overreaction by the Wikimedia community.

But ultimately, Wales's biggest mistake was that his position was incompatible with the emerging power structure and the new leadership model of the Wikimedia movement he himself helped develop. Had he not been out of line, the leadership transformation could have been more drawn out and he could have had larger influence on its execution, but the outcome would have been the same. Wikipedia, by Wales's design, chose the democratic model. Even though Wikipedia is not a democracy, it has developed democratic institutions and is governed, in principle, as a democratic community. The role of a constitutional monarch or any other single absolute decision maker was incongruous.

## The Point of No Return

Leadership is not necessarily a person-centered phenomenon; it is a fluid process enacted by the leader and the followers (Latour, 1986; Hollander, 1992). Well-performing self-managed virtual teams may not even need to rely on individual leadership (Lim & Chidambaram, 2011), and they are cause, ideology, or rules driven. Single-person leadership of self-managed teams is also often less effective than shared leadership (Solansky, 2008). Wikipedia relies on dispersed and shared leadership (Zhu, Kraut, Wang, & Kittur, 2011; Zhu, Kraut, & Kittur, 2012) in everyday task coordination. Yet there are clear benefits to having one charismatic leader in self-managed virtual communities. As Joseph Reagle points out,

> One reason for this efficiency is that the reputation of such leaders has an additional benefit of being useful in circumstances where a community is otherwise deadlocked; charismatic authority can intervene in circumstances in which there are multiple simultaneous coordination costs that are too expensive. (2007, p. 145)

Many debates and problems in the Wikimedia community suffer from the lack of one person who could resolve them by weighing in and using the credit of social trust. Indeed,

> the decentralization of political organizing may have wonderful implications for knowledge creation—Wikipedia is one example—but the reality is that decentralization itself is not a sufficient condition for successful political reform. In most cases, it's not even a desired condition. (Morozov, 2012, pp. 194–195)

For many reasons, the role of the founder is irreplaceable. No appointed executive director, regardless of his or her actual leadership skills and charisma, could achieve Wales's status, simply because he invented and initiated the movement. The benefits of the benevolent dictatorship model in open-collaboration communities are especially high, since unlike in totalitarian regimes all users are free to quit individually or cause a schism ("fork") and become a community, so all benevolent dictators are naturally limited in their authoritarianism. In this sense, direct leadership in open-collaboration communities is more demanding than in other organizations (M. E. Greiner, 2004), and coordination becomes crucial (Hemetsberger & Reinhardt, 2009). It is also essential in communities as large as the English Wikipedia. Still, such leadership must rely on structuring other participants' efforts through partnership and assisting in decision making (Skolik, 2012) and in negotiating rules and norms (Crowston, Heckman, Annabi, & Masango, 2005; Heckman et al., 2007).

In the previous chapters, I describe the advancing bureaucratization of Wikipedia, increased formalities, and further departure from the original principles (such as "ignore all rules"). All these phenomena are exacerbated by the transformation in personal leadership. The initial Wikipedia culture was typical for a start-up: entrepreneurial and oriented toward innovation (Bernard, 2009). These traits are not natural in the long run and require additional fostering, and bureaucracy is known to smother them (Sørensen, 2007; Girard, 2009). Transitions in leadership are particularly dangerous to these traits (Foley, 2008). The problem with the benevolent dictatorship model is that it does not allow for such a transition; one cannot be elected dictator. The only possible change is the one that Wikimedia experienced, to the democratic system, with no way back.

However, one unfortunate side effect of the antileadership rhetoric in Wikipedia culture is not that it may eliminate leaders (who emerge in all communities) but that it results in the community denying to have them and consequently prohibiting recruitment and solid legitimization of new leaders (Epstein, 2001; O'Neil, 2009). Wales's leadership however, has not declined but evolved. As already noted, the decision to stop managing enabled him to start leading. The events described in this chapter and his seemingly deliberate strategy of withdrawing from active involvement worked synergistically to limit his micromanagement, which was becoming incongruous with the democratic governance model, and allow him to exercise leadership on a larger scale and on a higher level.

The postindustrial revolution in organization designs has led to flatter structures, less hierarchy, and more liquid organizing (Bauman, 1998). The emerging postmodern culture of authority relies on shorter power distance and open expression of feelings (Hirschhorn, 1998). Both the incidents

I describe indicate that Wales's actions were rejected only when he was perceived as exerting traditional authoritarian leadership. The rejection, executed openly and without pardon, signified that the community adopted the new model. It did not signify the rejection of Wales in his leadership role.

Paradoxically, only less involvement in direct management helped him reach his higher leadership potential. This is because open-collaboration communities are particularly sensitive to the congruence of a leadership model (benevolent dictatorship or democracy) with the corresponding leadership practices (direct, hands-on approach or general vision and directing the movement on a large scale). While benevolent dictatorship involves close participation in the community, the democratic approach requires passing the micromanagement and smaller-scale actions to the community in full, which encourages higher-level engagement. Thus, it is the compatibility of the accepted leadership model with the leadership practices that seems to determine the model's effectiveness.

Wikipedia had evolved its egalitarian organizational design and was able to sustain it under the unique leadership of its creator. As leadership began to change, the design became unstable and sought a new equilibrium.

# 8

## THE KNOWLEDGE REVOLUTION
## AT THE GATES

In this book, I describe the results of a six-year ethnographic, participative re-search project on Wikipedia. I introduce the principles by which this commu-nity lives and show that the discourse of equality on Wikipedia also perpetuates the fears of authority. I explain how the theoretically ahierarchical system may increase the perception of inequality in practice and how the hierarchy is en-acted through community elections (the only frequent occasion for the com-munity at large to exercise its power). I show that although Wikipedia is often portrayed as collaborative and peaceful, it relies just as much on conflicts and disputes. I describe how the gradual and incremental increase in participation in editing determines both the attractiveness of this endeavor and its addictive-ness and, consequently, displays of irascibility. I explain how the seemingly cha-otic, anarchistic, and laissez-faire organization of cooperation on Wikipedia is, in fact, susceptible to extremely tight control through observation and registra-tion of all behavior, which structures the discourse of participants, and through procedures. I analyze the accumulation of bureaucracy in terms of the iron law of oligarchy, the need to establish and reinstate hierarchies, and the support of disproportionate technological power between veterans and newcomers. I also show how organizational control, so strict in other aspects, is more lenient in terms of credential checks as a result of a transformation of interpersonal trust and of trust in procedures. I describe how disregard for real-world cre-dentials and formal authority helps sustain the Wikipedia community, both by allowing an alternative authority-building pattern and by negating the ossified

structures of real-world knowledge generation. I study the internal stakeholders' composition of the Wikimedia movement and describe how it is influenced
by an advancing professionalization of the chapters. I consider the risk of a
major forking in the movement, analyze tensions and conflicts between the
key groups of interest (definitely ominous to a bystander, but mostly harmless,
considering that they are simply more explicit and exposed in radically open
cultures than in regular organizations), and reflect on the emerging, fluctuating
governance model of the movement that limits the influence of the Wikimedia
Foundation in spite of its current major role. Finally, I review the evolution of
Jimmy Wales's leadership on Wikipedia and explain how open-collaboration
communities require congruence between an organizational leadership model
(authoritative or egalitarian) and the exercise of leadership power (direct and
interventionist or general and visionary).

I now focus on two additional issues, both closely related to the previous
discussions but not addressed directly before: scholarly critique of the Wikipedia community and Wikipedia as an example of power-knowledge revolution. The latter is redefining the boundaries of social expertise and knowledge
hierarchies. Are open-collaboration communities the avant-garde of a movement liberating society from a neoliberal regime or the prelude to totalitarian
and ideological control? Additionally, I discuss the future of the Wikimedia
community.

## Hive Minds, Schmucks, Losers, and Other Misconceptions About Wikipedia

Some say that the contemporary Internet in general, and Wikipedia in particular, promotes amateurs and everyday Joes—that Wikipedia's "hive mind
mentality" and "digital Maoism" suppress human intelligence and dilute individual judgments and tastes (Lanier, 2006). Andrew Keen, the author of the
ominously titled *The Cult of the Amateur: How Today's Internet Is Killing Our
Culture* (2007), even states in an interview that no normal person would give
away labor for free and anonymously and that "only schmucks would do that.
Or losers" (quoted in Parvaz, 2011). As one of those schmucks or losers, and
possibly both, I am certainly biased, but I must point out that this argument is
rooted in the traditional point of view of attributing professionalism to formal
position rather than to skill and evaluation of the actual outcome (which, as
already mentioned, in the case of Wikipedia matches the commercial competi-

tion standards). One attribute of the postindustrial meritocracy is exactly such weighting of knowledge against titles. Wikipedia makes it possible to spread the weight of contributions until they are small enough that people are willing to offer what they do for free, without significant effort and with a major benefit for the whole community. Keen's contempt for this model indicates that he wants to believe the typically neoliberal economic paradigm that people are ruled mainly by self-interest, which excludes rational contribution to production of public good, even though open-collaboration communities are showing the opposite (Ostrom, 2000; Benkler, 2011). He also does not see the liberation in the new modes of knowledge production and the demise of the traditional ones (Scott et al., 1994). Wikipedia encompasses the capitalist mode of production and is the avant-garde of the emerging informational-communal approach (Barbrook, 2000; Hardt & Negri, 2001; O'Neil, 2011a; Firer-Blaess & Fuchs, 2013). Also, Keen apparently ignores the contexts in which "the wisdom of crowds" is particularly effective (Surowiecki, 2004) and seems to believe the Taylorist divide—some think and give orders, and others physically work and are the passive recipients of morsels of knowledge graciously given by the order givers—is still effective (Blackler, 1995).

Moreover, J. Lanier's and Keen's critique of Wikipedia assumes that the multiple authorship of Wikipedia articles dilutes authors' intellect and individuality and reduces them to a sort of a smart mob, composed of anonymous, chaotic, and contingent passersby, heavily relying on free-riding (R. Levine, 2011). While this argument sounds reasonable, it does not hold water in practice (Tumlin, Harris, Buchanan, Schmidt, & Johnson, 2007). It is obviously not true of Wikipedia, which relies equally on single-edit authors and on a stable, highly active community. As Yochai Benkler observes, "Wikipedia is not faceless, by and large. Its participants develop, mostly, persistent identities (even if not by real name) and communities around the definitions" (2006a).

Similarly, objections to the dispersed authorship model, expressed also by people sympathetic to Wikipedia's design, which depict Wikipedia as a "publish then filter" endeavor, as opposed to a traditional encyclopedia that relies on the "filter then publish" principle (Shirky, 2009, p. 98), may be considered at least partially inadequate, since "publishing" means fundamentally different things in the age of the Internet. Granted, anyone can make edits to Wikipedia, and the changes are visible instantly (more recently, changes introduced by new users on many Wikipedias do not appear until more established editors approve them). Yet one can argue just as well that Wikipedia is not a work that is "published" (a term related to temporal milestones more meaningful to a traditional press) but rather one in an ongoing process of creation (Priedhorsky et al., 2007). While open-source projects generally have frequent releases (Raymond, 1999/2004), Wikipedia is in continuous release mode (Luther & Bruckman, 2008). If an analogy to traditional encyclopedia production has to be made (and the sense of such an analogy is questionable when even the publishers of the most traditional encyclopedia, *Britannica*, decided in 2012 to cease publishing the paper edition; see Britannica Editors, 2012), one could just as well argue that on Wikipedia the subsequent edits from different people are the systematic layers of quality improvement. Instead of production stages of traditional encyclopedias, Wikipedia has thousands of quality control checks and "publication" never materializes. (It is a rare event for Wikipedia content to be frozen, sometimes with some editorial corrections, as was done in several DVD[1] publications relying entirely on Wikipedia content.)

Many academics object to Wikipedia merely because it challenges the traditional social construction of knowledge and its dissemination, in which the empowered academics are the ones who play the roles of crucial gatekeepers and disseminators (Eijkman, 2010). Indeed, the change in the role of custodian of knowledge may be the reason for both the academic disregard for Wikipedia and its attractiveness for people from outside academia. Paul du Gay, when introducing the approaches to identity in literature, insists that "we need to see how particular categories of person have been formed or 'made up' in specific contexts, at a particular time and through certain practical means" (2007, p. 25). The attractiveness of being a Wikipedian relies to a significant extent on users being able to assume an identity of knowledge creators, a role traditionally reserved for a highly privileged caste of academics. This is probably also why Wikipedia is not widely appreciated in scholarly circles. As Lawrence M. Sanger points out, "If Wikipedia fulfills its highest potential in terms of measurable quality, then experts will thereafter not need to be granted positions of special authority in order for humanity to have a resource that accurately tracks expert opinion" (2009, p. 56).

Consciously or not, many academics may perceive Wikipedia as a symbolic threat to their authority. Things become even worse when they start editing Wikipedia and have to face the fact that their hard-earned diplomas and titles do not help even a bit in discussions with other editors. Their discursive authority as well as knowledge, naturally, should still help in making their arguments stronger, but the aura of expertise is gone. Wikipedia redefines the modes of knowledge enactment and development by reconceptualizing it into a many-to-many relation and "participatory expertise" (Pfister, 2011, p. 229). The innovative construction of interpersonal trust and identity on Wikipedia stems from the need to discard the traditional hierarchy of knowledge production, so that the social organization of collaboration could work the way it does. In this sense, some disregard for academic titles (in terms of purely formal recognition of authority, without some actual expertise) is embedded in the philosophy of the movement.

While knowledge management may be just a fad in consulting in business literature (Jemielniak & Kociatkiewicz, 2009), management of knowledge through crowdsourcing has brought a successful redefinition of social knowledge boundaries, of which the Wikimedia movement is a part. The resulting inevitable redistribution of social power (Foucault, 1982) is probably even more significant in the long run than the parallel transformation of consumers of culture into its producers (Bruns, 2008). The new mode of knowledge production surpasses the traditional, hierarchical, turf-driven, and caste-like system that universities depend on (Gibbons, 2000; Godin & Gingras, 2000; Bartunek, 2011), being possibly more effective than research institutions at engaging the practitioners and society.

This knowledge- and power-distribution revolution may surprise and perhaps frighten many, which may be why some technology pundits and scholars are eager to predict the demise of Wikipedia. For instance, Eric Goldman, a professor of law at Santa Clara University, claimed in 2005 that "Wikipedia will fail within 5 years" (Goldman, 2005), because of its overly open nature, the gradual decrease in the community's enthusiasm, and its inability to counter spam and vandalism. As years pass, he repeats his prophecy but changes the timeline (N. Anderson, 2009).

Others, even though they do not expect Wikipedia's demise any time soon, perceive it as a cult (Arthur, 2005; Peters, 2007; Metz, 2008b). In the words of Sam Vaknin,

> All cults are the same: they spawn a hierarchy, sport arcane rules, suffer from paranoid insularity, do not tolerate dissent, criticism, and disagreement, and ascribe to themselves a cosmic grandiose mission. No cult is benign. All cults are run by individuals with narcissistic traits and the Wikipedia is no exception. (2010)

Still others, despite appreciating the merits of Wikipedia, see it as based on a system of injustice, power play, and domination (O'Neil, 2011a) and as a flawed knowledge community (Roberts & Peters, 2011).

These views notwithstanding, the perception of Wikipedia even in academic circles has improved over time, as has the perception of its quality (Shachaf, 2009), and scholars not only rely on it but also support it (Bateman & Logan, 2010; Heilman et al., 2011) and use it as a teaching tool (Konieczny, 2012), although many of them recognize that Wikipedia is a challenge to traditional academic authority (Eijkman, 2010). As Matthew Battles observes,

> Authority, after all, flows ultimately from results, not from such hierophantic trappings as degrees, editorial mastheads, and neoclassical columns. And if the underprivileged (or under-titled) among us are supposed to keep quiet, who will enforce their silence—the government? Universities and foundations? Internet service providers and media conglomerates? Are these the authorities—or their avatars in the form of vetted, credentialed content—to whom it should be our privilege to defer?
>
> Experience, expertise, and authority do retain their power on the web. What's evolving now are tools to discover and amplify individual expertise wherever it may emerge. (2007)

This corresponds well with Clay Shirky's observation:

> In fact what Wikipedia presages is a change in the nature of authority. Prior to Britannica, most encyclopaedias derived their authority from the author. Britannica came along and made the relatively radical assertion that you could vest authority in an institution. You trust Britannica, and then we in turn go out and get the people to write the articles. What Wikipedia suggests is that you can vest authority in a visible process. As long as you can see how Wikipedia's working, and can see that the results are acceptable, you can come over time to trust that. And that is a really profound challenge to our notions of what it means to be an institution, what it means to trust something, what it means to have authority in this society. (Quoted in Gauntlett, 2009, p. 42)

In a broader sense, Wikipedia, with all its flaws, is still an embodiment of a Habermasian rational discourse platform, emancipating communication of knowledge and allowing egalitarian knowledge creation and sharing and contradicting the thesis of information technology as a tool of social control and domination (Cammaerts, 2008; Hansen, Berente, & Lyytinen, 2009). It challenges the "monologic" expertise of dominant knowledge elites (Hartelius, 2010, p. 505): the communicative self-reflexivity, dialogical truth, and networked expertise of Wikipedia all stay in stark contrast to the traditional model, embodied by *Britannica*. As Joseph M. Reagle notes, the university, the academy, and scholarly society in general were each developed in response to its predecessor's failure to satisfy new needs for knowledge production and distribution (2010b, p. 154); the same may be said of Wikipedia.

In addition, Wikimedia projects in some ways resemble social entrepreneurship ventures (Clamp & Alhamis, 2010), even though they are not oriented at generating profit, as they are deadly competition to many similar commercially developed products. *Britannica* and more recently Wikitravel[2] have learned the hard way that volunteer-driven communities, dedicated to distributing knowledge for free and without advertising, can create products that are more appealing to readers and contributors. This is possible partly thanks to its governance model: relying on dispersed communities and editors, occasionally organized into chapters, but with a professional foundation responsible for backbone operations, as discussed in Chapter 6. Many commercial organizations over the last years have learned to draw from open-collaboration models (Westenholz, 2012).

## New Freedoms and Altruism or New Exploitation?

Participation in virtual communities of practice, such as free/libre-and-open-source-software (F/LOSS) projects and other open-collaboration communities, has major influence on enculturation and shaping the shared values of the participants. For example, the Debian hacker ethic is to a huge extent socially constructed and strengthened in communal interactions in opposition to the traditional market-based concept of intellectual property (Coleman & Hill, 2005). It revolves around the strong belief in personal freedom (Coleman & Golub, 2008).

Pekka Himanen describes the hacker ethic, a characteristic of the emerging network society (2001). This new paradigm is based on cooperation and joint production and is transforming the economy and society (Benkler, 2006b). Collaborative, altruistic efforts and peer equality play important roles. Also, "the basic organizational factor in life is not work or money but passion and the desire to create something socially valuable together" (p. 53).

This resonates with core Wikipedia community values (Antin, 2011). In fact, Wikipedians, similar to Christopher Kelty's (2008) "geeks" (including hackers, programmers, administrators), besides their encyclopedic work, spend much of their time discussing values, ideas, and Internet freedoms, and many are clearly ideology driven. This is one of the reasons why the Stop Online Piracy Act and Protect Intellectual Property Act protests, orchestrated by Jimmy Wales and described in Chapter 7, gained so much momentum. In this sense, the Wikimedia movement taps into the alternative-left critique of the capitalist system, similar to the Occupy Wall Street movement, opposing the neoliberal vision of the world (Hardt & Negri, 2001; Klein, 2007). As Martin Hilbert observes, Web 2.0 applications, including social networks and Wikipedia "have the potential to fulfill the promise of breaking with the longstanding democratic trade-off between group size (direct mass voting on predefined issues) and depth of argument (deliberation and discourse in a small group)" (2009, p. 87).

In this spirit, it is possible to perceive Wikipedia indeed as the avant-garde of the new modes of collaboration, questioning the current capitalist system and transforming markets and freedom through social production and open collaboration (Benkler, 2006b).

Yet, clearly, Wikipedia is also a sign of another phenomenon: prosumer capitalism. According to George Ritzer and Nathan Jurgenson (2010), prosumer capitalism is characterized by massive unpaid labor and products with no cost attached, resulting in abundance of goods that had previously been scarce. They perceive the Web 2.0 phenomenon, including Wikipedia, as happening in the wake of the new offensive of capitalism, perhaps even more exploitative than before. Instead of a digital utopia of equality, freedom, and culture of generosity (Tapscott & Williams, 2006), it may, as already noted, serve the increased surveillance, corporate control, and abuse through unpaid labor (Turner, 2006; Bauman, 2012; Morozov, 2012). The technological revolution of the new capitalism is just as much about giving freedom as it is about taking it away (Sennett, 2007). Online communities and social networks can be seen as both creating a public interaction space and obliterating the old, physical ones at the same time; digitalization eliminates social divisions and creates them (Bauman, 1998). We see the "use of technology as a form of societal rule" (Bauman, 1991, p. 150).

In this sense, the motivation systems, as well as the parahierarchies and social recognition structure of open-collaboration systems described in

Chapters 1 and 2, are potentially elements of normative control (Kunda, 1992) over participants: at first by luring users to contribute through making small investments of time at low stakes, allowing bite-size, fine-grained contributions, and later through influencing the values of participants and through ideological persuasion to contribute. Editing Wikipedia is often described as fun, just as virtual gaming communities often enforce the ideology of play (Kücklich, 2009) and commercial organizations rely on redefining work as fun (Fleming & Spicer, 2004, 2007; Sørensen & Spoelstra, 2012). Thus, that work on open-collaboration platforms is perceived as a hobby should not necessarily signify that it does not involve worker exploitation. While Wikipedia is a not-for-profit organization and exploitation of editors, if any, benefits society as a whole, other organizations also using crowdsourcing and user-generated content (as does TripAdvisor and IMDb) rely on elements of open-collaboration design, tested so well in the Wikipedia community, to maximize their revenues. This criticism of open-collaboration organization as a new form of making capital out of consumers and using them to create value for the producers does not apply directly to Wikipedia. Yet the thesis that the open-collaboration phenomenon leads univocally and definitely to liberating consumers from traditional neoliberal institutions and economics seems risky.

Moreover, the theoretical democratization of knowledge production may be simply a reenactment of the established system (König, 2012), as discussed in Chapter 2. As Eli E. Pariser's recent work convincingly shows, the free access to information may just as well be threatened by "filter bubbles" (2011) and corporate monopolization of knowledge, not only supporting the old establishment but also adding new layers to it. Wikipedia seems to be, willingly or not, in the middle of a major ideological clash:

> Today powerful and highly profitable corporations such as Microsoft and Google are battling for a greater presence and power on the internet. However, the orientation of capitalism and its goals—especially ever-increasing profits—are in conflict with the cyber-libertarianism that remains a strong presence online on sites such as Wikipedia, Linux, and Creative Commons communities. Thus, profit-making corporations cannot ride roughshod over the internet; they must find ways of adapting, at least for the moment, to this new web ethic. (Ritzer & Jurgenson, 2010, p. 23)

This may be why the Wikimedia community reacts wildly to attempts at censorship (even of semiporn or gore in encyclopedic contexts), organizes massive protests to protect Internet liberties, and jealously protects user privacy. Although the "digital nativity" of the new generation is exaggerated and somewhat nonreflexively repeated (Selwyn, 2009), there may be something to it. If it is applicable to anyone, it is the generation that has grown up using and occasionally editing Wikipedia, exposed also to a mass new media culture, one depending on consumer production (Deuze, 2009).

The contrasting philosophies (libertarianism vs. the new left; increasing human freedoms vs. the system of new oppressions; peer production as altruistic collective endeavor vs. being brainwashed into free labor) do not have to be mutually exclusive. Wikipedia may partly rely on normative and ideological control, yet the dark side of that control, observable in commercial organizations (Barley & Kunda, 2004; Fleming & Spicer, 2004), does not occur in Wikipedia because of the entirely voluntary and nonmonetary character of participation and the nonprofit character of its organization. Wikipedia may also be an example of "peer progressivism" (S. Johnson, 2012, p. 45), characteristic of the digital natives, and combine the concepts traditionally associated with the right (libertarianism, distributed intelligence prevailing over centralized planning) with the ones traditionally ascribed to the left (cooperative work, developing and protecting the commons and the public good).

## Where Do We Go from Here?

As I have shown in this book, the Wikimedia movement is a unique and fascinating phenomenon of spontaneous social ordering, self-regulation, and collective production for the common good. The Wikimedia community is deeply value driven; it is disputatious and quarrelsome but altruistic. Even though I am not aware of any good, culturally rich studies of the ideological involvement of Wikimedians, quite clearly they are often activists involved in other movements, too, even those not following radical ideologies related to their Internet presence. This radicalism is visible in the approaches to free speech (considered one of the most important values, as described in Chapter 7) and also to privacy. The hatred of censorship in any form is the main reason for the impasse in filtering of controversial content. Regarding privacy, an interesting though typical dichotomy can be observed: Wikimedians believe in the need for radical transparency and public access to most information, as long as it is not private and related to individuals. While all organizations of power (e.g., governments, corporations, nongovernmental organizations, Wikimedia movement committees) are expected to release as much information as possible and strive for transparency, all individuals have a radical right to protect their private information. This respect for privacy goes far; for instance, for many years, the Wikimedia Foundation required scans of IDs from candidates applying for roles of trust (e.g., those of a checkuser, steward, or an ombudsperson) but deleted them immediately after use and did not even store the names that were submitted.

Although this ideological stance will likely remain, many other challenges face the Wikimedia movement. One of the biggest is Wikimedia's need to catch up with new generations of editors, who expect the same usability and comfort they find on popular social networks. At the time of writing this book, a WYSIWYG editor is being introduced on the English Wikipedia, for iPhone and Android, allowing upload of pictures directly to the Commons repository. Other technological innovations and improvements are on the way.

But other challenges loom. The extremely low number of female editors and the significant underrepresentation of editors from the Global South have no easy solution but must be addressed at some point. Similarly, finding common ground with the academic world and coming to terms with it is an issue the whole movement will have to address.[3] Even if a solution is not always possible institutionally, reaching out to the academic world is important on the level of individual contributions.

As topic saturation nears and the quality of articles improves, it will become increasingly difficult to keep entry contribution at a low level of effort. Newcomers will eventually find it increasingly difficult to contribute to Wikipedia without doing major research, and initial contributions in particular will have to be easy to make the system of incremental commitment feasible. The Wikimedia movement as a whole is still far from this point, but increasing problems with editor retention may signal that becoming a Wikimedian is not as easy as it used to be (this is also because of the increased bureaucracy, informal hierarchies, and other processes described in the book).

Larger structural changes of the data may be required in the near future; however, they will be difficult to implement. Wikimedia projects in general rely on a traditional encyclopedic form of specific articles, sorted by categories and searchable by headwords. This structure does not include social networking for the reader, and it is not efficient. Wikipedia may include a marvelous article on St. Peter's Basilica in Rome that is useful for art students, for example, but it will not be equally convenient for use with Google Glass or easy to cut into digestible bites.

Additionally, currently Wikipedians assume the same general adult level of reading ability (even Simple Wikipedia does so, while using simplified language for nonnative speakers' convenience). At some point, Wikimedia projects may decide to diversify their articles in this respect and allow readers to decide for themselves which level of difficulty to see, consequently rewriting all articles in such a way that different levels of comprehension are allowed.

All of these and other changes will influence the social side of the community; however, they will not change one thing: Wikimedia currently is and will long remain a fascinating topic for researchers in anthropology, organization studies, management, sociology, media studies, and many other disciplines.

## Conclusion

This book is a result of a deeply participative and intimate immersion in an open-collaboration organization. Participation was used as a research method and is discussed in Appendix A. Wikipedia has a unique social organization, with peculiarities, dysfunctions, and problems but also with an amazing efficiency, openness, and egalitarian culture.

Wikipedia is an insanely ambitious project to compile all human knowledge in a single, organized, and structured piece of work and make it accessible for free to everyone. Although some authors believe that it is nearing completion (Rosen, 2012), according to other estimates it is far from it.[4] Whatever the practical saturation may be, there is still much to do when all languages and all projects are considered. Whether Wikipedia is truly open and egalitarian, whether it provides accurate information often enough or allows hoaxes to prevail too often, and whether its governance and structure can provide long-term stability, one thing is clear: the social organization of nonexpert work in this virtual, open-collaboration community is fascinating, unique, and inspiring for management and organization studies, and I hope it will be a topic of many more detailed analyses.

User Raul654 created a collection of "Laws of Wikipedia," in which he gathers both his own morsels of wisdom and those contributed by others (see [[User:Raul654/Raul's_laws]]). On March 21, 2006, he added "the zeroeth law of Wikipedia," of unknown attribution. It is a good summary of this ever-evolving, amazingly different, and surprisingly effective community and concludes this book: "The problem with Wikipedia is that it only works in practice. In theory, it can never work."

# APPENDIX A: METHODOLOGY

This publication is academic and, as such, has to explain its methodology. To keep the book more accessible for nonacademic readers, these explanations are in this appendix, which positions the research in relation to the literature and in a wider academic context. In addition, it is an introduction to ethnographic studies online.

## Ethnography and Going Native

*Common Knowledge?* is an ethnographic project. Since many similar academic papers present themselves as organizational ethnographies and this one does not, this requires more explanation. Sometimes a series of qualitative interviews and snapshot observations passes as ethnographic research. "A journey into the organizational bush is often little more than a safe and closely chaperoned form of anthropological tourism" (Bate, 1997, p. 1150). In rare cases, studies without longitudinal participation in the studied community are presented as ethnographic, perhaps in an attempt to make an impression of validity, and result in what S. Bate calls an "ethnographic pastiche" (Bate, 1997, p. 1151). Though many such studies may be interesting and valuable, carelessly applied labels dilute genuine ethnographic inquiry (Wolcott, 1990).

This book is a result of long-term, reflexive participative ethnographic research. It belongs to the anthropology of organization, a field of increasing interest in the academic community (Schwartzman, 1993; Wright, 1994; Kostera, 2007; Humphreys & Watson, 2009). The anthropology of organization assumes that ethnographic research requires extensive fieldwork combined with a variety of research methods meant to "grasp the native's point of view, his relation to life, to realize his vision of his world" (Malinowski, 1922/1961, p. 25).

I am a "native anthropologist" (Narayan, 1993) who had an extended presence in the studied community, which accepted me as a member. Traditional anthropology sometimes warns against studying one's own culture: "Fieldwork in a cultural context of which you already have intimate first-hand experience seems to be much more difficult than fieldwork which is approached from the naive viewpoint of a total stranger" (Leach, 1982, p. 124).

Anthropologists are advised to remain "professional strangers" (Agar, 1980) or "marginal natives" (Lobo, 1990; D. Walsh, 2004) and not to go native. However, such concerns have been discussed for a long time (Jarvie, 1969), and going native has some academic benefits (Hayano, 1979; Tresch, 2001). In fact, it may be considered desirable (Sperschneider & Bagger, 2003). John Van Maanen puts it this way: "Fieldwork of an ethnographic kind is authentic to the degree it approximates the stranger stepping into a culturally alien community to become, for a time and in an unpredictable way, an active part of the face-to-face relationships in that community" (1988/2011, p. 9).

Particularly in the case of a virtual community, where all members start as strangers, the experience of going fully native is indispensable (Gatson & Zweerink, 2004), and at the same time, the disadvantages of going native are largely neutralized. This experience goes far beyond the practical issues of material access:[1] being a fully active Wikipedian was quite likely the only way to gain the trust and friendship of other Wikipedians, so that they would share their insights and honest views, and to be able to discern the topics, discussions, and events that are important to the community.

An incredibly large volume of information constitutes the community's virtual life,[2] characterized also by its "deep diversity" of cultures and backgrounds (English-Lueck, 2011). In addition, the dynamics of a discussion is usually lost once the discussion is over. While it is possible to go through discussions retrospectively, they would be extremely difficult to follow for a person who has not been immersed in Wikipedia culture for a couple of years, who does not understand the context of disputes, and who cannot distinguish between recurring and new ones. Indeed, "insiderness [is] . . . the key to delving into the hidden crevices of the organization" (Labaree, 2002, p. 98). Beginners struggle even with understanding the language of the natives, but this obstacle is certainly easier to overcome than in traditional anthropological studies. Thus, retrospective studies conducted by non-Wikipedians are often shallow because of the hermetic nature of many of this electronic tribe's behaviors and the non-Wikipedian's lack of context (including off-Wikipedia discussions); outsiders have little access to community knowledge (Merton, 1972). Also, they tend to apply interpretive lenses borrowed from studies of other organizations and as a result may be prone to cognitive biases (for example, communal organizational tensions on Wikipedia are more likely to be construed as a sign of deep conflict than as radical openness and acceptance of the airing of opinions without fear of reprisal from upper levels).

This study benefits from autoethnographic insight (Hayano, 1979; Kanuha, 2000). It follows Barbara Czarniawska-Joerges's advice to keep an "anthropological frame of mind" (1992, p. 73), question the obvious explanations of the observed phenomena, and preserve the researcher's identity.

## The Use of First-Person Narrative

The presentation of the ethnographer's role in the field is vitally important for the written outcome of the research (Van Maanen, 1988/2011), and there are many strategies for presentation in a published ethnographic work (Geertz, 1988).

Ethnographers often suffer from a problem described by Clifford Geertz: they are torn between producing "author-saturated" and "author-evacuated" texts (1988, p. 9). Texts written from a first-person perspective bring the reader to the field. They give the reader the impression of being there, dramatizing the described events and legitimizing anthropological fieldwork. However, such a stylistic choice threatens the scientific status of the text itself, as academic research is traditionally written in third person. In the traditional approach, scholars, following the example set by the sciences, assume a stance of full disengagement from their subjective judgments. The careful avoidance of first-person narratives builds the academic standing of the text. Their work is realist in the sense of treating the studied cultures as natural, nonsocial phenomena and as if the researcher were merely reporting what he or she observed (Van Maanen, 1988/2011). This approach assumes that "eliminating the human scientist from the text is compatible with an assumption that the removal of possible researcher biases is both desirable and possible" (Golden-Biddle & Locke, 1997, p. 65).

Use of the third person in ethnographic accounts has been criticized (Hastrup, 1992; Bal, 1993; Denzin & Lincoln, 2003; Lincoln & Denzin, 2003). The obvious risk is that "much of that writing is simply not interesting to read because adherence to the model requires writers to silence their own voices, to view themselves as contaminants" (Richardson, 2001, p. 35), but bucking tradition is not a simple decision. Since ethnography has often been challenged as less than scientific and sometimes bordering on fiction (Silverman, 1975; Webster, 1982), choosing between first or third person is a serious dilemma.

Anthropologists have recognized the inherently political character of this problem (Clifford & Marcus, 1986): ethnography is always subjective because of the choosing involved in the quotations to present and events to report. As with any other academic writing, ethnography is not a report transmitting an objective reality, and removing the author from the text does not make the results more or less valid; it is simply a persuasive strategy of hiding the author behind a seemingly dispassionate account (Watson, 1995). This is true even of such seemingly impersonal fields as economics (McCloskey, 1998) or the sciences (Latour & Woolgar, 1979; Knorr-Cetina, 1999). Indeed, "the burden of authorship cannot be evaded, however heavy it may have grown; there is no possibility of displacing it onto 'method'" (Geertz, 1988, p. 140). When the researcher not only witnesses but also actively participates in events, obliterating the first person from the narrative for the sake of academic literary tradition seems to be a costly trade-off (Bochner, 2001).

This is probably why many ethnographic accounts are first-person narratives (Powdermaker, 1966). Similarly, in organizational ethnographies the use of "I" in the text is often justified (Czarniawska, 2004). Its use is relevant for narratives based on autoethnographic studies (L. Anderson, 2006; Denzin, 2006; Afonso & Taylor, 2009), in which an ethnographer reflects on his or her own experience.

Following this logic, I have not attempted to eliminate all sign of myself from this book. Most of the time and when describing the Wikipedia community, I use third person. When I report events I was involved in, I use a "confessional" form (Van Maanen, 1988/2011, p. 73), and when I cite my own experience or describe choices I made (for example, in this appendix), I occasionally switch the narrative to the first person to emphasize its ownership.

## Research Methods

This study relies on the interpretive paradigm (Burrell & Morgan, 1979). In line with Clifford Geertz's famous quote, drawing on Weberian comparison, this paradigm assumes that "man is an animal suspended in webs of significance he himself has spun," and the study of these webs "is not an experimental science in search of law, but an interpretive one in search of meaning" (Geertz, 1973, p. 5). The study assumes a theatrical metaphor (Goffman, 1959): organizational actors discursively enact their roles (Bowers & Iwi, 1993), cocreated dynamically by the ones performing them, and negotiate symbolic meanings of their worldviews (Blumer, 1986; Collins, 1990).

Typically for an ethnographic organizational study, this study takes culture to be a root metaphor (Smircich, 1983), which means that the community under consideration is understood as a culture (assuming that cultural processes are a useful key for understanding communal interactions), and the anthropological repertoire of methods to be most appropriate (Czarniawska-Joerges, 1992; Alvesson, 1995). Consequently, the studied culture is perceived performatively and not ostensively (Latour, 1986; D. Jemielniak, 2002), which means that it is analyzed without the use of a preconceptualized, theoretical model of culture; rather, the analysis aims at understanding the cognitive map and participants' perception of how the culture is organized. The study is oriented at the actual practices rather than at what may be modeled in principle (Feldman, 2000; Spicer, Alvesson, & Kärreman, 2009).

The socially constructed character of everyday reality (Berger & Luckman, 1967) assumes that any observation is deeply rooted in interpretation and that our perception of the world is always symbolic (Czarniawska, 2003); social reality is given meaning only through intersubjective negotiations (Schütz, 1967). The authenticity of the results in an objective, enlightened report is thus found in giving justice to the studied community's insight and in reliable, reflexive interpretation of the fieldwork (Cunliffe, 2003) rather than in a presentation of how it really is (Case, 2003).

The research methods used for the study are typical for ethnography (Nachmias & Frankfort-Nachmias, 1981/2001) and relied on triangulation (Denzin, 1978): participant observation, open-ended interviews, and case studies. As is common for anthropological inquiry (Atkinson & Hammersley, 1994), participant observation was the most extensively used method (Emerson, Fretz, & Shaw, 2001; Delamont, 2004). I took the stance of a member-researcher, trying to understand the community as a full-fledged participant, to gain deeper knowledge of its social construction than a casual nonparticipant observer could (Adler & Adler, 1987). The study started on November 14, 2006. Each day I would log in to Wikipedia to create articles, correct existing ones, or check the changes other people made and interact with Wikipedians in policy discussions, on article talk pages, and in debates on article or topic notability.

As time passed, I moved through all the ranks of the Wikipedia parahierarchy. In April 2007 I was elected an administrator on the Polish Wikipedia. I also started editing on the English Wikipedia and, to lesser extent, on several other Wikimedia projects. In 2008 I became one of a handful of bureaucrats on the Polish Wikipedia (see Chapter 2). I became one of six members of the Ombudsmen Commission for all Wikimedia projects in 2011. I stepped down from this position in February 2012 upon being elected a steward (the role with widest access to technical privileges, across all Wikimedia projects). In October 2012 I was elected to the Funds Dissemination Committee, a global advisory body at the Wikimedia Foundation, comprising seven Wikimedians from across the world and two nonvoting participants from the board of trustees, and was elected to be its inaugural chairman. In the course of my presence on Wikipedia I have ended up with a modest five-digit edit count. Over six years I spent about one hour on Wikipedia almost every day, participating, taking notes (Emerson, Fretz, & Shaw, 2001/2011), and observing the community—these hundreds of hours of ethnographic observation are my main source of insight. Although technically I have been active on over six hundred Wikimedia projects, most of my edits took place on the Polish Wikipedia, the English Wikipedia, Meta-Wiki (a wiki to coordinate all Wikimedia projects), and to a much smaller extent, the Commons (a repository of media files for all Wikimedia projects).

Additionally, the book relies on reflexive qualitative interviews (Alvesson, 2003), a method often accompanying observation (Darlington & Scott, 2003). Twenty-six interviews were conducted with Polish and English Wikipedia administrators (including five stewards and representatives of Wikimedia chapters). Five Wikimedia Foundation employees were also interviewed. All interviews were oral, either face to face or by Skype, except two that were conducted via text chat. Each lasted for about an hour and was unstructured (Whyte & Whyte, 1984). Transcripts of the interviews were prepared following the ethnomethodological procedure (Silverman, 2005): with maximal accuracy to the actual conversation, including pauses and mistakes. Unlike in grounded theory (Glaser & Strauss, 1967), but typically for ethnographic interviews (Atkinson & Hammersley, 1994), the collected data were used in a loosely structured way, to understand data collected from participative observation. NVivo 7 software was used to organize and categorize the interview excerpts.

Finally, this study relies on selected case studies (Denzin & Lincoln, 2003; Stake, 2005), which were particularly useful in analyzing events I was not able to observe personally (Eisenhardt, 1989) but that were important for understanding the shape of Wikipedia communities. Since I was able to access all the discussions after edits (and follow the exact timeline of the disputes and see the parts of the debates later deleted) and since I am a highly experienced Wikipedian, that I was not participating in them as they developed is a relatively minor flaw. The cases were selected on the basis of suggestions from veteran Wikipedians, and their description is a large part of this book. Combined with participant observation and interviews, the case studies allow wide triangulation of the field material (Baxter & Jack, 2008). The cases selected for the detailed analysis amount to 1.5 million words of discussions. The inherently textual nature of these cases and their storyline dynamics make their analysis close to narrative studies of organizations (Czarniawska, 2000; Boje, 2001; Kostera & Glinka, 2001; Kostera, 2006; Kociatkiewicz & Kostera, 2012).

The case study analyses and the participant observations for obvious reasons use the methodology of content analysis (Krippendorff, 2004; Hsieh & Shannon, 2005), which is typical for online research (Herring, 2010).

## Research Questions

Like most qualitative interpretive research (Marshall & Rossman, 2010), the study started not with a list of hypotheses but with primary initial questions (Silverman, 2005, p. 77):

- How do people perceive hierarchy and create a "career" in an ahierarchical environment? How are power and status enacted in open-collaboration projects? In what way is organizational control exerted in virtual communities, where there are no traditional motivational tools and where identities are fluid?
- How do members of open-collaboration projects balance the need for credential checks and trust in each other with following organizational procedures?
- Why are bureaucratic scripts created and enforced in a semianarchist virtual community that declares it despises such procedures?
- How can a community of dispersed volunteers disempower the organization (Wikimedia Foundation), which owns all the resources, including the platform that allows volunteers to communicate with each other?
- What governance principles and paradigms does a virtual open-collaboration community use?
- How do authority and leadership work in an organization that emphasizes egalitarianism and antileadership?
- What effect does leadership demise have on the organizational structure of Wikipedia? What kinds of conflicts escalate, and how are these conflicts resolved?
- In what way are open-collaboration projects driven by disagreement and discontent rather than the drive to cooperate and communicate? How are the effective rules of collaboration established in a community of users who have practically no common ground but instead have considerable diversity in education, country of origin, age, social class, culture, and so on, and only limited interaction possibilities?

All these questions were discussed in the study, using the example of the Wikipedia community.

## Virtual Ethnography

Some researchers consider conducting ethnographic research online to be distinctly different from regular, face-to-face fieldwork (Buchanan, 2004). In many respects, conducting fieldwork online is different from the archetypal study of an exotic tribe (Garcia, Standlee, Bechkoff, & Cui, 2009). The following are examples of differences:

- Physical copresence with the subjects is impossible at most times, and interaction in most cases must be through textual discourse (often even asynchronous); video-chatting is rare.
- Subjects have much more control over the construction of their persona and identities, and thus the presentation of self in everyday life (Goffman, 1959) is significantly different: some social stigmas (Goffman, 1963) are easily concealed (for instance, those related to gender, ethnicity, or physical impairment), while some are much more transparent (such as those related to literacy and vocabulary range).
- The issues of gaining access (Feldman, Bell, & Berger, 2003) and of nativity (both quite central to anthropological inquiry) are significantly different.
- The public and private spheres are fuzzy: many dialogues are conducted semi-privately with the implicit assumption that though they are publicly available (or available just to the community) in practice they would not be accessed by the general public.

In addition, the use of some research methods has to be modified; participant observation is not of people themselves but of the behavior of their avatars and personas (Schroeder & Axelsson, 2006), which is distinctive in a text-only environment (M. Williams, 2007).

Yet online communities are not less rich in interaction than the real (or rather, physically close) ones (Paccagnella, 1997). While many of the details of research conduct may be different, and the researcher has to approach the study differently, the similarities prevail. "Qualitative researchers who have thought carefully about internet ethnography accept that it should be employed and understood as part of a commitment to existing theoretical traditions" (Travers, 2009, p. 172), and in principle, "virtual ethnographies are just ethnographies" and "the argument that something new is going on, methodologically and substantively" is based on the sociological privileging of the traditional methods (Randall, Harper, & Rouncefield, 2007, p. 293).

This is why ethnography and its tools have been adapted to studies of online communities (Nocera, 2002). Since the 1990s ethnography has been attracting more and more anthropologists (E. G. Coleman, 2010a). It has been developed and accepted in the social sciences, where it is termed "virtual ethnography" (Hine, 2008; Hancock, Crain-Dorough, Parton, & Oescher, 2010), "connective ethnography" (Dirksen, Huizing, & Smit, 2010), "digital ethnography" (Murthy, 2008), "Internet ethnography" (Sade-Beck, 2008), or as Robert V. Kozinets aptly states, "netnography" (2002, 2010), though this last term may indicate a connection with the field that is less anthropological and more text analysis. Some anthropologists also took active part in the development of the free culture and free information movement (Kelty, 2004).

This distinctive variety of anthropological inquiry is an emerging, yet established, field of organizational anthropology (Boellstorff, 2008; Pragnell & Gatzidis, 2011; Steinmetz, 2012). Following these adaptations, this book assumes that virtual ethnography is a variation of traditional ethnography (which, in itself, is a varied method). Virtual reality is not an entity separate from the whole world of social interaction. Rather, it is a particular form of human activity (Beneito-Montagut, 2011), forming a field of particular human action that should not be arbitrarily separated from others (Ruhleder, 2000). As Christine Hine puts it, "All forms of interaction are ethnographically valid, not just the face to face. The shaping of the ethnographic object as it is made possible by the available technologies is the ethnography. This is ethnography, *in, of* and *through* the virtual" (2000, p. 65; emphasis in original).

I have prior experience in traditional organizational ethnography, in both fieldwork (D. Jemielniak, 2007, 2008; Hunter, Jemielniak, & Postuła, 2010) and methodology (Jemielniak & Kostera, 2010), and in netnographic research (D. Jemielniak, 2013a, 2013b), and thus I conducted this study by applying regular ethnography principles to the study of the Wikipedia virtual community (Daniel, 2010).

## Studying Two Wikipedias and Shielding Identities

One consideration when writing about the Wikipedia community is the use of direct quotations. According to Roy Langer and Suzanne C. Beckman (2005), online pseudonyms should be treated like real names for subject protection. In a way, Wikipedia nicknames do serve almost like real names in the community, to the extent that at physical meet ups, as well as on Facebook, on IRC, and in other interactions, Wikipedians often address each other by nickname, even if they know the other's real name. Thus, handling nicknames as if they were real identifiers does have some theoretical appeal.

However, following this stance would lead to major altering of all quotes. After all, search engines easily find direct quotations. Even searching for a string from a quotation can often track down the discussion. In fact, such backtracks are a sport among many readers of online studies (Kozinets, 2010). As a result, the standard procedure of using pseudonyms would not work.

However, using spatial metaphors for online research (e.g., speaking of virtual spaces) and adopting traditional human-subject rules for studying virtual communities does not have to be the only way of understanding Internet life (Bassett & O'Riordan, 2002), and possible alternatives include treating anything on the Internet as publicly available text. After all, online discussions are conducted with the assumption that they will be read by the general public and unidentified recipients (and this assumption heavily influences the ways people behave on Wikipedia, as described in Chapter 4). As a consequence, human-subject research ethics do not have to be applied and a researcher should not be concerned about direct quotations. Even in traditional ethnography, identifying organizations and subjects is often possible, and thus in virtual ethnography there should not be additional concerns beyond the standard protection of the subject's name and personal data (Gatson & Zweerink, 2004).

However, describing the conflicts in which I personally participated in a way that would allow identifying my former adversaries would be unfair and seem to border on a personal vendetta. Yet conflicts are important for understanding human behavior on Wikipedia. Even more useful is learning about the conflicts that I witnessed or even participated in (since such insight into social interaction and its dynamics is commonly one of the strong points of ethnography), and describing them with quotations is the most reasonable way to go about it.

Thus, to present the trajectory of a conflict from my own experience (see the prologue), I use only translated quotes from the Polish Wikipedia, as sometimes it could be assumed that the quoted material could have been directed to be seen by me, rather than the general community. With proper disguise of names, quotations are not easy to link to real people, and only those directly involved in the community and in the described situations may be able to. This approach satisfies Amy Bruckman's (2006) proposal to use different levels of disguise in studies of online communities. It also somewhat amends the power imbalance between me, the author and at the same time a participant in a conflict, and my adversaries (Boser, 2006). Throughout the rest of the book, however, the English Wikipedia is the subject because of its bigger size, greater familiarity to the reader, and higher internationalization. The assumption is made that public online discussions have been published for a general audience and do not require disguise of participants. Whenever "Wikipedia" is mentioned without specifying a project, the observation is general and applies to all Wikimedia projects I am familiar with.

Naturally, there are other, very good reasons to study more than one Wikipedia project. Comparing two Wikipedias in two different languages and cultures has important benefits. So far, most academic studies have focused on the English Wikipedia (Hara, Shachaf, & Hew, 2010), which is sometimes even misleadingly referred to as "the Wikipedia," as if the English Wikipedia were the only one out there, even though virtual communities significantly vary across Wikipedias and many of the "universal" laws observed by researchers of open-collaboration communities may be, in fact, local. Some studies find significant cultural differences across different Wikipedias (Pfeil, Zaphiris, & Ang, 2006), in both regular interaction patterns (Hara et al., 2010) and general conduct, specific for Wikipedia collaboration (Stvilia, Al-Faraj, & Yi, 2009; Nemoto & Gloor, 2011). Wikimedia projects hold independence in high regard, to the extent that trying to use one's status on a project to leverage status on a different one is a faux pas, and adopting regulations from other projects is regarded with suspicion (for example, on the Polish Wikipedia, attempts to copy English policies are pejoratively called "en-wikism"). As a result, differences among Wikipedias and other Wikimedia projects are sometimes large.

A minority of published studies describes some of the national variations, but few researchers have delved into two Wikipedia projects simultaneously and none so far in organization studies or in virtual ethnography. Yet if valid conclusions are to be drawn about such open-collaboration projects and the more universal character of internal relations in them (which is necessary if we are to transfer open-collaboration characteristics to other organizations or make generalizations about open-collaboration environments), it is important to take into account that some observed phenomena may be influenced by a national culture or language or simply result from a contingent event in one particular community's history. Many of the peculiarities, which some could attribute to the open-collaboration virtual form of organization, do not necessarily look the same way on different projects. Therefore, in this book special focus is given to observations shared by the Polish and the English Wikipedias. Major differences important for the discussion are emphasized.

Incidentally, according to a 2011 "Wikipedia Editors Study" conducted by the Wikimedia Foundation, the Polish Wikipedia community has the highest score of editor satisfaction (Wikimedia Foundation, 2011a), which makes it an instructive model.

All general rules and guidelines discussed in the book are from the English Wikipedia versions and wording (with acknowledgment of key differences, when important). Also, all general and nonpersonal discussions, cases, and events are taken verbatim from the English Wikipedia (without disguising names). However, some disputes and direct quotations from personal interactions with users that exemplify processes typical for both projects are disguised by selecting and translating them from the Polish Wikipedia, and their authors are also disguised. In this way the study can have a universal character and yet be fully ethical with respect to the people quoted in most sensitive situations (personal disputes and quarrels rather than open general discussions).

# APPENDIX B: GLOSSARY OF
# WIKIPEDIA SLANG

This appendix includes a selection of Wikipedia terms understandable to most experienced editors but cryptic to outsiders. The unabridged version can be found at [[WP:Glossary]].[1]

3RR   Abbreviation for three-revert rule.

Admin   Short for Administrator. A user with extra technical privileges for "custodial" work on Wikipedia—specifically, deleting and protecting pages, and blocking abusive users.

AfD, AFD   The [[WP:Articles_for_deletion]] page. The AfD of an article refers to the discussion wherein Wikipedians consider whether an article should be kept or deleted.

AGF, WP:AGF   Abbreviation for "assume good faith", a guideline whereby one should not assume that an unwanted or disputed edit was done maliciously.

ArbCom, Arbcom, ARBCOM   Abbreviation for [[WP:Arbitration_Committee]].

Arbitration   The final step in the dispute resolution process. *See also* [[WP:Arbitration _Committee]].

Article   An encyclopedia entry. All articles are pages, but there are also pages that are not articles, such as this one. *See also* [[WP:What_is_an_article]].

Autoconfirmed   A newly registered user is still subject to some of the same restrictions as anonymous users—for example, inability to move articles or edit semi-protected pages, although some restrictions, such as the restriction on anonymous users creating pages, are lifted. When a user is autoconfirmed, these restrictions end. Currently, a new user must make ten edits and wait four days to be autoconfirmed.

Bad faith nomination   A bad faith nomination is the nomination of a page, or more pages (usually for deletion at AFD) for disingenuous reasons such as making a point or vandalism.

Ban   Banning is the extreme, last resort action by which someone is prevented from editing Wikipedia for a certain length of time, limited or unlimited. Typical reasons for banning include a long history of biased edits (violation of NPOV), persistent adding of incorrect or doubtful material, refusal to cooperate with others, or extreme incivility and threats. Banned users are not necessarily blocked, however, it is one mechanism to enforce a ban. Any username or IP judged to be the same person can be blocked without any further reason. *See also* Block.

Banner    A banner is a template that is placed across the top of an article's talk page or at the top of a category to indicate specific details relating to the article or category's maintenance. They are often specifically linked to a WikiProject to indicate that the article or category falls within the jurisdiction of that project, but may also be related to article maintenance or protection. "Banner" may also simply mean the administrator who bans a troublesome editor.

Barnstar    Barnstars are a light-hearted system of awards given to Wikipedian editors by other editors to acknowledge good work or other positive contributions to Wikipedia. They take the form of an image posted to an editor's talk page, usually in the form of a five-pointed star. There is a wide variety of different types of barnstar, each indicating a different reason for the award having been given.

Be Bold, be bold, BOLD, WP:BOLD    The exhortation that users should try to improve articles and fix mistakes themselves by editing, rather than complain about them. *See* [[WP:Be_bold_in_updating_pages]].

BEANS, WP:BEANS    A reference to the essay on not warning people to do things they wouldn't have thought of doing (it just gives them ideas): Don't stuff beans up your nose.

Blanking    Removing all content from a page. Newcomers often do this accidentally. On the other hand, if blanking an article is done in bad faith, it is *vandalism*. If blanking is done to a vandalized brand-new page, it is maintenance, and the page will be deleted by an administrator within a few hours if no dispute arises. {{Delete}} should be added to the blanked page to draw attention to it, rather than just blanking it. Newcomers often mistake blanking for *deletion*.

Block, WP:BLOCK    Action by an administrator, removing from a certain IP address or username the ability to edit Wikipedia. Usually done against addresses that have engaged in vandalism or against users who have been banned; *see* [[WP:Blocking_policy]]. *See also* Ban.

BLP, WP:BLP    Abbreviation for [[WP:Biographies_of_living_persons]]—official Wikipedia policy, whereby articles about living people must be handled with great care.

Blue link, bluelink    A wikilink to an article that already exists shows up blue (or purple if it has been recently visited by that reader/editor). *See also* Sea of blue, Red link, [[WP:WikiProject_Red_Link_Recovery]].

Bot    A program that automatically or semi-automatically adds or edits Wikipedia-pages. *See* [[WP:Bots]], Vandalbot.

Broken link    A link to a nonexistent page, usually colored red, depending on your settings. May also refer to dead links. *See also* Edit link, Red link, [[WP:Red_link]].

Bureaucrat    A Wikipedia Administrator who has been entrusted with promoting users to Administrator status. *See also* 'Crat, [[WP:Bureaucrats]].

Cabal    Sometimes assumed to be a secretive organization responsible for the development of Wikipedia, the word is usually used as a sarcastic hint to *lighten up* when discussions seem to become a little too paranoid. Discussions involving the term may have links to POV / NPOV issues, admin problems, or pretty much anything to do with the foundation of Wikipedia. The term *TINC* ("There Is No Cabal") is occasionally encountered, used humorously in such a way as to suggest that maybe there is a cabal after all. The term is comparable to the use of the term SMOF in science fiction fandom. *Compare* Troll. *See also* m:Cabal,[2] [[There_Is_No_Cabal]], [[WP:Mediation_Cabal]].

Canvassing, WP:CANVAS    Canvassing is sending messages to multiple Wikipedians with the intent to inform them about a community discussion. Under certain conditions, canvassing is acceptable to notify other editors of ongoing discussions (*see* Friendly notices), but inappropriate messages, written to influence the outcome rather than to improve the quality of a discussion, are considered disruptive since they compromise the consensus building process. *See* [[WP:Canvassing]].

Cat, cat.    "Category" or "categorize". Often pluralized as "cats" or "cats."

Category    A category is a collection of pages automatically formed by the Wikipedia servers by analyzing category tags in articles. Category tags are in the form [[Category:Computers]]. The part after the ":" is the name of the Category. Adding a category tag causes a link to the category and any super-categories to go to the bottom of the page. As stated, it also results in the page being added to the category listing. A list of basic categories to browse through can be found at [[Category:Fundamental_categories]], though a more user-friendly way to find a category is at [[WP:Browse]].

CheckUser    An access level with which a user can see the IP addresses of logged-in users, usually to determine if someone is using sockpuppets to violate policy. Currently only granted to certain members of the Arbitration Committee and other trusted users.

Cleanup, cl    The process of repairing articles that contain errors of grammar, are poorly formatted, or contain irrelevant material. Cleanup generally requires only editing skills, as opposed to the specialized knowledge that is more often called for by pages needing attention. *See also* [[WP:Cleanup_process]].

Climbing the Reichstag    A humorous way of indicating that an editor has over-reacted during an argument such as an edit-war in order to gain some advantage. This has similar consequences to—and is as unwelcome as—WP:POINT (qv). *See also* [[Fathers_for_Justice#Activities]], [[WP:No_climbing_the_Reichstag_dressed_as _Spider-Man]].

cmt    Comment.

COI    Acronym for [[WP:Conflict_of_interest]].

Commons    Wikimedia Commons is an online repository of free-use images, sound and other media files.

Community Portal    One of Wikipedia's main pages. It can often be found on the sidebar (on the left side in most skins), and is a page that lists important notices, the collaboration of the week, outstanding tasks that need to be addressed, and several other useful bits of information and resources. The Community Portal is useful for picking an article or topic to work on or read.

Consensus, WP:CON    The mechanism by which all decisions on Wikipedia are nominally made. Not the same as a "majority vote" (cf [[WP:Polling_is_not_a _substitute_for_discussion]]).

Contribs, contributions    Short for contributions. A user has made these edits. *See* [[Help:User_contributions]].

Contributor    *See* Editor.

Copyedit    A change to an article that only affects formatting, grammar, and other presentational aspects. *See also* [[WP:Basic_copyediting]].

Copyvio, CopyVio, copy vio, copyviol    Copyright violation. Usually used in an edit summary when deleting copyrighted material added without complying with Wikipedia copyright verification procedures. *See also* CV, [[WP:Copyrights]].

'Crat    Short for Bureaucrat, used only occasionally.

CSB    WikiProject Countering systemic bias or, more rarely, an adjective for a topic of concern to the WikiProject, e.g., "This does not seem to be a CSB article." Systemic bias is the tendency for Wikipedia articles to be biased towards a European or American view of things, simply because most editors are European or American.

CSD, WP:CSD    Criteria for speedy deletion, a policy detailing the circumstances when articles etc. can be removed from Wikipedia without discussion. Also lists the templates needed to nominate something for speedy deletion.

CV, cv    Abbreviation of Copyvio.

Dablink, DAB link, etc.    1. Abbreviation of "disambiguation link"; a link that leads to a disambiguation page. 2. To disambiguate a link within the text of a page. 3. A link at the top of an article to one or more other articles with similar titles (a hatnote), or the addition of such.

Data dump    To import material from outside sources into Wikipedia without editing, formatting and linking (Wikifying). This is frowned upon by most Wikipedians, and is often a copyvio.

Dead-end page    Page that has no links to existing other pages, except interlanguage links. [[Special:DeadendPages]] lists them, but this function is disabled in some Wikimedia projects for performance reasons.

De-admin    *See* De-sysop.

Deletionist    Someone who actively attempts to delete pages that others prefer to keep. Deletionism is the idea that Wikipedia should follow the same rules for inclusion as existing paper encyclopedias (mostly Encyclopedia Britannica). Often used as a derogatory term. The term "inclusionist" for the opposite party is less used. *See also* m:deletionism, m:inclusionism, [[Deletionism_and_inclusionism_in _Wikipedia]].

Deprecated    1. Techie-speak for "tolerated in or supported by a system but not recommended (i.e., beware: may well be on the way out)". 2. The term is also used to refer to pages, templates or categories that have been orphaned or are no longer used. 3. In non-technical English, the word means, "deplored or strongly disapproved of".

De-sysop    Take away someone's sysop (Administrator) status. Used very rarely, in cases where someone has voluntarily elected to resign such status, or is judged to have misused their admin powers. *See also* [[WP:Requests_for_de-adminship]].

Developer, dev    Usually capitalized. A user who can make direct changes to Wikipedia's underlying software and possibly also the database, often being one of the Media-Wiki developers (see next definition) or other Wikimedia Foundation technicians. Technically, it is the highest user access level, but Developer privileges are generally only used at request. Sometimes referred to by other terms such as "system administrators" or "sysadmins", to distinguish from MediaWiki developers. *See also* m:Developers *for a list of developers and further information.* Usually not capitalized. One of the developers of the MediaWiki software; often but not always a Wikipedia Developer (in the above sense).

De-wikify, dewikify    To remove (de-link) some of the wikification of an article. This can be done to remove self-references or excessive common-noun wikification (also known as the sea of blue effect).

Diff    The difference between two versions of page, as displayed using the *Page history* feature, or from Recent Changes. The versions to compare are encoded in the URL, so you can make a link by copying and pasting it—for instance when discussing a change on an article's talk page.

Disambiguation, disambig    The process of resolving the conflict that occurs when articles about two or more different topics have the same natural title. *See also* Dab.

Disambiguation page, DAB page, dab page    A page that contains various meanings of a word, and refers to the pages where the various meanings are defined. In cases when there is a prevailing meaning of the term, disambiguation pages are named "subject (disambiguation)".

Edit conflict    Also, rarely "edconf". Appears if an edit is made to the page between when one opens it for editing and completes the edit. The later edit does not take effect, but the editor is prompted to merge their edit with the earlier one. Edit conflicts should not be confused with edit wars.

Editcountitis    A humorous term for having an unhealthy obsession with the number of edits that a person makes to Wikipedia, usually applied to one trying to make as many edits as possible. Often cited on Requests for Adminship regarding people who judge people on sheer edit count rather than personal merit.

Edit creep, editcreep, edit-creep    The tendency for high quality articles to degrade over time. Articles usually achieve good article or featured article recognition because a small core of people knew the subject well and researched it carefully. Subsequently, new readers continue to alter the page. The average contribution may weaken the piece through bad copyediting, poor syntax, recitation of popular misconceptions, or giving undue weight to a subordinate topic. (By way of analogy to scope creep.)

Edit summary    The contents of the "Summary:" field below the edit box on the "Edit this page" page.

Editor    Anyone who writes or modifies articles in a Wikipedia. That includes you. Other terms with the same meaning: contributor, user.

edit war    Two or more parties continually making their preferred changes to a page, each persistently undoing the changes made by the opposite party. Often, an edit war is the result of an argument on a talk page that could not be resolved. Edit wars are not permitted and may lead to blocks. Sometimes termed "revert war"; *see also* Three-revert rule.

External link, ext. ln., extlink, ext lk, EL, etc.    A link to a website not owned by Wikimedia. The alternatives are an internal link, wikilink or free link within Wikipedia, and an interwiki link to a sister project. *See also* [[WP:External_links]], [[WP:Spam]].

FA    Featured article, an article that has been selected as representing "the best of Wikipedia". Articles become featured articles when a FAC gets consensus for promotion.

Forest fire    A flame war which spreads, seemingly uncontrollably, beyond the pages where it began into unrelated articles' talk pages. A forest fire becomes progressively more difficult for any user to keep track of. On Wikipedia, this is less of a problem than on other wikis, due to well-established boundaries for user conduct, clear guidelines for article content, and a formal dispute resolution process. *See also* [[Wildfire]], http://meatballwiki.org/wiki/ForestFire.

Fork    A splitting of an entity to satisfy different groups of people—in Wikipedia, this can either mean a project-wide split, in which a group of users decides to take a project database and continue with it on their own site (which is perfectly legal under the GFDL, and one of an editor's least disputed rights), or the split of an article, usually to accommodate different POVs. The latter is often called a POV fork and generally regarded as highly undesirable.

GA    Good article.

Gdanzig    An edit war over which of several possible names should be used for a place. The word is a portmanteau of Gdańsk and Danzig, the two names about which a venerable edit war ensued. *See* [[Talk:Gdansk/Vote]].

Geogre's Law    A law attributed to User:Geogre (although he may not have been the first person, and has certainly not been the only person, to observe this correlation), and most frequently referred to in [[WP:Articles_for_deletion]]. Paraphrased, the law states that there exists a strong correlation between the lack of proper capitalization of a person's name in the title of a biographical article, and the failure of the subject of that article to satisfy the criteria for inclusion of biographies.

GF    Good faith, a tenet of Wikipedia.

Godwin's Law    Godwin's Law is particularly concerned with logical fallacies such as reductio ad Hitlerum, wherein an idea is unduly dismissed or rejected on the ground of it being associated with persons generally considered "evil". Godwin's Law is: "As an online discussion grows longer, the probability of a comparison involving Nazis or Hitler approaches 1." It is often cited as soon as it occurs as a flag that discussions have gone on too long or gotten out of hand on a particular topic.

Google test    Running sections or titles of articles through the Google search engine for various purposes. The four most common are to check for copyright violations, to determine which term among several is the most widely used, to decide whether a person is sufficiently notable to warrant an article and to check whether a questionable and obscure topic is real (as opposed to the idiosyncratic invention of a particular individual). *See also* Ghits, [[WP:Google_test]].

Hagiography    Wording that is excessively fulsome, adulatory or glowing in a biographical article, to the point of violating NPOV.

Handwaving, armwaving    An assertion not supported by evidence; most frequently seen in articles for deletion discussions, when editors may assert that a subject is notable, but fail to make a convincing case. Such arguments are usually given less weight. *See also* [[Handwave]].

History    All previous versions of an article, from its creation to its current state. Also called page history. *See also* [[Help:Page_history]].

Hopelessly POV    Describing an article which, in the opinion of some Wikipedians, is so closely tied to a particular point of view as to be inherently in violation of Wikipedia policy and unable to be made neutral. Other Wikipedians consider the accusation "hopelessly POV" as being merely an excuse to suppress certain points of view.

IANAL, IANaL    An abbreviation for "I Am Not a Lawyer", indicating that an editor is about to give their opinion on a legal matter as they understand it, although they are not professionally qualified to do so, and may not fully understand the law in question. May be generalized to other fields, e.g., *IANAA* (administrator), *IANAD* (doctor).

IAR, Ignore All Rules    A policy which states simply "If a rule prevents you from improving or maintaining Wikipedia, ignore it." There are several essays on what this means, including [[WP:What_"Ignore_all_rules"_means]].

IAW    An abbreviation for "in accordance with", as in "IAW WP:RS."

Inclusionist    A user who is of the opinion that Wikipedia should contain as much information as possible, often regardless of presentation or notability. There are varying degrees of Inclusionism—radical Inclusionists vote "Keep" on every AfD they come across, while more moderate ones merely express their desire for a wide variety of topics to be covered, even if they do not fit the standard criteria for inclusion in an encyclopedia, or if the articles in question have quality problems.

Infobox    A consistently formatted table which is present in articles with a common subject. *See* [[Help:Infobox]], [[WP:Manual_of_Style_(infoboxes)]] *for a how-to guide. See also* Navbox, Taxobox.

Interwiki    A link to a sister project; this can be an interlanguage link to a corresponding article in a different language in Wikipedia, or a link to a project such as Wikibooks, Meta, etc. The abbreviations iw or i/w are often used in edit summaries when an interwiki link has been added or changed.

IP, IP contributor, IP user, IP editor    An editor who contributes without an account. *See also* Anon.

IRC    Internet Relay Chat.

ITHAWO    I thought he already was one. Used about people listed in "admin" requests.

Janitor    *See* Admin.

Jimbo    Jimmy Wales, co-founder of Wikipedia.

Kill / Kill with fire / Kill with a stick    Dysphemisms for "deleting" a page, expressing some disgust for the existence of the page.

Link farm    Link farms are articles or sections of articles consisting entirely of external or internal links. Some pages consisting of internal links are acceptable (such as disambiguation pages and list articles); others are likely to be candidates for deletion, as are any consisting entirely of external links.

Link rot    Because websites change over time, many external links from Wikipedia to other sites cannot be guaranteed to remain active. When an article's links becomes outdated and no longer work, the article is said to have undergone *link rot*.

Listify    To delete a category and turn the contents into a list. Sometimes used in CFD discussions as shorthand for saying that "this group of articles would be better if presented as a list, rather than as a category."

Lugo    A meme associated with stagnation or the lack of sufficient updates on the Main page. It originated from an incident in 2008, when an image of President of Paraguay Fernando Lugo stayed up on the "In the news" section for well over a week. *See also* [[WP:Wikipedia_Signpost/2009-01-31/Dispatches]]—Wikipedia Signpost *article on the process and history of "In the news."*

Magic word, magicword, magic-word    A symbol recognized by the MediaWiki software and which when seen in the non-commented text of the page, triggers the software to do something other than display that symbol, or transclude a page with that name, but instead to use the symbol directly.

Main Page    The page to which every user not specifying an article is redirected. The Main Page contains links to current events, presents certain articles (like a featured article of the day and links to Wikipedia's newest articles), and serves as an entry point to browsing all articles by topic or other classification. Links to sister projects and other-language Wikipedias are also a prominent feature on the Main Page. Due to its high exposure, all content on the Main Page is protected.

Mainspace    The main article namespace (i.e., not a talk page, not a "Wikipedia:" page, not a "User:" page, etc.).

Mastodon    Refers to the fight or flight reflex that sometimes happens while editing Wikipedia. Generally mentioned to request for calm. "Nobody ever got trampled to death because they were editing an encyclopedia." Frequently misspelled "masta-don". *See also* [[WP:No_angry_mastodons]].

MC    The Mediation Committee. *See* [[WP:Mediation_Committee]].

Meat puppet    An account created only for the illegitimate strengthening of another user's position in votes or discussions. Unlike a sock puppet, the account is used by another person. Meat puppets are treated exactly like sock puppets in most cases, making the distinction between them largely academic.

MedCab, Medcab, MEDCAB    The Mediation Cabal. *See* [[WP:Mediation_Cabal]].

MedCom, Medcom, MEDCOM    The Mediation Committee. *See* [[WP:Mediation _Committee]].

Mediation    An attempt by a third party to resolve an edit war or other conflict be-tween users. There exists a [[WP:Mediation_Committee]] which can do so on a more or less official basis as the penultimate step in the [[WP:dispute_resolution]] process, and a [[WP:Mediation_Cabal]] which acts as an informal alternative. *See also* [[WP:What_is_mediation?]], [[WP:Mediation]].

MediaWiki    The software behind Wikipedia and its sister projects, as well as several projects not related to Wikimedia, and a namespace. *Contrast* Wikimedia. *See also* [[WP:MediaWiki]], [[WP:MediaWiki_namespace]].

Meh    Common edit summary used by many Wikipedians. Generally used for minor edits that no one is expected to care about. Also use (in edit summary or directly in talk page posts) in response to posts that the editor feels are uninteresting or point-less, or proposals not worth considering.

Merge    Taking the text of two pages, and turning it into a single page. *See* [[Help:Merging_and_moving_pages]].

Mergist    A user who adheres to the principle of Mergism, which is a compromise be-tween the Inclusionist and Deletionist principles. A Mergist is of the opinion that while many topics merit inclusion, not every topic deserves its own article, and tries to combine these "side" topics into longer, less specific articles.

Meta    A separate wiki used to discuss general Wikimedia matters. In the past, this has been called *Metapedia*, *Meta Wikipedia*, *Meta Wikimedia*, and many other combinations.

Meta page, meta-page   A page that provides information about Wikipedia. Meta pages are more correctly referred to as project namespace pages. Meta pages should not be confused with a page on Meta-Wikimedia.

Minor edit   A minor edit is one that the editor believes requires no review and could never be the subject of a dispute. An edit of this kind is marked in its page's revision history with a lower case, bolded "m" character (m).

Mirror   A website other than Wikipedia that uses content original to Wikipedia as a source for at least some of its content. *See also* [[WP:Mirrors_and_forks]].

Mop   A term used to refer to administrator duties (compare Janitor). Often seen in the phrase *to give someone a mop* (i.e., to make someone into an administrator).

MOS, MoS   Found in edit summaries to indicate that a change has been made to make an item comply with Wikipedia's standard writing style ("Manual of Style"). Often found in compound forms such as "MOSNUM" ("Manual of Style/Dates and numbers") and "MOSCAPS" ("Manual of Style/Capital letters"). *See also* NC, [[WP:Manual_of_Style]].

Move   Changing the name and location of an article because of a misspelling, violation of naming convention, misnomer, or inaccuracy. Involves either renaming the page or moving it and constructing a redirect to keep the original link intact. *See also* [[Help:Renaming_(moving)_a_page]].

Namespace   A way to classify pages. Wikipedia has namespaces for encyclopedia articles, pages about Wikipedia (project namespace), user pages (User:), special pages (Special:), template pages (Template:), and talk pages (Talk:, Wikipedia talk:, and User talk:), among others. *See also* [[WP:Namespace]].

Navbox, Navigation template   A navbox is a type of template placed at the bottom articles to enable the reader to navigate easily to other articles on related topics. *See also* Infobox, Taxobox.

Newbie test, noob test, newb test   An edit made by a newcomer to Wikipedia, just to see if "Edit this page" *really* does what it sounds like. Newcomers should use [[WP:Sandbox]] for this purpose. *See also* [[WP:Introduction]].

nom   Short for "nomination" or "nominator". Often found on deletion process pages as part of the phrase Delete per nom, indicating a voter's assent to and/or agreement with the main nomination for deletion.

NOR   The Wikipedia policy that No Original Research is allowed in citing sources in articles.

Notice board, noticeboard   A page that acts as a forum for a group of users, who use it to coordinate their editing. Most notice boards are by geographic location, like the UK Wikipedians' notice board; a notable exception is the Administrators' noticeboard.

NPOV, NpoV   Neutral point of view, or the agreement to present possibly subjective content in an objective, neutral, and substantiated manner, so as not to cause edit wars between opposing sides. As a verb, to remove biased statements or slanted phrasing. As an adjective, it indicates that an article complies with Wikipedia's NPOV policy.

Null edit   A null edit is made when an editor opens the edit window of a document then re-saves the page without having made any text changes. This is sometimes done as a lazy way to purge—to update the functioning of templates (which require articles containing them to be edited in order for any changes to take effect). The term also applies to making a very small, non-substantive change (e.g., removing an unneeded blank line or adding one) in order to get the article history to register a change, for the purpose of leaving an edit summary that responds to a previous one.

Nupedia   A Wikipedia predecessor project that shut down in 2003. It is currently inactive and there are no plans to resurrect it. *See also* [[WP:Nupedia_and_Wikipedia]].

OP   Abbreviation for Original post (or "Original poster"). Can also stand for Open Proxy. Or, in the context of IRC, "op" can refer to "ChanOp" (Channel Operator), and to "get ops" or "be opped" means to attain a higher access level within a channel.

Open Ticket Request System   Refers to the people and software that surround the handling of email sent to the Wikimedia Foundation.

Original post, original poster   In a discussion thread, refers to the topic/person/ message which started the discussion. Depending on context, OP may stand for either "original post" (the message which started the thread), or "original poster" (the person who started the thread). Often used on Wikipedia's discussion pages and commonly seen on the [[WP:Reference_desk]].

Original research   In Wikipedia, original research (sometimes abbreviated OR) is material added to articles that has not been published already by a reputable source. As an encyclopedia, Wikipedia is not the appropriate place to publish original research, nor can it be used for substantiation of article content.

Orphan, orphan article, orphaned article, orphan image, orphaned image   An *orphaned article* is an article with no links from other pages in the main article namespace. An *orphaned image* is an image with no links from any pages at all. You can view lists of orphaned articles and images. [[Category:Orphaned_articles]] contains orphaned articles organized by month. *See also* Wikiproject Orphanage.

OTRS   Abbreviation for Open Ticket Request System. *See also* [[WP:Volunteer _response_team]].

Parent; Parent category   A larger, more general category of which the category under discussion is a subcategory (for example, [[Category:Aquatic_organisms]] is a parent category of [[Category:Fish]]). *Compare* Child. *See also* [[Help:Categorization]].

Parent-only category   A category which only contains subcategories.

Patent nonsense   A humorous pejorative applied to articles that are either completely unintelligible or totally irrelevant.

Patrol   [[WP:Recent_changes_patrol]] and/or [[WP:New_page_patrol]]. May also be used as a synonym for "review closely".

PD   Material not presently under copyright and thus available for use without permission. Public domain.

Peer Review   A request to have fellow Wikipedians review and help improve an article. Wikipedia has a page specifically for posting such a request and offering up your work for review.

Permastub   Any stub article which is unlikely to grow to a more respectable size; an article on a subject about which little can ever be written. These articles are often potential candidates for merging into larger articles.

Permcat   A *permanent category*—that is, a category into which an article is assigned to aid reader navigation, as opposed to a temporary assignment relating to a process such as cleanup or stub sorting.

Permalink, permanent link   A link to a specific version of a Wikipedia page, which will not reflect later edits to the page.

Per, per nom, per $X$   A comment on a page such as RFA or AFD may be accompanied by the note "per nom", which means "for the reasons given by the nominator". Similarly, a comment may be noted "per X" where X is the name of one of the other commenters, or a reference to some page that explains the reasoning. *See also* [[WP:What_does_'per'_mean?]].

Personal attack   A comment that is not directed at content, but rather insults, demeans or threatens another editor (or a group of editors) personally, with obvious malice. To maintain a friendly and productive atmosphere, personal attacks are forbidden per Wikipedia policy and may be grounds for blocking in serious and/or repeated cases. *See also* [[WP:No_personal_attacks]], [[WP:Remove_personal_attacks]].

POINT, WP:POINT   "Thou shalt not deliberately skew any page, nor create or nominate for deletion any page, nor in any other way vandalize Wikipedia, in order to try to prove your point!". *See also* [[WP:Don't_disrupt_Wikipedia_to_illustrate_a _point]].

Pokémon test   A heuristic for assessing the relevance or legitimacy of prospective article topics, which holds that any topic more notable than the most obscure species of Pokémon may deserve a Wikipedia article.

POV, PoV   Point of view. Originally referred to each of many perspectives on an issue, which may need to be considered and balanced in an encyclopedic article. Today, more often used as a synonym for "biased", as in "That reply was POV, not neutral".

POV warrior, PoV warrior   An editor who aggressively distorts coverage of certain topics to suit his/her biases despite community norms of neutrality and the Wikipedia policy of NPOV.

Prejudice   As in, "*delete without prejudice*" and variations, based on the legal term. Deletion without prejudice indicates that there is a problem with the present version of the article (e.g., lack of sources) and that recreation of the article is viable if that problem is fixed. Deletion *with* prejudice indicates that there's a problem with the subject of the article, and that it should not be recreated in any form (although deletion review can overturn this).

Process page    A wikispace page dedicated to discussion and (usually) voting on specific pages or users, or for similar administrative reasons. Examples include CFD, RFA, and AFD.

Prod, PROD    Proposed deletion. A process by which articles that do not qualify for speedy deletion but are able to be uncontroversially deleted can be removed from Wikipedia without going through a full AfD process. Can be used as both a noun and a verb (*To prod an article*). *See also* [[WP:Guide_to_deletion]].

Project namespace    The project namespace is a namespace dedicated to providing information about Wikipedia. Pages in the project namespace always start with "Wikipedia:".

Protected page    This term indicates a page that cannot be edited except by administrators, or in some cases, established users. Usually this is done to cool down an edit war. *See also* [[WP:This_page_is_protected]].

The Pump    A nickname for [[WP:Village_pump]]. *See also* VP.

RA    [[WP:Requested_articles]], a place to ask people to create articles that should exist but do not.

RAA    Request for Administrator Attention.

Random page    The Random page link is on the left of each page for most skins. It will take you to a Wikipedia article that is chosen by a computer algorithm without any deliberate pattern or meaning to the choice.

Randy in Boise    A generic name for editors who don't give enough deference to experts.

RC    An abbreviation for Recent changes.

RC Patrol    A group of volunteer editors who examine Recent changes logs for vandalism and other undesirable edits.

Re    Remark or Regarding.

Reader-facing template    *See* [[WP:Neutral_point_of_view]].

Re-creation    A posting of the same or substantially the same text as a deleted article by a new user, or of the same text or different text of a deleted article by the original creator. Sometimes misspelled "recreation".

Recent changes    A dynamically generated page (found at Special:Recentchanges) that lists all edits in descending chronological order. Sometimes abbreviated as RC. Recent changes are checked regularly by editors doing RC patrol, which means checking all suspicious edits to catch vandalism as early as possible. Other ways of watching recent changes are the Recentchanges IRC channel, or CryptoDerk's Vandal Fighter, which announce changes in realtime.

**Redirect, redir**   A page title which, when requested, merely sends the reader to another page. This is used for synonyms and ease of linking. For example, *impressionist* might redirect to *impressionism. For an introduction to what a redirect is, see* [[Help:Redirect]]. *For the guidelines on handling redirects on Wikipedia, see* [[WP:Redirect]].

**Red link, redlink**   A wikilink to an article that does not exist shows up red. *See also* Blue link, [[WP:WikiProject_Red_Link_Recovery]], [[WP:Red_link]].

**Refactor**   To restructure a document, usually applied to the ordering and summarizing of talk pages. *See also* [[WP:Refactoring_talk_pages]].

**Reincarnation**   A new user account created by a banned user to evade the block. *See* Sock puppet.

**Rename**   "Renaming" may refer to a variety of operations on Wikipedia—*see* [[Help:Rename]].

**Repoint, re-point**   To change the destination article of a redirect, either to avoid a double redirect or to change the redirect so that it leads to a more appropriate article. The term retarget is also frequently used.

**Req**   Abbreviation for "Request".

**Rescope, re-scope**   To change the subject matter of an article, a template or—most frequently—a category to one that is more acceptable for editorial or encyclopedic purposes. If by doing so the subject area is broadened, the term *upscope* is sometimes used.

**Revdel**   Abbreviation for Revision deletion. *Not to be confused with Delrev, which is short for Deletion review, a completely different process.*

**Revert**   An edit that reverses edits made by someone else, thus restoring the prior version. *See also* [[Help:Reverting]].

**Revert war**   *See* Edit war.

**RfA, RFA**   Can mean [[WP:Requests_for_adminship]] or (rarely) [[WP:Requests_for _arbitration]], depending on the context. The latter is frequently abbreviated *RfAr* to avoid the ambiguity.

**RfAr, RFAR**   [[WP:Requests_for_arbitration]].

**RfB, RFB**   [[WP:Requests_for_bureaucratship]].

**RfC, RFC**   [[WP:Requests_for_comment]], part of the dispute resolution process. A request for comment is an informal process for soliciting input from Wikipedians about a question of article content or a user's conduct.

**RfD, RFD**   The [[WP:Redirects_for_deletion]] page.

**RfM, RFM**   Request for mediation, part of the dispute resolution process. *See also* [[WP:Requests_for_mediation]].

**Rm**   Remove. Used in edit summaries to indicate that a particular piece of text or formatting has been deleted.

Rmv    1. Remove (Rm) vandalism. Used in edit summaries when good edits were made after vandalism, requiring the editor to sort out the vandalism, as opposed to a simple reversion. *See also* Rvv. 2. Same as Rm.

Rogue admin    Accusatory term for a Wikipedia administrator, suggesting that the accused person systematically abuses their administrative access. Such accusations are rarely found to be justified or particularly productive. *See also* Rouge admin.

Rollback    To change a page back to the version before the last edit. Administrators and rollbackers have special tools to do this more easily. *See* [[WP:Rollback_feature]].

Rollbacker    A class of users who can use the rollback feature. This feature is automatically enabled for all administrators.

Rouge admin    A misspelling of "rogue admin" occasionally used by vandals and trolls. Now used jokingly by many Wikipedia administrators, usually to describe themselves performing actions that the affected users may not like (such as blocking vandals and deleting bogus pages).

RS    [[WP:Reliable_sources]]—a guideline that articles should be based on reliable published sources.

Rv    Revert. An edit summary indicating that the page has been reverted to a previous version, often because of vandalism. *See also* [[Help:Reverting]].

Rvt    Same as Rv.

Salt    (from "salt the earth") Administrators can prevent the creation of a page through the protection interface. This is useful for articles that have been deleted but repeatedly recreated. *See also* [[WP:SALT]].

Sandbox    A sandbox is a page that users may edit however they want. Though it is meant to help users experiment and gain familiarity with Wiki markup, the public sandbox at [[WP:Sandbox]] is often filled with strange things and patent nonsense. In addition to the public sandbox, users may create private sandboxes on subpages of their user page.

Sea of blue    The hard-to-read effect of far too many blue links in an article, caused by over-wikilinking. *See also* De-wikify.

Section editing    Using one of the "[edit]" links to the right of each section's title, one can get an edit window containing only the section of the page that's *below* the [edit] link. This makes it easier to find the exact spot where one wants to edit, and helps you avoid an edit conflict. You can turn section editing off in your preferences under the "Enable section editing via [edit] links" option.

Self-link    A Wikilink contained in an article that points the reader to that same article, e.g., linking *Vice President* in the article "Vice President". Such links are automatically displayed as strongly emphasized text rather than links, but the more complex case of a link which *redirects* to the same article is not, and should be de-wikified.

Self-ref, selfref, self-ref    When used in terms like "no self-refs", this refers to the guideline [[WP:Self-references_to_avoid]] whereby articles should generally not refer to the Wikipedia project directly or implicitly. Self-ref can also refer to the template {{selfref}}.

Self-revert    An editor self-reverts when he or she reverts or undoes an edit that he or she had previously made. This may be because the editor was merely making a test, or because the editor later realised his or her edit was faulty, or because he or she wishes to show good faith after a three-revert rule violation. *See* Revert.

SfD, SFD    The [[WP:Stub_types_for_deletion]] page.

Sharpen cat    To place an article within a more specific category, e.g., placing a biography article from [[Category:Kenya]] into [[Category:Kenyan_people]]. In addition, sh cat in edit summaries.

Sheep vote    A vote on Wikipedia that seems to be cast just to go along with the flow. E.g., on RfA, this can typically be a vote such as "Support because x, y, and z are supporting." The opposite is called a wolf vote.

SME    An acronym for subject matter expert.

Smerge    A contraction of "slight merge" or "selective merge", sometimes used in Articles for deletion discussions. This is for when a topic deserves mention in another article, but not to the extent and detail that is already included (a partial *merge and redirect*).

Snap    Retarget a double redirect to point to the ultimate target.

SNG    A Subject specific Notability Guideline, *see* [[Category:Wikipedia_notability _guidelines]].

Snowball clause    Sometimes entries on process pages are closed early when it becomes obvious that they have "a snowball's chance in Hell" of passing the process. This removal is "per the Snowball clause". The verb "snowballing" is sometimes used for this action.

Sock puppet, sock    Another user account created secretly by an existing Wikipedian, generally to manufacture the illusion of support in a vote or argument. Also, particularly on AfD, a friend of an existing Wikipedian who has created an account solely for the purpose of supporting that Wikipedian in a vote (this special case is often called a meat puppet). It is not always possible to tell the difference.

Soft redirect    A very short article or page that essentially points the reader in the direction of another page. Used in cases where a normal redirect is inappropriate for various reasons (e.g., it is a cross-wiki redirect).

SPA    Short for *Single Purpose Account*. If that single purpose is disruptive (e.g., vote stacking, or attacking some user) the account tends to be indefinitely blocked.

Spamectomy    Removing spam from an article so that it is less of a POV issue.

Speedy    Abbreviation for Speedy delete (or "speedy rename" as appropriate). Can also be used as a verb—e.g., *"I think the article should be speedied"*. "Speedy" on Wikipedia does not mean "now, immediately", but rather something that can be done without further discussion.

Speedy delete    Deletion of a page without prior discussion. Pages can be speedily deleted only under very specific circumstances; *see* [[WP:Criteria_for_speedy _deletion]] for those.

Speedy keep    The closing of a vote on a deletion wikispace page (like AFD) before the normal end of the voting period. This happens when the nomination has been faulty (e.g., a bad faith nomination) or when there is overwhelming evidence that the page should be kept (e.g., overwhelming support for keeping it, or a history of deletion attempts that have ended in the same way).

Split    Separating a single page into two or more pages.

Sprot, sprotect, sprotection    Short for *semi-protect[ion]*. Articles that are semi-protected cannot be edited by unregistered or newly registered users.

Steward    An Administrator who has been empowered to change any user's status on any Wikimedia Foundation project, including granting and revoking Administrator status and granting bureaucrat status. *See also* [[WP:Administrators#Stewards]].

Stub    An article considered too short to give an adequate introduction to a subject (often one paragraph or less). Stubs are marked with stub templates, a specific type of cleanup template, which add the articles to stub categories sorted by subject matter. *See also* [[WP:Find_or_fix_a_stub]], [[WP:Wikiproject_Stub_Sorting]].

Subarticle, sub-article    1. An article that has been split from an original, larger main article to keep the main article readable and to better develop the sub-topic of the split into a richer article in its own right. *Contrast* Subpage. *See also* [[WP:Summary _style]]. 2. A page in multi-page list that was split to reduce list article size. *See also* [[WP:Stand-alone_lists]].

Subpage, sub-page    A page connected to a parent page, such as Somepage/Arguments. You can only create subpages in certain namespaces. Do not use subpages in the main article space. *Contrast* Subarticle. *See also* [[WP:Subpages]].

Substub    A very short stub article, usually consisting of only one sentence.

SUL    Abbreviation for "Single user login", which refers to the process of unifying individual accounts with the same name across Wikimedia projects into one global account.

Sysop, Sys-op, Sys-Op    A less-used name for Administrator. *See also* De-sysop.

Systemic bias    In Wikipedian terms, this refers to the preponderance of Wikipedia articles relating to subjects specific to English-speaking and/or Western countries, as opposed to those from the rest of the world. It may also refer to a bias for articles that may be of particular interest to those who have an affinity towards computers and the Internet, since they are more likely to edit Wikipedia. *See also* [[WP:WikiProject_Countering_systemic_bias]].

Talk page    A page reserved for discussion of the page with which it is associated, such as the article page. All pages within Wikipedia (except pages in the Special namespace, and talk pages themselves) have talk pages attached to them.

Talk page stalker, TPS    A humorous term for an editor who involves themselves in discussions on other users' talk pages (often after a previous conversation with that user has left the page on the editor's Watchlist). TPS involvement should be constructive or humorous, and is distinguished from wikistalking.

Task force    A smaller group of editors in a WikiProject dedicated to a more specific field within the scope of the parent project. Task forces are located on WikiProject subpages. They generally have a less formal bureaucratic structure than full-fledged WikiProjects. *See also* [[WP:WikiProject_Council/Guide/Task_forces]].

Template    A way of automatically including the contents of one page within another page, used for boilerplate text, navigational aids, etc. *See also* [[WP:Template_namespace]].

Templatise, Templatize    To delete a list or category and turn the contents into a template, usually either a navbox or infobox. Sometimes used in CFD discussions as shorthand for saying that "this group of articles would be better if presented in template form rather than as a category." *See also* Listify.

Test edit    Same as newbie test.

Thread    A talk page discussion, usually with more than 2 indented replies. May refer to either a complete second level section (i.e., a section with heading surrounded by ==) of posts as is defined by talk page archiving bots. For this type of thread, the age is the time interval from the most recent post to current time. It can also refer to an individual sequence of indented paragraphs.

Three-revert rule    A rule whereby no one is allowed to revert a single article more than three times in one day (with a few exceptions).

TLDR, tl;dr    Short for "Too long; didn't read". For example where a reply to a query is *very* long and detailed. *See* [[WP:Too_long;_didn't_read]].

TINC    Short for "there is no cabal". *See* Cabal.

TOC, ToC    An article (or other page)'s *table of contents*, which lists the subsection headings within the page. This is usually close to the top left of the page, but may be placed at the top right, floated, or omitted entirely.

Trainwreck    A nomination of a group of related pages for deletion or renaming which fails due to the disparate nature or worth of the pages. The deletion process often becomes messy with editors wishing to keep some pages but delete or rename others. Usually the discussion is closed as a procedural "keep", with some or all of the pages later nominated separately. *See* for example [[WP:Articles_for_deletion/Warcraft_character_articles]].

Transwiki    Move a page to another Wikimedia project, in particular Wiktionary, Wikibooks, or Wikisource. *See also* m:Transwiki, [[WP:WikiProject_Transwiki]].

Troll    A user who incites or engages in disruptive behavior (trolling). There are some people who enjoy causing conflict, and there are those who make a hobby of it. However, these are few in number and one should *always* assume good faith in other editors. Calling someone a troll in a dispute is a bad idea; it has an effect similar to calling someone a Nazi—no further meaningful debate is likely to occur. *See also* m:What_is_a_troll?

Trout, trout-slapping    A rebuke.

Tweak    A small edit. *See* [[Tweaking]].

Tyop    A silly misspelling of typo. Used as an edit summary when correcting typos. *See also* [[WP:Typo]].

Umbrella nomination    A nomination (e.g., on CfD) that contains several items (e.g., categories) which are normally nominated individually. Can become a trainwreck.

Unencyclopedic    Saying that something is unencyclopedic to imply that it would not be expected to appear in an encyclopedia, and thus in Wikipedia. (One must remember however that Wikipedia is not a paper encyclopedia, and hence does not have the space limitations of a paper encyclopedia).

Unregistered user    *See* IP user.

Un-wiki    Going against the character of a Wiki. Usually, saying that something is "un-wiki" means that it makes editing more difficult or impossible.

Un-wikify, unwikify    Same as de-wikify.

Upmerge    A term frequently used on categories for discussion and stub types for deletion, it means "merge into parent category". In the case of stub types, this usually means to keep any associated template but to link it with the parent category rather than the category under discussion. In contexts such as [[WP:WikiProject_Stub _sorting/Proposals]], creating an upmerged template means a stub template, only, feeding into a more general stub type.

Upscope    A portmanteau of upmerge and rescope. *See* Rescope.

User    *See* Editor.

Userbox    A small box which is stored in the template space, and which includes a small piece of information about a user (such as "This user likes cheese"). Many users use userboxes on their user page, although some look down upon it. *See also* [[WP:Userboxes]].

Userfy    [[WP:Userfication]] is the process by which material posted in a Wikipedia article, project, or template space is moved into the user space: into a user page or subpage. A common case is where an inexperienced user who is not a notable person has created an article about himself/herself. The article would be deleted after userfying—moving its content to a user page.

User page    A personal page for Wikipedians. Most people use their pages to introduce themselves and to keep various personal notes and lists. They are also used by Wikipedians to communicate with each other via the user talk pages. The process of Registration does not generate user pages automatically. A user page is linked to as [[User:SomeUserNameHere|SomeUserNameHere]] and appears as SomeUserNameHere.

Vandal    One who engages in significant amounts of vandalism.

Vandalbot    Some kind of bot being used for vandalism or spamming. Recognizable by the fact that one or a few IP-addresses make many similar clearly vandalistic edits in a short time. In the worst cases, these have created or vandalized hundreds of pages in several Wikipedias in a time span of only minutes. *See also* m:Vandalbot.

Vandalism    Deliberate defacement of Wikipedia pages. This can be by deleting text or writing nonsense, bad language, etc. The term is sometimes improperly used to discredit the views of an opponent in edit wars. Vandalism can be reported at [[WP:Administrator_intervention_against_vandalism]].

VandalProof    A tool for finding and removing vandalism. *See also* [[User:AmiDaniel/VandalProof]].

VFD    Used to refer to the "Votes for deletion" page. Although this has been replaced with "AFD" ([[WP:AFD]]), you may still see the term in older talk pages.

Village pump    The main community forum of Wikipedia (found at [[WP:Village _pump]]), where proposals, policy changes, technical problems and other internals are announced and discussed in front of a wider audience than a topic-specific page would have.

VP    Shorthand for Village pump or for VandalProof.

Wall of text    An unusually long paragraph, presenting a solid block of text of a dozen or more lines. Walls of text are visually unappealing and difficult to read. A wall of text in an article may simply be a sign of an inexperienced editor unfamiliar with Wikipedia markup, or may be a sign of a more serious issue such as copy-and-paste copyright violation. A wall of text in a talk page may be taken to be a sign of soap-boxing or shotgun argumentation. *See also* [[WP:Too_long;_didn't_read]] (TLDR, TL:DR, [[WP:TLDR]]).

Watchlist    A set of pages selected by the user, who can then click on My watchlist to see recent changes to those pages. *See also* [[Help:Watching_pages]].

Weasel words    Phrases such as "Some say that . . ." or "It has been argued . . ." that introduce a point of view without attributing it more specifically. *See also* [[WP:Neutral _point_of_view#Attributing_and_substantiating_biased_statements]].

Wheel war    A dispute between Wikipedia administrators who use the privileges of Wikipedia administrators (such as blocking) as weapons in an edit war. *See also* [[Wheel_war]].

WikiBlame    A tool for searching past versions of a particular article for a particular string of text. Usually used to determine who added the string of text. It is an external tool, available at wikipedia.ramselehof.de/wikiblame.php or via the "Revision history search" link on the article's history page.

Wikibreak, wikivacation, Wikiholiday, Wiki-break, etc.    When a Wikipedian takes a break from Wikipedia.

WikiCrime, wikicrime    An egregious case of or clear pattern of editing that violates Wikipedia policies, such as vandalism, spam, disruptive editing, tendentious editing, canvassing, hoaxing, adding unverifiable information, self-aggrandizement or promotion, removing well-sourced or adding unsourced information to suit personal biases, etc.

WikiFairy, Wikifaerie, Wiki-fairy, etc.    A Wikipedian who beautifies wiki entries by organizing messy articles, and adding style, color and graphics. The efforts of Wiki-Fairies are normally welcome, though they do not necessarily create new articles or affect the substantive content of the articles they edit. WikiFairies are considered to be basically friendly, like WikiGnomes. *See also* WikiOgre.

Wikify, wfy, wikiize, wiki-ise, etc.    To format using Wiki markup (as opposed to plain text or HTML). It commonly refers to adding internal links to material (Wikilinks) but is not limited to just that. To wikify an article could refer to applying any form of wiki-markup, such as standard headings and layout, including the addition of infoboxes and other templates, or bolding/italicizing of text. Noun: wikification; gerund: wikifying. *See also* [[WP:How_to_edit_a_page]], [[Category:Articles _that_need_to_be_wikified, [[WP:WikiProject_Wikify]], [[WP:Guide_to_layout]], [[WP:Make_only_links_relevant_to_the_context]].

WikiGnome, wikignome, Wiki-Gnome, wiki-gnome, etc.    A Wikipedian who makes minor, helpful edits without clamoring for attention or praise for what they did. *See also* WikiFairy, WikiOgre.

WikiHate, wikihate    Counterproductive editing attitude and behavior, especially tendentious, biased and personally antagonistic types of edit-warring.

Wikilawyering    Attempting to inappropriately rely on technicalities in a legalistic manner with respect to [[WP:Policies]] or [[WP:Arbitration]].

Wikilink, wl    A link to another Wikipedia page or to an anchor on the same page, as opposed to an external link. For policy, *see* [[WP:Only_make_links_that_ are_relevant_to_the_context]] and [[WP:Build_the_web]]. For mechanics, *see* [[WP:Canonicalization]], [[Help:Section#Section_linking]], [[WP:How _to_edit_a_page#Links_and_URLs]], and [[WP:Citing_sources/Further_consi derations#Wikilinks_to_full_references]]. *See also* Free link and Piped link.

WikiLove, wikilove    A general spirit of collegiality and mutual understanding among Wikipedians. The term pre-dates Wikipedia. WikiLove is achieved through wiki-quette, civility, assumption of good faith about other editors, neutrality, respect for policies and guidelines, and calm editing and discussion.

Wiki markup, wikitext, wiki text, wiki-text, etc.    Code like HTML, but simplified and more convenient, for example "boldfaced text" instead of <B>boldfaced text</B>. It is the source code stored in the database and shown in the edit box. Searching by the Wikipedia software is done in the wikitext, as opposed to searching by external major search engines, which is done in the resulting HTML. The size of a page is the size of the wikitext. *See also* Wikitext, [[Help:Wiki_markup]], [[WP:How_to_edit _a_page]], [[WP:Guide_to_layout]].

Wikimedia    Properly Wikimedia Foundation, Inc. (WMF), a non-profit organization that provides a legal, financial, and organizational framework for Wikipedia and its sister projects and provides the necessary hardware. *Contrast* MediaWiki.

WikiOgre, Wiki-ogre, wikiogre, etc.    A Wikipedian who makes large edits from time to time but generally keeps to WikiGnomery. *See also* WikiFairy

Wikiportal    Pages intended to be the main pages for Wikipedians interested in a specific area of knowledge, helping both to find the information on the specific topic and to develop articles connected with it. *See also* [[WP:Portal]].

Wikipediholic, Wikiholic    A wikipedian who obsesses over the project to the point where interacting with Wikipedia becomes akin to a psychological addiction.

WikiProject    An active group of Wikipedia editors working together to improve a specific group of articles, usually those on one or more related topics. This often involves an attempt to standardize the content and style of the articles using an agreed standard format.

Wikiquette    The etiquette of working with others on Wikipedia. *See also* [[WP:Etiquette]].

Wikiquote    A Wikipedia sister project to create a free online collection of quotations.

Wikislap    Providing someone with the URL of a Wikipedia article when he or she expresses a lack of knowledge about a particular topic.

Wikisource    A Wikipedia sister project to create a free online compendium of primary source texts.

Wikispace    The Wikipedia namespace. *See* [[WP:Namespace#Pseudo-namespaces]], [[WP:Shortcuts]] (Wikipedia:WP).

Wikispam    Articles or sections created to promote a product or other meme. Spamming can also include adding extraneous or irrelevant links to promote an outside site, particularly for commercial purposes.

Wikistalking, wikihounding    The singling out of one or more editors, and joining discussions on multiple pages or topics they may edit or multiple debates where they contribute, in order to repeatedly confront or inhibit their work, with an apparent aim of creating irritation, annoyance or distress to the other editor. Note that editors can and do follow others in good faith with constructive intent; it is the manner and motivation which distinguishes wikistalking.

Wikistress, Wiki-Stress, wiki-stress, etc.    Personal stress or tension induced by editing Wikipedia, or more often by being involved in minor conflict with another editor. Some users maintain a Wikistress meter on their user page. *See* Wikistress template ([[Template:Wstress3d]]), The Bosch Wikistress Meter ([[Template:Boschmeter]]), [[Wikistress]].

WikiTerrorism, wikiterrorism, WikiTerror, wikiterror   A melodramatic term for the act of purposely trying to damage Wikipedia on a large scale. It can be vandalism, but it could include trolling, edit warring, or anything that could disrupt Wikipedia on a large scale. WikiTerrorism could also be "blitzing" Wikipedia, or vandalizing several articles in rapid succession. Such actions should be reported immediately to administrators and will usually be blocked. Some may consider this term in bad taste or hyperbolic.

Wiktionary, wikt.   A Wikipedia sister project to create a free online dictionary of every language.

WMF   *See* Wikimedia.

Wolf vote   A vote on Wikipedia which seems to be cast just to go against the flow. E.g., on RfA, this can typically be a vote such as "Oppose because x, y, and z are supporting." The opposite is called a sheep vote.

WP   1. Common abbreviation for Wikipedia, especially for pages in the Wikipedia namespace. *See also* [[WP:Namespace#Pseudo-namespaces]], [[WP:Shortcuts]]. 2. Also sometimes used as an abbreviation for WikiProject (*see also* WPP).

# NOTES

## PROLOGUE

1. I purposefully avoid providing citations to these discussions to protect the subjects.

2. For ease of reference, all citations to the English Wikipedia are presented in a shortened format. For example, [[WP:Size_comparisons]] can be found at https://en.wikipedia.org/wiki/WP:Size_comparisons (or https://en.wikipedia.org/wiki/Wikipedia:Size_comparisons, because "WP" is a shortcut to "Wikipedia"). Double square brackets are characteristic of the markup code of wiki technology, often used by people to collaborate in creating and modifying content on the web. They allow easy visual differentiation of this type of citation.

## INTRODUCTION

1. The ethnographic study discussed in this book took place in 2006–2012, when I was particularly active on the Polish Wikipedia (where I was elected an administrator and a bureaucrat—roles are described in more detail in Chapter 2) and the English Wikipedia, which both serve as the basis of the analysis. I was also elected by the global Wikimedia community to serve as one of about forty stewards worldwide, and thus some of the conclusions rely on international observations and participation.

2. Doing ethnographic research from the inside, through going native, traditionally has been considered less legitimate or valid than an outsider approach. However, over the last twenty years this approach has been recognized as legitimate and as having its own advantages. A more detailed discussion of methodology is included in Appendix A.

3. Reputation building is also rapidly growing in importance in everyday life because of the increased popularity of collaborative consumption (Botsman & Rogers, 2010).

4. Wikipedias are the most popular projects within the Wikimedia Foundation, but there are many others, such as Wiktionaries, Wikinews, Wikiversities, Wikibooks, and Wikiquotes, all organized on the basis of similar community principles and run from Wikimedia Foundation computer servers. Wikileaks.org has no relation with Wikimedia projects and since 2010 does not even use MediaWiki software. For the purposes of this book, "Wikipedia" refers to the English and the Polish Wikipedias, and "Wikimedia"

refers to all projects run under the Wikimedia Foundation umbrella. The Wikimedia Foundation is an American nonprofit charitable organization established in 2003 to run Wikipedia and other projects, and it owns the related trademarks and domain names. The foundation is discussed in further detail in Chapter 6.

5. The meaning of the word "community" is elusive. Wikipedians use it both to describe the members of the general Wikimedia movement worldwide and to refer to people involved in their local projects.

6. For a long list of other criticisms, see [[WP:Criticisms]].

7. This very well might have been the reason for the so-called Seigenthaler incident, when for four months the biography of John Seigenthaler, a well-known American journalist, contained a sentence implying his involvement in John Kennedy's assassination ([[Wikipedia_biography_controversy]]). This hoax, corrected well before it was described by Seigenthaler in *USA Today* (Seigenthaler, 2005), caused a major scandal and a lapse of trust in Wikipedia in 2005. While there is no denying that the incident showed a weakness in the system of social creation of knowledge when faced with malicious hoaxers, and many measures have been taken since then to address the issue, it is still quite clear that the misinformation would have been corrected much more quickly if it had been planted in a highly popular article (e.g., in the description of the assassination itself). Similarly, a massive hoax about the "Bicholim conflict," a made-up war described on Wikipedia in 2007 and unsuspected till December 2012 (Morris, 2013a), would most likely not have survived if it had been about a topic of more interest to most readers.

8. This was, for example, the unfortunate, though ironic, case for Taner Akcam, a history professor from Turkey. Because of his research on the Armenian genocide, Turkish nationalists planted information that he was a terrorist in his biography on Wikipedia. As a result, he was detained in the Montreal airport by officers who had seen the bio. After sorting out the misunderstanding, Akcam continued his travel, only to be detained again in the United States two days later for the same reason (Suddath, 2011). This story shows not only that hoaxes take place on Wikipedia but also that information on Wikipedia is extremely powerful.

## CHAPTER 1

1. See more on the milestone event in the accounts of Kovitz and Sanger at [[User:BenKovitz#The_conversation_at_the_taco_stand]].

2. As of April 8, 2013, of Wikipedians who had declared their command of languages, which most do, 1,954 specified that they could contribute with a basic level of English; 6,151, declared that they were at an intermediate level; 12,200 were at an advanced level; 6,547 were at a near-native level (including me); 4,465 were at a professional level; and 30,929 were at a native level. Categories are taken from [[Category:User_en]].

3. The statistical measures of Wikipedia growth become even more complicated when one has to decide what constitutes an article. For quite a while in the official statistics, only articles with at least one comma were counted. This obviously placed non-European languages at a disadvantage. Currently, a different measure is applied in

MediaWiki software (version 1.18 and later), but earlier versions are still in use. For more information, see "Manual:Article count," 2013.

4. Retrieved August 14, 2013, from http://en.wikichecker.com/.

5. Retrieved August 14, 2013, from http://toolserver.org/~emijrp/wikimedia counter/.

6. Retrieved August 28, 2012, from http://reportcard.wmflabs.org.

7. Although some researchers (Buss & Strauss, 2009) do not consider wikis to be online communities because they shift focus from social networking to knowledge creation, Wikimedia projects, with their interactions, socializing, group identity, and perception of belonging, especially for registered users, satisfy the criteria, as does any other community in the open-source and open-collaboration movement (M. Castells, 2001; Von Krogh, Spaeth, & Lakhani, 2003; S. Weber, 2004).

8. It may be worth noting that besides significant efforts from the Wikimedia Foundation to close the gender gap, there are other initiatives that address the problem, such as WikiChix (see http://geekfeminism.wikia.com/wiki/WikiChix), which was created in 2006 to allow female editors of Wikipedia to discuss their perceptions of gender bias and means of minimizing it. To read more on systemic bias on Wikipedia, visit [[WP:BIAS]].

9. All abbreviated rules correspond with their article titles on the English Wikipedia. This rule, for example, can be found under [[WP:NPA]].

10. I do not provide a citation to the discussion, because the person is editing under his own name and is still a Wikimedia Foundation employee.

11. An infobox is a table, graphically separated from the main body of the article, summarizing the main data about the described person or phenomenon and typically used in biographies.

12. For more on definitions of free cultural works and free licenses, see "Definition," 2008.

13. Notably, "History of Poland (1945–89)" and "Polish Culture during World War II" are among them.

14. For a list of types and categories of userboxes on the English Wikipedia, see [[WP:Userboxes/Gallery]].

## CHAPTER 2

1. The organizational archetype of a trickster has a long tradition and has been studied from different angles (see Czarniawska-Joerges, 1998; Gabriel, 1995; D. Jemielniak, 2008a; Kociatkiewicz & Kostera, 2010).

2. I have been elected as an administrator and a bureaucrat on Polish Wikipedia and later as a steward for all Wikimedia projects (within this role I have been required to take one of any of the other roles of trust on these projects, which do not have functionaries assigned to them).

3. On the Polish, English, and many other Wikipedias such support is also required in administrator elections, but the exact requirements are regulated by each Wikipedia separately; for instance, the Japanese Wikipedia requires 75 percent support for election to local community roles.

4. The exact number of administrators on the English Wikipedia is difficult to establish for several reasons. First, in the beginnings of Wikipedia some foundation staff members were given not a staff flag but an admin flag. Second, in some statistics, bots (programs that automate tasks) are included, and in some they are not. Finally, sometimes when accounts are renamed, the old and the new account are both counted (as if there are two admins, when in fact there is one). As of August 2013, 2,197 accounts have performed administrative actions (see [[User:JamesR/AdminStats]]), and there are 1,438 administrators (see [[WP:Administrators]]).

5. Justin Knapp (editing as "koavf"), reached one million edits in April 2012 (Horn, 2012). In recognition, Jimbo Wales stated, "I hereby proclaim, in my usual authoritarian and bossy manner, that today (April 20) shall forever be known as Justin Knapp Day" (see [[WP:Justin_Knapp_Day]]).

6. On some projects, for instance, the Swedish Wikipedia, administrators are re-elected every year.

7. The voluntary-work and immaterial-labor phenomena, typical for open-collaboration and F/LOSS communities and related to the gift-economy character of the postcapitalist turn, may be also perceived as a new way of exerting control over production and ideological persuasion to performing free labor (Terranova, 2000), one decoded and reconverted into a script of profit (Deleuze & Guattari, 1972/2004).

## CHAPTER 3

1. The title of this chapter repeats the title of an article ("Mourir pour Danzig?") by Marcel Déat, a French nationalist and socialist, published in 1938 in the newspaper *L'Œuvre* and widely discussed at that time not only in France but also in other European countries. The article argued that France should not respect the alliance with Poland and should not go to war with Germany if Poland was attacked. See more at [[Marcel_Déat]].

2. See the popular cartoon "Duty Calls" by Randall Munroe at http://xkcd.com/386/.

3. In a recent PR-related controversy involving a Wikipedian, in September 2012 Roger Bamkin, a director and the treasurer of Wikimedia United Kingdom, appeared to be pushing articles about Gibraltar to the front page of the English Wikipedia, in the "Did You Know" section (with an unprecedented frequency of every couple of days), while working as a paid consultant for the government of Gibraltar (Blue, 2012a). If he was, it was a conflict of interest and could lead to others promoting and privileging a nonneutral point of view for compensation. As a result, the U.K. chapter was investigated by the Wikimedia Foundation, and temporary ineligibility for Wikimedia fund donations was considered (Blue, 2012b). The U.K. chapter hired Compass Partnership consulting agency to conduct an external audit and introduced procedures to prevent similar conflicts of interest. See [[WP:Wikipedia_Signpost/2013-02-11/News_and_ notes]]. An even bigger PR-related scandal occurred in 2013, when an extensive network of paid advocacy articles on Wikipedia, created by a commercial PR company, was revealed. See [[WP:Wikipedia_Signpost/2013-10-09/News_and_notes]].

4. She described her interest in a conversation during the Wikimania 2012 conference in Washington on July 12. Her interest is evidenced by the list of readings published on her blog at http://suegardner.org/books-i-like/ (as of August 15, 2013, eleven books about Quakers and twelve on other topics are listed).

5. It is also one of the wars listed on the "Wikipedia:Lamest edit wars" page (see [[WP:Lamest_edit_wars]]). Other of the painfully long battles on the English Wikipedia with additional Polish flavor include a debate on whether Chopin was Polish, Polish-French, French-Polish, or perhaps just French and whether his name should be written "Szopen," following the Polish transcription, and whether Nicolaus Copernicus was Polish, German, or Prussian. Other examples of heated feuds that did not make it to the list of the lamest edit wars but could qualify include whether Marie Curie (or Maria Skłodowska-Curie) should be considered Polish, Polish-French, or Polish-born French. A long-lasting war (which I took occasional part in) was over what countries are in Central Europe and according to what sources.

6. Godwin's Law of Nazi Analogies is an argument made by Mike Godwin in 1990 stating that any online discussion, given enough time, eventually degenerates into comparisons to Hitler or the Nazis. Some discussion forums and newsgroups have a tradition that whoever invokes the Nazi or Adolf Hitler analogy automatically loses the argument. See [[Godwin's_law]].

7. One of Wales's comments in the discussion, from October 2003, is archived at http://lists.wikimedia.org/pipermail/wikipedia-l/2003-October/012896.html.

8. See [[Wikipedia_talk:Naming_conventions_(disputed_place_names)/Archive_1]]; [[Wikipedia_talk:Naming_conventions_(geographic_names)/Archive_1]]; and [[Talk:Gdansk/Naming_convention]].

9. The *Wikipedia Signpost* is a community-driven and community-written newspaper of the English Wikipedia. It is available at [[WP:Wikipedia_Signpost]].

10. A sock-puppet is an account created by a user to make a false impression of wider support for some point of view.

11. Incidentally, or perhaps also a little because of this peace, the city of Gdańsk competed with Oxford and Amsterdam to serve as a host city for Wikimania 2010. It won, to become the sixth city in the world to organize a Wikimania annual international conference.

12. For instance, articles related to the topic of rape may be relatively less developed than others and emphasize different issues than they would if females were not underrepresented (Szymanski, Devlin, Chrisler, & Vyse, 1993; Verberg, Wood, Desmarais, & Senn, 2000). Also, Western views and approaches are more likely to be reflected. For example, in a discussion on an article on Todd Akin, a Republican nominee for a U.S. Senate seat in 2012, who said in an interview that after "legitimate rape" women often do not get pregnant, quite a few disputants minimized this controversy and did not consider it important enough to be mentioned in the lead of the article. Also, an article on "legitimate rape" was created to redirect to coverage of this incident, despite some editors pointing out that the term "legitimate rape" should be reserved for phenomena

such as legal acceptance of marital rape in some jurisdictions and the historical droit du seigneur (the right of first night) rather than for a one-time event in American politics.

13. To be fair, experienced Wikipedians often distance themselves from newcomers, as described in Chapter 4.

14. For an analysis, see [[User:Piotrus/Morsels_of_wikiwisdom#On_the_import ance_of_wikipolitics]].

## CHAPTER 4

1. WikiProjects also have an important role in creating microcommunities. These are virtual venues gathering people of similar interests, so that they can discuss inter- pretations and standards, as well as serve as ad hoc consultants if somebody from the general Wikipedia population needs advice on their topic of expertise. The WikiProject for sociology can be found at [[Portal:Sociology]]. WikiProjects often run WikiPortals, which are article aggregators for particular topics.

2. Most editors' amount and patterns of editing on the English Wikipedia, as well as quantity, quality, and nature of activities on Wikipedia, do not change over time. Thus, from their first edits it is possible to predict with reasonable accuracy who of the new editors may become power editors; in other words, "Wikipedians are born, not made" (Panciera, Halfaker, & Terveen, 2009).

3. Wikipedia rules and policies do not apply to communication on other IRC channels and on the open e-mail lists, even though they are just as public as Wikipedia discussions.

4. Additionally, the lack of an automated notification system (surely technically trivial to introduce) increases the sacrifice editors have to make to follow their dialogues and underprivileges newcomers who may be unaware that replies will be on their inter- locutor's talk page. The editors' sacrifice contributes to the egalitarian system of power, discussed more widely in Chapter 2.

5. Interestingly, from 2004 to 2007 a voluntary Association of Members' Advocates existed on Wikipedia to help in dispute resolution, but it was eventually shut down because of slowness of operation and the perception of many Wikipedians that it was overly bureaucratic and prone to wikilawyering (see [[WP:Association_of_Members' _Advocates]]).

6. Ostrom's principles related to smaller communities, and it can be assumed that Wikipedia is a pioneer in addressing many of the social organization problems of scale and that not all principles of open-collaboration communities may be fully applicable to it.

## CHAPTER 5

1. Essjay's original talk page no longer exists, but this post has been archived at http://www.wikipedia-watch.org/essjay.html.

2. This post is archived at http://en.wikipedia.org/w/index.php?title=User_talk:Ess jay&oldid=112480415#Slashdot.

3. This post is archived at http://en.wikipedia.org/w/index.php?title=User_ talk:Essjay&oldid=112480415.

## CHAPTER 6

1. For a useful taxonomy of contributions to Wikimedia projects, see "Research:Contribution Taxonomy Project," 2012.

2. I wrote these words two days after I was appointed one of seven members of the FDC, and I was later elected chair. I hope that this book's organizational analysis is unaffected by this role, but the reader should be aware of a potential bias. This position is unpaid.

3. See the discussion beginning with the post at http://lists.wikimedia.org/piper mail/wikimedia-l/2012-October/122236.html.

4. For quotations from interviewees who chose to remain anonymous, I do not provide names or dates to protect those subjects.

5. These views were expressed in the official presentation of the board of trustees during the Wikimania conference in Washington on July 14, 2012.

6. This strategic change was approved by the board of trustees on October 26, 2012, as described in "Vote," 2013 and discussed with the community in "User:Sue Gardner," 2012.

7. See the post at http://lists.wikimedia.org/pipermail/wikimedia-l/2012 -October/122260.html.

8. See a post of the letter at http://lists.wikimedia.org/pipermail/foundation-l/2011 -August/067163.html.

9. See, for example, the post at http://lists.wikimedia.org/pipermail/founda tion-l/2011-August/067195.html.

10. See the discussion beginning with the post at http://lists.wikimedia.org/ pipermail/foundation-l/2011-April/065229.html.

11. See, for example, the situation described at [[WP:Administrators'_noticeboard/ Archive242#Antonio_Pizzigati]].

12. For the full text of the protest manifesto (in Italian), see "Wikipedia:Comunicato," 2011.

13. See "Wikimedia Forum/Italian Wikimedia," 2012, and the discussion beginning with the post at http://lists.wikimedia.org/pipermail/foundation-l/2011-October/069191 .html.

14. See the post at http://lists.wikimedia.org/pipermail/foundation-l/2011 -October/069258.html.

15. After the strike the Russian Arbitration Committee decided that the strike had been agreed on too hastily, without the proper community consensus, and two admin- istrators involved in the situation were demoted. See the post at http://lists.wikimedia .org/pipermail/wikimedia-l/2012-December/122895.html.

16. The referendum engaged over twenty-four thousand voters, making it clear that there is support for some form of image filtering. See "Image Filter Referendum," 2011.

17. For discussions on controversial content, see "Controversial Content," 2012.

18. See http://lists.wikimedia.org/pipermail/wikimedia-l/2012-October/122426 .html.

19. As in any organization, occasional governance tensions occur. This is so mostly when the scope of authority and its practical execution between each body within the community have to be established—for example, the rights of the Arbitration Committee, prerogatives of stewards on local projects, and division of responsibilities between the global Ombudsman Commission and a local audit subcommittee.

## CHAPTER 7

1. A nickname possibly indicating both Wales's desire for informality and his working-class origins.

2. Notability policies on the "Wikipedia:Biographies of Living Persons" page that were later developed help avoid such lengthy discussions now (see [[WP:Biographies _of_living_persons]]).

3. There is now a closed e-mail list (internal-l) for some WMF staff, representatives of the chapters, and handpicked known and well-established Wikipedians.

4. Administrators on Wikiversity are called "custodians," but I use the more common form of the function's name to avoid confusion.

5. See his post at http://wikipediareview.com/index.php?showtopic=28227&st=0& p=216249&#entry216249.

6. Meta-Wiki, often simply called "Meta," is a separate wiki, available at http://meta .wikimedia.org, dedicated to serving all other Wikimedia wikis in terms of policy discussions, debates, cross-wiki antivandalism, steward elections, and so on.

7. The image is available at http://commons.wikimedia.org/wiki/File:2011052622242 9!F%C3%A9licien_Rops_-_Sainte-Thérèse.png.

8. In March 2010 the German Wikipedia decided against limiting the type of material presented on the main page and, in spite of protests from many readers, kept an article with a close-up photo of a vagina. The internal discussion, spiked by angry comments from readers, was over seventy-three thousand words but led to no clear veto of the article being featured (see "Wikipedia Diskussion," 2013). Similarly, in spite of many protests and discussions, the cartoons of prophet Muhammad published by the Danish newspaper *Jyllands-Posten* in 2005 have been kept on the English Wikipedia in the article "*Jyllands-Posten* Muhammad Cartoons Controversy," even though they are highly offensive to Muslims and even though the original publication resulted in violent protests and acts of terrorism (see [[Jyllands-Posten_Muhammad_cartoons_controversy]]). In general, Wikimedia communities are unable to reach consensus on how to allow any form of image filtering (for a good summary of many debates in the community, see "Controversial Content," 2012, especially the timeline).

9. Images removed from the Commons disappear from all articles in Wikimedia projects. This is a result of a special script that ensures that articles show images instead of empty links. However, to restore deleted images requires manually inserting them, one by one, in each article.

10. All quotes in the discussion come from the foundation e-mail list, unless stated otherwise. The archive is available at http://lists.wikimedia.org/pipermail/foun dation-l/2010-May/thread.html#57891.

11. To follow the discussions and the development of this initiative, see [[User _talk:Jimbo_Wales/Archive_91#Request_for_Comment:_SOPA_and_a_strike]] and [[WP:SOPA_initiative]].

12. For a list of these communities, see [[WP:SOPA_initiative/Actions_by_other _communities]].

13. The Commons community seems to be somewhat hostile to Wales. In 2013 one of the Commons bureaucrats who had previously been in conflict with Wales uploaded a picture of Wales painted with a penis by an Australian artist (going by the stage name Pricasso), along with a video documenting the process. Wales considered this an act of harassment and mobbing (Morris, 2013b). However, the Commons community voted that the picture is notable and should not be deleted. See "Commons:Deletion Requests," 2013.

## CHAPTER 8

1. See http://dumps.wikimedia.org/dvd.html.

2. Wikitravel, a commercial website hosted by Internet Brands, has a community of volunteers to develop a travel advisory wiki-guide. However, in 2012 a significant part of the community decided to partner with Wikivoyage, a German fork of Wikitravel (created in 2004 as a result of dissatisfaction with Wikitravel's decision to run ads), and together came under the Wikimedia Foundation umbrella. Since Wikitravel content was accessible through a data dump (allowed by Creative Commons license, although disabled shortly thereafter by Internet Brands), the new website, running under the brand of Wikivoyage, took over both the content and the crucial part of the Wikitravel community, leaving Internet Brands in a very difficult strategic position (Cohen, 2012; see also [[Wikivoyage]]).

3. Small steps in this area are being made. For example, the American Sociological Association is calling on its members to improve and develop better Wikipedia articles; see http://www.asanet.org/about/wiki_Initiative.cfm.

4. The user Emijrp estimates the completion of Wikipedia as of August 2013 to be near 4 percent, basing the estimation on the number of different topics, the number of articles that are "red linked" (mentioned and linked in other articles but not yet covered), and other factors. See [[User:Emijrp/All_human_knowledge]].

## APPENDIX A

1. Having administrator and steward privileges allowed me to access articles and talk pages that had been removed from Wikipedia and thus led to an understanding of how the rules of deletion and exclusion work in practice, not just in policy.

2. As of October 2013, there are over 4.3 million articles on the English Wikipedia alone, but the community's life happens elsewhere. In addition to encyclopedic articles there are over twenty-seven million other pages (see [[WP:Size_of_Wikipedia]]), such as article talk pages, categories, and redirects—millions of pages, many of them containing dozens of thousands of words and containing discussions between users, voting pages, opinions, rules and regulations, essays, polls, or just anecdotes meant for other

Wikipedians. There is even a daily, community-written newspaper ([[WP:Wikipedia _Signpost]])! The sheer size of the written culture of the English and other Wikipedias, independent from articles and rarely accessed by others, is enormous. It is probably impossible to read all these pages in a lifetime, and experienced Wikipedians limit themselves to mainstream discussions and debates. Also, the more important a discussion or opinion is, the more likely it is to draw attention from the community and be linked to in mainstream discussions, many of which begin or are at least referred to in the Village Pump ([[WP:Village_pump]]), which is an announcement board and sometimes a general discussion page.

## APPENDIX B

1. Besides this brief introduction, all content in this glossary is quoted from Wikipedia (with occasional minor additional clarifications) under the Creative Commons Attribution-ShareAlike 3.0 Unported License, and this appendix as a whole can be shared under the same provisions. See [[WP:Text_of_Creative_Commons_Attribution -ShareAlike_3.0_Unported_License]].

2. Cross-references that begin with "m:" refer to the Meta-Wiki page for the term after the colon. For example, "m:Cabal" is short for http://meta.wikimedia.org/wiki/ Cabal.

# REFERENCES

Aaltonen, A., & Lanzara, G. F. (2010, April 7–10). *Unpacking Wikipedia governance: The emergence of a bureaucracy of peers?* Paper presented at the Third Latin American and European Meeting on Organisation Studies, Buenos Aires.

Adams, T., & Smith, S. A. (Eds.). (2008). *Electronic tribes: The virtual worlds of geeks, gamers, shamans, and scammers.* Austin: University of Texas Press.

Adler, P. A., & Adler, P. (1987). *Membership roles in field research* (Vol. 6). Newbury Park, CA: Sage.

Afonso, E. Z. F., & Taylor, P. C. (2009). Critical autoethnographic inquiry for culture-sensitive professional development. *Reflective Practice, 10*(2), 273–283.

Agar, M. (1980). *The professional stranger: An informal introduction to ethnography.* New York: Academic Press.

Albrechtslund, A. (2008). Online social networking as participatory surveillance. *First Monday, 13*(3). Retrieved from http://firstmonday.org/ojs/index.php/fm/article/viewArticle/2142/1949

Alvesson, M. (1995). *Cultural perspectives on organizations.* Cambridge, England: Cambridge University Press.

Alvesson, M. (2003). Beyond neopositivists, romantics, and localists: A reflexive approach to interviews in organizational research. *The Academy of Management Review, 28*(1), 13–33.

Amichai-Hamburger, Y., Lamdan, N., Madiel, R., & Hayat, T. (2008). Personality characteristics of Wikipedia members. *CyberPsychology and Behavior, 11*(6), 679–681.

Anderson, J. J. (2011). *Wikipedia: The company and its founders.* Minneapolis, MN: Essential Library.

Anderson, L. (2006). Analytic autoethnography. *Journal of Contemporary Ethnography, 35*(4), 373–395.

Anderson, N. (2009, February 12). Doomed: Why Wikipedia will fail. *Ars Technica.* Retrieved from http://arstechnica.com/business/2009/2002/doomed-why-wikipedia-will-fail/

Anthony, D., Smith, S. W., & Williamson, T. (2007, April). *The quality of open source production: Zealots and Good Samaritans in the case of Wikipedia* (Technical Report TR2007-606). Retrieved from Department of Computer Science, Dartmouth, website: http://www.cs.dartmouth.edu/reports/TR2007-606.pdf

Anthony, D., Smith, S. W., & Williamson, T. (2009). Reputation and reliability in collective goods: The case of the online encyclopedia Wikipedia. *Rationality and Society,* 21(3), 283–306.

Antin, J. (2011). My kind of people? Perceptions about Wikipedia contributors and their motivations. In *Proceedings of the SIGCHI Conference on Human Factors in Computing Systems* (pp. 3411–3420). New York: ACM.

Antin, J., & Cheshire, C. (2010, February 6–10). *Readers are not free-riders: Reading as a form of participation on Wikipedia.* Paper presented at the Computer Supported Cooperative Work conference, Savannah, GA.

Argyris, C. (1973). *On organizations of the future.* Beverly Hills, CA: Sage.

Arnstein, S. R. (1969). A ladder of citizen participation. *Journal of the American Institute of Planners,* 35(4), 216–224.

Arthur, C. (2005, December 14). Log on and join in, but beware the web cults. *The Guardian.* Retrieved from http://www.theguardian.com/technology/2005/dec/15/wikipedia.web20

Arthur, C. (2012). *Digital wars: Apple, Google, Microsoft and the battle for the Internet.* London: Kogan Page.

Ashton, D. (2011). Awarding the self in Wikipedia: Identity work and the disclosure of knowledge. *First Monday,* 16(1–3). Retrieved from http://firstmonday.org/article/view/3156/2747

Atkinson, P., & Hammersley, M. (1994). Ethnography and participant observation. In N. K. Denzin & Y. S. Lincoln (Eds.), *Handbook of qualitative research* (Vol. 1, pp. 248–261). Thousand Oaks, CA: Sage.

Autier, F. (2001, July 5–7). *Bureaucracy vs. adhocracy: A case of overdramatisation?* Paper presented at the European Group for Organizational Studies conference, Lyon, France. Retrieved from http://citeseerx.ist.psu.edu/viewdoc/download?doi=10.1.1.155.4590&rep=rep1&type=pdf

Avgitidou, S. (2009). Participation, roles and processes in a collaborative action research project: A reflexive account of the facilitator. *Educational Action Research,* 17(4), 585–600.

Ayers, P., Matthews, C., & Yates, B. (2008). *How Wikipedia works: And how you can be a part of it.* San Francisco: No Starch Press.

Bailenson, J. N., & Beall, A. C. (2006). Transformed social interaction: Exploring the digital plasticity of avatars. In R. Schroeder & A.-S. Axelsson (Eds.), *Avatars at work and play* (pp. 1–16). Dordrecht, Netherlands: Springer.

Bailey, D., & Neilsen, E. H. (1992). Creating a bureau-adhocracy: Integrating standardized and innovative services in a professional work group. *Human Relations,* 45(7), 687–710.

Bal, M. (1993). First person, second person, same person: Narrative as epistemology. *New Literary History,* 24(2), 293–320.

Ball, K., & Wilson, D. C. (2000). Power, control and computer-based performance monitoring: Repertoires, resistance and subjectivities. *Organization Studies,* 21(3), 539–565.

Barbrook, R. (1998). The hi-tech gift economy. *First Monday, 3*(12). Retrieved from http://pear.accc.uic.edu/ojs/index.php/fm/article/viewArticle/631/552

Barbrook, R. (2000). Cyber-communism: How the Americans are superseding capitalism in cyberspace. *Science as Culture, 9*(1), 5–40.

Barker, J. R. (1993). Tightening the iron cage: Concertive control in self-managing teams. *Administrative Science Quarterly, 38*(3), 408–437.

Barley, S. R., & Kunda, G. (2001). Bringing work back in. *Organization Science, 12*(1), 76–95.

Barley, S. R., & Kunda, G. (2004). *Gurus, hired guns, and warm bodies: Itinerant experts in a knowledge economy.* Princeton, NJ: Princeton University Press.

Barnard, A. (1983). Contemporary hunter-gatherers: Current theoretical issues in ecology and social organization. *Annual Review of Anthropology, 12*, 193–214.

Barnett, E. (2010, May 11). Wikipedia porn row sees founder give up his editing privileges. *The Telegraph.* Retrieved from http://www.telegraph.co.uk/technology/wikipedia/7711486/Wikipedia-porn-row-sees-founder-give-up-his-editing-privileges.html

Bartunek, J. M. (2011). What has happened to mode 2? *British Journal of Management, 22*(3), 555–558.

Bass, B. M., & Shackleton, V. J. (1979). Industrial democracy and participative management: A case for a synthesis. *Academy of Management Review, 4*(3), 393–404.

Bassett, E. H., & O'Riordan, K. (2002). Ethics of Internet research: Contesting the human subjects research model. *Ethics and Information Technology, 4*(3), 233–247.

Bate, S. (1997). Whatever happened to organizational anthropology? A review of the field of organizational ethnography and anthropological studies. *Human Relations, 50*(9), 1147–1175.

Bateman, A., & Logan, D. W. (2010). Time to underpin Wikipedia wisdom. *Nature, 468*(7325), 765–765.

Battles, M. (2007, June 13). Authority of a new kind *Encyclopaedia Britannica Blog.* Retrieved from http://www.britannica.com/blogs/2007/2006/authority-of-a-new-kind/

Bauman, Z. (1987/1998). *Prawodawcy i tłumacze* [Legislators and interpreters: On modernity, post-modernity and intellectuals]. Warsaw, Poland: Wydawnictwo IFiS PAN.

Bauman, Z. (1989/2000). *Modernity and the Holocaust.* Ithaca, NY: Cornell University Press.

Bauman, Z. (1991). The social manipulation of morality: Moralizing actors, adiaphorizing action. *Theory, Culture and Society, 8*(1), 137–151.

Bauman, Z. (1998). *Liquid modernity.* Cambridge, England: Polity Press.

Bauman, Z. (2001). *Community: Seeking safety in an insecure world.* London: Polity Press.

Bauman, Z. (2005). *Liquid life.* Cambridge, England: Polity Press.

Bauman, Z. (2007). *Liquid times: Living in an age of uncertainty.* Cambridge, England: Polity Press.

Bauman, Z. (2012, August 5). Do Facebook and Twitter help spread democracy and human rights? *Social Europe Journal*. Retrieved from http://www.social-europe .eu/2012/2005/do-facebook-and-twitter-help-spread-democracy-and-human -rights/

Bauman, Z., & Lyon, D. (2012). *Liquid surveillance: A conversation*. Cambridge, England: Polity Press.

Bauwens, M. (2008, January 7). Is something fundamentally wrong with Wikipedia governance processes? *P2P Foundation*. Retrieved from http://blog.p2pfounda tion.net/is-something-fundamentally-wrong-with-wikipedia-governance -processes/2008/01/07

Baxter, P., & Jack, S. (2008). Qualitative case study methodology: Study design and implementation for novice researchers. *The Qualitative Report, 13*(4), 544–559.

Baytiyeh, H., & Pfaffman, J. (2010). Volunteers in Wikipedia: Why the community matters. *Educational Technology and Society, 13*(2), 128–140.

Bell, B. S., & Kozlowski, S. W. J. (2002). A typology of virtual teams. *Group and Organization Management, 27*(1), 14–49.

Beneito-Montagut, R. (2011). Ethnography goes online: Towards a user-centred methodology to research interpersonal communication on the Internet. *Qualitative Research, 11*(6), 716–735.

Benevolent dictator. (2013, April 27). *Wikimedia*. Retrieved August 23, 2013, from http:// meta.wikimedia.org/wiki/Benevolent_dictator

Benkler, Y. (2002). Coase's penguin, or, Linux and "the nature of the firm." *Yale Law Journal, 112*(3), 369–446.

Benkler, Y. (2006a). Extracting signal from noisy spin. *The Edge*. Retrieved from http:// www.edge.org/discourse/digital_maoism.html

Benkler, Y. (2006b). *The wealth of networks: How social production transforms markets and freedom*. New Haven, CT: Yale University Press.

Benkler, Y. (2011). *The penguin and the leviathan: How cooperation triumphs over self-interest*. New York: Crown Business.

Benkler, Y., & Nissenbaum, H. (2006). Commons-based peer production and virtue. *Journal of Political Philosophy, 14*(4), 394–419.

Berger, P. L., & Luckman, T. (1967). *The social construction of reality: A treatise in the sociology of knowledge*. Garden City, NY: Doubleday.

Bergquist, M., & Ljungberg, J. (2001). The power of gifts: Organizing social relationships in open source communities. *Information Systems Journal, 11*(4), 305–320.

Bernard, C. (2009). Cultural innovation in software design: The new impact of innovation planning methods. *Journal of Business Strategy, 30*(2–3), 57–69.

Berry, D. M. (2008). *Copy, rip, burn: The politics of copyleft and open source*. London: Pluto Press.

Berstein, J. (2011, February 3). Wikipedia's benevolent dictator. *New Statesman*. Retrieved from http://www.newstatesman.com/digital/2011/01/jimmy-wales-wikipedia-site

Beschastnikh, I., Kriplean, T., & McDonald, D. W. (2008). Wikipedian self-governance in action: Motivating the policy lens. In E. Adar, M. Hurst, T. Finin, N. S. Glance,

N. Nicolov, & B. L. Tseng (Eds.), *Proceedings of the Second International Conference on Weblogs and Social Media* (pp. 27–35). Menlo Park, CA: AAAI Press.

Bianchi, A. J., Kang, S. M., & Stewart, D. (2010). The organizational selection of status characteristics: Status evaluations in an open source community. *Organization Science.* doi:10.1287/orsc.1100.0580

Billings, M., & Watts, L. A. (2010). Understanding dispute resolution online: Using text to reflect personal and substantive issues in conflict. In *CHI '10: Proceedings of the SIGCHI Conference on Human Factors in Computing Systems* (pp. 1447–1456). New York: ACM.

Bjørn, P., & Ngwenyama, O. (2010). Technology alignment: A new area in virtual team research. *IEEE Transactions on Professional Communication, 53*(4), 382–400.

Black, L. W., Welser, H. T., Cosley, D., & DeGroot, J. M. (2011). Self-governance through group discussion in Wikipedia: Measuring deliberation in online groups. *Small Group Research, 42*(5), 595–634.

Blackler, F. (1995). Knowledge, knowledge work and organizations: An overview and interpretation. *Organization Studies, 16*(6), 1021–1046.

Blankenhorn, D. (2010, May 12). Long past time for Wikimedia to grow up. *ZDNet.* Retrieved from http://www.zdnet.com/blog/open-source/long-past-time-for-wikimedia-to-grow-up/6466

Blau, P. M. (1964). *Exchange and power in social life.* New York: Wiley.

Blau, P. M., & Scott, W. R. (1962). *Formal organizations: A comparative approach.* Stanford, CA: Stanford Business Books.

Blue, V. (2012a, September 18). Corruption in Wikiland? Paid PR scandal erupts at Wikipedia. *Cnet.* Retrieved from http://news.cnet.com/8301-1023_3-57514677-93/corruption-in-wikiland-paid-pr-scandal-erupts-at-wikipedia/

Blue, V. (2012b, October 1). Wikimedia U.K. faces ethics probe, funding squeeze. *Cnet.* Retrieved from http://news.cnet.com/8301-1023_3-57523024-93/wikimedia-u.k-faces-ethics-probe-funding-squeeze/

Blumer, H. (1986). *Symbolic interactionism: Perspective and method.* Berkeley: University of California Press.

Board of Trustees. (2013, August 11). *Wikimedia.* Retrieved August 15, 2013, from http://wikimediafoundation.org/wiki/Board_of_Trustees

Bochner, A. P. (2001). Narrative's virtues. *Qualitative Inquiry, 7*(2), 131–157.

Boehlert, E. (2009). *Bloggers on the bus: How the Internet changed politics and the press.* New York: Free Press.

Boeker, W., & Karichalil, R. (2002). Entrepreneurial transitions: Factors influencing founder departure. *Academy of Management Journal, 45*(3), 818–826.

Boellstorff, T. (2008). *Coming of age in second life: An anthropologist explores the virtually human.* Princeton, NJ: Princeton University Press.

Boje, D. M. (2001). *Narrative methods for organizational and communication research.* London: Sage.

Bonaccorsi, A., & Rossi, C. (2003). Why open source software can succeed. *Research Policy, 32*(7), 1243–1258.

Boser, S. (2006). Ethics and power in community-campus partnerships for research. *Action Research, 4*(1), 9–21.

Bossewitch, J., & Sinnreich, A. (2013). The end of forgetting: Strategic agency beyond the panopticon. *New Media and Society, 15*(2), 224–242.

Botsman, R., & Rogers, R. (2010). *What's mine is yours: The rise of collaborative consumption.* New York: HarperBusiness.

Bourne, D., & Özbilgin, M. F. (2008). Strategies for combating gendered perceptions of careers. *Career Development International, 13*(4), 320–332.

Bowers, J., & Iwi, K. (1993). The discursive construction of society. *Discourse and Society, 4*(3), 357–393.

Braverman, H. (1974). *Labor and monopoly capital: The degradation of work in the twentieth century.* New York: Monthly Review Press.

Brincker, B., & Gundelach, P. (2010). A la carte community: Identity and values in the open source software project TYPO3. *Scandinavian Journal of Information Systems, 22*(1), 27–44.

Britannica Editors. (2012, March 13). Change: It's okay. Really. *Encyclopaedia Britannica Blog.* Retrieved from http://www.britannica.com/blogs/2012/03/change/

Bruckman, A. (2006). Teaching students to study online communities ethically. *Journal of Information Ethics, 15*(2), 82–98.

Bruns, A. (2008). *Blogs, Wikipedia, Second Life, and beyond: From production to produsage.* New York: Peter Lang.

Brunton, F. (2012). Constitutive interference: Spam and online communities. *Representations, 117*(1), 30–58.

Bryant, S. L., Forte, A., & Bruckman, A. (2005). Becoming Wikipedian: Transformation of participation in a collaborative online encyclopedia. In *Proceedings of the 2005 International ACM SIGGROUP Conference on Supporting Group Work* (pp. 1–10). New York: ACM.

Bryson, J. M., & Anderson, S. R. (2000). Applying large-group interaction methods in the planning and implementation of major change efforts. *Public Administration Review, 60*(2), 143–162.

Buchanan, E. A. (Ed.). (2004). *Readings in virtual research ethics: Issues and controversies.* Hershey, PA: Information Science.

Bug 30208—Trial for restricting non-autoconfirmed users from creating new articles on enwiki. (2013, January 31). *Bugzilla.* Retrieved August 21, 2013, from http://bugzilla.wikimedia.org/show_bug.cgi?id=30208

Burke, M., & Kraut, R. (2008). Taking up the mop: Identifying future Wikipedia administrators. In *CHI '08 Extended Abstracts on Human Factors in Computing Systems* (pp. 3441–3446). New York: ACM.

Burrell, G. (1997). *Pandemonium: Towards a retro-organization theory.* London: Sage.

Burrell, G., & Morgan, G. (1979). *Sociological paradigms and organisational analysis: Elements of the sociology of corporate life.* London: Heinemann.

Burris, B. H. (1989). Technocratic organization and control. *Organization Studies, 10*(1), 1–22.

Burson, M. C. (2001). Finding clarity in the midst of conflict: Facilitating dialogue and skillful discussion using a model from the Quaker tradition. *Group Facilitation, 4*, 23–29.

Buss, A., & Strauss, N. (2009). *Online community handbook: Building your business and brand on the web.* Berkeley, CA: New Riders.

Butler, B., Joyce, E., & Pike, J. (2008). Don't look now, but we've created a bureaucracy: The nature and roles of policies and rules in Wikipedia. In *CHI '08: Proceedings of the SIGCHI Conference on Human Factors in Computing Systems* (pp 1101–1110). New York: ACM.

Butler, B., Sproull, L., Kiesler, S., & Kraut, R. (2007). Community effort in online groups: Who does the work and why? In S. Weisband (Ed.), *Leadership at a distance: Research in technologically-supported work.* Mahwah, NJ: Lawrence Erlbaum.

Bywater, M. (2011, February 7). Wikipedia: This is a man's world. *The Independent.* Retrieved from http://www.independent.co.uk/life-style/gadgets-and-tech/features/wikipedia-this-is-a-mans-world-2206207.html

Cairncross, F. (2001). *The death of distance: How the communications revolution is changing our lives.* Boston: Harvard Business School Press.

Callahan, E. S., & Herring, S. C. (2011). Cultural bias in Wikipedia content on famous persons. *Journal of the American Society for Information Science and Technology, 62*(10), 1899–1915.

Cammaerts, B. (2008). Critiques on the participatory potentials of Web 2.0. *Communication, Culture and Critique, 1*(4), 358–377.

Campbell, J. (1995). *Understanding John Dewey: Nature and cooperative intelligence.* Chicago: Open Court.

Cao, R., Chuah, K. B., Chao, Y. C., Kwong, K. F., & Law, M. Y. (2012). The role of facilitators in project action learning implementation. *The Learning Organization, 19*(5), 414–427.

Carr, N. G. (2007, May 29). The ignorance of crowds. *Strategy and Business.* Retrieved from http://www.strategy-business.com/article/07204?pg=all

Carstensen, T. (2009). Gender trouble in Web 2.0: Gender perspectives on social network sites, wikis and weblogs. *International Journal of Gender, Science and Technology, 1*(1), 106–127.

Carte, T. A., Chidambaram, L., & Becker, A. (2006). Emergent leadership in self-managed virtual teams. *Group Decision and Negotiation, 15*(4), 323–343.

Case, P. (2003). From objectivity to subjectivity: Pursuing *subjective authenticity* in organizational research. In R. I. Westwood & S. Clegg (Eds.), *Debating organization: Point-counterpoint in organization studies* (pp. 156–180). Malden, MA: Blackwell.

Castells, M. (1996). *The rise of the network society.* Cambridge, MA: Blackwell.

Castronova, E. (2005). *Synthetic worlds: The business and culture of online games.* Chicago: University of Chicago Press.

Cheliotis, G. (2009). From open source to open content: Organization, licensing and decision processes in open cultural production. *Decision Support Systems, 47*(3), 229–244.

Chen, S. (2010). Wikipedia: A republic of science democratized. *Albany Law Journal of Science and Technology, 20*(2), 247–325.

Chen, S. (2011). The Wikimedia Foundation and the self-governing Wikipedia community: A dynamic relationship under constant negotiation. In G. Lovink & N. Tkacz (Eds.), *Critical point of view: A Wikipedia reader*. Amsterdam: Institute of Network Cultures.

Cheney, G. (2002). *Values at work: Employee participation meets market pressure at Mondragon*. Ithaca, NY: ILR Press.

Cheshire, C. (2011). Online trust, trustworthiness, or assurance? *Dædalus, the Journal of the American Academy of Arts and Sciences, 140*(4), 49–58.

Chesney, T. (2006). An empirical examination of Wikipedia's credibility. *First Monday, 11*(11). Retrieved from http://firstmonday.org/htbin/cgiwrap/bin/ojs/index.php/fm/article/view/1413/1331

Choi, B., Alexander, K., Kraut, R. E., & Levine, J. M. (2010). Socialization tactics in Wikipedia and their effects. In *CSCW '10: Proceedings of the 2010 ACM Conference on Computer Supported Cooperative Work* (pp. 107–116). New York: ACM.

Chozick, A. (2012, July 9). Tech and media elite are likely to debate piracy. *The New York Times*. Retrieved from http://www.nytimes.com/2012/07/10/business/media/tech-and-media-elite-are-likely-to-debate-piracy.html?pagewanted=all&_r=0

Chu, F., Kolodny, A., Maital, S., & Perlmutter, D. (2004). The innovation paradox: Reconciling creativity and discipline: How winning organizations combine inspiration with perspiration. In *Engineering Management Conference, 2004 Proceedings*. New York: IEEE International.

Ciesielska, M. (2010). *Hybrid organisations: A study of the open source–business setting*. Copenhagen, Denmark: Copenhagen Business School.

Ciesielska, M., & Iskoujina, Z. (2012). Trust as a success factor in open innovation: The case of Nokia and GNOME. In D. Jemielniak & A. Marks (Eds.), *Managing dynamic technology-oriented businesses: High-tech organizations and workplaces* (pp. 11–29). Hershey, PA: IGI Global.

Ciffolilli, A. (2003). Phantom authority, self-selective recruitment and retention of members in virtual communities: The case of Wikipedia. *First Monday, 8*(12). Retrieved from http://firstmonday.org/article/view/1108/1028

Clamp, C. A., & Alhamis, I. (2010). Social entrepreneurship in the Mondragon Cooperative Corporation and the challenges of successful replication. *Journal of Entrepreneurship, 19*(2), 149–177.

Clifford, J., & Marcus, G. E. (Eds.). (1986). *Writing culture: The poetics and politics of ethnography*. Berkeley: University of California Press.

Cobb, A. T., Stephens, C., & Watson, G. (2001). Beyond structure: The role of social accounts in implementing ideal control. *Human Relations, 54*(9), 1123–1153.

Cohen, N. (2007, March 5). A contributor to Wikipedia has his fictional side. *The New York Times*. Retrieved from http://www.nytimes.com/2007/03/05/technology/05wikipedia.html?ref=business

Cohen, N. (2012, September 9). Travel site built on wiki ethos now bedevils its owner. *The New York Times.* Retrieved from http://www.nytimes.com/2012/09/10/business/media/once-a-profit-dream-wikitravel-now-bedevils-owner.html

Coleman, E. G. (2001). High-tech guilds in the era of global capital. *Anthropology of Work Review, 22*(1), 28–32.

Coleman, E. G. (2009). Code is speech: Legal tinkering, expertise, and protest among free and open source software developers. *Cultural Anthropology, 24*(3), 420–454.

Coleman, E. G. (2010a). Ethnographic approaches to digital media. *Annual Review of Anthropology, 39,* 487–505.

Coleman, E. G. (2010b). The hacker conference: A ritual condensation and celebration of a lifeworld. *Anthropological Quarterly, 83*(1), 47–72.

Coleman, E. G. (2011). Hacker politics and publics. *Public Culture, 23*(3), 511–516.

Coleman, E. G. (2013). *Coding freedom.* Princeton, NJ: Princeton University Press.

Coleman, E. G., & Golub, A. (2008). Hacker practice. *Anthropological Theory, 8*(3), 255–277.

Coleman, E. G., & Hill, B. M. (2004). How free became open and everything else under the sun. *M/C: A Journal of Media and Culture, 7*(3). Retrieved from http://journal.media-culture.org.au/0406/02_Coleman-Hill.php

Coleman, E. G., & Hill, B. M. (2005). The social production of ethics in Debian and free software communities: Anthropological lessons for vocational ethics. In S. Koch (Ed.), *Free/open source software development.* Hershey, PA: Idea Group.

Coleman, J. S. (1980). Authority systems. *Public Opinion Quarterly, 44*(2), 143–163.

Collier, B., & Bear, J. (2012). Conflict, criticism, or confidence: An empirical examination of the gender gap in Wikipedia contributions. In *CSCW '12: Proceedings of the ACM 2012 Conference on Computer Supported Cooperative Work* (pp. 383–392). New York: ACM.

Collier, B., & Kraut, R. (2012, April 18–20). *Leading the collective: Social capital and the development of leaders in core-periphery organizations.* Paper presented at the Collective Intelligence conference, Cambridge, MA.

Collier, B., Burke, M., Kittur, N., & Kraut, R. (2010). Promoting good management: Governance, promotion, and leadership in open collaboration communities. In *ICIS 2010 Proceedings.* Retrieved from http://aisel.aisnet.org/icis2010_submissions/220/

Collins, R. (1990). Market closure and the conflict theory of the professions. In M. Burrage & R. Torstendahl (Eds.), *Professions in theory and history: Rethinking the study of the professions.* London: Sage.

Commons talk:Sexual content. (2013, August 17). *Wikimedia Commons.* Retrieved August 22, 2013, from http://commons.wikimedia.org/wiki/Commons_talk:Sexual_content/Archive_4

Commons:Deletion requests/file:Jimmy Wales by Pricasso.jpg. (2013, August 20). *Wikimedia Commons.* Retrieved August 22, 2013, from http://commons.wikimedia.org/wiki/Commons:Deletion_requests/File:Jimmy_Wales_by_Pricasso.jpg

Community Logo/Request for consultation. (2013, October 29). *Wikimedia*. Retrieved November 7, 2013, from http://meta.wikimedia.org/wiki/Community_Logo/Request_for_consultation

Conlon, M. P. (2007). An examination of initiation, organization, participation, leadership, and control of successful open source software development projects. *Information Systems Education Journal, 5*(38), 1–13.

Constant, D., Sproull, L., & Kiesler, S. (1996). The kindness of strangers: The usefulness of electronic weak ties for technical advice. *Organization Science, 7*(2), 119–135.

Controversial content. (2012, January 25). *Wikimedia*. Retrieved August 22, 2013, from http://meta.wikimedia.org/wiki/Controversial_content

Correa, P., Correa, A., & Askanas, M. (2006). *Wikipedia: A techno-cult of ignorance.* Thornhill, Ontario: Akronos. Retrieved from http://www.aetherometry.com/Electronic_Publications/Politics_of_Science/Antiwikipedia/awp_index.html

Coser, L. A. (1957). Social conflict and the theory of social change. *The British Journal of Sociology, 8*(3), 197–207.

Courpasson, D. (2000). Managerial strategies of domination: Power in soft bureaucracies. *Organization Studies, 21*(1), 141–161.

Crombie, A. (1985). The nature and types of search conferences. *International Journal of Lifelong Education, 4*(1), 3–33.

Crovitz, L. G. (2010, December 6). Julian Assange, information anarchist. *The Wall Street Journal*. Retrieved from http://topics.wsj.com/article/SB10001424052748703989004575653113548361870.html

Crowston, K., & Howison, J. (2006). Hierarchy and centralization in free and open source software team communications. *Knowledge, Technology and Policy, 18*(4), 65–85.

Crowston, K., Heckman, R., Annabi, H., & Masango, C. (2005). A structurational perspective on leadership in free/libre open source software teams. In M. Scotto & G. Succi (Eds.), *Proceedings of the First International Conference on Open Source Systems* (pp. 9–15). Retrieved from http://oss2005.case.unibz.it/Resources/Proceedings/OSS2005Proceedings.pdf

Crowston, K., Jullien, N., & Ortega, F. (2012, August 31). *Is Wikipedia inefficient? Modelling effort and participation in Wikipedia.* Paper presented at the Hawaii International Conference on System Sciences, Grand Wailea, HA. Retrieved from http://papers.ssrn.com/sol3/papers.cfm?abstract_id=1960696

Cunliffe, A. L. (2002). Reflexive dialogical practice in management learning. *Management Learning, 33*(1), 35–61.

Cunliffe, A. L. (2003). Reflexive inquiry in organizational research: Questions and possibilities. *Human Relations, 56*(8), 983–1003.

Czarniawska, B. (2000). *The uses of narrative in organization research.* Gothenburg, Sweden: Gothenburg Research Institute.

Czarniawska, B. (2003). Social constructionism and organizational studies. In R. I. Westwood & S. Clegg (Eds.), *Debating organization: Point-counterpoint in organization studies* (pp. 128–140). Malden, MA: Blackwell.

Czarniawska, B. (2004). *Narratives in social science research*. London: Sage.

Czarniawska-Joerges, B. (1992). *Exploring complex organizations: A cultural perspective*. Newbury Park, CA: Sage.

Czarniawska-Joerges, B. (1998). *Narrative approach in organization studies*. Thousand Oaks, CA: Sage.

Da Cunha, J. V., & Orlikowski, W. J. (2008). Performing catharsis: The use of online discussion forums in organizational change. *Information and Organization, 18*(2), 132–156.

Dahlander, L., Frederiksen, L., & Rullani, F. (2008). Online communities and open innovation. *Industry and Innovation, 15*(2), 115–123.

Daniel, B. K. (2010). *Handbook of research on methods and techniques for studying virtual communities: Paradigms and phenomena* (Vol. 1). Hershey, PA: Information Science Reference.

Danzig. (2001, October 17). *Wikipedia*. Retrieved November 7, 2013, from https://en.wikipedia.org/w/index.php?title=Danzig&oldid=362994153

Darlington, Y., & Scott, D. (2003). *Qualitative research in practice: Stories from the field*. Crows Nest, Australia: Allen & Unwin.

De Jong, B. A., & Elfring, T. (2010). How does trust affect the performance of ongoing teams? The mediating role of reflexivity, monitoring, and effort. *The Academy of Management Journal, 53*(3), 535–549.

De Laat, P. B. (2007). Governance of open source software: State of the art. *Journal of Management and Governance, 11*(2), 165–177.

De Laat, P. B. (2012). Coercion or empowerment? Moderation of content in Wikipedia as "essentially contested" bureaucratic rules. *Ethics and Information Technology, 14*, 123–135.

De Vugt, G. (2010). Dare to edit! The politics of Wikipedia. *Ephemera, 10*(1), 64–76.

Definition of free cultural works. (2008, December 1). Retrieved August 14, 2013, from http://freedomdefined.org/Definition

Delamont, S. (2004). Ethnography and participant observation. In C. Seale, G. Gobo, J. F. Gubrium, & D. Silverman (Eds.), *Qualitative research practice* (pp. 217–229). Thousand Oaks, CA: Sage.

Deleuze, G., & Guattari, F. (1972/2004). *Anti-Oedipus: Capitalism and schizophrenia*. London: Continuum.

Demil, B., & Lecocq, X. (2006). Neither market nor hierarchy nor network: The emergence of bazaar governance. *Organization Studies, 27*(10), 1447–1466.

Denzin, N. K. (1978). *The research act*. New York: McGraw-Hill.

Denzin, N. K. (2006). Analytic autoethnography, or déjà vu all over again. *Journal of Contemporary Ethnography, 35*(4), 419.

Denzin, N. K., & Lincoln, Y. S. (2003). *Strategies of qualitative inquiry* (2nd ed.). Thousand Oaks, CA: Sage.

DeTienne, D. R. (2010). Entrepreneurial exit as a critical component of the entrepreneurial process: Theoretical development. *Journal of Business Venturing, 25*(2), 203–215.

Deuze, M. (2009). Media industries, work and life. *European Journal of Communication*, 24(4), 467–480.

Difference between revisions of "Wikiversity:Community Review/Wikimedia Ethics:Ethical Breaching Experiments." (2010, March 16). *Wikiversity*. Retrieved November 8, 2013, from https://en.wikiversity.org/w/index.php?title=Wikiversity%3ACommunity_Review%2FWikimedia_Ethics%3AEthical_Breaching_Experiments&diff=545159&oldid=545155

Dirksen, V., Huizing, A., & Smit, B. (2010). "Piling on layers of understanding": The use of connective ethnography for the study of (online) work practices. *New Media and Society*, 12(7), 1045–1063.

Dobosz-Bourne, D., & Kostera, M. (2007). The quest for quality: Translation of a mythical idea. *Journal of Organizational Change Management*, 20(1), 60–73.

Donath, J. S. (1999). Identity and deception in the virtual community. In M. A. Smith & P. Kollock (Eds.), *Communities in cyberspace* (pp. 29–59). New York: Routledge.

Dondio, P., Barrett, S., Weber, S., & Seigneur, J. (2006). Extracting trust from domain analysis: A case study on the Wikipedia project. *Autonomic and Trusted Computing*, 4158, 362–373.

Dreyfus, H. L., & Rabinow, P. (1983). *Michel Foucault: Beyond structuralism and hermeneutics* (2nd ed.). Chicago: University of Chicago Press.

Drucker, P. F. (1993). *Post-capitalist society* (1st ed.). New York: Harper Business.

Du Gay, P. (2007). *Organizing identity: Persons and organizations "after theory."* Los Angeles: Sage.

Du Gay, P. (Ed.). (2005). *The values of bureaucracy*. Oxford, England: Oxford University Press.

Eijkman, H. (2010). Academics and Wikipedia: Reframing Web 2.0+ as a disruptor of traditional academic power-knowledge arrangements. *Campus-Wide Information Systems*, 27(3), 173–185.

Eisenhardt, K. M. (1989). Building theories from case study research. *Academy of Management Review*, 14(4), 532–550.

Elkington, J., & Beloe, S. (2010). The twenty-first century NGO. In T. P. Lyon (Ed.), *Good cop/bad cop: Environmental NGOs and their strategies toward business* (pp. 17–47). London: Routledge.

Emerson, R. M., Fretz, R. I., & Shaw, L. L. (2001). Participant observation and fieldnotes. In P. Atkinson, A. Coffey, S. Delamont, J. Lofland, & L. Lofland (Eds.), *Handbook of ethnography* (pp. 352–368). Thousand Oaks, CA: Sage.

Emerson, R. M., Fretz, R. I., & Shaw, L. L. (2001/2011). *Writing ethnographic fieldnotes*. Chicago: University of Chicago Press.

English-Lueck, J. (2011). Prototyping self in Silicon Valley: Deep diversity as a framework for anthropological inquiry. *Anthropological Theory*, 11(1), 89–106.

English-Lueck, J. A., Darrah, C. N., & Saveri, A. (2002). Trusting strangers: Work relationships in four high-tech communities. *Information, Communication and Society*, 5(1), 90–108.

Enyedy, E., & Tkacz, N. (2011). "Good luck with your WikiPAIDdia": Reflections on the 2002 fork of the Spanish Wikipedia. In G. Lovink & N. Tkacz (Eds.), *Critical point of view: A Wikipedia reader* (pp. 110–118). Amsterdam: Institute of Network Cultures.

Epstein, B. (2001). Anarchism and the anti-globalization movement. *Monthly Review, 54*(4), 1–14.

Etzioni, A. (1959). Authority structure and organizational effectiveness. *Administrative Science Quarterly, 4*(1), 43–67.

Famiglietti, A. (2011). The right to fork: A historical survey of de/centralization in Wikipedia. In G. Lovink & N. Tkacz (Eds.), *Critical point of view: A Wikipedia reader* (pp. 296–308). Amsterdam: Institute of Network Cultures.

Famiglietti, A. (2012). The pentad of cruft: A taxonomy of rhetoric used by Wikipedia editors based on the dramatism of Kenneth Burke. *First Monday, 17*(9). Retrieved from http://www.uic.edu/htbin/cgiwrap/bin/ojs/index.php/fm/article/view/4082/3294

Feldman, M. S. (2000). Organizational routines as a source of continuous change. *Organization Science, 11*(6), 611–629.

Feldman, M. S., Bell, J., & Berger, M. T. (2003). *Gaining access: A practical and theoretical guide for qualitative researchers.* Walnut Creek, CA: AltaMira Press.

Filipacchi, A. (2013, April 24). Wikipedia's sexism toward female novelists. *The New York Times.* Retrieved from http://www.nytimes.com/2013/04/28/opinion/sunday/wikipedias-sexism-toward-female-novelists.html

Finkelstein, S. (2008, March 26). Wikipedia's school for scandal has plenty more secrets to reveal. *The Guardian.* Retrieved from http://www.guardian.co.uk/technology/2008/mar/27/wikipedia.scandal

Firer-Blaess, S., & Fuchs, C. (2013). Wikipedia: An info-communist manifesto. *Television and New Media.* Advance online publication. doi:10.1177/1527476412450193

Flanagin, A. J., & Metzger, M. J. (2011). From Encyclopædia Britannica to Wikipedia. *Information, Communication and Society, 14*(3), 355–374.

Fleming, P., & Spicer, A. (2004). "You can checkout anytime, but you can never leave": Spatial boundaries in a high commitment organization. *Human Relations, 57*(1), 75–94.

Fleming, P., & Spicer, A. (2007). *Contesting the corporation: Struggle, power and resistance in organizations.* Cambridge, England: Cambridge University Press.

Foley, M. J. (2008). *Microsoft 2.0: How Microsoft plans to stay relevant in the post-Gates era.* New York: Wiley.

Forte, A., & Bruckman, A. (2005, November 6). *Why do people write for Wikipedia? Incentives to contribute to open-content publishing.* Paper presented at the GROUP 2005 Workshop: Sustaining Community: The Role and Design of Incentive Mechanisms in Online Systems, Sanibel Island, FL. Retrieved from http://jellis.org/work/group2005/papers/forteBruckmanIncentivesGroup.pdf

Forte, A., & Bruckman, A. (2008). Scaling consensus: Increasing decentralization in Wikipedia governance. In *HICSS '08: Proceedings of the 41st Annual Hawaii International Conference on System Sciences* (p. 157). Washington, DC: IEEE

Computer Society. Retrieved from http://dlc.dlib.indiana.edu/dlc/bitstream/handle/10535/5638/ForteBruckmanScalingConsensus.pdf

Forte, A., Kittur, N., Larco, V., Zhu, H., Bruckman, A., & Kraut, R. E. (2012). Coordination and beyond: Social functions of groups in open content production. In *CSCW '12: Proceedings of the ACM 2012 Conference on Computer Supported Cooperative Work* (pp. 417–426). New York: ACM.

Forte, A., Larco, V., & Bruckman, A. (2009). Decentralization in Wikipedia governance. *Journal of Management Information Systems, 26*(1), 49–72.

Foucault, M. (1977). *Discipline and Punish*. New York: Pantheon.

Foucault, M. (1982). The subject and power. In H. L. Dreyfus & P. Rabinow (Eds.), *Michel Foucault, beyond structuralism and hermeneutics*. London: Harvester Wheatsheaf.

Founding principles. (2004, May 3). *Wikimedia*. Retrieved November 8, 2013, from http://meta.wikimedia.org/w/index.php?title=Founding_principles&oldid=46234

Fox, A. (1974). *Beyond contract: Work, power and trust relations*. London: Faber & Faber.

Franco, V., Piirto, R., Hu, H. Y., Lewenstein, B., Underwood, R., & Vidal, N. (1995). Anatomy of a flame: Conflict and community building on the Internet. *Technology and Society Magazine, IEEE, 14*(2), 12–21.

Fréard, D., Denis, A., Détienne, F., Baker, M., Quignard, M., & Barcellini, F. (2010). In The role of argumentation in online epistemic communities: The anatomy of a conflict in Wikipedia. In *ECCE '10: Proceedings of the 28th Annual European Conference on Cognitive Ergonomics* (pp. 91–98). New York: ACM.

Freeman, J. (1972). The tyranny of structurelessness. *Berkeley Journal of Sociology, 17*, 151–164.

Frickel, S., & Gross, N. (2005). A general theory of scientific/intellectual movements. *American Sociological Review, 70*(2), 204–232.

Fuggetta, A. (2003). Open source software—an evaluation. *Journal of Systems and Software, 66*(1), 77–90.

Gallivan, M. J. (2008). Striking a balance between trust and control in a virtual organization: A content analysis of open source software case studies. *Information Systems Journal, 11*(4), 277–304.

Gambetta, D. (1988). *Trust: Making and breaking cooperative relations*. New York: Blackwell.

Garcia, A. C., Standlee, A. I., Bechkoff, J., & Cui, Y. (2009). Ethnographic approaches to the Internet and computer-mediated communication. *Journal of Contemporary Ethnography, 38*(1), 52–84.

Gardner, S. (2011, January 13). Wikipedia at 10: A web pioneer worth defending. *The Guardian*. Retrieved from http://www.theguardian.com/commentisfree/cifamerica/2011/jan/12/wikipedia-internet

Garud, R., Jain, S., & Tuertscher, P. (2008). Incomplete by design and designing for incompleteness. *Organization Studies, 29*(3), 351–371.

Garzarelli, G., & Galoppini, R. (2003). *Capability coordination in modular organization: Voluntary FS/OSS production and the case of Debian GNU/Linux*. EconPapers. Retrieved from http://econpapers.repec.org/paper/wpawuwpio/0312005.htm

Gatson, S. N., & Zweerink, A. (2004). Ethnography online: "Natives" practising and in-
scribing community. *Qualitative Research, 4*(2), 179–200.

Gauntlett, D. (2009). Case study: Wikipedia. In G. Creeber & R. Martin (Eds.), *Digital
cultures: Understanding New Media* (pp. 41–45). Berkshire, England: Open University
Press.

Gdansk. (2001a, November 11). *Internet Archive Wayback Machine.* Retrieved from
http://web.archive.org/web/20011111155718/http://www.wikipedia.com/wiki/
Gdansk

Gdańsk. (2001b, November 19). *Wikipedia.* Retrieved from http://en.wikipedia.org/w/
index.php?title=Gda%C5%84sk&oldid=333254700

Gdańsk: Difference between revisions. (2002a, June 28). *Wikipedia.* Retrieved
November 7, 2013, from https://en.wikipedia.org/w/index.php?title=Gda%C5%84s
k&diff=prev&oldid=107671

Gdańsk: Difference between revisions. (2002b, June 29). *Wikipedia.* Retrieved
November 7, 2013, from https://en.wikipedia.org/w/index.php?title=Gda%C5%84s
k&diff=next&oldid=107930

Gdańsk: Difference between revisions. (2004, February 10). *Wikipedia.* Retrieved
November 7, 2013, from https://en.wikipedia.org/w/index.php?title=Gda%C5%84sk
&diff=2355452&oldid=2355317

Gdańsk: Difference between revisions. (2012, June 26). *Wikipedia.* Retrieved November 7,
2013, from https://en.wikipedia.org/w/index.php?title=Gda%C5%84sk&diff=49939
0993&oldid=499387188

Gedajlovic, E., Lubatkin, M. H., & Schulze, W. S. (2004). Crossing the threshold from
founder management to professional management: A governance perspective.
*Journal of Management Studies, 41*(5), 899–912.

Geertz, C. (1973). *The interpretation of cultures.* New York: Basic Books.

Geertz, C. (1988). *Works and lives: The anthropologist as author.* Stanford, CA: Stanford
University Press.

Geiger, R. S. (2011). The lives of bots. In G. Lovink & N. Tkacz (Eds.), *Critical point of
view: A Wikipedia reader* (pp. 78–93). Amsterdam: Institute of Network Cultures.

Geiger, R. S., & Ribes, D. (2010). The work of sustaining order in Wikipedia: The banning of a vandal. In *CSCW '10: Proceedings of the 2010 ACM Conference on Computer
Supported Cooperative Work* (pp. 117–126). New York: ACM.

Geiger, R. S., Halfaker, A., Pinchuk, M., & Walling, S. (2012). Defense mechanism or
socialization tactic? Improving Wikipedia's notifications to rejected contributors. In
*Proceedings of the Sixth International AAAI Conference on Weblogs and Social Media*
(pp. 122–129). Palo Alto, CA: AAAI Press.

Gentry, M. E. (1982). Consensus as a form of decision making. *Journal of Sociology and
Social Welfare, 9*(2), 233–244.

George, A. (2007). Avoiding tragedy in the wiki-commons. *Virginia Journal of Law and
Technology, 12*(8), 1–42.

Gibbons, M. (2000). Mode 2 society and the emergence of context-sensitive science.
*Science and Public Policy, 27*(3), 159–163.

Gibson, C. B., & Cohen, S. G. (2003). *Virtual teams that work: Creating conditions for virtual team effectiveness*. San Francisco: Jossey-Bass.

Giles, J. (2005). Internet encyclopaedias go head to head. *Nature, 438,* 900–901.

Gillmor, D. (2004). *We the media: Grassroots journalism by the people, for the people*. Sebastopol, CA: O'Reilly Media.

Girard, B. (2009). *The Google way: How one company is revolutionizing management as we know it*. San Francisco: No Starch Press.

Glaser, B. G., & Strauss, A. L. (1967). *The discovery of grounded theory: Strategies for qualitative research*. Hawthorne, NY: Aldine de Gruyter.

Glasford, D. E., Dovidio, J. F., & Pratto, F. (2009). I continue to feel so good about us: Ingroup identification and the use of social identity—enhancing strategies to reduce intragroup dissonance. *Personality and Social Psychology Bulletin, 35*(4), 415–427.

Glott, R., Schmidt, P., & Ghosh, R. (2010). *Wikipedia survey: Overview of results*. Retrieved from United Nations University Merit website: http://wikipediasurvey .org/docs/Wikipedia_Overview_15March2010-FINAL.pdf

Godin, B., & Gingras, Y. (2000). The place of universities in the system of knowledge production. *Research Policy, 29*(2), 273–278.

Goffman, E. (1959). *The presentation of self in everyday life*. Garden City, NY: Doubleday.

Goffman, E. (1963). *Stigma: Notes on the management of spoiled identity*. Englewood Cliffs, NJ: Prentice Hall.

Golden-Biddle, K., & Locke, K. D. (1997). *Composing qualitative research*. Thousand Oaks, CA: Sage.

Goldman, E. (2005, December 5). Wikipedia will fail within 5 years *Technology and Marketing Law Blog*. Retrieved from http://blog.ericgoldman.org/archives/2005/12/ wikipedia_will.htm

Goldspink, C. (2010). Normative behaviour in Wikipedia. *Information, Communication and Society, 13*(5), 652–673.

Gómez, V., Kappen, H. J., & Kaltenbrunner, A. (2011). Modeling the structure and evolution of discussion cascades. In *Proceedings of the 22nd ACM Conference on Hypertext and Hypermedia* (pp. 181–190). New York: ACM.

Gorbatai, A. D. (2011a). *Aligning collective production with demand: Evidence from Wikipedia*. Retrieved from http://faculty.chicagobooth.edu/workshops/orgs -markets/past/pdf/gorbatai.pdf

Gorbatai, A. D. (2011b). Exploring underproduction in Wikipedia. In *WikiSym '11: Proceedings of the 7th International Symposium on Wikis and Open Collaboration* (pp. 205–206). New York: ACM.

Gorbatai, A. D., & Jemielniak, D. (2012, August 6). *The role of conflict and norms in the collective production of Wikipedia*. Paper presented at the Academy of Management, Boston, MA.

Gouldner, A. W. (1960). The norm of reciprocity: A preliminary statement. *American Sociological Review, 25*(2), 161–178.

Granovetter, M. (1985). Economic action and social structure: The problem of embeddedness. *American Journal of Sociology, 91*(3), 481–510.

Granovetter, M. S. (1973). The strength of weak ties. *American Journal of Sociology, 78*(6), 1360–1380.

Grant, R. M. (2010). *Contemporary strategy analysis.* New York: Wiley.

Green, M. C., & Carpenter, J. M. (2011). Trust, deception, and identity on the Internet. In Z. Birchmeier, B. Dietz-Uhler, & G. Stasser (Eds.), *Strategic uses of social technology: An interactive perspective of social psychology* (pp. 40–62). Cambridge, England: Cambridge University Press.

Greenwood, D. J., & Levin, M. (2001). Re-organizing universities and "knowing how": University restructuring and knowledge creation for the 21st century. *Organization, 8*(2), 433–440.

Greenwood, D. J., González Santos, J. L., & Cantón, J. (1991). *Industrial democracy as process: Participatory action research in the Fagor Cooperative Group of Mondragón.* Assen, Netherlands: Van Gorcum Arbetslivscentrum.

Greenwood, F. (2012, July 23). Wikimania 2012: The singularity, and Wikipedians not being what you think. *Faine Opines* blog. Retrieved from http://fainegreenwood .com/2012/07/23/wikimania-2012-the-singularity-and-wikipedians-not-being -what-you-think/

Greiner, L. E. (1972, July–August). Evolution and revolution as organizations grow. *Harvard Business Review,* 37–46.

Greiner, M. E. (2004). Leadership behavior in virtual communities. In *Seventh Annual Conference of the Southern Association for Information Systems: 2004 Proceedings* (pp. 97–104). Savannah, GA: SAIS. Retrieved from http://sais.aisnet.org/sais2004/ Greiner.pdf

Grossman, W. (2001). *From anarchy to power: The net comes of age.* New York: NYU Press.

Gruber, J., & Trickett, E. J. (1987). Can we empower others? The paradox of empowerment in the governing of an alternative public school. *American Journal of Community Psychology, 15*(3), 353–371.

Guo, C., & Musso, J. A. (2007). Representation in nonprofit and voluntary organizations: A conceptual framework. *Nonprofit and Voluntary Sector Quarterly, 36*(2), 308–326.

Hafner, K. (2007, August 19). Seeing corporate fingerprints in Wikipedia edits. *The New York Times.* Retrieved from http://www.nytimes.com/2007/08/19/tech nology/19wikipedia.html

Haley, H., & Sidanius, J. (2005). Person-organization congruence and the maintenance of group-based social hierarchy: A social dominance perspective. *Group Processes and Intergroup Relations, 8*(2), 187–203.

Halfaker, A. (2012, March 27). Kids these days: The quality of new Wikipedia editors over time *Wikimedia Community Blog.* Retrieved from http://blog.wikimedia .org/2012/2003/2027/analysis-of-the-quality-of-newcomers-in-wikipedia-over-time/

Halfaker, A., & Riedl, J. (2012). Bots and cyborgs: Wikipedia's immune system. *Computer, 45*(3), 79–82.

Halfaker, A., Geiger, R. S., Morgan, J., & Riedl, J. (2013). The rise and decline of an open collaboration community: How Wikipedia's reaction to sudden popularity is causing its decline. *American Behavioral Scientist, 57*(5), 664–688.

Halfaker, A., Kittur, A., & Riedl, J. (2011). Don't bite the newbies: How reverts affect the quantity and quality of Wikipedia work. In *WikiSym '11: Proceedings of the 7th International Symposium on Wikis and Open Collaboration* (pp. 163–172). New York: ACM.

Halfaker, A., Kittur, A., Kraut, R., & Riedl, J. (2009). A jury of your peers: Quality, experience and ownership in Wikipedia. In *Proceedings of WikiSym 2009: The 5th International Symposium on Wikis* (p. 115). New York: ACM. Retrieved from http://www.wikisym.org/ws2009/Proceedings/p115-halfaker.pdf

Hambrick, D. C., & Crozier, L. M. (1985). Stumblers and stars in the management of rapid growth. *Journal of Business Venturing, 1*(1), 31–45.

Hammwöhner, R. (2007). Interlingual aspects of Wikipedia's quality. In M. A. Robbert, R. O'Hare, M. L. Markus, & B. D. Klein (Eds.), *Proceedings of the 12th International Conference on Information Quality* (pp. 477–488). Cambridge, MA: MIT.

Hancock, R., Crain-Dorough, M., Parton, B., & Oescher, J. (2010). Understanding and using virtual ethnography in virtual environments. In B. K. Daniel (Ed.), *Handbook of Research on Methods and Techniques for Studying Virtual Communities: Paradigms and Phenomena* (Vol. 1, pp. 457–468). Hershey, PA: Information Science Reference.

Hansen, S., Berente, N., & Lyytinen, K. (2009). Wikipedia, critical social theory, and the possibility of rational discourse. *The Information Society, 25*(1), 38–59.

Hara, N., Shachaf, P., & Hew, K. F. (2010). Cross-cultural analysis of the Wikipedia community. *Journal of the American Society for Information Science and Technology, 61*(10), 2097–2108.

Hardt, M., & Negri, A. (2001). *Empire*. Cambridge, MA: Harvard University Press.

Hare, A. P. (1973). Group decision by consensus: Reaching unity in the Society of Friends. *Sociological Inquiry, 43*(1), 75–84.

Hartelius, E. J. (2010). Wikipedia and the emergence of dialogic expertise. *Southern Communication Journal, 75*(5), 505–526.

Hastrup, K. (1992). Writing ethnography: State of the art. In J. Okely & H. Callaway (Eds.), *Anthropology and Autobiography* (pp. 116–133). Abingdon, England: Routledge.

Hayano, D. M. (1979). Auto-ethnography: Paradigms, problems, and prospects. *Human Organization, 38*(1), 99–104.

Hecht, B., & Gergle, D. (2010). The tower of Babel meets web 2.0: User-generated content and its applications in a multilingual context. In *Proceedings of the SIGCHI Conference on Human Factors in Computing Systems* (pp. 291–300). New York: ACM.

Heckman, R., Crowston, K., & Misiolek, N. (2007). A structurational perspective on leadership in virtual teams. In K. Crowston, S. Sieber, & E. Wynn (Eds.), *Virtuality and Virtualization* (Vol. 236, pp. 151–168). Boston: Springer.

Heilman, J. M., Kemmann, E., Bonert, M., Chatterjee, A., Ragar, B., Beards, G. M., et al. (2011). Wikipedia: A key tool for global public health promotion. *Journal of Medical Internet Research, 13*(1). Retrieved from http://www.jmir.org/2011/1/e14/

Heller, K. J. (1996). Power, subjectification and resistance in Foucault. *SubStance, 25*(1), 78–110.

Hemetsberger, A., & Reinhardt, C. (2009). Collective development in open-source communities: An activity theoretical perspective on successful online collaboration. *Organization Studies, 30*(9), 987–1008.

Herman, R. D., & Renz, D. O. (1997). Multiple constituencies and the social construction of nonprofit organization effectiveness. *Nonprofit and Voluntary Sector Quarterly, 26*(2), 185–206.

Hernandez, S. (2006). Striving for control: Democracy and oligarchy at a Mexican cooperative. *Economic and Industrial Democracy, 27*(1), 105–135.

Herring, S. C. (2010). Web content analysis: Expanding the paradigm. In J. Hunsinger, L. Klastrup, & M. Allen (Eds.), *International Handbook of Internet Research*. London: Springer.

Herzberg, F. M., Mausner, B., & Bloch-Snyderman, B. (1959). *The Motivation to Work*. New York: Wiley.

Hilbert, M. (2009). The maturing concept of e-democracy: From e-voting and online consultations to democratic value out of jumbled online chatter. *Journal of Information Technology and Politics, 6*(2), 87–110.

Hill, B. M. (2005, June 29). Towards a standard of freedom: Creative commons and the free software movement. Retrieved from http://mako.cc/writing/toward_a_standard_of_freedom.html

Hill, B. M., & Monroy-Hernández, A. (2013). The remixing dilemma: The trade-off between generativity and originality. *American Behavioral Scientist, 57*(5), 643–663.

Hill, B. M., & Shaw, A. (2013). The Wikipedia gender gap revisited: Characterizing survey response bias with propensity score estimation. *PLOS One*. Retrieved from http://www.plosone.org/article/info%3Adoi%2F10.1371%2Fjournal.pone.0065782

Hill, B. M., Shaw, A., & Benkler, Y. (2013). Status, social signaling and collective action in a peer production community. Unpublished manuscript, Berkman Center for Internet and Society working paper, Cambridge, MA.

Himanen, P. (2001). The hacker ethic and the spirit of the information age. New York: Random House.

Hine, C. (2000). *Virtual ethnography*. Thousand Oaks, CA: Sage.

Hine, C. (2008). Virtual ethnography: Modes, varieties, affordances. In N. Fielding, R. M. Lee, & G. Blank (Eds.), *The SAGE Handbook of Online Research Methods* (pp. 257–270). Los Angeles: Sage.

Hippel, E. V. (1988). *The sources of innovation*. New York: Oxford University Press.

Hirschhorn, L. (1998). *Reworking authority: Leading and following in a post-modern organization*. Cambridge, MA: MIT Press.

Hock, D. (2005). *One from many: Visa and the rise of chaordic organization*. San Francisco: Berrett-Koehler.

Hoffman, D. A., & Mehra, S. K. (2009). Wikitruth through wikiorder. *Emory Law Journal, 59*(1), 151–209.

Hoffmann, W. H., Neumann, K., & Speckbacher, G. (2010). The effect of interorganizational trust on make-or-cooperate decisions: Disentangling opportunism-dependent and opportunism-independent effects of trust. *European Management Review, 7*(2), 101–115.

Holck, J., & Jørgensen, N. (2007). Continuous integration and quality assurance: A case study of two open source projects. *Australasian Journal of Information Systems, 11*(1), 40–53.

Hollander, E. P. (1958). Conformity, status, and idiosyncrasy credit. *Psychological Review, 65*(2), 117–127.

Hollander, E. P. (1992). The essential interdependence of leadership and followership. *Current Directions in Psychological Science, 1*(2), 71–75.

Horn, L. (2012, April 20). Seven years, one million edits, zero dollars: Wikipedia's flat broke superstar. *Gizmodo.* Retrieved from http://gizmodo.com/5903743/seven -years-one-million-edits-zero-dollars-wikipedias-flat-broke-superstar-editor

Hough, A. (2012, March 11). Jimmy Wales: Wikipedia chief to advise Whitehall on policy. *The Telegraph.* Retrieved 2012 from http://www.telegraph.co.uk/technology/wikipe dia/9137339/Jimmy-Wales-Wikipedia-chief-to-advise-Whitehall-on-policy.html

Hsieh, H. F., & Shannon, S. E. (2005). Three approaches to qualitative content analysis. *Qualitative Health Research, 15*(9), 1277–1288.

Humphreys, M., & Watson, T. J. (2009). Ethnographic practices: From "writing-up ethnographic research" to "writing ethnography." In S. Ybema, D. Yanow, H. Wels, & F. H. Kamsteeg (Eds.), *Organizational ethnography: Studying the complexities of everyday organizational life* (pp. 40–55). London: Sage.

Hunter, C., Jemielniak, D., & Postuła, A. (2010). Temporal and spatial shifts within playful work. *Journal of Organizational Change Management, 23*(1), 87–102.

Huse, M. (2003). Renewing management and governance: New paradigms of governance? *Journal of Management and Governance, 7*(3), 211–221.

Iba, T., Nemoto, K., Peters, B., & Gloor, P. A. (2010). Analyzing the creative editing behavior of Wikipedia editors: Through dynamic social network analysis. *Procedia: Social and Behavioral Sciences, 2*(4), 6441–6456.

Image filter referendum/results. (2011, October 22). *Wikimedia.* Retrieved August 22, 2013, from http://meta.wikimedia.org/wiki/Image_filter_referendum/Results/en

Isenhart, M. W., & Spangle, M. (2000). *Collaborative approaches to resolving conflict.* Thousand Oaks, CA: Sage.

Jahnke, I. (2010). Dynamics of social roles in a knowledge management community. *Computers in Human Behavior, 26*(4), 533–546.

Jarvie, I. C. (1969). The problem of ethical integrity in participant observation. *Current Anthropology, 10*(5), 505–508.

Jayaraman, N., Khorana, A., Nelling, E., & Covin, J. (2000). CEO founder status and firm financial performance. *Strategic Management Journal, 21*(12), 1215–1224.

Jemielniak, D. (2002). Kultura—odkrywana czy konstruowana? *Master of Business Administration, 2*(55), 28–30.

Jemielniak, D. (2006). The management science as a practical field: In support of action research. *The International Journal of Knowledge, Culture and Change Management 6*(3), 163–170.

Jemielniak, D. (2007). Managers as lazy, stupid careerists? Contestation and stereotypes among software engineers. *Journal of Organizational Change Management, 20*(4), 491–508.

Jemielniak, D. (2008). Software engineers or artists: Programmers' identity choices. *Tamara Journal for Critical Organization Inquiry, 7*(1), 20–36.

Jemielniak, D. (2009). Time as symbolic currency in knowledge work. *Information and Organization, 19,* 277–293.

Jemielniak, D. (2010). W obronie biurokracji. *Master of Business Administration, 2*(103), 72–79.

Jemielniak, D. (2012). *The new knowledge workers.* Cheltenham, England: Edward Elgar.

Jemielniak, D. (2013a). Netnografia, czyli etnografia wirtualna: Nowa forma badań etnograficznych. *Prakseologia, 153,* 97–115.

Jemielniak, D. (2013b). *Życie wirtualnych dzikich.* Warsaw, Poland: Poltext.

Jemielniak, D., & Gorbatai, A. (2012). *Power and status on Wikipedia.* Unpublished manuscript, Berkman Center for Internet and Society, Harvard University, Cambridge, MA.

Jemielniak, D., & Kociatkiewicz, J. (2009). Knowledge management: Fad or enduring organizational concept? In D. Jemielniak & J. Kociatkiewicz (Eds.), *Handbook of Research on Knowledge-Intensive Organizations.* Hershey, PA: Information Science Reference.

Jemielniak, D., & Kostera, M. (2010). Narratives of irony and failure in ethnographic work. *Canadian Journal of Administrative Sciences, 27*(4), 335–347.

Jemielniak, J. (2011). The place of arbitration in online proceedings as a simulacrum. In A. Wagner & L. Cheng (Eds.), *Exploring Courtroom Discourse: The Language of Power and Control* (pp. 251–262). Furnham, England: Ashgate.

Jemielniak, J., & Mikłaszewicz, P. (2010). Capturing the change: Universalising tendencies in legal interpretation. In J. Jemielniak and P. Mikłaszewicz (Eds.), *Interpretation of law in the global world: From particularism to a universal approach* (pp. 1–27). Heidelberg, Germany: Springer.

Jensen, C., & Scacchi, W. (2010). Governance in open source software development projects: A comparative multi-level analysis. *IFIP Advances in Information and Communication Technology, 319,* 130–142.

Jessop, B. (2010). Metagovernance. In M. Bevir (Ed.), *The SAGE handbook of governance.* London: Sage.

Johnson, D. G. (1997). Ethics online. *Communications of the ACM, 40*(1), 60–65.

Johnson, S. (2012). *Future perfect: The case for progress in a networked age.* New York: Riverhead.

Jones, G. R., & George, J. M. (1998). The experience and evolution of trust: Implications for cooperation and teamwork. *Academy of Management Review, 23*(3), 531–546.

Jones, T. M., & Bowie, N. E. (1998). Moral hazards on the road to the "virtual" corporation. *Business Ethics Quarterly, 8*(2), 273–292.

Kamm, O. (2007, August 16). Wisdom? More like dumbness of the crowds. *Oliver Kamm* blog. Retrieved from http://oliverkamm.typepad.com/blog/2007/08/wisdom-more-lik.html

Kane, G. C. (2009, August). It's a network, not an encyclopedia: A social network perspective on Wikipedia collaboration. *Academy of Management Proceedings*, 1–6. Retrieved from http://www.profkane.com/uploads/7/9/1/3/79137/sn_wiki_bpp _aom.pdf

Kane, G. C., and Ransbotham, S. (2012, April 18–20). *Collaborative development in Wikipedia*. Paper presented at the Collective Intelligence 2012 conference, Cambridge, MA. Retrieved from http://arxiv.org/pdf/1204.3352.pdf

Kane, G. C., Majchrzak, A., Johnson, J., & Chenisern, L. (2009, December 15–18). *A longitudinal model of perspective making and perspective taking within fluid online collectives*. Paper presented at the Thirtieth International Conference on Information Systems, Phoenix, AZ. Retrieved from http://community.mis.temple.edu/seminars/ files/2010/11/jerry2.pdf

Kanuha, V. K. (2000). "Being" native versus "going native": Conducting social work research as an insider. *Social Work*, *45*(5), 439–447.

Kapiszewski, K. (2011). Więcej niż pasja. *Przegląd*, *41*. Retrieved from http://www .przeglad-tygodnik.pl/pl/artykul/wiecej-niz-pasja

Karatzogianni, A., & Kuntsman, A. (Eds.). (2012). *Digital cultures and the politics of emotion: Feelings, affect and technological change*. London: Palgrave.

Kearns, K. P. (1994). The strategic management of accountability in nonprofit organizations: An analytical framework. *Public Administration Review*, *54*(2), 185–192.

Keegan, B., & Gergle, D. (2010). Egalitarians at the gate: One-sided gatekeeping practices in social media. In *CSCW '10: Proceedings of the 2010 ACM conference on Computer Supported Cooperative Work* (pp. 131–134). New York: ACM. Retrieved from http:// research.microsoft.com/en-us/um/redmond/groups/connect/cscw_10/docs/p131.pdf

Keegan, B., Gergle, D., & Contractor, N. (2011). Hot off the wiki: Dynamics, practices, and structures in Wikipedia's coverage of the Tohoku catastrophes. In *WikiSym '11: Proceedings of the 7th International Symposium on Wikis and Open Collaboration* (pp. 105–113). New York: ACM. Retrieved from http://www.wikisym.org/ws2011/ _media/proceedings%253Ap105-keegan.pdf

Keegan, B., Gergle, D., & Contractor, N. (2012). Do editors or articles drive collaboration? Multilevel statistical network analysis of Wikipedia coauthorship. In *CSCS '12: Proceedings of the ACM 2012 Conference on Computer Supported Cooperative Work* (pp. 427–436). New York: ACM.

Keen, A. (2007). *The cult of the amateur: How today's Internet is killing our culture*. New York: Broadway Business.

Kelty, C. M. (2001). Free software/free science. *First Monday*, *6*(12). Retrieved from http://firstmonday.org/ojs/index.php/fm/article/viewArticle/902/811

Kelty, C. M. (2004). Punt to culture. *Anthropological Quarterly*, *77*(3), 547–558.

Kelty, C. M. (2006). *The scale of norms: Free software and the theories of gift exchange*. Unpublished manuscript. Retrieved from http://kelty.org/or/papers/unpublishable/ Kelty-Gifts-Dec-2006-Revised.pdf

Kelty, C. M. (2008). Geeks, social imaginaries, and recursive publics. *Cultural Anthropology*, *20*(2), 185–214.

Kelty, C. M. (2010). Theorising the practices of free software: The movement. In B. Bräuchler & J. Postill (Eds.), *Theorising Media and Practice* (pp. 281–302). Oxford, England: Berghahn Books.

Kemp, R. (2010). Open source software (OSS) governance in the organisation. *Computer Law and Security Review, 26*(3), 309–316.

Kendall, L. (2011). Community and the Internet. In M. Consalvo & C. Ess (Eds.), *The handbook of Internet studies*. Oxford, England: Wiley-Blackwell.

Kerr, J. L. (2004). The limits of organizational democracy. *The Academy of Management Executive, 18*(3), 81–95.

Kiel: Difference between revisions. (n.d.). *Wikipedia.* Retrieved from http://en.wikipedia .org/w/index.php?title=Kiel&diff=2839601&oldid=2838532

Kim, S. (2002). Participative management and job satisfaction: Lessons for management leadership. *Public Administration Review, 62*(2), 231–241.

Kittur, A., & Kraut, R. E. (2008). Harnessing the wisdom of crowds in Wikipedia: Quality through coordination. In *CSCW '08: Proceedings of the 2008 ACM Conference on Computer Supported Cooperative Work* (pp. 37–46). New York: ACM.

Kittur, A., Chi, E., Pendleton, B. A., Suh, B., & Mytkowicz, T. (2007, April 28–May 3). *Power of the few vs. wisdom of the crowd: Wikipedia and the rise of the bourgeoisie.* Paper presented at the Twenty-Fifth Annual ACM Conference on Human Factors in Computing Systems, San Jose, CA. Retrieved from http://edouard-lopez.com/fac/ ICPS%20-%20S7/Complexit%C3%A9/2008-Wikipedia-As-A-Complex-System/ Power%20of%20the%20Few%20vs.%20Wisdom%20of%20the%20Crowd%3A%20 Wikipedia%20and%20the%20Rise%20of%20the%20Bourgeoisie.pdf

Klein, N. (2000). *No logo: No space, no choice, no jobs; Taking aim at the brand bullies.* Toronto: A. A. Knopf Canada.

Klein, N. (2007). *The shock doctrine: The rise of disaster capitalism.* New York: Metropolitan Books/Henry Holt.

Knights, D., Noble, F., Vurdubakis, T., & Willmott, H. (2001). Chasing shadows: Control, virtuality and the production of trust. *Organization Studies, 22*(2), 311–326.

Knorr-Cetina, K. (1999). *Epistemic cultures: How the sciences make knowledge.* Cambridge, MA: Harvard University Press.

Koch, C. (2004). The tyranny of projects: Teamworking, knowledge production and management in consulting engineering. *Economic and Industrial Democracy, 25*(2), 277–300.

Kociatkiewicz, J., & Kostera, M. (2012). The speed of experience: The co-narrative method in experience economy education. *British Journal of Management, 23*(4), 474–488.

Kogut, B., & Metiu, A. (2001). Open-source software development and distributed innovation. *Oxford Review of Economic Policy, 17*(2), 248–264.

Konieczny, P. (2009a). Governance, organization, and democracy on the Internet: The Iron Law and the evolution of Wikipedia. *Sociological Forum, 24*(1), 162–192.

Konieczny, P. (2009b). Wikipedia: Community or social movement? *Interface: A Journal for and about Social Movements, 1*(2), 212–232.

Konieczny, P. (2010). Adhocratic governance in the Internet age: A case of Wikipedia. *Journal of Information Technology and Politics, 7*(4), 263–283.

Konieczny, P. (2012). Wikis and Wikipedia as a teaching tool: Five years later. *First Monday, 17*(9). Retrieved from: http://firstmonday.org/htbin/cgiwrap/bin/ojs/index.php/fm/article/viewArticle/3583/3313

König, R. (2012). Wikipedia: Between lay participation and elite knowledge representation. *Information, Communication and Society, 16*(2), 160–177.

Kostakis, V. (2010). Identifying and understanding the problems of Wikipedia's peer governance: The case of inclusionists versus deletionists. *First Monday, 15*(3). Retrieved from http://firstmonday.org/ojs/index.php/fm/article/view/2613/2479

Kostera, M. (2006). The narrative collage as research method. *Storytelling, Self, Society, 2*(2), 5–27.

Kostera, M. (2007). *Organizational ethnography. Methods and inspirations.* Lund, Sweden: Studentlitteratur.

Kostera, M., & Glinka, B. (2001). Budget as logos: The rhetorics of the Polish press. *Organization, 8*(4), 647–682.

Kozinets, R. V. (2002). The field behind the screen: Using netnography for marketing research in online communities. *Journal of Marketing Research, 39*(1), 61–72.

Kozinets, R. V. (2010). *Netnography: Doing ethnographic research online.* Los Angeles: Sage.

Kriplean, T., Beschastnikh, I., & McDonald, D. W. (2008). Articulations of wikiwork: Uncovering valued work in Wikipedia through barnstars. In *CSCW '08: Proceedings of the 2008 ACM Conference on Computer Supported Cooperative Work* (pp. 47–56). New York: ACM. Retrieved from http://dub.washington.edu/djangosite/media/papers/tmpZ77p1r.pdf

Kriplean, T., Beschastnikh, I., McDonald, D. W., & Golder, S. A. (2007). Community, consensus, coercion, control: CS*W or how policy mediates mass participation. In *Proceedings of the 2007 International ACM Conference on Supporting Group Work* (pp. 167–176). New York: ACM. Retrieved from http://dub.washington.edu/djangosite/media/papers/tmpzq4PJB.pdf

Krippendorff, K. (2004). *Content analysis: An introduction to its methodology.* Thousand Oaks, CA: Sage.

Krupa, Y., Vercouter, L., Hübner, J., & Herzig, A. (2009). Trust based evaluation of Wikipedia's contributors: Engineering societies in the agents world X. In H. Aldewereld, V. Dignum, & G. Picard (Eds.), *Lecture Notes in Computer Science* (Vol. 5881, pp. 148–161). Berlin, Germany: Springer.

Kücklich, J. R. (2009). Virtual worlds and their discontents precarious sovereignty, governmentality, and the ideology of play. *Games and Culture, 4*(4), 340–352.

Kumar, J. A. (2010). Forking, leadership control and social capital in open innovation. In *Proceedings of the IEEE International Conference on Management of Innovation and Technology (ICMIT)* (pp. 720–725). St. Louis, MO: IEEE.

Kunda, G. (1992). *Engineering culture: Control and commitment in a high-tech corporation* (Rev. ed.). Philadelphia: Temple University Press.

Kuznetsov, S. (2006). Motivations of contributors to Wikipedia. *ACM SIGCAS Computers and Society, 36*(2). Retrieved from https://dl.acm.org/citation.cfm? id=1215943

Kwan, M., & Ramachandran, D. (2009). Trust and online reputation systems. In J. Golbeck (Ed.), *Computing with Social Trust* (pp. 287–311). London: Springer.

Labaree, R. V. (2002). The risk of "going observationalist": Negotiating the hidden dilemmas of being an insider participant observer. *Qualitative Research, 2*(1), 97–122.

Lakhani, K. R., & Von Hippel, E. (2003). How open source software works. *Research Policy, 32*(6), 923–943.

Lakhani, K., & Wolf, R. (2003). Why hackers do what they do: Understanding motivation and effort in free/open source software projects. In J. Feller, B. Fitzgerald, S. A. Hissam, & K. R. Lakhani (Eds.), *Perspectives on free and open source software.* Cambridge, MA: MIT Press.

Lam, S. K., & Riedl, J. (2011). The past, present, and future of Wikipedia. *Computer, 44*(3), 87–90.

Lam, S. K., Uduwage, A., Dong, Z., Sen, S., Musicant, D. R., Terveen, L., et al. (2011). WP:Clubhouse? An exploration of Wikipedia's gender imbalance. In *WikiSym '11: Proceedings of the 7th International Symposium on Wikis and Open Collaboration.* New York: ACM.

Lampe, C., Wash, R., Velasquez, A., & Ozkaya, E. (2010). Motivations to participate in online communities. In *CHI '10: Proceedings of the SIGCHIConference on Human Factors in Computing Systems* (pp. 1927–1936). New York: ACM.

Lampel, J., & Bhalla, A. (2007). The role of status seeking in online communities: Giving the gift of experience. *Journal of Computer-Mediated Communication, 12*(2), 434–455.

Land, M. B. (2009). Networked activism. *Harvard Human Rights Journal, 22*, 205–243.

Langer, R., & Beckman, S. C. (2005). Sensitive research topics: Netnography revisited. *Qualitative Market Research: An International Journal, 8*(2), 189–203.

Laniado, D., & Tasso, R. (2011). Co-authorship 2.0: Patterns of collaboration in Wikipedia. In *HT '11: Proceedings of the 22nd ACM Conference on Hypertext and Hypermedia* (pp. 201–210). New York: ACM.

Laniado, D., Tasso, R., Volkovich, Y., & Kaltenbrunner, A. (2011). When the Wikipedians talk: Network and tree structure of Wikipedia discussion pages. In *Proceedings of the Fifth International Conference on Weblogs and Social Media* (pp. 177–184). Menlo Park, CA: AAAI Press. Retrieved from http://www.aaai.org/ocs/index.php/ICWSM/ ICWSM11/paper/viewFile/2764/3301

Lanier, J. (2006, May 29). Digital Maoism: The hazards of the new online collectivism. *The Edge.* Retrieved from http://www.edge.org/3rd_culture/lanier06/lanier06 _index.html

Latour, B. (1986). The powers of association. In J. Law (Ed.), *Power, action and belief: A new sociology of knowledge?* London: Routledge & Kegan Paul.

Latour, B., & Woolgar, S. (1979). *Laboratory life: The social construction of scientific facts.* Beverly Hills, CA: Sage.

Lattemann, C., & Stieglitz, S. (2005). Framework for governance in open source communities. In *HICSS '05: Proceedings of the 38th Annual Hawaii International Conference on System Sciences* (p. 192.1). Washington, DC: IEEE Computer Society.

Latusek, D., & Cook, K. S. (2012). Trust in transitions. *Kyklos, 65*(4), 512–525.

Latusek, D., & Gerbasi, A. (Eds.). (2010). *Trust and technology in a ubiquitous modern environment: Theoretical and methodological perspectives.* Hershey, PA: Information Science Reference.

Latusek, D., & Jemielniak, D. (2007). (Dis)trust in software projects: A thrice told tale; On dynamic relationships between software engineers, IT project managers, and customers. *The International Journal of Technology, Knowledge, and Society, 3*(10), 117–125.

Lave, J., & Wenger, E. (1991). *Situated learning: Legitimate peripheral participation.* Cambridge, England: Cambridge University Press.

Leach, E. (1982). *Social anthropology.* Oxford, England: Oxford University Press.

Lee, E. J., & Jang, J. (2010). Profiling Good Samaritans in online knowledge forums: Effects of affiliative tendency, self-esteem, and public individuation on knowledge sharing. *Computers in Human Behavior, 26*(6), 1336–1344.

Lee, H. (2005). Behavioral strategies for dealing with flaming in an online forum. *The Sociological Quarterly, 46*(2), 385–403.

Lerner, J., & Tirole, J. (2002). Some simple economics of open source. *The Journal of Industrial Economics, 50*(2), 197–234.

Leskovec, J., Huttenlocher, D., & Kleinberg, J. (2010). Governance in social media: A case study of the Wikipedia promotion process. In *Proceedings of the Fourth International Conference on Weblogs and Social Media* (pp. 98–105). Menlo Park, CA: AAAI Press. Retrieved from http://www.aaai.org/ocs/index.php/ICWSM/ICWSM10/paper/view File/1485/1841

Lesser, E., Fontaine, M., & Slusher, J. (Eds.). (2012). *Knowledge and communities.* London: Routledge.

Lessig, L. (1999). *Code: And other laws of cyberspace.* New York: Perseus.

Lessig, L. (2001). *The future of ideas. The fate of the commons in the connected world.* New York: Random House.

Lessig, L. (2004). *Free culture: How big media uses technology and the law to lock down culture and control creativity.* New York: Penguin Press.

Lessig, L. (2008). Remix making art and commerce thrive in the hybrid economy. Retrieved from http://www.archive.org/details/LawrenceLessigRemix

Levine, R. (2011). *Free ride.* New York: Doubleday.

Levine, S. (2008). The full-time guild master. *Intersect: The Stanford Journal of Science, Technology and Society, 1*(1), 36–42.

Levy, S. (1984). *Hackers: Heroes of the computer revolution.* Garden City, NY: Doubleday.

Lewin, A., & Stephens, C. (1994). Designing postindustrial organizations. In G. P. Huber & W. H. Glick (Eds.), *Organizational change and redesign: Ideas and insights for improving performance* (pp. 393–409). New York: Oxford University Press.

Li, Q. (2009). Towards a better understanding of group forking dynamics in virtual contexts. In *Proceedings of the ACM 2009 International Conference on Supporting Group Work* (pp. 381–382). New York: ACM.

Lih, A. (2004, April 16–17). *Wikipedia as participatory journalism: Reliable sources? Metrics for evaluating collaborative media as a news resource.* Paper presented at the Fifth International Symposium on Online Journalism, Austin, TX.

Lih, A. (2009). *The Wikipedia revolution: How a bunch of nobodies created the world's greatest encyclopedia.* New York: Hyperion.

Lim, J. Y. K., & Chidambaram, L. (2011). A longitudinal comparison of leader-follower relationships between high and low performing self-managed work teams in virtual settings. In *HICSS '11: Proceedings of the 2011 44th Hawaii International Conference on System Sciences* (pp. 1–10). Washington, DC: IEEE Computer Society.

Limits to configuration changes. (2013, July 30). *Wikimedia.* Retrieved August 22, 2013, from http://meta.wikimedia.org/wiki/Ignoring_community_consensus

Lincoln, Y. S., & Denzin, N. K. (Eds.). (2003). *Turning points in qualitative research: Tying knots in a handkerchief* (Vol. 3). Walnut Creek, CA: Altamira Press.

List of largest wikis. (2013, January 21). *Wikimedia.* Retrieved January 21, 2013, from http://meta.wikimedia.org/wiki/List_of_largest_wikis

Lobo, L. (1990). Becoming a marginal native. *Anthropos, 85,* 125–138.

Local chapters. (2013, July 12). *Wikimedia.* Retrieved August 21, 2013, from https://wikimediafoundation.org/wiki/Local_chapters

Louis, M. R. (1994). In the manner of friends: Learnings from Quaker practice for organizational renewal. *Journal of Organizational Change Management, 7*(1), 42–60.

Lucassen, T., Dijkstra, R., & Schraagen, J. M. (2012). Readability of Wikipedia. *First Monday, 17*(9). Retrieved from http://www.uic.edu/htbin/cgiwrap/bin/ojs/index.php/fm/article/view/3916/3297

Łuczewski, M. (2012). *Odwieczny naród.* Toruń, Poland: UMK-FNP.

Luther, K., & Bruckman, A. (2008). Leadership in online creative collaboration. In *CSCW '08: Proceedings of the 2008 ACM Conference on Computer supported cooperative work* (pp. 343–352). New York: ACM.

Malinowski, B. (1922/1961). *Argonauts of the western Pacific.* New York: E. P. Dutton.

Mallet, S. (1975). *Essays on the new working class.* St. Louis, MO: Telos Press.

Malone, T. W., Laubacher, R., & Dellarocas, C. (2010). The collective intelligence genome. *MIT Sloan Management Review, 51*(3), 21–31.

Manual:Article count. (2013, June 7). *MediaWiki.* Retrieved August 14, 2013, from http://www.mediawiki.org/wiki/Manual:Article_count

Marks, A., & Lockyer, C. (2004). Producing knowledge: The use of the project team as a vehicle for knowledge and skill acquisition for software employees. *Economic and Industrial Democracy, 25*(2), 219–245.

Markus, M. L. (2007). The governance of free/open source software projects: Monolithic, multidimensional, or configurational? *Journal of Management and Governance, 11*(2), 151–163.

Marshall, C., & Rossman, G. B. (2010). *Designing qualitative research*. Thousand Oaks, CA: Sage.

Martin, K. (2007, December 18). The other shoe drops. *Nonbovine Ruminations* blog. Retrieved from http://nonbovine-ruminations.blogspot.com/2007/12/other-shoe -drops.html

Mateos-Garcia, J., & Steinmueller, W. (2006, October 26–27). *Open, but how much? Growth, conflict and institutional evolution in Wikipedia and Debian*. Paper presented at the DIME International Conference on Communities of Practice, Durham, England. Retrieved from http://www.dime-eu.org/files/active/1/cops2006_Mateos -Garcia_Steinmueller.pdf

Mateos-Garcia, J., & Steinmueller, W. E. (2008). The institutions of open source software: Examining the Debian community. *Information Economics and Policy, 20*(4), 333–344.

Matzat, U. (2010). Reducing problems of sociability in online communities: Integrating online communication with offline interaction. *American Behavioral Scientist, 53*(8), 1170–1193.

Mauss, M. (1954/2001). *The gift: Form and reason for exchange in archaic societies*. London: Routledge.

Mazzarella, W. (2006). Internet x-ray: E-governance, transparency, and the politics of immediation in India. *Public Culture, 18*(3), 473.

McCloskey, D. N. (1998). *The rhetoric of economics*. Madison: University of Wisconsin Press.

McEvily, B. (2011). Reorganizing the boundaries of trust: From discrete alternatives to hybrid forms. *Organization Science, 22*(5). Retrieved from http://dx.doi.org/10.1287/ orsc.1110.0649

Merton, R. K. (1938). Science and the social order. *Philosophy of Science, 5*(3), 321–337.

Merton, R. K. (1972). Insiders and outsiders: A chapter in the sociology of knowledge. *American Journal of Sociology, 78*(1), 9–47.

Metz, C. (2007, December 4). Secret mailing list rocks Wikipedia. *The Register*. Retrieved from http://www.theregister.co.uk/2007/12/04/wikipedia_secret_mailing/

Metz, C. (2008a, March 5). Ex-Wikipedia staffer harpoons Wales over expenses. *The Register*. Retrieved from http://www.theregister.co.uk/2008/03/05/jimmy_wales _and_danny_wool/

Metz, C. (2008b, March 6). Why you should care that Jimmy Wales ignores reality. *The Register*. Retrieved from http://www.theregister.co.uk/2008/03/06/a_model_wiki pedian/

Metz, C. (2010, May 9). Jimbo Wales exiles "porn" from Wikiland. *The Register*. Retrieved from http://www.theregister.co.uk/2010/05/09/wikimedia_pron_purge/

Meyer, J. W., & Rowan, B. (1977). Institutionalized organizations: Formal structure as myth and ceremony. *The American Journal of Sociology, 83*(2), 340–363.

Meyer, R. (2012, July 16). 3 Charts that show how Wikipedia is running out of admins. *The Atlantic*. Retrieved from http://www.theatlantic.com/technology/archive/2012/07/ 3-charts-that-show-how-wikipedia-is-running-out-of-admins/259829/

Meyerson, D., & Weick, K. E. (1996). Swift trust and temporary groups. In R. M. Kramer & T. R. Tyler (Eds.), *Trust in organizations: Frontiers of theory and research* (pp. 166–195). Thousand Oaks, CA: Sage.

Mintzberg, H., & McHugh, A. (1985). Strategy formation in an adhocracy. *Administrative Science Quarterly, 30*(2), 160–197.

Miyazaki, H. (2006). *The method of hope: Anthropology, philosophy, and Fijian knowledge.* Stanford, CA: Stanford University Press.

Mockus, A., Fielding, R. T., & Herbsleb, J. (2000). A case study of open source software development: The Apache server. In *ICSE '00: Proceedings of the 22nd International Conference on Software Engineering* (pp. 263–272). New York: ACM.

Morand, D. A. (1996). Dominance, deference, and egalitarianism in organizational interaction: A sociolinguistic analysis of power and politeness. *Organization Science, 7*(5), 544–556.

Morell, M. F. (2009, August 26–28). *The governance of digital commons: Wikimedia governance case study.* Paper presented at the Wikimania conference, Buenos Aires, Argentina. Retrieved from http://wikimania2009.wikimedia.org/wiki/Proceedings: 195

Morell, M. F. (2010). Participation in online creation communities: Ecosystemic participation? In *Conference Proceedings of JITP 2010: The Politics of Open Source* (pp. 270–295). Retrieved from http://scholarworks.umass.edu/jitpc2010/1/

Morell, M. F. (2011a, June 30–June 1). *An introductory historical contextualization of online creation communities for the building of digital commons: The emergence of a free culture movement.* Paper presented at the Sixth Open Knowledge Conference, Berlin, Germany.

Morell, M. F. (2011b). The Wikimedia Foundation and the governance of Wikipedia's infrastructure historical trajectories and its hybrid character. In G. Lovink & N. Tkacz (Eds.), *Critical Point of View: A Wikipedia Reader* (pp. 325–341). Amsterdam: Institute of Network Cultures.

Morozov, E. (2012). *The net delusion: The dark side of Internet freedom.* New York: Public Affairs.

Morris, K. (2013a, January 1). After a half-decade, massive Wikipedia hoax finally exposed. *The Daily Dot.* Retrieved from http://www.dailydot.com/news/wikipedia -bicholim-conflict-hoax-deleted/

Morris, K. (2013b, June 25). How Wikimedia Commons became a massive amateur porn hub. *The Daily Dot.* Retrieved from http://www.dailydot.com/technology/wikime dia-commons-photos-jimmy-wales-broken/

Müller-Birn, C., Dobusch, L., & Herbsleb, J. D. (2013). Work-to-rule: The emergence of algorithmic governance in Wikipedia. In *C&T '13: Proceedings of the 6th International Conference on Communities and Technologies* (pp. 80–89). New York: ACM.

Muller-Seitz, G., & Reger, G. (2010). "Wikipedia, the Free Encyclopedia" as a role model? Lessons for open innovation from an exploratory examination of the supposedly democratic-anarchic nature of Wikipedia. *International Journal of Technology Management, 52*(3), 457–476.

Murthy, D. (2008). Digital ethnography an examination of the use of new technologies for social research. *Sociology, 42*(5), 837–855.

Nachmias, D., & Frankfort-Nachmias, C. (1981/2001). *Metody badawcze w naukach społecznych* [Research methods in the social sciences]. Warsaw, Poland: Zysk i ska.

Nahapiet, J., Gratton, L., & Rocha, H. O. (2005). Knowledge and relationships: When cooperation is the norm. *European Management Review, 2*(1), 3–14.

Narayan, K. (1993). How native is a "native" anthropologist? *American Anthropologist, 95*(3), 671–686.

Narayan, S., & Cheshire, C. (2010). Not too long to read: The tldr interface for exploring and navigating large-scale discussion spaces. In *HICSS '10: Proceedings of the 2010 43rd Hawaii International Conference on System Sciences*(pp. 1–10). Washington, DC: IEEE Computer Society. Retrieved from http://people.ischool.berkeley.edu/~coye/Pubs/ConferenceProceedings/Narayan_Cheshire_TLDR.pdf

Nemoto, K., & Gloor, P. A. (2011). Analyzing cultural differences in collaborative innovation networks by analyzing editing behavior in different-language Wikipedias. *Procedia: Social and Behavioral Sciences, 26*, 180–190.

Nemoto, K., Gloor, P., & Laubacher, R. (2011). Social capital increases efficiency of collaboration among Wikipedia editors. In *HT '11: Proceedings of the 22nd ACM Conference on Hypertext and Hypermedia* (pp. 231–240). New York: ACM.

Neus, A., & Scherf, P. (2005). Opening minds: Cultural change with the introduction of open-source collaboration methods. *IBM Systems Journal, 44*(2), 215–225.

Newell, S., & Swan, J. (2000). Trust and inter-organizational networking. *Human Relations, 53*(10), 1287–1328.

Niederer, S., & van Dijck, J. (2010). Wisdom of the crowd or technicity of content? Wikipedia as a sociotechnical system. *New Media and Society, 12*(8), 1368–1387.

Nocera, J. L. A. (2002). Ethnography and hermeneutics in cybercultural research accessing IRC virtual communities. *Journal of Computer-Mediated Communication, 7*(2). doi:10.1111/j.1083-6101.2002.tb00146.x

Nov, O. (2007). What motivates wikipedians? *Communications of the ACM, 50*(11), 60–64.

Nyman, L., & Mikkonen, T. (2011). To fork or not to fork: Fork motivations in SourceForge projects. *Open Source Systems: Grounding Research, 365*, 259–268.

Nyman, L., Mikkonen, T., Lindman, J., & Fougère, M. (2011). Forking: The invisible hand of sustainability in open source software. In I. Hammouda & B. Lundell (Eds.), *Proceedings of SOS 2011: Towards Sustainable Open Source* (pp. 1–5). Tampere, Finland: Tampere University of Technology. Retrieved from http://tutopen.cs.tut.fi/sos11/papers/SOS11_proceedings.pdf#page=9

O'Mahony, S. (2003). Guarding the commons: How community managed software projects protect their work. *Research Policy, 32*(7), 1179–1198.

O'Mahony, S. (2007). The governance of open source initiatives: What does it mean to be community managed? *Journal of Management and Governance, 11*(2), 139–150.

Oboler, A., Steinberg, G., & Stern, R. (2010). The framing of political NGOs in Wikipedia through criticism elimination. *Journal of Information Technology and Politics, 7*(4), 284–299.

Oels, A. (2002). Investigating the emotional roller-coaster ride: A case study–based assessment of the Future Search Conference design. *Systems Research and Behavioral Science, 19*(4), 347–355.

O'Leary, M., Orlikowski, W., & Yates, J. (2002). Distributed work over the centuries: Trust and control in the Hudson's Bay Company. In P. J. Hinds & S. Kiesler (Eds.), *Distributed work* (pp. 1670–1826). Cambridge, MA: MIT Press.

Olson, D. R. (1990). Thinking about interpretation: A reply to Snyder. *Interchange, 21*(3), 56–60.

O'Mahony, S., & Bechky, B. A. (2008). Boundary organizations: Enabling collaboration among unexpected allies. *Administrative Science Quarterly, 53*(3), 422–459.

O'Mahony, S., & Ferraro, F. (2007). The emergence of governance in an open source community. *The Academy of Management Journal, 50*(5), 1079–1106.

O'Neil, M. (2009). *Cyberchiefs: Autonomy and authority in online tribes.* New York: Pluto Press.

O'Neil, M. (2010). Shirky and Sanger, or the costs of crowdsourcing. *Journal of Science Communication, 9*(1), 1–6.

O'Neil, M. (2011a). The sociology of critique in Wikipedia. *Critical Studies in Peer Production, 1*(2). Retrieved from http://peerproduction.net/issues/issue-0/peer-reviewed-papers/sociology-of-critique/

O'Neil, M. (2011b). Wikipedia and authority. In G. Lovink & N. Tkacz (Eds.), *Critical point of view: A Wikipedia reader* (pp. 309–324). Amsterdam: Institute of Network Cultures.

Ong, W. J. (2002). *Orality and literacy.* London: Routledge.

Orlikowski, W. J. (2002). Knowing in practice: Enacting a collective capability in distributed organizing. *Organization Science, 13*(3), 249–273.

Ortega, F. (2009). *Wikipedia: A quantitative analysis.* Unpublished doctoral dissertation, GSyC/Libresoft, Universidad Rey Juan Carlos, Madrid, Spain.

Ortega, F., & Gonzalez-Barahona, J. M. (2007). Quantitative analysis of the Wikipedia community of users. In *WikiSym '07: Proceedings of the 2007 International Symposium on Wikis* (pp. 75–86). New York: ACM.

Ortega, F., Gonzalez-Barahona, J. M., & Robles, G. (2008). On the inequality of contributions to Wikipedia. In *HICSS '08: Proceedings of the 41st Annual Hawaii International Conference on System Sciences* (p. 304). Washington, DC: IEEE Computer Society.

Ortega, F., Izquierdo-Cortazar, D., Gonzalez-Barahona, J. M., & Robles, G. (2009). On the analysis of contributions from privileged users in virtual open communities. In *HICSS '09: Proceedings of the 42nd Hawaii International Conference on System Sciences* (pp. 1–10). Washington, DC: IEEE Computer Society. Retrieved from http://www.computer.org/csdl/proceedings/hicss/2009/3450/00/01-03-03.pdf

Orton-Johnson, K. (2007). The online student: Lurking, chatting, flaming and joking. *Sociological Research Online, 12*(6). Retrieved from http://www.socresonline.org.uk/12/6/3.html

Ostroff, F. (1999). *The horizontal organization: What the organization of the future looks like and how it delivers value to customers.* Oxford: Oxford University Press.

Ostrom, E. (1990). *Governing the commons: The evolution of institutions for collective action*. Cambridge, England: Cambridge University Press.

Ostrom, E. (2000). Collective action and the evolution of social norms. *The Journal of Economic Perspectives, 14*(3), 137–158.

Oxley, M., Morgan, J. T., Zachry, M., & Hutchinson, B. (2010, July 7–9). *"What i know is . . .": Establishing credibility on Wikipedia talk pages*. Paper presented at the Sixth International Symposium on Wikis and Open Collaboration, Gdańsk, Poland.

Paccagnella, L. (1997). Getting the seats of your pants dirty: Strategies for ethnographic research on virtual communities. *Journal of Computer-Mediated Communication, 3*(1). doi:10.1111/j.1083-6101.1997.tb00065.x

Panciera, K., Halfaker, A., & Terveen, L. (2009). *Wikipedians are born, not made: A study of power editors on Wikipedia*. Paper presented at the GROUP '09 Proceedings of the ACM 2009 International conference on Supporting Group Work, New York.

Pariser, E. E. (2011). *The filter bubble: What the Internet is hiding from you*. New York: Penguin Press.

Parvaz, D. (2011, January 15). Look it up: Wikipedia turns 10. *AlJazeera*. Retrieved from http://www.aljazeera.com/indepth/features/2011/01/201111571716655385.html

Pegg, D., & Wright, D. (2011, December 8). Wikipedia founder attacks Bell Pottinger for "ethical blindness." *The Independent*. Retrieved from http://www.independent.co.uk/news/uk/politics/wikipedia-founder-attacks-bell-pottinger-for-ethical-blindness-6273836.html

Pentzold, C. (2011). Imagining the Wikipedia community: What do Wikipedia authors mean when they write about their "community"? *New Media and Society, 13*(5), 704–721.

Perlow, L. A. (1998). Boundary control: The social ordering of work and family time in a high-tech corporation. *Administrative Science Quarterly, 43*(2), 328–357.

Peters, P. (2007, January 18). Lesson #2: Procedure vs content, or "You didn't genuflect deeply enough." *Live Journal*. Retrieved from http://parkerpeters.livejournal.com/1195.html

Petition to Jimbo. (2013, April 27). *Wikimedia*. Retrieved August 23, 2013, from http://meta.wikimedia.org/wiki/Petition_to_Jimbo

Pettigrew, A. M. (1990). Longitudinal field research on change: Theory and practice. *Organization Science, 1*(3), 267–292.

Pfaffenberger, B. (1996). "If I want it, it's OK": Usenet and the (outer) limits of free speech. *The Information Society, 12*(4), 365–386.

Pfeil, U., Zaphiris, P., & Ang, C. S. (2006). Cultural differences in collaborative authoring of Wikipedia. *Journal of Computer-Mediated Communication, 12*(1), 88–113.

Pfister, D. S. (2011). Networked expertise in the era of many-to-many communication: On Wikipedia and invention. *Social Epistemology, 25*(3), 217–231.

Piskorski, M. J., & Gorbatai, A. D. (2011). *Testing Coleman's social-norm enforcement mechanism: Evidence from Wikipedia*. Harvard Business School (working paper 11-055). Retrieved September 7, 2011, from http://www.hbs.edu/research/pdf/11-055.pdf

Potts, J., Hartley, J., Banks, J., Burgess, J., Cobcroft, R., Cunningham, S., et al. (2008). Consumer co-creation and situated creativity. *Industry and Innovation, 15*(5), 459–474.

Powdermaker, H. (1966). *Stranger and friend: The way of an anthropologist* (Vol. 410). New York: Norton.

Powell, W. W. (1991). Neither market nor hierarchy: Network forms of organization. *Research in Organizational Behavior 12*, 295–336.

Pragnell, C., & Gatzidis, C. (2011). Addiction in World of Warcraft: A virtual ethnography study. In H. H. Yang & S. C.-Y. Yuen (Eds.), *Handbook of Research on Practices and Outcomes in Virtual Worlds and Environments* (Vol. 1, pp. 54–74). Hershey, PA: Information Science Reference.

Prasarnphanich, P., & Wagner, C. (2008, February 26–29). *Creating critical mass in collaboration systems: Insights from Wikipedia.* Paper presented at the Second IEEE International Conference on Digital Ecosystems and Technologies, Phitsanulok, Thailand.

Preece, J., & Shneiderman, B. (2009). The reader-to-leader framework: Motivating technology-mediated social participation. *AIS Transactions on Human-Computer Interaction, 1*(1), 13–32.

Priedhorsky, R., Chen, J., Lam, S. T. K., Panciera, K., Terveen, L., & Riedl, J. (2007). Creating, destroying, and restoring value in Wikipedia. In *Proceedings of the 2007 International ACM Conference on Supporting Group Work* (pp. 259–268). New York: ACM.

Project-wide protests. (2013, March 30). *Wikimedia.* Retrieved August 22, 2013, from http://meta.wikimedia.org/wiki/Project-wide_protests

Pursuer, R., & Cabana, S. (1998). *The self-managing organisation: How leading companies are transforming the work of teams for real impact.* New York: Free Press.

Rad, H. S., & Barbosa, D. (2012, August 27–29). *Identifying controversial articles in Wikipedia: A comparative study.* Paper presented at the WikiSym conference, Linz, Austria.

Rad, H. S., Makazhanov, A., Rafiei, D., & Barbosa, D. (2012). Leveraging editor collaboration patterns in Wikipedia. In *HT '12: Proceedings of the 23rd ACM Conference on Hypertext and Social Media* (pp. 13–22). New York: ACM.

Rafaeli, S., & Ariel, Y. (2008). Online motivational factors: Incentives for participation and contribution in Wikipedia. In A. Barak (Ed.), *Psychological aspects of cyberspace: Theory, research, applications* (pp. 243–267). Cambridge, England: Cambridge University Press.

Randall, D., Harper, R., & Rouncefield, M. (2007). *Fieldwork for design: Theory and practice.* London: Springer-Verlag.

Ransbotham, S., & Kane, G. C. (2011). Membership turnover and collaboration success in online communities: Explaining rises and falls from grace in Wikipedia. *MIS Quarterly—Management Information Systems, 35*(3), 613–627.

Raymond, E. S. (1998). Homesteading the noosphere. *First Monday, 3*(10). Retrieved from http://firstmonday.org/htbin/cgiwrap/bin/ojs/index.php/fm/article/view Article/621/542

Raymond, E. S. (1999). The cathedral and the bazaar. *Knowledge, Technology and Policy, 12*(3), 23–49.

Raymond, E. S. (1999/2004). *The cathedral and the bazaar.* Beijing, China: O'Reilly.

Rayton, D. (1972). *Shop floor democracy in action.* Nottingham, England: Russell Press.

Read, B. (2007, March 9). Wikipedia fights bogus credentials. *The Chronicle of Higher Education* blog. Retrieved from http://chronicle.com/blogs/wiredcampus/wiki pedia-fights-bogus-credentials/2888

Readings, B. (1996). *The university in ruins.* Cambridge, MA: Harvard University Press.

Reagle, J. M. (2004). Open content communities. *M/C: A Journal of Media and Culture, 7*(3). Retrieved from http://journal.media-culture.org.au/0406/06_Reagle .rft.php

Reagle, J. M. (2007). Do as I do: Authorial leadership in Wikipedia. In *WikiSym '07: Proceedings of the 2007 International Symposium on Wikis* (pp. 143–156). New York: ACM. Retrieved from http://www.wikisym.org/ws2007/_publish/Reagle _WikiSym2007_WikipediaAuthorialLeadership.pdf

Reagle, J. M. (2010a). "Be nice": Wikipedia norms for supportive communication. *New Review of Hypermedia and Multimedia, 16*(1–2), 161–180.

Reagle, J. M. (2010b). *Good faith collaboration: The culture of Wikipedia.* Cambridge, MA: MIT Press.

Reagle, J. M. (2013). "Free as in sexist?" Free culture and the gender gap. *First Monday, 18*(1). Retrieved from http://www.uic.edu/htbin/cgiwrap/bin/ojs/index.php/fm/ article/view/4291/3381

Reagle, J. M., & Rhue, L. (2011). Gender bias in Wikipedia and Britannica. *International Journal of Communication, 5,* 1138–1158.

Reavley, N., Mackinnon, A., Morgan, A., Alvarez-Jimenez, M., Hetrick, S., Killackey, E., et al. (2012). Quality of information sources about mental disorders: A comparison of Wikipedia with centrally controlled web and printed sources. *Psychological Medicine, 48*(8), 1753–1762.

Rehn, A. (2004). The politics of contraband: The honor economies of the warez scene. *Journal of Socio-Economics, 33*(3), 359–374.

Requests for comment/remove founder flag. (2013, July 5). *Wikimedia.* Retrieved August 23, 2013, from https://meta.wikimedia.org/wiki/Requests_for_comment/Remove _Founder_flag

Research talk:Dynamics of online interactions and behavior. (2012, January 25). *Wikimedia.* Retrieved August 22, 2013, from http://meta.wikimedia.org/wiki/ Research_talk:Dynamics_of_Online_Interactions_and_Behavior

Research:Contribution Taxonomy Project. (2012, November 16). *Wikimedia.* Retrieved August 15, 2013, from http://meta.wikimedia.org/wiki/Research:Contribution _Taxonomy_Project

Research:Dynamics of online interactions and behavior. (2012, July 10). *Wikimedia.* Retrieved August 22, 2013, from http://meta.wikimedia.org/wiki/ Research:Dynamics_of_Online_Interactions_and_Behavior

Restivo, M., & van de Rijt, A. (2012). Experimental study of informal rewards in peer production. *PLoS ONE, 7*(3). Retrieved from http://dx.plos.org/10.1371/journal .pone.0034358

Rheingold, H. (1994). *The virtual community: Surfing the Internet.* London: Minerva.

Richardson, L. (2001). Getting personal: Writing-stories. *International Journal of Qualitative Studies in Education, 14*(1), 33–38.

Riggio, R. E., & Orr, S. S. (2004). *Improving leadership in nonprofit organizations.* San Francisco: Jossey-Bass.

Ritzer, G., & Jurgenson, N. (2010). Production, consumption, prosumption: The nature of capitalism in the age of the digital "prosumer." *Journal of Consumer Culture, 10*(1), 13–36.

Rivington, J. (2007, April 25). Wikipedia guns for Britannica extermination. *TechRadar.* Retrieved from http://www.techradar.com/news/internet/broadband/wikipedia -guns-for-britannica-extermination-132792

Roberts, P., & Peters, M. A. (2011). From Castalia to Wikipedia: Openness and closure in knowledge communities. *E-Learning and Digital Media, 8*(1), 36–46.

Robertson, M., & Swan, J. (2004). Going public: The emergence and effects of soft bureaucracy within a knowledge-intensive firm. *Organization, 11*(1), 123–148.

Rosen, M. (1985/1991). Breakfast at Spiro's: Dramaturgy and dominance. In P. J. Frost, L. F. Moore, M. R. Louis, C. C. Lundberg, & J. Martin (Eds.), *Reframing Organizational Culture.* Newbury Park, CA: Sage.

Rosen, R. J. (2012, October 25). Surmounting the insurmountable: Wikipedia is nearing completion, in a sense. *The Atlantic.* Retrieved from http://www.theatlantic .com/technology/archive/2012/2010/surmounting-the-insurmountable-wikipedia-is -nearing-completion-in-a-sense/264111/

Roth, P. (2012, September 7). An open letter to Wikipedia. *The New Yorker.* Retrieved from http://www.newyorker.com/online/blogs/books/2012/09/an-open-letter-to -wikipedia.html

Rothschild-Whitt, J. (1979). The collectivist organization: An alternative to rational-bureaucratic models. *American Sociological Review, 44*(4), 509–527.

Rubenson, G. C., & Gupta, A. K. (1992). Replacing the founder: Exploding the myth of the entrepreneur's disease. *Business Horizons, 35*(6), 53–57.

Ruhleder, K. (2000). The virtual ethnographer: Fieldwork in distributed electronic environments. *Field Methods, 12*(3), 3–17.

Rutter, K. A. (2003). From measuring clouds to active listening. *Management Learning, 34*(4), 465–480.

Sade-Beck, L. (2008). Internet ethnography: Online and offline. *International Journal of Qualitative Methods, 3*(2), 45–51.

Sadowski, B. M., Sadowski-Rasters, G., & Duysters, G. (2008). Transition of governance in a mature open software source community: Evidence from the Debian case. *Information Economics and Policy, 20*(4), 323–332.

Sanger, L. M. (2009). The fate of expertise after Wikipedia. *Episteme, 6*(1), 52–73.

Santana, A., & Wood, D. J. (2009). Transparency and social responsibility issues for Wikipedia. *Ethics and Information Technology, 11*(2), 133–144.

Schachaf, P., & Hara, N. (2010). Beyond vandalism: Trolls in Wikipedia. *Journal of Information Science, 36*(3), 357–370.

Schafft, K. A., & Greenwood, D. J. (2003). Promises and dilemmas of participation: Action research, search conference methodology, and community development. *Community Development, 34*(1), 18–35.

Schiff, S. (2006, July 31). Know it all: Can Wikipedia conquer expertise? *The New Yorker.* Retrieved from http://www.newyorker.com/archive/2006/07/31/060731fa_fact

Schoorman, F. D., Mayer, R. C., & Davis, J. H. (2007). An integrative model of organizational trust: Past, present, and future. *The Academy of Management Review, 32*(2), 344–354.

Schroeder, R., & Axelsson, A. S. (2006). *Avatars at work and play: Collaboration and interaction in shared virtual environments* (Vol. 34). Dordrecht, Netherlands: Springer.

Schütz, A. (1967). *The phenomenology of the social world.* Evanston, IL: Northwestern University Press.

Schwartzman, H. (1993). *Ethnography in organizations.* Newbury Park, CA: Sage.

Scott, P., Gibbons, M., Nowotny, H., Limoges, C., Trow, M., & Schwartzman, S. (1994). *The new production of knowledge: The dynamics of science and research in contemporary societies.* Newbury Park, CA: Sage.

Seigenthaler, J. (2005, November 29). A false Wikipedia "biography." *USA Today.* Retrieved from http://www.usatoday.com/news/opinion/editorials/2005-11-29-wikipedia-edit_x.htm

Selwyn, N. (2009). The digital native: Myth and reality. *Aslib Proceedings: New Information Perspectives, 61*(4), 364–379.

Sennett, R. (2007). *The culture of the new capitalism.* New Haven, CT: Yale University Press.

Shachaf, P. (2009). The paradox of expertise: Is the Wikipedia Reference Desk as good as your library? *Journal of Documentation, 65*(6), 977–996.

Shah, S. K. (2006). Motivation, governance, and the viability of hybrid forms in open source software development. *Management Science, 52*(7), 1000–1014.

Shankbone, D. (2007, June 7). Nobody's safe in cyberspace. *The Brooklyn rail: Critical perspectives on arts, politics, and culture.* Retrieved from http://www.brooklynrail.org/2008/06/express/nobodys-safe-in-cyber-space

Shapiro, F. R. (2008, July 21). Quote . . . misquote. *The New York Times.* Retrieved from http://www.nytimes.com/2008/07/21/magazine/27wwwl-guestsafire-t.html?_r=0

Shapiro, S. P. (1987). The social control of impersonal trust. *American Journal of Sociology, 93*(3), 623–658.

Sharir, M., & Lerner, M. (2006). Gauging the success of social ventures initiated by individual social entrepreneurs. *Journal of World Business, 41*(1), 6–20.

Shaw, A. (2012). Centralized and decentralized gatekeeping in an open online collective. *Politics and Society, 40*(3), 349–388.

Sheeran, M. J. (1983). *Beyond majority rule: Voteless decisions in the religious Society of Friends*. Philadelphia: Philadelphia Yearly Meeting of the Religious Society of Friends.

Shirky, C. (2005). Epilogue: Open source outside the domain of software. In J. Feller, B. Fitzgerald, S. A. Hissam, & K. R. Lakhani (Eds.), *Perspectives on free and open source software*. Cambridge, MA: MIT Press.

Shirky, C. (2009). *Here comes everybody: The power of organizing without organizations*. New York: Penguin.

Shirky, C. (2012, November 12). Napster, Udacity, and the academy. *Clay Shirky* blog. Retrieved from http://www.shirky.com/weblog/2012/2011/napster-udacity-and-the -academy/

Shore, C., & Wright, S. (1999). Audit culture and anthropology: Neo-liberalism in British higher education. *The Journal of the Royal Anthropological Institute, 5*(4), 557–575.

Shubik, M. (1971). The dollar auction game: A paradox in noncooperative behavior and escalation. *Journal of Conflict Resolution, 15*(1), 109–111.

Silverman, D. (1975). *Reading Castaneda: A prologue to the social sciences*. London: Routledge.

Silverman, D. (2005). *Doing qualitative research: A practical handbook* (2nd ed.). London: Sage.

Simmonds, T. (2010). Common knowledge? The rise of Creative Commons licensing. *Legal Information Management, 10*(03), 162–165.

Singel, R. (2009, May 29). Wikipedia bans Church of Scientology. *Wired*. Retrieved from http://www.wired.com/business/2009/05/wikipedia-bans-church-of-scientology/

Sitkin, S. B., & Roth, N. L. (1993). Explaining the limited effectiveness of legalistic "remedies" for trust/distrust. *Organization Science, 4*(3), 367–392.

Skolik, S. (2012). Partnership and leadership as main relationship in Wikimedia projects. In C. B. Illés (Ed.), *Human resource management and corporate competitiveness*. Gödöllő, Hungary: Szent Istvan University Publishing.

Smircich, L. (1983). Concepts of culture and organizational analysis. *Administrative Science Quarterly, 28*(3), 339–358.

Solansky, S. T. (2008). Leadership style and team processes in self-managed teams. *Journal of Leadership and Organizational Studies, 14*(4), 332–341.

Sørensen, B. M., & Spoelstra, S. (2012). Play at work: Continuation, intervention and usurpation. *Organization, 19*(1), 81–97.

Sørensen, J. B. (2007). Bureaucracy and entrepreneurship: Workplace effects on entrepreneurial entry. *Administrative Science Quarterly, 52*(3), 387–412.

Sperschneider, W., & Bagger, K. (2003). Ethnographic fieldwork under industrial constraints: Toward design-in-context. *International Journal of Human-Computer Interaction, 15*(1), 41–50.

Spicer, A., Alvesson, M., & Kärreman, D. (2009). Critical performativity: The unfinished business of critical management studies. *Human Relations, 62*(4), 537–560.

Staff and contractors. (2013, March 20). *Wikimedia*. Retrieved August 15, 2013, from http://wikimediafoundation.org/wiki/Staff_and_contractors?showall=1

Stake, R. E. (2005). Qualitative case studies. In N. K. Denzin & Y. S. Lincoln (Eds.), *Handbook of qualitative research* (Vol. 3, pp. 443–466). Thousand Oaks, CA: Sage.

Starling, Tim. (2010, December 14). Old Wikipedia backups discovered. Retrieved from http://marc.info/?l=wikien-l&m=129234207124074

Staw, B. M. (1981). The escalation of commitment to a course of action. *Academy of Management Review, 6*(4), 577–587.

Steinmetz, K. F. (2012). Message received: Virtual ethnography in online message boards. *International Journal of Qualitative Methods, 11*(1), 26–39.

Stewards/confirm/2009. (2009, February 10). *Wikimedia*. Retrieved August 23, 2013, from https://meta.wikimedia.org/wiki/Stewards/confirm/2009#Jimbo_Wales

Stewart, D. (2005). Social status in an open-source community. *American Sociological Review, 70*(5), 823–842.

Stewart, K. J., & Gosain, S. (2006). The impact of ideology on effectiveness in open source software development teams. *MIS Quarterly, 30*(2), 291–314.

Stvilia, B., Al-Faraj, A., & Yi, Y. J. (2009). Issues of cross-contextual information quality evaluation: The case of Arabic, English, and Korean Wikipedias. *Library and Information Science Research, 31*(4), 232–239.

Stvilia, B., Twidale, M. B., Smith, L. C., & Gasser, L. (2008). Information quality work organization in Wikipedia. *Journal of the American Society for Information Science and Technology, 59*(6), 983–1001.

Suddath, C. (2011, January 13). History professor deemed security threat. *Time*. Retrieved from http://www.time.com/time/specials/packages/article/0,28804, 2042333_2042334_2042574,00.html

Suh, B., Convertino, G., Chi, E. H., & Pirolli, P. (2009). The singularity is not near: Slowing growth of Wikipedia. In *WikiSym '09: Proceedings of the 5th International Symposium on Wikis and Open Collaboration*. New York: ACM. Retrieved from http://www.parc.com/content/attachments/singularity-is-not-near.pdf

Sumi, R., Yasseri, T., Rung, A., Kornai, A., & Kertész, J. (2011, October 9–11). *Characterization and prediction of Wikipedia edit wars*. Paper presented at the IEEE International Conference on Privacy, Security, Risk, and Trust, and IEEE International Conference on Social Computing, Boston.

Sun, Y., Fang, Y., & Lim, K. H. (2011). Understanding sustained participation in transactional virtual communities. *Decision Support Systems, 53*(1), 12–22.

Sundin, O. (2011). Janitors of knowledge: Constructing knowledge in the everyday life of Wikipedia editors. *Journal of Documentation, 67*(5), 840–862.

Surowiecki, J. (2004). *The wisdom of crowds*. New York: Anchor Books.

Swartz, A. (2006, September 4). Who writes Wikipedia? *Raw Thought* blog. Retrieved from http://www.aaronsw.com/weblog/whowriteswikipedia

Szymanski, L. A., Devlin, A. S., Chrisler, J. C., & Vyse, S. A. (1993). Gender role and attitudes toward rape in male and female college students. *Sex Roles, 29*(1), 37–57.

Talk:Access to nonpublic information policy. (2013, November 7). *Wikimedia*. Retrieved November 7, 2013, from http://meta.wikimedia.org/wiki/Talk:Access_to_nonpub lic_information_policy

Talk:Benevolent dictator. (2011, October 22). *Wikimedia*. Retrieved August 23, 2013, from http://meta.wikimedia.org/wiki/Talk:Benevolent_dictator

Talk:Wikimedia Chapters Association. (2013, May 10). *Wikimedia*. Retrieved August 22, 2013, from http://meta.wikimedia.org/wiki/Talk:Wikimedia_Chapters_Association#WMF_Board_letter_regarding_the_Chapters_Association

Tapscott, D., & Williams, A. D. (2006). *Wikinomics: How mass collaboration changes everything*. New York: Portfolio Trade.

Taylor, T., Martin, B. N., Hutchinson, S., & Jinks, M. (2007). Examination of leadership practices of principals identified as servant leaders. *International Journal of Leadership in Education, 10*(4), 401–419.

Terranova, T. (2000). Producing culture for the digital economy. *Social Text, 63*(18), 33–58.

Thau, S., Crossley, C., Bennett, R. J., & Sczesny, S. (2007). The relationship between trust, attachment, and antisocial work behaviors. *Human Relations, 60*(8), 1155–1179.

Thom-Santelli, J., Cosley, D. R., & Gay, G. (2009). What's mine is mine: Territoriality in collaborative authoring. In *CHI '09: Proceedings of the SIGCHI Conference on Human Factors in Computing Systems* (pp. 1481–1484). New York: ACM.

Tkacz, N. (2010). Wikipedia and the politics of mass collaboration. *Journal of Media and Communication, 2*(2), 41–53.

Tkacz, N. (2011). The politics of forking paths. In G. Lovink & N. Tkacz (Eds.), *Critical point of view: A Wikipedia reader*. Amsterdam: Institute of Network Cultures.

Toffler, A. (1980). *The third wave*. New York: Morrow.

Török, J., Iñiguez, G., Yasseri, T., San Miguel, M., Kaski, K., & Kertész, J. (2013). Opinions, conflicts, and consensus: Modeling social dynamics in a collaborative environment. *Physical Review Letters, 110*(8). Retrieved from http://arxiv.org/pdf/1207.4914.pdf

Travers, M. (2009). New methods, old problems: A sceptical view of innovation in qualitative research. *Qualitative Research, 9*(2), 161–179.

Tresch, J. (2001). On going native. *Philosophy of the Social Sciences, 31*(3), 302–322.

Trist, E. (1983). Referent organizations and the development of inter-organizational domains. *Human Relations, 36*(3), 269–284.

Tumlin, M., Harris, S. R., Buchanan, H., Schmidt, K., & Johnson, K. (2007). Collectivism vs. individualism in a wiki world: Librarians respond to Jaron Lanier's essay "Digital Maoism: The hazards of the new online collectivism." *Serials Review, 33*(1), 45–53.

Turek, P., Wierzbicki, A., Nielek, R., Hupa, A., & Datta, A. (2010). Learning about the quality of teamwork from wikiteams. In *Proceedings of the 2010 IEEE Second International Conference on Social Computing* (pp. 17–24). Washington, DC: IEEE Computer Society.

Turner, F. (2006). *From counterculture to cyberculture: Stewart Brand, the Whole Earth Network, and the rise of digital utopianism*. Chicago: University of Chicago Press.

User talk:Jimbo Wales/Archive. (2010, May 9). *Wikimedia Commons*. Retrieved August 22, 2013, from http://commons.wikimedia.org/wiki/User_talk:Jimbo_Wales/Archive

User talk:Jimbo Wales/Archive/2010/5. (2010, June 5). *Wikimedia Commons*. Retrieved November 8, 2013, from https://commons.wikimedia.org/wiki/User_talk:Jimbo _Wales/Archive/2010/5

User talk:Jimbo Wales/Difference between revisions. (2011, August 24). Wikipedia. Retrieved November 6, 2013, from https://en.wikipedia.org/w/index.php?title=User _talk%3AJimbo_Wales&diff=446424770&oldid=446419156

User talk:John Cline: Difference between revisions. (2011, March 18). *Wikipedia*. Retrieved November 6, 2013, from http://en.wikipedia.org/w/index.php?title=User _talk%3AMy76Strat&action=historysubmit&diff=419433563&oldid=419433552

User talk:Sue Gardner/Narrowing focus. (2012, December 24). *Wikimedia*. Retrieved August 22, 2013, from http://meta.wikimedia.org/wiki/User_talk:Sue_Gardner/ Narrowing_focus

User:Sue Gardner/Narrowing focus. (2012, October 18). *Wikimedia*. Retrieved August 21, 2013, from http://meta.wikimedia.org/wiki/User:Sue_Gardner/Narrowing_focus

Vaknin, S. (2010, May). The Wikipedia cult [Interview by Daniel Tynan]. *Global Politician*. Retrieved from http://www.globalpolitician.com/26423-wikipedia-cult -jimmy-wales

Van Maanen, J. (1988/2011). *Tales of the field: On writing ethnography* (2nd ed.). Chicago: University of Chicago Press.

Van Rossum, G. (2008, July 31). Origin of BDFL. *All Things Pythonic* blog. Retrieved from http://www.artima.com/weblogs/viewpost.jsp?thread=235725

Verberg, N., Wood, E., Desmarais, S., & Senn, C. (2000). Gender differences in survey respondents' written definitions of date rape. *Canadian Journal of Human Sexuality, 9*(3), 181–190.

Viégas, F. B., Wattenberg, M., Kriss, J., & van Ham, F. (2007). Talk before you type: Coordination in Wikipedia. In *HICSS '07: Proceedings of the 40th Annual Hawaii International Conference on System Sciences* (p. 78). Washington, DC: IEEE Computer Society.

Viggiani, F. A. (1991). *Democratic hierarchies in the workplace.* Unpublished doctoral dissertation. Cornell University, Ithaca, NY.

Viggiani, F. A. (1997). Democratic hierarchies in the workplace: Structural dilemmas and organizational action. *Economic and Industrial Democracy, 18*(2), 231–260.

Viggiani, F. A. (2011). Organization development and democratization of the firm. *Business and Social Sciences Review, 1*(1), 21–40.

Viseur, R. (2012). Forks impacts and motivations in free and open source projects. *International Journal of Advanced Computer Science and Applications, 3*(2), 117–122.

Von Hippel, E., & Von Krogh, G. (2003). Open source software and the "private-collective" innovation model: Issues for organization science. *Organization Science, 14*(2), 209–223.

Vote:Narrowing Focus. (2013, March 25). *Wikimedia*. Retrieved August 21, 2013, from http://wikimediafoundation.org/wiki/Vote:Narrowing_Focus

Wakefield, R. L., Leidner, D. E., & Garrison, G. (2008). A model of conflict, leadership, and performance in virtual teams. *Information Systems Research, 19*(4), 434–455.

Wales, J. (2012, June 24). Richard O'Dwyer and the new Internet war. *The Guardian.* Retrieved from http://www.guardian.co.uk/commentisfree/2012/jun/24/richard-o-dwyer-my-petition

Walling, S. (2011, April 15). How much do new editors actually improve Wikipedia? *Wikimedia Community Blog.* Retrieved from http://blog.wikimedia.org/2011/04/15/neweditorsquality/

Walsh, D. (2004). Doing ethnography. In C. Seale (Ed.), *Researching society and culture* (pp. 225–238). Newbury Park, CA: Sage.

Walsh, J. (2011, October 4). Regarding recent events on Italian Wikipedia. *Wikimedia Global Blog.* Retrieved from http://blog.wikimedia.org/2011/10/04/regarding-recent-events-on-italian-wikipedia

Walsh, J. (2012, January 2). Wikimedia fundraiser concludes with record breaking donations. *Wikimedia Foundation Fundraiser Blog.* Retrieved from https://blog.wikimedia.org/c/fundraiser-2011

Wasko, M. M., & Faraj, S. (2000). "It is what one does": Why people participate and help others in electronic communities of practice. *The Journal of Strategic Information Systems, 9*(2), 155–173.

Wasko, M. M., & Faraj, S. (2005). Why should I share? Examining social capital and knowledge contribution in electronic networks of practice. *MIS Quarterly, 29*(1), 35–57.

Wasko, M. M., Teigland, R., & Faraj, S. (2009). The provision of online public goods: Examining social structure in an electronic network of practice. *Decision Support Systems, 47*(3), 254–265.

Waters, N. L. (2007). Why you can't cite Wikipedia in my class. *Communications of the ACM, 50*(9), 15–17.

Watson, T. J. (1995). Shaping the story: Rhetoric, persuasion and creative writing in organisational ethnography. *Studies in Cultures, Organizations and Societies, 1*(2), 301–311.

WCA budget—Draft 01. (2012). Retrieved from http://upload.wikimedia.org/wikipedia/meta/e/ef/20120710-_budget_WCA_draft.pdf

Weber, M. (1947). *The theory of social and economic organization.* Glencoe, IL: Free Press.

Weber, S. (2004). *The success of open source.* Cambridge, MA: Harvard University Press.

Webster, S. (1982). Dialogue and fiction in ethnography. *Dialectical Anthropology, 7*(2), 91–114.

Welcome to Citizendium. (2013, August 15). *Citizendium.* Retrieved August 15, 2013, from http://en.citizendium.org

Welham, J., & Lakhani, N. (2009, June 8). Wikipedia sentinel quits after "sock-puppeting" scandal. *The New Zealand Herald.* Retrieved from http://www.nzherald.co.nz/technology/news/article.cfm?c_id=5&objectid=10577178

Wellman, B. (2002). Little boxes, glocalization, and networked individualism. In M. Tanabe, P. V. D. Besselaar, & T. Ishida (Eds.), *Digital cities II: Computational and sociological approaches* (pp. 10–25). Berlin, Germany: Springer Verlag.

Welser, H. T., Cosley, D., Kossinets, G., Lin, A., Dokshin, F., Gay, G., et al. (2011). Finding social roles in Wikipedia. In *Proceedings of the 2011 iConference* (pp. 122–129). New York: ACM.

Werker, E., & Ahmed, F. Z. (2008). What do nongovernmental organizations do? *The Journal of Economic Perspectives, 22*(2), 73–92.

Westenholz, A. (2006). Identity work and meaning arena: Beyond actor/structure and micro/macro distinctions in an empirical analysis of IT workers. *American Behavioral Scientist, 49*(7), 1015–1029.

Westenholz, A. (Ed.). (2012). *The Janus face of commercial open source software communities: An investigation into institutional (non)work by interacting institutional actors.* Copenhagen, Denmark: Copenhagen Business School.

Whyte, W. F., & Whyte, K. K. (1984). *Learning from the field: A guide from experience.* Beverly Hills, CA: Sage.

Whyte, W. F., & Whyte, K. K. (1991). *Making Mondragon: The growth and dynamics of the worker cooperative complex* (2nd, rev. ed.). Ithaca, NY: ILR Press.

Wikimedia Chapters Association. (2013, August 18). *Wikimedia.* Retrieved August 21, 2013, from http://meta.wikimedia.org/wiki/Wikimedia_Chapters_Association

Wikimedia Chapters Association/Berlin Agreement. (2013, February 6). *Wikimedia.* Retrieved August 21, 2013, from http://meta.wikimedia.org/wiki/Berlin_Agreement

Wikimedia Chapters Association/Charter. (2013, July 8). *Wikimedia.* Retrieved August 21, 2013, from http://meta.wikimedia.org/wiki/Wikimedia_Chapters_Association_Charter

Wikimedia Deutschland. (2013, August 1). *Wikimedia.* Retrieved August 21, 2013, from http://meta.wikimedia.org/wiki/Wikimedia_Deutschland

Wikimedia Forum/Italian Wikimedia. (2012, October 28). *Wikimedia.* Retrieved August 22, 2013, from http://meta.wikimedia.org/wiki/Wikimedia_Forum/Italian_Wikipedia#Close_the_Italian_chapter

Wikimedia Foundation. (2011a, April). *Wikipedia Editors Study.* Retrieved from http://upload.wikimedia.org/wikipedia/commons/7/76/Editor_Survey_Report_-_April_2011.pdf

Wikimedia Foundation. (2011b, August 15). Editor trends study. *Wikimedia Strategic Planning.* Retrieved August 14, 2013, from http://strategy.wikimedia.org/wiki/Editor_Trends_Study

Wikimedia Foundation. (2012). *Wikimedia Foundation: 2012–13 Annual Plan.* Retrieved from https://upload.wikimedia.org/wikipedia/foundation/4/4f/2012-13_Wikimedia_Foundation_Plan_FINAL_FOR_WEBSITE.pdf

Wikinews:Water cooler. (2012, August). *Wikinews.* Retrieved August 22, 2013, from http://en.wikinews.org/wiki/Wikinews:Water_cooler/miscellaneous/archives/2012/August#WN_fork_open_globe_is_no_more...

Wikipedia. (2012, January 29). *Encyc.* Retrieved August 15, 2013, from http://encyc.org/wiki/Wikipedia

Wikipedia Diskussion:Hauptseite/Vulva. (2013, May 19). *Wikipedia.* Retrieved August 15, 2013, from http://de.wikipedia.org/wiki/Wikipedia_Diskussion:Hauptseite/Vulva

Wikipedia:Comunicato 4 ottobre 2011. (2011, October 8). *Wikipedia*. Retrieved August 22, 2013, from http://it.wikipedia.org/w/index.php?title=Wikipedia:Comunicato_4_ottobre_2011/en&oldid=43993454

Wikipedia:Encuestas/2011/sobre el filtro de imágenes. (2011, December 13). *Wikipedia*. Retrieved August 22, 2013, from http://es.wikipedia.org/wiki/Wikipedia:Encuestas/2011/Sobre_el_filtro_de_imágenes

Wikipedia:Meinungsbilder/Einführung persönlicher Bildfilter. (2012, August 18). *Wikipedia*. Retrieved August 22, 2013, from http://de.wikipedia.org/wiki/Wikipedia:Meinungsbilder/Einführung_persönlicher_Bildfilter

Wikipédia:Sondage/Installation d'un Filtre d'image. (2013, February 3). *Wikipedia*. Retrieved August 22, 2013, from http://fr.wikipedia.org/wiki/Wikip%C3%A9dia:Sondage/Installation_d%27un_Filtre_d%27image

Wikipedia talk:Requests for adminship: Difference between revisions. (2011, September 1). *Wikipedia*. Retrieved November 6, 2013, from https://en.wikipedia.org/w/index.php?title=Wikipedia_talk:Requests_for_adminship&diff=prev&oldid=447859630

Wikipedia:Wikipedia-fork. (2013, August 13). *Wikipedia*. Retrieved August 22, 2013, from http://de.wikipedia.org/wiki/Wikipedia:Wikipedia-Fork

Wikiversity:Community Review/Wikimedia Ethics:Ethical Breaching Experiments. (2011, July 2). *Wikiversity*. Retrieved November 8, 2013, from https://en.wikiversity.org/wiki/Wikiversity:Community_Review/Wikimedia_Ethics:Ethical_Breaching_Experiments

Wikiversity:Community Review/Wikimedia Ethics:Ethical Breaching Experiments/Sue Gardner. (2010, March 24). *Wikiversity*. Retrieved November 8, 2013, from https://en.wikiversity.org/wiki/Wikiversity:Community_Review/Wikimedia_Ethics:Ethical_Breaching_Experiments/Sue_Gardner

Willard, G. E., Krueger, D. A., & Feeser, H. R. (1992). In order to grow, must the founder go: A comparison of performance between founder and non-founder managed high-growth manufacturing firms. *Journal of Business Venturing, 7*(3), 181–194.

Williams, C. (2012, August 2). Wikipedia charity chairman resigns after pornography row. *The Telegraph*. Retrieved from http://www.telegraph.co.uk/technology/wikipedia/9447161/Wikipedia-charity-chairman-resigns-after-pornography-row.html

Williams, M. (2007). Avatar watching: Participant observation in graphical online environments. *Qualitative Research, 7*(1), 5–24.

Williams, T. A. (1979). The search conference in active adaptive planning. *The Journal of Applied Behavioral Science, 15*(4), 470–483.

Winter, J. (2010a, May 10). Despite content purge, pornographic images remain on Wikimedia. *FoxNews*. Retrieved from http://www.foxnews.com/scitech/2010/05/10/porn-wikipedia-illegal-content-remains/

Winter, J. (2010b, May 14). Exclusive: Shakeup at Wikipedia in wake of porn purge. *FoxNews*. Retrieved from http://www.foxnews.com/scitech/2010/05/14/exclusive-shake-wikipedia-porn-pressure/

Winter, J. (2010c, April 27). Wikipedia distributing child porn, co-founder tells FBI. *FoxNews*. Retrieved from http://www.foxnews.com/scitech/2010/04/27/wikipedia-child-porn-larry-sanger-fbi/

Wolcott, H. F. (1990). Making a study "more ethnographic." *Journal of Contemporary Ethnography, 19*(1), 44–72.

Wright, S. (1994). *Anthropology of organizations*. London: Routledge.

Yang, H. L., & Lai, C. Y. (2010). Motivations of Wikipedia content contributors. *Computers in Human Behavior, 26*(6), 1377–1383.

Yasseri, T., & Kertész, J. (2013). Value production in a collaborative environment. *Journal of Statistical Physics, 151*(3–4), 414–439.

Yasseri, T., Spoerri, A., Graham, M., & Kertész, J. (in press). The most controversial topics in Wikipedia: A multilingual and geographical analysis. In P. Fichman & N. Hara (Eds.), *Global Wikipedia: International and cross-cultural issues in online collaboration*. Lanham, MD: Scarecrow Press.

Yasseri, T., Sumi, R., Rung, A., Kornai, A., & Kertész, J. (2012). Dynamics of conflicts in Wikipedia. *PLoS ONE, 7*(6). Retrieved from http://arxiv.org/abs/1202.3643

Yoo, Y., & Alavi, M. (2004). Emergent leadership in virtual teams: What do emergent leaders do? *Information and Organization, 14*(1), 27–58.

Zhang, W., & Kramarae, C. (2008). Feminist invitational collaboration in a digital age: Looking over disciplinary and national borders. *Women and Language, 31*(2), 8–19.

Zhu, H., Kraut, R. E., Wang, Y. C., & Kittur, A. (2011). Identifying shared leadership in Wikipedia. In *CHI '11: Proceedings of the SIGCHI Conference on Human Factors in Computing Systems* (pp. 3431–3434). New York: ACM.

Zhu, H., Kraut, R., & Kittur, A. (2012). Effectiveness of shared leadership in online communities. In *CSCW '12: proceedings of the ACM 2012 Conference on Computer Supported Cooperative Work* (pp. 407–416). New York: ACM.

Zittrain, J. (2008). *The Future of the Internet and how to stop it*. New Haven, CT: Yale University Press.

Zlatić, V., Božičević, M., Štefančić, H., & Domazet, M. (2006). Wikipedias: Collaborative web-based encyclopedias as complex networks. *Physical Review E, 74*(1). Retrieved from http://impact.asu.edu/~mcn/cse591sp07/zlatic-2006.pdf

# INDEX

comments: proper etiquette for, 18; protocol for deleting or altering, 94, 95; during RfAs, 42–43, 90, 92–93. *See also* edit wars; RFCs (requests for comment)

common-pool resource management, 102

Commons, Wikimedia, 92; and child pornography incident, 167–171; culture of, 177; deleted images on, 234n9; direct upload of pictures to, 191; relationship with Jimmy Wales, 177, 235n13

common sense, 96

communication transparency, 92

community ambassadors, 137

community-building role of conflict, 82

community logo trademarking, 139

community of Wikipedia, 4; as "community of dissensus," 84; community ties as more important than member ties, 85–86; as egalitarian but with closely controlled members, 86–87; "us versus them" mentality among, 89

competition as exacerbating editcountitis, 40

conflict/disagreement: "as addictive as cocaine," 77; in board of trustees, 129; and consensus, 67, 80, 97, 149; as fostering creativity and innovation, 84; on foundational issues, 162; freedom of open, 57; and purposeful rule violation and trolling, 82; typology of trajectories of, 78–81, 79; Wikipedia driven by, 60, 77–78, 84, 125. *See also* dispute/conflict resolution process; edit wars; forking

conflict of interest (COI) rule, 19, 230n3

"connective ethnography," 199

consensus: CCC rule, 75; CONEXCEPT rule, 171–172; CON norm, 18–19; as constructing shared perspectives, 24; during Gdańsk/Danzig edit war, 70–71, 74–76, 78; polls only to help determine, 63; to prevent forking, 145; Quaker methods of, 62, 63; role of facilitator in, 83; seeking truth or, 80; and silence as agreement, 67, 149; and Wikipedia policy, 62–63

Conservapedia, 5

consumer coproduction, 2

content disputes, 61–64, 76–78. *See also* Gdańsk/Danzig edit war

content policies, 20–22

control: through procedures, 96–99; through revisions tracking, 87–92, 88; through structured discourse, 92–96

controversial-content filtering: as censorship, 152, 190; and child pornography, 167–173; and German Wikipedia vagina photo, 234n8; inability to reach consensus on, 234n8; referendum on, 145–146, 233n16; Sue Gardner on, 145–146

Cook, Karen S., 124

"copyleft" philosophy, 2

copyright violations (CV) rule, 22

core and noncore activities, 132

Coser, Lewis A., 84

Creative Commons, 189

credentials, 105–106; alternatives to verification of, 120–124; bureaucratic scripts as substituting for, 108; community poll on, 116–117, 119; and Essjay controversy, 111–114; and integrity of information, 108; as more important than personal identity, 107; on relevance of external, 116, 121; trust and control of, 117–120; and validity of article content, 107; Wales's proposal on, 115–116

creep, instruction, 96

cult, Wikipedia as, 185

*The Cult of the Amateur* (Keen), 182

cult-of-the-amateur accusations, 29

culture, Wikipedia as a, 196

Cunningham, Ward, 10

Curie, Marie, edit war over, 231n5

CV (copyright violations) rule, 22

cyber-libertarianism, 189

Danish cartoons controversy, 234n8

Dank (user), 48

Dayewalker (user), 42–43, 90

Dcoetzee (admin), 170

DDL intercettazioni (Italian wiretapping bill), 140

Déat, Marcel, 230n1

Debian community, 174–175, 187

personal attacks (NPA rule), 17–18, 94
personal user awards, 27
Peters, Parker, 51
Ph.D. claims and egalitarian ideal, 112, 116
PIPA (Protect Intellectual Property Act,
    U.S.), 141, 172, 188
placeholder phrases, 95
plagiarizing from Wikipedia, 22
Pluto controversy, 77
POINT (illustrating a point) rule, 20
policies. *See* rules/norms/policies
Polish edit wars on English Wikipedia,
    231n5. *See also* Gdańsk/Danzig edit war
Polish Wikipedia, 12, 201–202; accused of
    gender/sexuality bias, 5; admin recall
    procedures on, 49–50, 55; articles per
    capita on, 12; banning of most prolific
    editor on, 81; basic rules and norms
    of, 17, 98–99; criticisms of admins on,
    53–54; elections within, 35; and gender
    bias in describing members of parlia-
    ment, 21–22; mediation on, 83; number
    of administrators on, 36; number of
    bureaucrats on, 41; number of RfAs on,
    37; and requirements for sources, 21; RfA
    process on, 41, 44, 46; RfA rejection for
    homophobic comment on, 130; RFCs
    (requests for comment) on, 61; software
    support for diacriticals in, 136; status of
    admins on, 46–47; talk pages on, 92–94;
    userboxes on, 26
political views. *See* religious/political views
polling: on blackout to protest SOPA and
    PIPA, 172–173; cheating in, 74–75; con-
    troversial-content filtering referendum,
    145–146; on credential verification, 116; in
    Gdańsk/Danzig edit war, 74–75, 78; and
    "not a substitute for discussion" (POLL)
    norm, 18–19, 63; straw polls, 63; use of
    banner space to announce, 138
Poor, Ed (admin, bureaucrat), 69–70
pornography issue, 167–173
Portuguese Wikipedia, 12
postindustrial meritocracy, 4, 183
power/empowerment: collaboration and,
    80; decentralized nature of, 150; defined,
    56; forking as form of, 146; leaders

lacking direct power, 157, 159; loss of,
    by academics, 184; power play within
    Wikipedia, 31; and questions of owner-
    ship, 144–145
premodern communal controls, 100
Pricasso, 235n13
principles shared across Wikimedia, 98
privacy, individual, 191
Privatemusings (user), 164–166
"private-1" mailing lists, 53
procedural rationality, focus on, 151
professionalization: entrepreneur's exit as
    component of, 154; of social movements,
    134–135
programming/developers: and comparisons
    with Linus, Apache, Perl, 161, 175; and
    dangers of changes without discussion,
    136–137; developers not understanding
    global impact of changes, 137; and oppo-
    sition to community decision on article
    creation, 142–143; and setting priorities
    for bugs, 136; WMF and programming
    errors, 135–136
project development advisory council, pro-
    posal to form, 164
project-wide protest procedures, 142
proper behavior guidelines, 99
prosumer capitalism, 188
Prot (Wikipedia editor), vii–xiii
Protect Intellectual Property Act (PIPA,
    U.S.), 141, 172, 188
pseudonyms: information page on, 117; use
    of, by Essjay, 111–113; use of, in this book,
    200–201
PSI award, 27
publication, meaning of, 184
published source requirement, 21
"publish then filter" or vice versa, 183

Quakers (Society of Friends), 62, 63; role of
    clerk, 82

radical autonomy, 103
Rafaeli, Sheizaf, 32
range blocks, 137
Rangell, Sue, 41
rational discourse platform, 186

schisms/forking, 126, 133, 144–148, 179
schmucks and losers, free labor only for, 182
Search Conference method, 63–64, 83
search engines, 146–147, 200, 209
secret ballot proposals, 44
"secret" e-mail list issue, 53
Seer (admin), x
Seigenthaler, John, 228n7
self-organization, 150–151
self-promotion, 88
semiautomatic corrections, 38
servant-leadership model, 174
service awards, 26
sexism in categorization, 16
Sheeran, Michael, 62
Shirky, Clay, 60, 149, 186
"Show preview," 95
*Signpost, Wikipedia,* 74, 139, 235–236n2
Simple Wikipedia, 192
Sinnreich, Aram, 103
slang and abbreviations: glossary of, 203–225; as intimidating to newcomers, 102, 122; status enhanced by knowledge of, 123
Snottywong (user), 142–143
social dominance strategies, 52–54
socialization among Wikipedians, 24
social signaling through user pages, 27–28
societal rule, technology as form of, 188
Society of Friends, 62
sociotechnical communities (STC), 123
sociotechnical system, 100
sock-puppetry, 118, 164, 231n10
"soft bureaucracies," 151
software application, quality of, 40
SOPA (Stop Online Piracy Act, U.S.), 141, 172, 188
Space Cadet (editor), 68
Spanish Wikipedia (Enciclopedia Libre), 12, 15, 35, 146, 148
"specific-expertise" seats on board of trustees, 129
stalemate conflict trajectory, 79, 80–81, 83
stalking, 110–111, 113–114
Stallman, Richard, 175
Starling, Tim, 65
start-up culture, 179

status: of adminship, 46–48, 140; as available to nonexperts, 29, 106; based on peer recognition, 22–23, 30; "big men" must show modesty to maintain, 31; and egalitarianism, 55–57; and fake credentials, 113, 119; featured- and good-article designations and, 24; gradations of, 32; issues with Wales's, 162–170, 178; as lock-in mechanism, 55; rules apply to all levels of, 18, 157; service awards demonstrating, 26–27; speed leading to greater, 40; stewards' ability to remove, 34; and understanding rules and slang, 123
STC (sociotechnical communities), 123
steward(s), 33–35, 36, 197; competition among, 40; need for programmer communication with, 137; number of, 41; as "slaves," 46; and Wales's status, 33, 165–166, 168, 177
stigmas as easy to conceal online, 117–118, 199
Stop Online Piracy Act (SOPA, U.S.), 141, 172, 188
stratification, 31–32, 85, 101–103, 115
straw polls, 63
structured discourse, control through, 92–96
stubs, 12–13
suppression, 34
surveys, 14–17. *See also Wikipedia Editors Study* (Wikimedia Foundation)
Swedish Wikipedia, 12, 230n6
swift trust, 119
symmetric control by peers, 100
Szopen (user), 65–66, 68, 74
Szopen/Chopin edit wars, 231n5

talk pages, 25, 86, 91–96
tarantula picture in arachnophobia article, 76–77
Taylorism, 39, 183
teams, self-managed virtual, 4, 119, 174, 178
technocratic control, 119
Teigland, Robin, 85
tendentious editing, 99
Thekohser (user), 165
theopenglobe.org, 145